War Powers of the President and Congress
Who Holds the Arrows and Olive Branch?

VIRGINIA LEGAL STUDIES are sponsored by the School of Law of the University of Virginia for the publication of meritorious original works, symposia, and reprints in law and related fields.

Studies Editors; Carl McFarland, 1967–73
Richard B. Lillich, 1973–

War Powers
of the President
and Congress

Who Holds the Arrows
and Olive Branch?

W. TAYLOR REVELEY III

University Press of Virginia
Charlottesville

THE UNIVERSITY PRESS OF VIRGINIA
Copyright © 1981 by the Rector and Visitors
of the University of Virginia

First published 1981

Library of Congress Cataloging in Publication Data

Reveley, W. Taylor
  Who holds the arrows and olive branch?

  (Virginia legal studies)
  Includes index.
  1. War and emergency powers—United States—History.
I. Title. II. Series. JK339.R48 342.73′041 80-29046 ISBN 0-8139-0808-6

Printed in the United States of America

To Helen

CONTENTS

Acknowledgments

The seeds for this book were sown in 1967. They have grown fitfully ever since with the exception of thirteen highly productive months in 1972-73, when I was an International Affairs Fellow of the Council on Foreign Relations and a Fellow of the Woodrow Wilson International Center for Scholars.

My first encounter with the war powers came in law school under the aegis of A. E. Dick Howard. I grappled with whether President Johnson might constitutionally keep fighting in Vietnam if Congress voted to stop. The subject proved to be fascinating, sparsely analyzed, and well worth further pursuit.

Pursuit was first encouraged by Daniel J. Meador, while I was on his faculty, and thereafter by John Norton Moore, who pointed me toward the Council on Foreign Relations. The Council and Wilson Center jointly funded a year's research and writing in New York City and Washington, D.C. The time in New York included a month at Columbia Law School via Abraham D. Sofaer, who was then beginning his superb work on the war powers. Warm thanks go to these people, as well as to John Temple Swing of the Council, and Benjamin H. Read and James H. Billington of the Wilson Center, for their aid and comfort. Equally warm thanks are due my law firm, Hunton & Williams, especially George C. Freeman, Jr., and his team. They set me wholly free for thirteen months to pursue this book and indulged my episodic efforts to finish it after returning.

A number of other organizations and events have been important to the venture. Without their impetus to thought and action, my efforts would have been much the poorer. Among them have been a Symposium at the University of Virginia Law School on *The Constitution and the Use of Military Force Abroad* (1969) and a resulting *Commentary*, 10 VA. J. INT'L LAW 58 (1969); preceded and followed by work on *Presidential*

Warmaking: Constitutional Prerogative or Usurpation? 55 VA.
L. REV. 1243 (1969); then *Testimony, War Powers Hearings Before a Subcomm. of the House Comm. on Foreign Affairs*, 93d
Cong., 1st Sess. 224 (1973); work as a member and rapporteur
of the American Society of International Law's Panel on *The
Constitution and the Conduct of American Foreign Policy*
(1973-74); a chapter on *Constitutional Aspects of United States
Participation in Foreign Internal Conflicts* in LAW AND CIVIL
WAR IN THE MODERN WORLD (John Norton Moore ed. 1974);
Testimony on Constitutional Aspects of Congressional-
Executive Relations before the federal Commission on the Organization of the Government for the Conduct of Foreign Policy (1974); a preview of this book's Chapters III-V in *Constitutional Allocations of the War Powers Between the
President and Congress: 1787-1788*, 15 VA. J. INT'L LAW 73
(1973); work as a conferee and rapporteur on the war powers
for the Roscoe Pound-American Trial Lawyers Foundation's
Conference on Powers of the Presidency (1975); and a chapter
on *The Power to Make War* in THE CONSTITUTION AND THE CONDUCT OF FOREIGN POLICY (Francis O. Wilcox & Richard A. Frank
eds. 1976).

The manuscript benefited from the review of many. The
substantive insights of John F. Murphy, William B. Spong, Jr.,
Julius Stone, Frederick S. Tipson, and Eugene P. Trani have
been extremely helpful, though I remain responsible for all sins
of substantive omission or commission. W. Richard Smyser
gave "the Arrows and Olive Branch" to the title. Ruth D. Kaufman provided valuable editorial suggestions, and Richard D.
Lillich guided the manuscript through the mysteries of the Virginia Legal Studies series.

Dennis A. Michaud helped research developments from
1789 to 1960. Kathleen A. Farrell cite-checked the manuscript,
with help from Bradley C. Reeves and Charles A. Anderson, Jr.
The typing was borne, successively, by Marjorie Doughty, Lydia Nunez, Karen Parrish, and Betty Ewers. Without all of their
labors production would still be underway.

Nor would the end have come without the good humor and
support of my wife. The way is not easy for the family of some-

one trying to finish a book and practice law more or less simultaneously. Helen ensured that everyone bore up, for which I am deeply grateful.

Richmond, Virginia   W. TAYLOR REVELEY III

War Powers of the President and Congress
Who Holds the Arrows and Olive Branch?

INTRODUCTION

Road Map and Résumé

FOR NEARLY two centuries the war powers have bedeviled a host of Presidents, Congressmen, and those few judges willing to deal with them in court. Through all, the nature of these powers has remained more unsettled perhaps than any other mainstream of American constitutional law. New efforts to lessen the mystery, this book included, have come in the wake of the Indochina War.

Reminder that an author should be read "for his wheat, sorting out his chaff," is especially appropriate to these efforts.[1] Thoughtful consideration of the war powers is difficult. They raise many complex issues. The information needed to resolve them is disturbingly varied and voluminous. Then, too, passions on war-power issues historically run high. Attempts to settle them are most often inspired by national trauma: a Civil War, a Versailles Treaty, or Vietnam. Thus, danger always exists of simplistic analyses centered on only a few of the pertinent questions, supported by congenial slivers of precedent, and given direction by a visceral reaction to the latest trauma. These inherent opportunities for error bear watching. The reader can proceed with the necessary caution if he knows where the author is going. The following introductory comments provide a road map and résumé.

Chapter I begins with a number of threshold questions. What exactly do we mean by the "war powers"? Who has tried to control them since the Constitution took effect in 1789? Why has controversy persisted over where control properly lies? And, do war-power issues have greater importance to the country's well-being now than ever before?

The chapter then narrows the focus from the war powers

writ large to those of the President and Congress. In later pages, the focus is narrowed again to the purely military prerogatives of the two branches, and still later to their respective authority over the commitment of American forces to combat.

The main work of Chapter I, however, is to erect the framework on which an understanding of the war powers will be built in subsequent pages. A striking number of issues exist even when attention is limited to the President and Congress. Identifying these issues and fixing their relationship to one another are crucial to a systematic grasp of the problem at hand. A central ambition of this book, accordingly, is the development of a framework that lays out for orderly consideration all of the issues important to the division of the war powers between the President and Congress. Chapter I takes the first step. It describes the basic factual circumstances (or variables) that combine to create the numerous contexts in which the authority of each branch must be determined. Like most skeletons, the chapter is dry. But dry or moist, the way will not be easy, nor the burden light for any who skim Chapter I only to read on and find its framework pervasive and never fully reiterated.

Then comes an extended look at what seem to have been the four main influences on the division of authority over war and peace between the President and Congress: (1) the text of the Constitution's war-power provisions, (2) the purposes of those who wrote and ratified the text in 1787-88, (3) evolving beliefs since 1789 about what the Constitution requires, and—irrespective of text, purposes, and evolving beliefs—(4) the various allocations of control over the war powers that have existed *in fact* between the President and Congress during the past two centuries.

Determinants (1) and (2) need no more introduction at this point. They are reasonably straightforward guides for constitutional interpretation. Determinants (3) and (4) are more convoluted. Together they make up what is generally termed "practice," or "usage." As later pages indicate, practice has been shaped not only by the constitutional text and debates but also by factors of three other sorts: the hazard, pace, and complexity of America's international circumstances at any particular time; the respective institutional capabilities of the President and Congress to cope with these changing circumstances; and the shifting balance of political strength between the two branches, which has helped the President at times and Congress at others to greater control over war and peace.

It is historical fact that all of these factors have contributed to the allocation of the war powers between the President and Congress. More important, they will all continue to contribute, barring a radical change in American habits. This does not inexorably doom us to wander amid constitutional confusion, obtaining firm direction only from gusts of realpolitik. The pages to come are premised on the dual notions that constitutional answers are both possible and vital to the country's health. The possibility of constitutional answers, however, does hinge on taking into account all of the determinants, the historical and political as well as the more purely legal. The working out of the necessary constitutional mechanics will occupy us throughout.

Chapter II begins an exploration of these determinants, starting with the most authoritative: the text of the Constitution's war-power provisions. The chapter finds strong signs of congressional dominance but not proof beyond a reasonable doubt. The constitutional text is too ambiguous at critical points for that, too prone to competing grants of authority to the President and Congress, and simply silent about which branch is to possess yet other crucial powers.

Chapters III through V pursue the intentions of the Framers and Ratifiers, finding in their debates even clearer evidence that Congress is to control most American decisions about war and peace. But the nature of the constitutional conventions and the behavior of former Framers and Ratifiers once government began under the Constitution create severe doubt that the specifics of the 1787-88 debates should dictate the division of the war powers between the two branches. Appropriately more influential are the underlying ends or objectives that can be abstracted from the specifics of these debates. These seminal purposes of the Framers and Ratifiers do demand our close attention.

Chapters VI, VII, and XI look at practice from 1789 to date.

They identify the dynamics of an erratic but phenomenal growth in presidential power over war and peace, as compared to what might reasonably have been expected in 1787-88. The process started immediately with Washington's administration but has never destroyed the capacity of Congress periodically to reassert its influence. Nor has it seriously eroded widespread belief that constitutionally Congress is at least the President's equal in matters of war and peace.

During this exploration of war-power determinants, as many pages go to the two years in which the Framers and Ratifiers were active as to the next two centuries. The disparity is premeditated. War-power history is anything but the simple series of vignettes in which it has usually been served up. A book of this length cannot remedy past ills by capturing the full sweep of pertinent developments since 1787. A reasonable try can be made at capturing the flavor of the most important single phase of that progress, however, the Framers' and Ratifiers' work. The details on 1787-88 can then provide a microcosm of the rich but opaque details that characterize much of the war powers' evolution.

There are other reasons also for emphasizing the Constitutional Fathers. Their debates are the most fertile source of ammunition for protagonists contending over the constitutional allocation of authority between the President and Congress. Thus their debates have been among the most misused of war-power precedent. A thorough account of what seems in fact to have occurred during the national and state conventions, taken out of the mouths of the participants themselves when possible, is the most effective antidote. A thorough account of 1787-88 is also engaging on two other scores: for its insight into the somewhat oblivious fashion with which the Framers and Ratifiers shaped constitutional provisions that have proved to be of immense importance, and for the related insight into the surprising extent to which the Framers' and Ratifiers' war-peace concerns did not mirror our own—and the equally fascinating extent to which they did.

At Chapter VIII the emphasis shifts from an account of the country's war-power past to recommendations about its future.

The underlying objectives sought by the Framers and Ratifiers are considered in light of today's circumstances. The chapter argues that, if anything, these ends are more responsive now to national needs than they were in 1787-88 and intervening years. Conflicts are found to exist among certain of the ends (*e.g.*, between the necessity that America have a capacity for speed and secrecy in matters of war and peace, on the one hand, and the necessity for consensus and democratic control, on the other). The chapter seeks to resolve these conflicts by proposing a staggered timing for when emphasis should go toward realizing particular objectives. Chapter VIII concludes with an assessment of the different capabilities of the President and Congress to realize the various war-power ends.

Taking into account all that has gone before, Chapter IX recommends an interpretation of the Constitution's war-power provisions. The resulting allocation of authority involves less control for Congress than the Framers and Ratifiers expected, but also less control for the President than most executives in this century and a number before have actually exercised.

Constitutional answers that lack any realistic chance of becoming settled law do little to dispel the mystery now shrouding the war powers. Chapter X turns to how the recommendations might become hard law. A touch of reform to rationalize legislative participation in decisions about war and peace would be helpful, coupled with a statute setting out basic ways for the President and Congress to collaborate in these matters and with a judicial willingness to decide war-power cases. Chapter XI examines the War Powers Resolution of 1973 and later developments for signs of movement in the recommended direction.

CHAPTER I

Old Controversies of

New Importance

RONALD REAGAN enjoys far more sweeping control over American war and peace than George Washington did, and Washington came to wield strikingly greater authority than had been expected for the President during the constitutional conventions of 1787-88. The dominant trend in war-power practice has been presidential aggrandizement. True, the process has not been linear between administrations or even within them— compare Lincoln's war powers with those of Andrew Johnson or the prerogatives of the early Nixon presidency with those of his last year in the White House. But over the course of nearly two hundred years, presidential war powers have grown radically.

It is too early to tell whether the conjunction of Indochina and Watergate (and the ensuing War Powers Resolution of 1973) marked a permanent reduction in those powers as they existed when Lyndon Johnson took office. Even should that be the case, post-Nixon Presidents are still likely to have more authority over war and peace than the Framers and Ratifiers anticipated and than the text of the Constitution suggests when read without the benefit of two hundred years of practice.

Old Controversies

Since the government began under the Constitution in 1789, struggles over the war powers have erupted constantly between the President and Congress. By 1815 the United States had fought an array of Indians, in effect foreign enemies; the two greatest powers of the day, France and Britain; and the rapacious Barbary States, Tripoli and Algiers. The Republic had skirted hostilities with Spain while pressing to relieve her of Florida. It was not a pacific area.

The respective constitutional prerogatives of the President and Congress over war and peace were of consuming concern to Americans while Washington, John Adams, and Madison held office. Nor have there been any administrations since in which the nature of these prerogatives has not been debated with some heat. The struggle caused by Indochina, though classic, has ample precedent. Controversy has persisted in part because Americans have frequently had to decide whether to fight. Decisions to use armed force have been made well over a hundred times since 1789, and decisions against its use at least as often. Persistence also reflects the weighty nature of the subject. Profound consequences may accompany the use or non-use of armed force. Disputes of corresponding intensity have arisen over the extent to which each branch is entitled to set policy.

Passion and dogged adherence to positions aroused on this account have been given new edge precisely because the disputes have concerned separation of powers. Presidential and congressional zeal in defense of real or imagined prerogatives is traditionally acute. And argument over the allocation of war powers conjures up two of our most cherished political bugbears: the fear that American democracy will perish, choked by presidential tyranny, and the obverse dread that it will smother amid congressional indecision and parochialism. With stakes so high, partisans have been loath to leave the constitutional fray.

Persistence has resulted, too, from the accumulation of unresolved controversies. Constitutional uncertainties about the division of the war powers between the President and Congress have not been cured by formal amendment, and, unlike most other areas of constitutional confusion, there has been very little light shed here by judicial decisions. Moreover, post-1789 practice regarding the division is often inconsistent. Most plausible and many quaint allocations of the war powers between the two branches are supported by one bit of precedent or another. Contrary divisions of control have existed in fact, and contradictory statements have been made by different men about what sorts of allocations are required. With unsettling frequency the same luminaries (Madison and Hamilton without peer) have varied their constitutional conclusions with changing times.

Such flux has been encouraged by our general tendency to collapse the *constitutional* question of where decision-making control lies into the *policy* question of what we would like the President or Congress to do about a pending situation. This emphasis on immediate result rather than on long-term constitutional structure has been with us since 1789, but never so emphatically as when the Cold War went sour in Indochina, curdling the prevailing taste for presidential prerogative. Inevitably, then, recurrent disputes over the war powers of the two branches has fueled future controversy almost as often as they have resulted in case-by-case definition of how authority is to be split between them.

President versus Congress has posed the most persistent war-power issues, but by no means the only ones. The House of Representatives has fought for a share of the Senate's special war-peace authority, lusting especially for a hand in international agreements. The President and Senate have fought over their respective foreign-affairs prerogatives, again focusing on treaty making. In the twentieth century only Versailles rivals Vietnam for generating uproar within the federal government.

On another plane entirely has been controversy over the scope of the *country's* war powers, to what extent they are constitutionally limited by (1) state and individual rights, (2) the separation of authority among the President, Senate, and House, and (3) international law. The Framers and Ratifiers of the Constitution, in fact, did not focus on the allocation of war powers between the President and Congress but on their division between the national government and the states. The Constitution explicitly denies the states certain diplomatic and military powers, while specifically granting the states, not the President, the right to take up arms to repel sudden enemy

attacks without prior congressional authorization. Though the
federal-state conflict over war powers receded to secondary
importance after 1789, it continued to brake national authority
throughout the nineteenth century. As late as World War I,
federal commitment of state militia to foreign wars was still
being attacked as unconstitutional.

Quite likely the states retain a few hard-core rights that limit
national war powers, even after the passing of most other
vestiges of federalism. Barring national calamity, for instance,
it seems that the federal government could not deprive a state
of republican government so as to assist a national war effort.
And states can even now affect American war and peace by the
way in which they treat foreigners within their territory.

The future of individual rights as a brake on national war
powers seems brighter. Admittedly, after the Sedition Act of
our Naval War with France, limits on habeas corpus during the
Civil War, restrictions on speech and property of the First and
Second World Wars, the latter's ethnic concentration camps,
and the generally meager protection given individual rights
even during times of peace before the Warren Court, a case
could have been made in recent years that these rights, like
those of the states, exerted scant control on the national war
powers. Intervening decisions of the Supreme Court suggest
that explicit guarantees in the Bill of Rights do bear even on
federal military action abroad. The extent to which the Constitution protects individuals against national decisions during
acute military emergency, nonetheless, remains an open
question. The civil-liberty judgments of the Warren Court
were not made under such constitutionally trying conditions.

Turning to the separation of powers, the fact that war-peace
authority is split among the President, House, and Senate has at
times broken our national capacity to act. Some have hailed the
ensuing paralysis as constitutional checks and balances at their
finest. More often, the paralysis has been decried as a defect
to be fixed by any available constitutional theory. Thus the
President and Senate have long argued that the House has a
constitutional duty to implement treaties, even when it had no
voice in their making. Similarly, Versailles spurred suggestion

that the separation of powers may not be used to block America's discharge of its international obligations; that is, neither the President, Congress as a whole, nor either of its houses may constitutionally defeat action by the rest of the government to meet the country's responsibilities abroad. To-day's variant of this Versailles argument, responding to Vietnam, reads international law into the Constitution to restrain national authority to use force. Under it, the United States may not constitutionally wield its war powers in violation of the law of nations, even if both the President and Congress want to.

Granted, the efficacy of our government of separated powers hinges on cooperation among the President, Senate, and House. Granted also, one means of controlling American military action would be to make unconstitutional any use of it that violates international law. Nonetheless, with rare exceptions, the Constitution now permits the President or either congressional house to use their powers freely to hamstring foreign undertakings by the rest of the government. And for now, it allows the United States to make war or peace despite international law, so long as our policy is set by the appropriate American authorities. Whether both of these realities should be reversed is among the inquiries here.

Two facets of the war powers remain: the role of the federal judiciary and the role of other federal personnel, most often military subordinates of the President who embark on war or peace action unauthorized by him or Congress. The courts have resolved controversies affecting foreign interests, and they have defined the constitutional war powers of the national government. In the process judges have handed down very few rulings provocative to other nations. And while their definition of national war powers, as against state or individual challenge, has been significant, courts have usually avoided cases involving the rights of the President or Congress to control these federal powers. Wielding one abstention doctrine or another, judges successfully withstood an unprecedented surge of opportunity to define these rights in Indochina cases.

Unauthorized decision making by federal subordinates has been important mainly as an occasion for renewed executive-legislative struggle, especially if one branch but not the other has repudiated the deed. President Monroe's tribulations with Congress following an 1818 incursion by Andrew Jackson into Spanish Florida provides a seminal case. With twentieth-century advances in communications between the field and the White House, unauthorized action by isolated commanders and diplomats has largely ended. The problem lingers on in more subtle form whenever today's bureaucracy has policies of its own to push.

New Importance

While the war powers present no novel constitutional issues, since the Second World War they have presented issues of wholly new dimensions. True, during the first generation under the Constitution, the country suffered the trials of a small, weak nation caught up, if at a distance, in the wars of the prevailing superpowers. The country nonetheless was significantly shielded by geography, the limited military technology of its potential foes, the virtual nonexistence of American capacity to intervene abroad, and our slight economic interdependence with other nations. During most of the nineteenth century, America was even further sheltered by the rise of a European balance of power for which it had no direct responsibility.

Especially during the last three decades, we have had a threefold change in circumstances: in our capacity and in our will to use force abroad and in the consequences of that use. The purely physical ability of postwar America to commit its military abroad in large or small numbers, swiftly or slowly, for days or years, vastly exceeds the country's conflict capacity before 1941. America's willingness to intervene abroad also stands in revolutionary contrast to a previous tradition of non-involvement except to trade, defend American citizens and property beset abroad, expand our boundaries, and police the Caribbean. Today's military technology, balance of power, and international interdependence no longer permit us to regard war-peace policy casually. Indochina perhaps will lessen the militancy with which the United States works out its salvation along with the rest of the world, but not the awareness that American well-being depends heavily on that of other nations.

Ironically coupled with this new capacity and will to use force abroad are consequences of intervention that defy prediction and risk catastrophe more relentlessly than ever before. Since 1945 the pace, complexity, and hazard of foreign affairs have grown exponentially. A misstep invites troubles unimagined when the United States was safe behind its ocean moats. Even the time when weak states might be "policed" with little risk of violating international law and political sensibilities has passed. No more with relative impunity may the American military punish backward peoples who have attacked our citizens and property, or pursue criminals across the borders of weak states, or occupy and administer dissolute Caribbean countries. The war powers do indeed pose old controversies of new importance. More than at any time since 1789, we need to understand and order the process by which this country decides when and how to use its military abroad.

Control over Policy and Tools

At the outset, what exactly do the "war powers" include? No one answer is cast in constitutional stone. Most realistically viewed, these powers range widely. At a minimum they speak to military prerogatives: for instance, control over raising, organizing, and supporting troops, their command, and disbanding; over when and why to fight, military strategy, and tactics; and over the terms and timing of peace. More broadly understood, the war powers refer to prerogatives over *all* American actions that significantly affect when the country must make military decisions and what they will be. Where, for example, has the Constitution placed authority over American policy on the treatment of aliens, on neutrality in other nations' conflicts, on territorial claims and concessions? Use of the military is usually begun under circumstances that make resort to it hard to resist. Pressures for commitment exist that often could have been mitigated had different American policies been pursued during the formative period. Thus, control over American policy on war and peace involves more than a voice in eleventh-hour decisions whether to commit troops. Further, nonmilitary policy provides vital support to armed efforts once underway—trade with an enemy ceases during war and its renewal aids peace.

Inescapably, also, the war powers speak to authority over *tools* (*e.g.*, men, money, and treaties) essential to carry out *policy*. In a government of separated powers, there is no guarantee that a decision maker will have equal authority both to initiate policy and to provide the tools necessary to implement it.

An unholy number of issues are subsumed in the question *how* control is allocated among the various pretenders to the war powers. To place some bounds on our inquiry, we will look only at the issues raised by division of these powers between the President and Congress. Even then the issues are legion, because the war powers must be allocated in specific factual contexts. No one split of authority between the President and Congress governs all of these situations any more than a single legal consequence arises when one person kills another. Homicide's factual contexts range from premeditated murder to accidental killing. Important distinctions exist even within the former—eliminating a business rival being less tolerable than cannibalism among the shipwrecked. Similarly, questions concerning authority over war and peace arise in distinct factual contexts, each posing a different issue and many receiving different answers as to the respective powers of the President and Congress. There is no "approved" list of factual variables that bear on the division of control between the two branches. History suggests, however, that seven sorts of facts have been especially important. Their outlines follow.

Variable One: The Type of Action

The breadth of policy pertinent to American war and peace has already been suggested. It runs from use of all possible armed force through limited military measures to unarmed action (diplomatic, economic, and the like). The respective prerogatives of the President and Congress are strongly affected by the type of action involved. For now, a list of the principal types important to the war powers will do.

Military Action

Only one of the following steps involves outright combat. The others, even if "bloodless," can nonetheless cost the country dearly—more dearly than armed action that involves only piddling fighting from start to finish. Some such bloodless ventures risk American involvement in major hostilities. Others have profound economic, political, legal, or moral consequences despite the absence of combat, for example, those stemming from an American invasion and occupation of an unwilling but impotent state. Defense or aggression is most successful, of course, when accomplished without the necessity for battle. Listed below, then, are various types of military action over which control must be divided between the President and Congress:

1. Changing the size, weapons, or readiness of the armed forces, *e.g.*, increasing the army by ten divisions through mobilization of reserves, suddenly floating global fleets against a tradition of simple coastal defense, replacing existing nuclear missiles with more sophisticated weapons, or merely raising the level of alert for strategic bombers.

2. Deploying the military anywhere on land, sea, or air for short periods, including on the borders or within the territories of other states, *e.g.*, moving radar command aircraft and naval task forces closer to potential foes, or having military units remain at foreign bases after their scheduled departure date. Such deployment can occur while American forces are still within our boundaries—massing troops on the Mexican border. This sort of action also includes outright invasion of another state's territory, so long as the undertaking is bloodless and brief.

3. Stationing the military in foreign territory for long periods, whether as an occupying or allied force.

4. Using the military to govern territory newly acquired by the United States.

5. Sending military personnel to train or advise foreign armed forces, whether those of another nation, insurgent group, or international organization.

6. Allowing merchant ships to arm themselves against attack by international outlaws or by the forces of another state. Also, providing private vessels with military protection on each vessel or by convoy. And tracking the movements of foreign war ships thought hostile to American or other friendly vessels.

7. Airlifting persons or matériel across disputed or hostile territory.

8. Searching or seizing foreign citizens or property on land or sea. By the same token, forcing their ships to port or aircraft to earth for search or seizure.

9. Blockading foreign territory by land, sea, or air.

10. Intelligence operations in or against other states.

11. Verbal or written threats or assurances about the circumstances in which the United States will take military action to help or hurt other countries, insurgent groups, or international organizations, whether delivered by declarations of American policy, through formal agreements with foreign entities, by the demeanor or words of American officials, or by some other sign of national intent.

12. Formal declarations of war.

13. Combat, from a few shots to major hostilities, involving armed attack on foreign persons or property by the regular American military, our secret agents, or foreign mercenaries, and involving overt or covert action.

Nonmilitary Action with Impact on War and Peace
Emphasis properly goes to the military ventures just listed. Use or nonuse of the armed forces has no peer in shaping war and peace. The provocative potential of nonmilitary action, moreover, tends to vary more with the times—territorial claims and concessions have largely lost their sting today (barring a rush to annex the oceans) though they were potent during the 1800s. Nonetheless, action regarding many matters other than the

purely military has always been important to our war and peace. Listed below are various nonmilitary subjects with whose control the war powers are concerned:

1. Aliens when they are neither military nor diplomatic personnel: the terms of their entry and stay in this country, of their naturalization and extradition.

2. American individuals, organizations, and businesses abroad: the terms of their exit from and reentry to this country, *e.g.*, whether they may participate in Olympics abroad, their regulation while outside America, and their treatment by foreign governments, *e.g.*, whether they are held hostage.

3. Apologies whatever the affront: demands that they be made to the United States, and their offering or refusal by America to other governments.

4. Economic claims whatever their basis: the definition, prosecution, or waiver of American claims, public or private, against other states, and the satisfaction or rejection of foreign claims against America.

5. Fiscal or monetary policy with international effect.

6. Foreign aid: money, matériel, and civilian personnel.

7. Foreign officials and troops: the terms of their American entry, stay, and exit.

8. Ideological and political operations by this country abroad and by other states in America: their existence and nature.

9. International law: its recognition by the United States and our adherence to or violation of it.

10. International conferences, summits, and ad hoc joint-ventures: American political participation.

11. International organizations: American membership, political participation, financial support, and adherence to or disregard of the organizations' recommendations or orders.

12. Neutrality in foreign conflicts.

13. Recognition by this country of new states, new govern-

ments, belligerents, and the making or breaking of diplomatic relations with them.

14. Technology and scientific data: the terms of their flow into and out of this country.

15. Territorial claims and concessions by the United States.

16. Trade policy.

17. Verbal or written threats and assurances about the circumstances in which America will take nonmilitary action of any of the sorts above to help or hurt other states, international ventures or organizations.

Variable Two: Purpose of the Action

It also matters to the war powers of the President and Congress *why* action is taken. Is the country seeking to repel an ongoing attack on American territory, to rescue our citizens attacked abroad, to defend an ally against internal subversion, to enforce international law's ban on piracy, to obey a U.N. call for collective security?

Historically, two sorts of purpose have proved especially important: (1) response to attack and (2) enforcement of laws. Suppressing domestic insurrection involves both. As regards other sorts of attacks to which America may wish to respond, the assault could fall on territory, persons, or property. The territory attacked might be American or foreign. If American, we might hold clear title to it, or it might be claimed by another state as well, and if the latter, our claim might be recognized by both the President and Congress or by the President alone. The attack might be by open or covert invasion, or by domestic rebels. Persons and property assaulted might be American or foreign, civilian or military, and they could be attacked on American or foreign territory, on the open sea, or in international airspace. Finally, the attack might be physical or only paper, for instance, verbal or written saber rattling, even a formal declaration of war not physically implemented.

Basic response options are equally varied. The United States could (a) preemptively strike and destroy a foreign force before it can attack, or remove to safety the intended victim of its attack; (b) meet and repel an ongoing assault; (c) engage in hot pursuit of the erstwhile attacker to destroy his capacity for immediate renewal of assault; (d) recapture any territory, person, or property seized by him; (e) take short-term punitive action or reprisals against the attacker; or (f) take offensive action against him on a scale disproportionate to that of the attack, after his capacity for imminent assault has ended and reprisals against him have been completed.

The prime laws for enforcement are congressional statutes, joint resolutions, declarations of war, and the like. Historically, the enforcement of treaties has also had considerable war-power significance. Other possibilities include (a) international law, for instance, any government's right to attack pirates, or to protect persons from mob violence on foreign territory at the request of host officials unable themselves to maintain order, or to take military steps against attack coming from the territory of a third state unable or unwilling to prevent it; (b) presidential agreements with foreign powers, for example, pacts among neighboring nations allowing hot pursuit of outlaws across their respective borders, or agreements with enemy states on the terms and conditions of cease-fire; and (c) *inchoate* foreign interests of the United States identified by the Executive alone, that is, foreign policy objectives not set out in any congressional act, treaty, principle of international law, or formal presidential agreement with another country (whatever these inchoate interests may be, whether desire for territorial gain, military bases, or the credibility of American commitments).

Variable Three: Costs of the Action

Beyond the type of action in question and its purpose, the costs that it imposes on the country affect each branch's prerogative to set policy. Such burdens have several dimensions. First, magnitude: All costs are not equal. It is important to know, for example, whether a physical loss of a few lives or millions is at stake. Second, immediacy: War-peace steps must often be begun before much, if any, of their potential harm has concretely developed. To the extent that projected rather than

known costs are in question, distinctions must be drawn between the degrees of risk present. Further, the greater the potential harm, the more rapidly its risks become significant;
slight chance of nuclear exchange outweighs the near certainty
of small-scale conventional combat.

Third, the kind of harm involved: Destruction out of a can-
non's mouth does not bound the possibilities. In addition to
such physical harm there are a variety of economic, political,
legal, moral, and social ills. We have already noted that in some
situations bloodless military action can hurt the country more
than actual combat. Among the important sorts of costs are:

1. Physical loss through death or injury to all touched by the
action, but especially American citizens.

2. Economic loss to all affected, again particularly Americans in both their foreign and domestic interests. Economic
harm may range from destruction of possessions and means of
production to heightened taxation, inflation and trade deficits.

3. Diminished legal rights for Americans at home and
abroad, for instance, the draft with its burdens on personal
freedom, earnings, schooling, and safety; censorship; and the
loss of treaty privileges abroad.

4. Diversion of resources and energy from other uses at
home and abroad, thus war-induced slackening of steps to improve the quality of life.

5. Harm to the political, legal, and moral effectiveness of the
federal government if its action is thought by many Americans
to violate constitutional or international law, to be immoral, or
to make no sense as a matter of policy.

6. Harm to the foreign interests of the United States, including its physical security, if other states think our action violates
international law or makes no sense as a matter of policy.

7. Finally, social and political disruption at home and
abroad stemming from the American venture, for example,
riots protesting government policy.

In this century particularly, there have been rumblings that
the only sorts of action which count for war-power purposes

are actual combat, formal declarations of war, and measures termed "war" by international law (whether declared or not) and thus that the only sorts of costs which affect the war powers are those caused by such action. Similarly, there has been suggestion that only costs of great magnitude and immediacy are relevant, small or potential harm having no bearing. But the language of the Constitution, the gloss given it by the Framers and Ratifiers, and practice since 1789 support a broader understanding of the relevant action and costs. The country has worried about the division of authority between the President and Congress when costs stemmed from many different types of action and when these costs were small or simply potential.

Variable Four: A Need for Speed or Secrecy

Swift or secret action has often been thought essential, for instance, to negotiations with foreign states, intelligence operations, preemptive American strikes against imminent attack, blunting ongoing enemy assault, hot pursuit of miscreants, rescue of their victims, and punishment of an aggressor while he remains receptive to reprisal as something other than a clarion to renewed combat. As we shall see, in league with variable number two (purpose), the need for speed or secrecy has freed Presidents at times when variable number three (costs) might otherwise have encouraged them to obtain prior congressional approval before acting. Thus "emergency" uses of force have generally joined a response-to-attack purpose with an assumed necessity for quick or covert action if purpose is to be well effected.

Variable Five: The Phase of Action

We have been talking about action as if it were a monolithic process. This oversimplifies reality. Like other events, steps involving war and peace pass through three stages that are important themselves to how the war powers are divided. First comes *initiation*: (a) gathering information indicating a need for action and alternative ways in which it can be taken, a prime function of groups such as the Central Intelligence Agency and American embassies abroad; (b) recommending which alternative best serves the national interest, a responsibility often assumed by executive staff members, the National Security Council, and congressional committees and leaders; (c) choosing that alternative which those in authority believe offers the country the greatest benefit at the least cost; (d) providing tools necessary to get the venture underway, that is, men, money, possibly international agreements with allies or international organizations, certainly communications with foreign entities, and perhaps the enactment of domestic regulations such as draft laws.

Once the action has been initiated, it enters a period of *conduct*. Then policies governing the venture must be interpreted to see what they call for in evolving circumstances; strategy and tactics to execute these policies must be set, and additional implementing tools provided as necessary.

Finally, there comes a third phase: the *limitation or termination* of the action. This phase involves the review of developments to date and decision either that the initial objectives have been realized, that they were defective from the outset, or that changed circumstances have undone them. The governing decisions of the action are then modified or the venture wholly ended. Ending an action poses a number of separate problems. If it involved major combat, steps must be taken concerning the terms and timing of cease-fire, prisoner exchange, the extent of American withdrawal from theaters of combat, the resolution of economic claims between the belligerents, whether to resume diplomatic relations and treaty obligations with the former enemy, when to end civil and economic restraints and executive emergency powers in the United States, and whether to grant amnesty to draft dodgers, to name a few.

Variable Six: The Tools
Essential to Implement Policy

American action does not spring spontaneously into being when the President or Congress speaks or writes something down on paper. Policy must be effected by tools. Five have been especially important to action for war and peace:

1. Personnel: Policy is implemented by people, from infantry privates to special diplomatic agents, who may or may not be in federal service when the need for them arises.

2. Money: The funds may already lie in the Treasury earmarked for action of the sort in question, or they may still rest untaxed in private pockets.

3. Agreements with other states or international organizations: American action often depends on covenants with foreign entities, whether by treaty or the timely nod of a presidential head.

4. Channels of communication between the United States and other governments, international organizations, or foreign citizens: Whether to exchange information, negotiate, threaten, or assure, this country's steps toward war or peace hinge heavily on use of such channels.

5. Regulations governing the conduct of private American citizens: American policy is frequently dependent on draft laws, neutrality provisions, wartime censorship, the suspension of habeas corpus during military emergency, and the like.

The arbiter of tools can sway policy just as soon as the means it controls become indispensable, and possibly sooner in anticipation of their coming indispensability. Allocation of the war powers is simplest when the type of action and tools in question suggest control for the same branch. Later pages make clear that this simplicity is rare. Policy initiative for the Executive has often evolved in response to the type of the action in question (*e.g.*, threats and assurances to other nations) without corresponding growth in presidential control over all of the necessary implementing tools: That the President may state a policy does not necessarily mean that he has authority to raise the men and funds, conclude the international agreements, and adopt the domestic regulations necessary to execute it. At the same time, his raw power to use tools *in hand* to shape events has often left the legislators supine by the time additional means under their control became essential: That Congress can slam the Treasury on military action begun unilaterally by the Executive is significant only if the legislators' will to do it has survived his fait accompli.

Variable Seven: The Extent of Congressional-Executive Involvement

A final fact affecting the war powers is the extent to which each branch is involved in setting the policy at issue. Is the President fixing it while Congress remains silent, or vice-versa? Have both branches taken explicit but contrary positions, or have they adopted a common policy? It will suffice for now to flesh out these possibilities.

What is the President's prerogative to set policy when Congress as a whole remains legislatively silent about the matter; that is, when no prior statute, joint resolution, or treaty explicitly authorizes the Executive's action, and no explicit ratification is given it after the fact? This need not mean (1) an absence of comment by individual Congressmen or committees, (2) a lack of effort to have legislation passed (including measures that, had they been adopted, would have limited or forbidden the President's policy), (3) no passage of explicit "sense" resolutions by one or both houses, or (4) the refusal to provide tools essential to implement the Executive's policy. Excluded only is a binding expression of congressional sentiment about the policy itself.

Assuming such congressional silence, the President could recommend action to Congress, give the legislators a reasonable time in which to vote yea or nay, and then, confronted by their inertia, act as he thinks best with no further resort to them. Or, after acting first on his own authority, he could report immediately what he had done to Congress and give it a reasonable time to ratify, limit, or terminate his policy. When still confronted with failure by the House and Senate to take a position, he might set policy thereafter as he thinks best, with no further resort to Congress, or with periodic reports to it. Or, conversely, he might terminate the action himself on the ground that he lacked legislative backing.

Similarly, the President could act as sparingly as possible until he has an opportunity to report to Congress and seek its approval. His options would then be the same as those just noted: Faced with congressional silence, he might govern the action thereafter with no further resort to the legislators, govern it but report periodically to them, or end it immediately for lack of their approval. Finally, of course, the President could simply act without prior or post resort to the legislators.

What, in turn, is Congress's prerogative when it legislates about war and peace without the President's recommendation, signature, or veto; that is, when he participates as passively as his constitutional duty to take care that the laws be faithfully executed permits. Obviously, if Congress votes against action, he need do nothing at all. If the vote is for action, the President's willingness to execute policy which became law without his taking part in the legislative process is analogous to Congress's providing tools to implement executive policy, or the legislators' refusing to vote restraints on it. In either case the passive branch has not expressly approved the active branch's steps. Even if Congress rarely acts on matters of war and peace without executive recommendation, signature, or veto, the scope of the legislators' capacity to do so remains an important element in the division of the war powers between the two branches. Congressional initiative could be crucial to spur an incompetent or weak Executive, as well as to spur the hesitant subordinates of a disabled or venal one.

What are the two branches' prerogatives when both act, but at one another's jugulars; that is, when despite the President's recommendation Congress refuses to authorize a particular war-peace policy or when over the Executive's veto the legislators direct that particular steps be taken? Open policy conflict between the two branches poses the fundamental war-power problem, because then presidential and congressional authority must be determined unalloyed, without the support of the other branch's silence or acquiescence. There are three core possibilities. (a) The President could act as he thinks best, to the point of ignoring contrary congressional acts or treating them as advisory only; in other words, no matter what authority Congress had to legislate while the President was silent, Congress has no prerogative over the matter once he takes a contrary position. (b) Just the reverse: Congress could control policy as it sees fit, rejecting the President's recommendations and overriding his vetoes; no matter what authority the President had to set policy while Congress remained silent, his control ends when the legislators take an explicit position to the contrary. (c) Or the two branches might have concurrent authority, the assent of each being necessary to change the status quo. Concurrent authority would preclude the beginning of action without their joint agreement, on the one hand, and the limitation or termination of any ongoing venture without similar agreement, on the other hand—Congress might not commit America to war over the President's veto, nor might he end our involvement in conflict if Congress voted its continuation.

Finally, there is the more happy situation of *explicit* interbranch accord. Agreement can come either through prior approval of a proposed venture by the President *and* Congress or by one's after-the-fact ratification of the other's action. Congress is represented either by majorities in both houses or the Senate by two-thirds of its members when treaties are at stake. The approval may speak directly to a particular action or to a class of ventures within which it clearly falls. Thus Congress might pass, and the President sign, legislation authorizing armed action against a particular nest of pirates, or the two branches might opt for legislation authorizing expeditions against pirates wherever and whenever they come to the Executive's attention.

Agreement between the branches poses a special set of warpower issues. Must particular types of action be approved by specific sorts of instruments? For instance, does a declaration of war provide the only constitutional means by which the President and Congress may commit American forces to large-scale combat. Similarly, to what extent may the President and Senate, bypassing the House, commit the country to war-peace action by treaty? An even more ubiquitous bone of contention since 1789 has been the extent to which Congress may delegate authority to the President to set American policy as he sees fit. A related issue arises if both branches agree to a particular course of action on the happening of certain future events—a congressional joint resolution signed by the President providing that the United States shall automatically be at war with any nation that physically attacks Great Britain. The constitutionality of such contingent agreement has been attacked, as with congressional delegations to the President, on the ground that it eliminates a weighing of costs and benefits at the moment of truth, important because their balance can have altered since the time both branches chose the policy in question.

Then there are questions of ratification. Does it matter how long after the fact one branch signals its approval of the other's fait accompli? May ratification cure action otherwise unconstitutional as beyond the single authority of the active branch? Is it significant if the active branch obtains ratification through misleading or false information or under the pressure of a contrived deadline? In short, the Constitution's war-power problems are eased but not wholly swept away when the two branches explicitly agree. Of course, too, their agreement poses most purely the question of the *nation's* war powers. Recall the possible limits on those powers from state and individual prerogatives and international law.

In varying combinations, the seven variables identified above produce a hefty number of situations in which the Constitution must divide the war powers between the President and Congress. Fortunately, the number of allocational outcomes is more modest. They were previewed during comment on the last variable. Thus the President may set policy as he sees fit when Congress is silent *if* the facts at hand involve X, Y, or Z combination of action, purpose, costs, need for speed or secrecy, phase, and tools. And so on for the legislators' prerogative when the Executive is passive, as well as for the war powers of each branch when they are at odds or in explicit agreement. Now that all these variables have been loosed, it may help to draw them together in an illustrative conundrum:

Sketch of a Typical War-Power Problem

Variables	*Constitutional Issues*
Type of Action: Proposed deployment of American marines on foreign soil	Given these facts and the Constitution's war-power requirements, what is the constitutional allocation of control between the two branches? For example:
Purpose: To rescue American citizens from imminent physical attack	

Sketch of a Typical War-Power Problem (*cont.*)

Variables	Constitutional Issues
Costs: Unavoidable political and legal liabilities, because entry of the marines would be explicitly opposed by the government of the country in which the Americans are threatened; potential physical and economic costs, as the deployment would seriously risk significant combat with local troops and confrontation with their great power supporter	(1) Does the President have an absolute prerogative to act as he thinks most in the national interest?
Need for Speed or Secrecy: Speed crucial to successful rescue of the endangered Americans, and secret preparation of the deployment useful to minimize the risk of combat	Or (2) is his prerogative conditioned upon (a) his prior unsuccessful effort to obtain congressional approval, or upon (b) his report to Congress immediately after committing the marines, coupled with his willingness to accept congressional limits on, or end to, his initiative?
Phase: Initiation of the venture	Or (3) should the President withhold the marines because he lacks prior congressional approval, even if it is denied by inaction rather than a negative vote?
Tools: Marines already raised, funded, and generally available to the commander in chief	
Congressional - Executive Involvement: President prepared to act but Congress has taken no position and seems unlikely to act	

CHAPTER II

The Constitutional Text

IF WE could find a man in the state of nature and have him first scan the war-power provisions of the Constitution and then look at war-power practice since 1789, he would marvel at how much Presidents have spun out of so little. On its face, the text tilts decisively toward Congress. Comparison of Articles I and IV with Article II shows that most of the specific grants of authority run to Congress. The pertinent provisions appear in Appendix A. Reading them straight through provides an insight that nothing else can into how the Constitution itself divides the war powers. The sequence in which the text assigns authority to each branch, the location of certain provisions relative to others, and the simple weight of the words devoted to Congress as opposed to the President are telling, as is the precise language of the grants.

In addition, provision for suspending habeas corpus during military emergency is set out in the legislative, not the executive, article of the Constitution. And state war powers are placed with the congressional grants, rather than in Article IV with other state concerns. Also indicative of broad authority over foreign affairs is the grant in Article I to Congress of control over matters with transnational effect though little impact on war and peace, such as the mails, patents, and copyrights.

Moreover, of those few specific grants of power given to the President, two of the most important (over treaties and major federal appointments) he shares with the Senate. Thus the text supports argument that, in those war-peace areas where policy and tools are not committed to the legislative process, they are held jointly by the President and the Senate (the executive element of Congress), except for certain ministerial functions most efficiently left to one man, for instance, military command and law enforcement, and, except for powers of limited war-peace importance, such as granting pardons and commissions.

Provisions giving Congress and the President weapons with which to coerce one another again run heavily toward the legislators. Under Articles I and II the Executive can try to mold Congress through information and recommendations, by the veto, and through calling or not calling special sessions. He can attack the legislators in his public statements, but lacks authority to remove them from office. The text, on the other hand, allows Congress to negate all of these executive spurs, and the President with them. Under its Article I legislative authority, Congress may supply its own information and recommendations and override presidential vetoes. It may also refuse to pass legislation dear to the Executive, and it can investigate other branches of government preparatory to lawmaking or while overseeing the execution of existing acts. Either or both houses may pass resolutions censuring the President, and together they can dispose of him "and all Civil Officers of the United States" through impeachment.

But more important in the real world than the congressional dominance suggested by the text has been the fact that the language does not unavoidably preclude broad presidential prerogative. Congressional control is not established beyond a reasonable doubt. There are three grounds for uncertainty about the text's meaning, to which we now turn.

Many words and phrases in the Constitution's war-peace provisions are generality itself. They are neither self-defining nor susceptible to one meaning applicable in all circumstances. Each generality, accordingly, can be made concrete in many ways. And whether expansively or narrowly construed, each has a number of different meanings, reflecting the factual differences in the war-power contexts that it governs. Thus, whether an ample reading of the declaration-of-war clause is linked with a spare interpretation of the commander-in-chief proviso, or vice-versa, the meaning given both provisions will vary with the type of action in question, its purpose and costs, whether there is a need for speed or secrecy, the tools required to implement it, and so on. "A word is not a crystal, transparent and unchanged," Mr. Justice Holmes suggested. Rather, he said, "it is the skin of a living thought and may vary greatly in color and content according to the circumstances and the time in which it is used."[1] While this cannot fairly be said of all words, it certainly fits many of the crucial provisions in the war-power text.

Doubt also exists because the text gives certain powers to the President and others to Congress that can be read to cover the same areas in mutually exclusive fashions.[2] These competing grants permit each branch to claim authority over many common aspects of the war powers. Edward S. Corwin spoke of "logical incompatibles" and said that the "Constitution, considered only for its affirmative grants of powers capable of affecting the issue, is an invitation to struggle for the privilege of directing American foreign policy."[3]

In fairness to the text, illogic and struggle do not have to characterize its affirmative grants. Struggle rises to fever pitch only when expansive readings are given to ill-defined Article II powers of the President, that is, when the clauses dealing with executive power, law enforcement, and military command are construed to involve the President in areas over which Article I has given Congress more explicit grants of authority. Competition is greatly lessened when congressional authority is read generously and presidential sparingly, for the Constitution provides the Executive with far fewer clearly defined responsibilities than it does Congress.

In addition to ill-defined, frequently competitive provisions, there are also numerous gaps in the war-power provisions. Though the text deals quite directly with some of the issues described in Chapter I, it conspicuously fails to speak to others, as we shall see.

Type of Action

Article I gives Congress authority "[t]o declare War" and "grant Letters of Marque and Reprisal." This language squarely

addresses the allocation of control over American involvement
in actual combat, but what concretely does it mean? "War" can
be read to cover any fighting, even if only a few shots are fired.
Or it can be restricted to significant hostilities, with various
constitutional measures for significance. Similarly, "marque
and reprisal" can be understood as shorthand for small-scale,
limited fighting and thus as confirmation that "war" covers all
combat, whatever its scale. But the text also permits us to dismiss "marque and reprisal" as a mode of private warfare long
since given up by the world and irrelevant today.

Equally unclear is what the text means when it says that Congress has the power "to declare" war. Read most stingily, "to
declare" gives the legislators nothing other than the right to *recognize* by formal declaration that a state of war exists. More
generously viewed, they are entitled to authorize war before
this country physically fights, although their approval may be
only an eleventh-hour gesture. Or "to declare" can be equated
with general authority over the commencement of war, including a say in steps leading to it on the assumption that when the
text grants a power it also grants authority over the decisions
that shape the context in which the power will be exercised.

What about congressional control over bloodless uses of the
military, from deployment on? The Article I, Section 8 proviso
that Congress is "[t]o make Rules for the Government and Regulation of the land and naval Forces" is relevant, as are provisions on "war" and "marque and reprisal." No self-evident
meaning graces "government and regulation." Though this language is most easily read to cover such matters as rules for military organization and discipline, it can also be read to cover
how the armed forces are used, especially their deployment
and stationing. "Government," in particular, supports expansive interpretation.

It is also possible to extrapolate "war" and "marque and reprisal" into congressional control over almost all bloodless uses
of the military, or to stop at various intermediate points. The
language accepts legislative authority over any use that *risks* or
precedes combat, with various understandings of how great
the risk of combat must be and how severe the potential fight-

ing. At a minimum, bloodless preparatory action appears to fall within the meaning of "war" in the Article I, Section 10 proviso that the states, unauthorized by Congress, may not "engage in War" unless "in such *imminent* Danger as will not admit of delay." Or, more broadly understood, "war" and "marque and reprisal" can be totally cut loose from the concept of combat and extended to any use of the military that imposes costs on the country: for example, the economic, political, legal, and moral penalties stemming from American occupation of a reluctant but weak state. Most favorably construed for Congress, then, "war" and "marque and reprisal" require legislative control as soon as any use of the military slightly risks even modest costs to the country, whatever their nature. Least favorably construed for Congress, "war" covers none of the bloodless uses and is limited to ongoing, large-scale combat, possibly just a formal declaration that such hostilities exist. "Marque and reprisal," in turn, are dismissed as anachronism.

What can the text do for presidential claims to authority over the various types of military action? Read narrowly, nothing. Then no provisions exist suggesting that the President may unilaterally make decisions concerning the use of the military as an instrument of American policy. So read, his most direct claim to power—designation as commander in chief—carries with it no policymaking authority, except as setting strategy and tactics amounts to policymaking. Under this interpretation, the commander-in-chief clause simply confers command on the President as first general and admiral.

Read more broadly, the injunction that "[t]he President shall be Commander in Chief of the Army and Navy of the United States, and of the Militia of the several States, when called into the actual Service of the United States" has almost limitless potential. At its apex, it carries plenary authority over all military action except that incontestably given to Congress: raising and supporting the armed forces, perhaps their organization, formal declarations of war, and letters of marque and reprisal.

Presidential claims to military control gain further textual support from the executive-power clause broadly construed and from an expansive reading of Article II, Section 3, that the

President "shall take Care that the Laws be faithfully executed." The latter, of course, may amount only to a presidential duty to enforce the precise terms of legislation or treaties.
Or it can be grandly construed, first, to empower the President
to use the military to enforce congressional acts or treaties that
themselves say nothing about such armed execution. Second,
"laws" can be read to include not just congressional directives
and treaties but also American international agreements made
solely on presidential authority, other international rights and
duties of the country, and even inchoate foreign policy objectives. Finally a sweeping "take-care" interpretation can accommodate presidential definition of which international rights
and duties, and which inchoate foreign policy objectives, are to
be classified as "laws." Thus, once the President has identified
an American security interest as "law," he may then "take care"
that it be "faithfully executed" via military force.

Recognition and diplomatic relations provide apt examples
of textual uncertainty regarding *nonmilitary* action with war-
peace consequences. Once again the terms used are ambiguous, and once again competing grants of authority are made to
the two branches.

A leap to congressional control over recognition and diplomatic relations may take flight from any of a number of textual
bases. First, it may be assumed (though the Constitution is silent about the matter) that the United States as a sovereign nation has power over its formal relations with other countries,
and Congress in turn has constitutional authority to make all
laws "necessary and proper for carrying into Execution" the
powers of the federal government. Second, most of the Constitution's specific grants of control over action related to war and
peace are given to the legislators, thereby suggesting Congress
as the repository of control over any such action not explicitly
mentioned. Third, provisions defining the war-power authority of the states appear in Section 10 of the congressional article,
another sign that Congress is the war-power sump to which
flows control denied the states and from which flow only specific derogations of legislative authority in favor of either the
states or the President. Of like locational import is Article I,

Section 9, clause 2, dealing with suspension of habeas corpus during military emergency. Fourth, the reference in Article II, Section 2, to "Officers of the United States" can be read to require either Senate confirmation or congressional authorization for the appointment of all American representatives to other countries. Finally, decisions about recognition or diplomatic relations may lead to hostilities, and the declaration-of-war clause can be construed to give Congress control not only over an American decision to fight but also over any other action that affects the likelihood of war, such as making and breaking ties with other countries.

Turning to the Executive, language that he "shall receive Ambassadors and other public Ministers" bears directly on recognition and diplomatic relations. But to what effect? At one pole, the text can be understood simply to describe a ceremonial function assigned to the President to avoid the inconvenience of assembling Congress to receive diplomats. Under this resolution of ambiguity, the language confers not a power over American diplomacy but a ceremonial duty to handle one byproduct of decision to have ties with a foreign power, whichever branch has made that decision. At the other pole is a reading which first interprets the reception of "ambassadors and other public ministers" to mean executive control over the presence in America of any foreign official, and then couples this prerogative with the presidential-senatorial appointment of American diplomats, to give the Executive complete sway over our policy on recognition and diplomatic relations.

Also important is the Article II, Section 1 declaration that "[t]he executive Power shall be vested in a President of the United States of America." Pregnantly absent from this language is the "herein granted" qualifying the equivalent Article I, Section 1 proviso that "[a]ll legislative Powers *herein granted* shall be vested in a Congress of the United States." Despite the missing "herein," Article II, Section 1, can be construed merely to give the American chief executive a title and his power a name. Definition of the content of that power is provided, under this interpretation, by the affirmative (or enumerated) grants stated elsewhere. Such a narrow construction of the executive-power clause, of course, provides no base from which to extrapolate presidential prerogative over much of anything.

On the other hand, a great deal may be divined from the missing "herein." Pushed to its outer limits, the executive-power clause can be read to authorize the President to act for the national good restrained only by specific grants of power to Congress, the courts or states, or by specific limitations on presidential and national prerogatives. So magnified, the clause ensures executive control over recognition and diplomatic relations suggested by the language on appointing and receiving diplomats.

One last contender for control over these sorts of action remains. The Senate with the President has textual possibilities. Control over major federal appointments is shared by the two, as is treaty making. Moreover, one reading of advice and consent by the Senate during the treaty process calls for full senatorial as well as presidential involvement in American negotiations with other nations. And "treaties" can be seen as the *sole* mechanism by which this country makes international agreements. From joint executive-senatorial control over diplomatic staffing and the full process of making agreements with other countries, it is but a short leap to their joint stewardship over all aspects of American foreign affairs not otherwise explicitly allocated by the Constitution. Under this reading, recognition and diplomatic relations fall naturally among the decisions to be made by the President and Senators gathered in executive council.

That the Constitution speaks squarely to some types of war-peace action and not to others is clear by now. Doubt about how to bridge the gaps accommodates contradictory textual constructions of the sort just noted.[4] The constitutional language dealing with military action is especially spare. Changing the size or composition of the armed forces and changing weaponry do receive direct mention in the authority given Congress over raising, supporting, and regulating the military in Article I, Section 8, clauses 12-17. Searching and seizing foreign citizens and property are brushed by congressional powers to define and punish crimes on the high seas and offenses against the law of nations, to make rules for captures on land and water, and to grant letters of marque and reprisal.

But for all the other sorts of military action, we have only the language in Article I, Section 8, that Congress may "declare War" and "grant Letters of Marque and Reprisal," and in Section 10 that "[n]o State shall, without the consent of Congress, . . . engage in War, unless actually invaded, or in such imminent Danger as will not admit of delay." These provisions ignore most bloodless uses of American armed force: deployment, stationing, occupation and governance, advising foreign troops, arming merchantmen, convoys, airlifts, blockades, intelligence operations, verbal or written threats and assurances, and the like. Power to govern such action must be drawn from aspects of the text that say nothing directly about them.

Of nonmilitary action, the text ignores this country's demanding or granting international apologies; the definition, prosecution, or waiver of American economic claims against other governments or American response to foreign claims; the terms for the entry, stay, and exit of foreign troops in America; this country's ideological and political operations abroad; American participation in international ventures and organizations; our neutrality in foreign conflicts; and threats and assurances about the circumstances in which the United States will use nonmilitary means to hurt or help other countries or international organizations.

In addition to these complete gaps, reference is partial at best to a range of other nonmilitary action. The only specific language on the treatment of aliens empowers Congress to establish a uniform rule of naturalization; there is nothing about setting the terms for the entry, stay, and exit of aliens, including such matters as extradition and immigration policy, nor about this country's regulation of Americans abroad or its interchange with foreign governments regarding their treatment. The only explicit provisions on international fiscal and monetary policy deal with congressional authority to coin money and to determine the value of American and foreign currency. Nothing is said about foreign aid, except as it falls under congressional power to dispose of American property. Adherence by the United States to international law has one fleeting mention in congressional authority to define and punish crimes on the high seas and offenses against the law of nations.

As we have seen, for the diverse action involved in American recognition of foreign states, governments, and belligerents, and in diplomatic relations with them, there are only two provisions squarely on point: that the President and Senate shall appoint American ambassadors and that the Executive shall receive ministers from abroad. Nothing is said about the presence in or passage through the United States of foreign officials, other than that the President is to receive foreign ambassadors. And there is no mention of territorial claims or concessions by this country over land, sea, continental shelf, air, or space, other than that Congress controls the disposal of American territory and the admission of new states to the Union.

Purpose

Article I, Section 8, authorizes Congress to tax to "provide for the common Defence," to punish crimes on the high seas and offenses against international law, and to call "forth the Militia to execute the Laws of the Union, suppress Insurrections and repel Invasions." Section 8 also states without qualification that Congress may raise armies and a navy, declare war, and grant letters of marque and reprisal. And this section is virtually as unqualified in its authority to Congress "[t]o make all Laws . . . necessary and proper for carrying into Execution" federal powers. Thus, while the text creates some question as to the uses to which the militia may be put and arguably the constitutional right of Congress to tax for aggressive war, it does not suggest that congressional authority over the war powers is affected by the purpose behind legislative action so far as the division of these powers between the legislators and the President is concerned.

The purpose behind executive action is equally irrelevant if the executive-power, commander-in-chief, and take-care clauses are squeezed to the limits of textual tolerance to produce presidential prerogative over all military action except a few types clearly given to Congress. If these clauses are given a less cosmic cast, search ensues for purposes permitting the President to act on his own. The textual elements of a law-enforcement justification have already been sketched.[5]

Response to attack is also a perennial favorite. Although the states may engage "without the Consent of Congress . . .in War . . . [if] actually invaded, or in such imminent Danger as will not admit of delays," there is no equivalent language authorizing executive response to either ongoing or imminent attack. Still, in light of the commander-in-chief clause and of the use of "declare" rather than a more fulsome verb like "make" in the declaration-of-war grant to Congress, the text supports executive response to sudden foreign attack on America, pending an opportunity for Congress to take action. Further support comes in Article IV, Section 4, which states that "[t]he United States . . . shall protect each of [the States] against Invasion." The President can be understood as the initial agent by which "[t]he United States" provides protection.[6]

Costs

As with purpose, the costs of action have textual significance for unilateral executive action. Unlike purpose, justification by costs involves limits on congressional authority—those that can be derived from a narrow reading of "war." If war means serious combat, the text permits extrapolation to presidential control over (1) all bloodless uses of the military, no matter how compelling their nonphysical costs, except for those few uses explicitly assigned to Congress, (2) military action that simply risks significant combat, and (3) those ventures that involve battle with minimal toll in life, limb, and property.

Need for Speed or Secrecy

Article II, Section 3, provides that "on extraordinary Occasions" the President may find it necessary to "convene both Houses, or either of them," thus recognizing that the legislators may not be sitting when the need for American use of force becomes acute. The other textual bases for executive action premised on a need for speed were just noted during discussion of response to attack. The states, of course, are the beneficiaries of the Constitution's only explicit indication that a need for speed may justify combat unauthorized by Congress. To the extent that the text mentions secrecy at all, the beneficiary is Congress. Article I, Section 5, provides that each House may exempt from the published journal of its proceedings "such Parts as may in their Judgment require Secrecy." Secrecy as justification for executive action must be drawn from executive-power and commander-in-chief language.

Phase

The Constitution says more about initiation and conduct than termination. Language with a clearly commencement cast exists. "All Bills for raising Revenue shall originate in the House of Representatives." "The Congress shall have Power . . . To declare War [and] grant Letters of Marque and Reprisal." The President "shall have Power, by and with the Advice and Consent of the Senate, to make Treaties." The problem is not that the text fails to speak to initiation but that it does so with studied ambiguity. For instance, the provisos cited leave unclear the extent to which the President and Senate, as opposed to the President and Congress as a whole, control the initiation of action that requires approval of a treaty *and* appropriation of implementing funds. And they raise doubt whether the President and Senate, versus the President and Congress, may commit the country to war by international agreement.

The text is more precise regarding conduct. The President holds the executive power. He is enjoined faithfully to execute the laws, and made commander in chief. He "may require the Opinion, in writing, of the principal Officer in each of the executive Departments, upon any Subject relating to the Duties of their respective Offices," and the text permits argument that the President may remove federal personnel engaged in "executive" tasks, though their appointment requires senatorial or congressional approval. In combination, and generously understood, these provisions readily support presidential conduct of national affairs.

When narrowly construed they still confer authority over the execution of American policy, but as an agent of the legislators. Agents may be instructed in the interpretation of their mandate, in the strategy and tactics of its execution, and in the care and tending of subordinate executive personnel. Thus, under one reading of the text, the President's authority over conduct may be contingent upon the absence of contrary, even nit-picking instructions from Congress.

If the language is more naturally read to make conduct a presidential preserve, textual difficulties then arise over the boundary between conduct, on the one hand, and initiation or termination, on the other. Executive interpretation and application of a congressional mandate may range so far afield as to become pure policymaking and tool providing. Conversely, legislative policymaking and tool providing may become so detailed that they impinge on presidential strategy and tactics. The text is not sensitive to where the lines are drawn.

It becomes wholly opaque regarding termination. Innocence suggests that control over ending action will track authority over beginning it. As a general proposition perhaps, but not with sufficient regularity to establish a reliable rule. With the help of executive control over conduct, extrapolation to executive control over termination has outstripped presidential claims to similar dominance over initiation. For example, the constitutional language can be read to support a presidential end to wars, treaties, and appointments that are also textually thought to be beyond unilateral beginning by the Executive.

The text also permits questions about how Congress may stop action begun by the President under authority delegated to him by the legislators or begun without obtaining prior congressional approval (and thus without giving both the Senate and the House a chance to vote no). The text can be read to require termination by the ordinary legislative process, with the congressional disapproval subject to executive veto. Or it can be understood to permit Congress to call a halt by concurrent resolution: majority vote in both houses without the possibility of presidential veto. The language conceivably accepts termination by majority disapproval in one house alone.

Extent of Congressional-
Executive Involvement

The language also ignores the effect of congressional inaction on presidential prerogative. It is any interpreter's judgment whether the President, when the legislators pass no relevant act, may pursue policies that would be beyond him were they to vote no. Or whether there are aspects of war-peace action immune to congressional control even if the President is willing to obey any directive that becomes law without his signature.

Similarly ignored are the situations that arise when Congress legislates against the President's recommendation and over his veto. Are there times when the Executive may ignore congressional prohibitions—when the commander in chief wishes to repel enemy attack on American territory and the legislators have voted to surrender? Are there occasions when the Executive may ignore congressional conditions—when the President wishes to use nuclear weapons in a conflict for which Congress voted only conventional arms? Are there times when the Executive may balk at specific action ordered by Congress —armed intervention by this country in a foreign war that the President thinks dead wrong? Answers of many sorts may be sculpted out of the text.

Though occasionally more direct, the language remains malleable on the constitutional requirements for agreement between the two branches. Other than the impeachment provisions, nothing appears concerning the one obtaining the consent of the other by misrepresenting facts or manipulating events. Some language does exist on the form in which agreement may be expressed, but its meaning is typically ambiguous. Because Congress shall have power "[t]o declare War," it can be concluded that only a formal declaration of war will suffice. Or, relying on the reference in Article I, Section 7, to laws, orders, resolutions, and votes, the text accepts flexibility in the form of agreement, so long as the instrument is approved by both houses of Congress and the President. The text is not clear whether a treaty, though the supreme law of the land, may authorize hostilities, since the House of Representatives has no part in treaty making but an equal say with the Senate in all explicit military powers. Nor is the text clear whether armed force as a means of execution may be read into every measure approved by Congress or the Senate, or whether authorization for violent implementation must be expressed. The text takes on none of the ratification unknowns. And it leaves vague the extent to which the President and Congress may delegate decision-making power either to the other branch or future events.[7]

Tools

Recall that the President or Congress may not have the same degree of control over both essential elements of action: setting policy and providing tools to implement it.

Personnel

Concerning personnel, Congress is overwhelmingly endowed compared to the President. The legislators have their complex of authority over raising and regulating the armed forces; the Senate shares appointment authority with the President over "Ambassadors . . . and all other Officers of the United States, whose Appointments are not herein otherwise provided for, and which shall be established by Law," and Congress as a whole under Article II, Section 2, "may by Law vest the Appointment of such inferior Officers, as they think proper, in the President alone . . . or in the Heads of Departments." Article I, Section 8, clause 18, empowers Congress "[t]o make all Laws which shall be necessary and proper for carrying into Execution [its] Powers, and all other Powers vested by this Constitution in the Government of the United States, or in any Department or Officer thereof," not least of all the Executive branch. Finally, the legislators may remove by impeachment the "President, Vice President and all Civil Officers of the United States" if they are convicted of "Treason, Bribery, or other high Crimes and Misdemeanors." The President has only his joint appointment prerogative with the Senate; the "Power to fill up all Vacancies that may happen during the Recess of the Senate"; whatever control Congress may vote him over lesser officers; and the proviso that he "shall Commission all the Officers of the United States."

Relying on these provisions, a strong textual case can be made that Congress controls the raising and disbanding, the organizational structure, and the disciplinary rules for all federal personnel, including those in the Executive branch, except as (1) some federal officers exist by constitutional fiat, for example, the President, (2) he shares appointment power with the Senate, and (3) presidential rights can be drawn from the executive-power, commander-in-chief, and take-care clauses.

Extrapolation makes little progress toward the President's raising federal personnel other than special diplomatic agents. It has to read narrowly "Officers of the United States" whose appointment must be approved by the Senate or authorized by Congress. "Officers" can be extended to include all who do federal business, or only those with fixed terms and conditions of office, assured compensation from the Treasury, and so forth. The more rigid the definition of an "officer," of course, the greater the President's freedom to create ad hoc personnel. Extrapolation is more amenable to control by the commander in chief over the organization and discipline of the armed forces, once raised; and to control by the chief executive and law enforcer over the organization and discipline of other federal personnel, once employed, especially those engaged in the conduct of American foreign relations. And since the text says nothing about the removal of "officers of the United States" other than by impeachment, it is possible to fashion a presidential right to fire those doing "executive" business, even when their appointment required senatorial consent. The text does not tolerate, however, the President's firing other federal employees.

Money

There is little confusion about this tool. Article I flatly gives Congress control over raising federal funds, authorizing their expenditure, and appropriating them from the Treasury. These fiscal powers are explicitly reiterated in the military context: Congress may tax to "provide for the common Defence"; Congress is "[t]o . . . support Armies" and "[t]o . . . maintain a Navy." The only express limit on its hold over money does not result from a competing grant of authority to the President but from an indirect restraint on his power as commander in chief: Although Congress may create standing armies, "no Appropriation of Money to that Use shall be for a longer Term than two Years."

Textual uncertainties center simply on the bounds of acknowledged legislative prerogative: to what degree Congress may wield its power of the purse to limit executive prerogative —for example, by conditioning the funding of the State Department on presidential nomination as Secretary of State of a man favored by Congress, or by ordering the President to loan money to another government—and to what degree Congress owes the Executive, as a coordinate branch of government, certain minimal operating funds.

Extrapolation from the take-care clause can produce a bit of prerogative for the Executive over whether to spend all, or any, of what Congress has provided, even when the spending legislation in no way infringes his constitutional rights. The text is amenable to presidential discretion to stop spending when a job authorized by Congress can be accomplished for less than the amount appropriated. If, however, the Executive never begins spending or stops before the congressional purpose is fulfilled, then he must act on the basis of some "higher" law. The take-care clause can conceivably be milked to produce such law, whether prior legislation that the President deems in conflict with the present spending measure or his own view of the national good. The text, however, seems clearly to preclude executive foot-dragging if Congress expressly orders that money be spent.

International Agreement
Acutely vague language returns regarding control over international agreements. Article II, Section 2, states that the President "shall have Power, by and with the Advice and Consent of the Senate, to make Treaties, provided two thirds of the Senators present concur." The text leaves open whether treaties are the *only* constitutional means by which the United States may make international agreements; or whether the President and Congress together, or the Executive solely on his own authority, may covenant with other countries.

Assuming that the treaty form is used, little about its mechanics is revealed by the requirement that the President "make" the agreement "by and with the advice and consent of the Senate." Good men and true can differ whether this language requires executive-senatorial concurrence on the occasion for negotiations with another state, who the negotiators shall be, and on instructions to them regarding terms, strategy, and tactics. The Article I, Section 6 proviso that "no Person holding any Office under the United States, shall be a Member of either House during his Continuance in Office" creates doubt whether Senators may be negotiators. Nor is it clear whether the President must meet personally with the Senate to receive its advice and consent, communicate through an agent, send a written message, or whether he may wholly ignore the Senators during the negotiating process. The language is equally vague about the power of the Senate to amend, rather than reject outright, a draft treaty submitted to it, or about the binding effect of prior senatorial approval of negotiating instructions if a draft agreement faithful to them is presented the Senate for approval. The text also ignores whether the President must renegotiate an agreement amended by the Senate or whether he has any obligation to ratify even treaties approved without change by the Senators.

No respite from ambiguity lies on the other side of treaty making. The text says nothing about the allocation of control over the interpretation of treaties once in effect nor about their modification or abrogation. Disagreement can be especially rife about the latter, with possible terminators the President alone, the President and Senate jointly, Congress alone, or the President and Congress via legislation or by concurrent resolution approving executive action.

The role of the House of Representatives in treaty making has its fair share of textual uncertainties, too. During the early years of the Republic, many Representatives read the language to preclude treaties on matters about which Congress as a whole has constitutional authority to legislate. Since such aggrandizement of Article I, Section 8, at the expense of Article II, Section 2, would gut the treaty power, the Senate and President have insisted that treaties provide an alternative means of rule making in areas otherwise committed to the legislative process.

The Representatives have stood more resolutely on a treaty-veto understanding of Article I, Section 7: "All Bills for raising Revenue shall originate in the House of Representatives." This language, so read, permits the House to hamstring treaty negotiations by refusing to vote necessary supporting funds or to void a ratified treaty by fiscal deprivation. Counterinterpretation leaves the Representatives' appropriations power, like their legislative authority, subject to language committing treaty making to the President and Senate. The most successful textual advance by the House into international agreements, however, comes by reading the treaty clause to permit pacts via congressional-executive agreement rather than through a treaty, and by reading congressional legislative authority to cover any matter within reach of an American international agreement.

Foreign Communications

The President's textual case is strongest here. Language most related to the channels by which the United States communicates officially with foreigners (that on appointing and receiving diplomats) is plausibly read to support executive authority over channels of communication, if not over policymaking concerning recognition or diplomatic relations. Equally important, so long as the issue remains control over the mechanical process of communication rather than over the substance of the message, the take-care clause readily backs presidential authority to execute national policy via communication with foreigners, even if that policy is wholly made by Congress.

Counterinterpretation begins with the facts of life. Communication often amounts to more than a mechanical process. The medium frequently becomes the message, as the timing, tone, and precise channel of exchange often carry more weight than the actual message. Further, information gained from communication between the United States and other countries may be essential to policymaking in the first instance and to its timely modification as circumstances change, both for our government and others. Simply by dint of control over the channels of communication, the controller is likely to receive a handle on policymaking and an influence with other states not otherwise his. It follows that the textual readings supporting authority for Congress or the Senate over recognition and diplomatic relations can be turned to support shared authority for Congress or the Senate with the President over official channels of foreign communications.

Regulations Governing Private American Conduct

This tool, like most others, textually leans toward Congress. Rules governing private conduct, especially when they are backed by criminal sanctions and affect behavior in this country, are legislative in nature. Article I puts legislative power in Congress and suggests its complete control over rule making by the necessary-and-proper clause. The proviso that "[t]he Privilege of the Writ of Habeas Corpus shall not be suspended, unless when in Cases of Rebellion or Invasion the public Safety may require it" is placed in Article I, Section 9, amid limitations on congressional power to legislate, thus suggesting that it is for Congress to make any rules suspending civil liberties under the brunt of military emergency. The only analogous authority for the President comes in his Article II, Section 2 "Power to Grant Reprieves and Pardons for Offenses against the United States, except in Cases of Impeachment."

Though regulations affecting private American conduct are legislative in nature, and thus arguably bounded by the Article I grant of legislative power to Congress, other constitutional language suggests that the legislators need not monopolize rule making. Article VI makes American treaties, as well as congressional acts, the "supreme Law of the Land," thereby permitting the Senate and President together to make rules by international agreement. And Article II, Section 2, does not preclude making international agreements on presidential authority alone. Executive orders or proclamations provide another mechanism for issuing regulations, and a presidential right to promulgate orders of one sort or another seems inherent in constitutional language establishing the presidency as an independent, operative branch of government. Accordingly, though the occasions for rule making by treaty, executive agreement, or executive order may be more restricted than those for rule making by act of Congress, the text can be read to give a measure of control over this tool to the Senate and President jointly and the Executive alone, as well as to the legislative process.[8]

Necessity for Interbranch Cooperation

The Constitution does impose one iron demand on the President and Congress: that they cooperate if any sustained venture for war or peace is to succeed. Even if congressional authority is most broadly construed, Congress must work its will through the legislative process, and the President is very much part of that process. Under Article II, Section 3, he determines when to call Congress into special session, should it not be sitting on "extraordinary Occasions." Also under Section 3 he may provide Congress with information on the state of the Union and recommend such "Measures as he shall judge necessary and expedient." And under Article I, Section 7, he may veto any measure that the legislators wish to have become law of the land. Accordingly, the text limits congressional control by the President's discretion over special sessions, his right to importune the legislators, and his capacity to force them to raise a two-thirds vote in both houses to overcome his opposition. The constitutional role of the Executive in the legislative process has been sparingly construed at times, but its presence is textually assured. Too, he has at least an equal voice with the Senate over appointments and treaties. And even were the bulk of his remaining constitutional powers seen as those of a congressional agent, the indispensability of an agent grows with the ponderousness of his master and the scope of his assignments.

On the other hand, if executive authority is read to take maximum advantage of generality, competition among grants, and gaps, it still cannot give the President total control over American war and peace. There are many important matters—trade controls and money, to cite an important area of policy and a crucial tool—that require congressional consent under the unavoidable terms of the text. With less extreme readings of the Constitution, of course, the mutual dependence of the two branches becomes more pronounced. That reality provides some comfort when the text slips into ambiguity before concrete war-power problems.[9]

CHAPTER III

The Framers and Ratifiers

THE CONSTITUTION was drafted and ratified to achieve specific objectives. Thus evidence of the Framers' and Ratifiers' purposes weighs heavily in assigning precise content to the text's uncertainties.

Sources of Intent

In ferreting out these purposes, our principal guidance comes from the constitutional provisions themselves and from debates at the 1787-88 conventions. We are entitled to range beyond the text and debates to look at three other sources as well. First is the historical and intellectual context in which the Framers and Ratifiers lived. Context suggests the evils against which the Constitution is meant to guard and definitions for its generalities. The Framers and Ratifiers, well read in history and political theory, seemed eager to take both into account in molding their new govenment.[1]

Equally important are publications issued during the ratification process construing the Constitution in attempts either to encourage or block its acceptance. Far and away the most significant was *The Federalist Papers*. Attention centers on it, but with several grains of salt. *The Federalist* lacks the authoritative status of debates in the Philadelphia and state conventions. It was promotional literature, devoted to rebutting the "Gorgons, Hydras, and Chimeras dire," seen in the proposed Constitution by its foes.[2] And *The Federalist* almost surely did not have the same impact on the constitutional understandings of the Ratifiers as it has had on the views of subsequent generations. As McLaughlin wrote in 1935: "[T]hese essays were probably of service in winning support of the Constitution; but the extent of that service we naturally cannot measure. For much immediate practical effect they were perhaps too learned, too free from passion . . . . *The Federalist* probably had more effect after the new government went into operation than in the days of uncertainty when the fate of the union seemed to hang in the balance . . . ."[3]

A third source of intent is contemporaneous construction, that is, the reading given to the Constitution once it went into effect by men who participated in its framing and ratification and by their contemporaries. During heated debate in 1831 over whether the President might constitutionally create special diplomatic agents, Senator Livingston made classic recourse to contemporaneous construction, arguing that the interpretation which he favored

was made in the earliest years of the Federal Government, by the man who presided in the convention which made that constitution, acting with the advice and assistance of the leading members of that body, all fresh from its discussion; men who had taken prominent parts in every question that arose. Yet, by those men, with this perfect and recent knowledge of the constitution, acting under the solemn obligation to preserve it inviolate, and without any possible motive to make them forget their duty, was this first precedent set; without a single doubt on the mind that it was correct; without protest, without even remark. A precedent going the full length of that which is now unhesitatingly called a lawless, unconstitutional usurpation; bearing the present act out in all its parts, and in some points going much beyond it.[4]

Contemporaneous construction must be gingerly handled, however. There is no reason to believe that the Framers and Ratifiers became more clear as to their purposes after their conventions than during them. Further, the constitutional understandings of certain of the leading figures of 1787-88 shifted over time, in response to emerging government realities and to passing political exigencies. For these reasons, contemporaneous construction is as much an element of practice since 1789 as it is direct evidence of intent.

It will be useful to look in some detail at the context in which the Framers and Ratifiers met. They were influenced especially by prior British and American practice.

British Experience

The Constitutional Fathers turned for their historical lessons to Greece and Rome, France, Holland, the Holy Roman Empire, and others, but above all to England. Hamilton, speaking of "the exclusion of military establishments in time of peace," noted that "as a national sentiment it must be traced to those habits of thinking which we derive from the nation from whom the inhabitants of these states have in general sprung."[5]

The Crown controlled British foreign and military affairs with little parliamentary check until the seventeenth century. Then, wielding the power of the purse, the legislators moved to radically reduce royal prerogative over these areas. During the course of a century of Stuart absolutism, civil war, Commonwealth, Restoration, and Glorious Revolution, Parliament confirmed its authority over levying taxes, including those for military ends; established its right to condition military appropriations, for instance, by voting funds for use only in disbanding the army; and acquired control over raising and maintaining standing armies in time of peace. The legislators also enlarged their say in foreign affairs, particularly treaty making. Following the Restoration, the Crown's authority as commander in chief proved only a sometime thing, buttressed ironically by public distaste for the military policy of John Churchill, the duke of Marlborough. He governed British use of force in the early 1700s when the War of the Spanish Succession coincided with the weak reign of Queen Anne, using his strength in the field and Parliament to pursue campaigns unpopular with most of his countrymen. Finally, the emerging authority of the cabinet and its responsibility to Parliament grew steadily during the 1700s, until by the time of our Philadelphia Convention there remained little purely royal prerogative over British foreign and military affairs.[6] Significantly, the legislators controlled British policy through statutory requests that the Crown act "by and with the advice and consent" of Parliament. The colonial legislatures in America used "advice and consent" similarly.[7]

The Framers and Ratifiers did not dwell on the emerging executive-in-Parliament, though there was some awareness of its existence.[8] To the extent that the rise of the cabinet was perceived, it very likely was viewed as an abuse of the separation of legislative and executive powers, a principle dear to the Constitutional Fathers and to the political theorists whom they favored.[9] Primary attention went to seventeenth-century lessons[10] and thus to executive despotism and its legislative remedies. The potential tyranny of standing armies during peace was stressed, and the burdens of ill-advised royal wars noted.[11] The king was frequently portrayed as having great foreign and military authority, an exemplar of what the American Executive was not to be.[12]

In their concern to contain executive power with legislative, the Framers and Ratifiers may well have been influenced by Whig theorists, as well as by their concept of British constitutional history.[13] They were also aware of the distinction drawn by theorists, principally Locke, between purely executive prerogative, on the one hand, and federative authority on the other, the former concerning law enforcement and the latter the conduct of external affairs, including war and peace. They knew, too, of the theorists' emphasis on the institutional advantages of the executive in handling foreign and military matters.[14]

Another important European influence on the Constitutional Fathers concerned the character of war: whether it might be entered without a formal declaration, at what levels of force it might arise, and the role of marque and reprisal in its prosecution. Theorists known to educated Americans in the 1780s, especially Grotius, Pufendorf, Vattel, and Burlamaqui, differed over whether a declaration was necessary to initiate unjust war, but agreed that none was needed to enter defensive hostilities. They examined in detail undeclared or "imperfect" war, noting that it was generally limited in scope, designed to redress grievances, and prosecuted through restricted government action or private war making under letters of marque and reprisal. They agreed further that it could easily lead to outright or "perfect" war.[15]

Public naval reprisals, in fact, had gone before British wars with the Dutch in 1652 and 1664, the Spanish in 1739, and the

French in 1756. And undeclared war was the norm in eighteenth-century European practice, a reality brought home to Americans when Britain's Seven Years' War with France began on this continent.[16] Thus the Framers and Ratifiers knew that war might be limited or general, that marque and reprisal were a means of waging limited hostilities, and that even major conflict generally began without prior declaration.

American Experience

America ceased to be a colony, wrote Edward Corwin, "with the belief prevalent that 'the executive magistracy' was the natural enemy, the legislative assembly the natural friend of liberty . . . ."[17] "Fear of a return of Executive authority like that exercised by the Royal Governors or by the King," according to Charles Warren, "had been ever present in the States from the beginning of the Revolution."[18] Part of the American antipathy for executive authority no doubt stemmed from the fact that the colonial assemblies were locally chosen and the royal governors appointed by London.[19] Another measure of it resulted from the colonists' distaste for British use of troops to enforce unpopular policies, especially economic. That use came to be attributed to the Crown and reinforced the aversion to peacetime armies born of seventeenth-century experience in Britain. The Declaration of Independence captured prevailing distrust of armed executives:

The history of the present King of Great Britain is a history of repeated injuries and usurpations, all having in direct object the establishment of an absolute Tyranny over these States . . . .

He has kept among us, in times of peace, Standing Armies without the consent of our legislature.

He has affected to render the Military independent of and superior to the Civil Power.

These themes recurred frequently in the years leading to the Constitution, along with a strong preference for militia rather than standing armies as America's peacetime military deterrent.[20]

The Continental Congresses responded to fear of executives by having none formally. Though the presiding officer of Congress was termed "The President," he mainly chaired debate. The legislators, acting through their unicameral assembly and various committees and boards established by it, sought to execute national affairs.[21] They did find it necessary to appoint a commander in chief for the American revolutionary forces and chose George Washington on June 19, 1775, instructing him, however, "punctually to observe and follow such orders and directions, from time to time, as you shall receive from this or a future Congress . . . or a committee of Congress, for that purpose appointed." The legislators then appointed various bodies to oversee the war effort, and were prone early in the conflict to instruct Washington in the minutia of its conduct.[22]

The Articles of Confederation came into effect on March 1, 1781, without a national administrator, except as the executive existed in Congress and its agents. Executive departments responsible to Congress did begin to appear in 1781, including Secretaries of Foreign Affairs and War,[23] but the Confederation had no need to allocate war powers between executive and legislative branches. The Articles simply gave Congress "the sole and exclusive right and power of determining on peace and war" and of "making rules for the government and regulation of the . . . land and naval forces, and for directing their operations."[24] Congress also largely controlled letters of marque and reprisal, though the states could issue them under certain circumstances. Ambiguity about the meaning of the word "declare" in the war-power context began then, since the Articles spoke of Congress's "determining on war" but of state marque and reprisal after a congressional "declaration of war."[25] It appears that "determine" and "declare" were used interchangeably.

State constitutions after 1776 proved less extreme in their rejection of executive authority, but not very much less. Independent state executives were created with narrow powers, and sometimes with the requirement that they govern in tandem with a council—a postrevolutionary adaptation of one means of containing colonial governors. Executive councils had long been in America, often associated with the upper house of the legislature.[26]

Care was taken that the executives not, "under any pretence, exercise any power or prerogative, by virtue of any law, statute or custome of England," and in the early state constitutions executive authority was largely symbolic.[27] In Madison's words, "The Executives of the States are in general little more than Cyphers; the legislators omnipotent."[28]

Nonetheless, almost every state made its governor commander in chief of the local militia, pursuant to legislative direction. The pertinent provision of the Massachusetts Constitution of 1780 (which Hamilton in *The Federalist, No. 69,* found more expansive in empowering the executive than the equivalent clause in the federal Constitution) named the governor "commander-in-chief of the army and navy" with power to "repel, resist, expel" invaders of Massachusetts, and "with all these and other powers incident to the offices of captain-general and commander-in-chief, and admiral, to be exercised agreeable to the rules and regulations of the constitution and the laws of the land and not otherwise."[29]

Out of this national and state experience there seems to have emerged little dissatisfaction with legislative control over decisions whether to go to war or make peace. Even in colonial times the legislators had dominated these determinations,[30] one way or another. They wholly controlled them thereafter. Nor had fear of executive usurpation lessened dramatically by 1787-88, particularly should a standing army during peace be at executive disposal. But there had by that time developed growing awareness that legislatures could be tyrannical, too, and that Congress to date had lacked the capacity to execute policy efficiently, especially foreign and military policy. There was related awareness that the legislatures had not been at their best during crises.

Concern over legislative tyranny had been sparked by the excesses of state assemblies.[31] Madison in *The Federalist, No. 48,* reminded his readers that the dangers of legislative misrule had escaped the "founders of our republics," so that "they seem never for a moment to have turned their eyes from the danger to liberty from the overgrown and all-grasping prerogative of an hereditary magistrate . . . . They seem never to have rec-

ollected the danger from legislative usurpations, which by assembling all power in the same hands, must lead to the same
tyranny as is threatened by executive usurpations." A national
executive was needed to check and balance Congress.

Disenchantment with legislative capacity to *conduct* military and foreign affairs, as opposed to legislative control over
whether America was to go to war or make peace, was pronounced by 1787. As early as 1775 Congress had conceded a
measure of institutional weakness in orders to General Washington issued just the day after he had been told to obey the legislature in all things. The second-round orders acknowledged
that "whereas all particulars cannot be foreseen, nor positive
instructions for such emergencies so beforehand given but that
many things must be left to your prudent and discreet management . . . ."[32] As the conflict progressed and congressional
efforts to conduct it proved less and less fruitful, the legislators
relied increasingly on Washington, especially during times of
dire emergency.[33] Consensus formed that, though Congress
might decide on war and peace, a separate executive was
needed to effect the decision via unified military command.

The legislators were not much more successful in their discharge of the nonmilitary aspects of foreign affairs. Ad hoc
congressional committees tried to handle various diplomatic
and treaty initiatives. Backbiting among committee members,
lapses of essential confidentiality, and frequent failure to delegate adequate operational authority to agents were endemic.[34]
And even under the Confederation voting in Congress continued to be by states irrespective of population, with congressional delegates elected annually by the state legislatures, and a
nine-vote majority required to approve treaties.[35] The yearly
assemblies limped along as had their predecessors, "essentially
. . . as councils of ambassadorial delegates from a group of
federated states."[36]

By 1787 it was apparent to most interested Americans that
the national legislature as then constituted could not effectively
execute diplomatic or military policy. A part of the difficulty
lay in the stranglehold of individual states on congressional action and in the absence of any group within Congress com-

posed of a few legislators with long tenure and ensured continuity. Congress restructured was expected to become a more potent executive force.[37] But there also was strong, though by no means universal, sentiment that effective implementation of American policy would require as well a national administrator, independent to one degree or another from the legislature.

Despite this sentiment the Constitutional Fathers spent precious little time on what authority the national administrator should have over foreign affairs, war and peace included. At issue in 1787-88 were far more basic questions about what sort of executive to carve out of existing congressional government—would it be single or plural, act with or without a council, have veto power, how would it be chosen, for what term and with what possibility of reelection? These issues were rarely considered with an eye to the respective roles of the President and Congress in determining American policy. To a large extent they were merely another manifestation of the state-national conflict, the federalists favoring a stronger Executive than the states righters.

That conflict was the transcendent problem for the Framers and Ratifiers. In 1787 it took eighteen days to move from Boston to Georgia. Economic and governmental divisions further separated the American people. The country was little more than "a loose confederation of states, rife with sectional secession movements."[38] Its constitutional necessities were, first, an allocation of authority between the national government and states that would create a viable union, and, second, a division of national authority between the representatives of the large and small states that would ensure ratification of the new plan of government.

Not surprisingly, when the Framers and Ratifiers felt they had to grapple with questions of war and peace, the emphasis was on the states, not on congressional-executive powers. Danger to the nation from state excesses in foreign affairs had provided important impetus to the Constitutional Convention. Since colonial days the states had been loath to subordinate their immediate individual interests to the common good. They were reluctant to bear their fair share of military burdens unless actually attacked, but prone themselves to incite Indians, European powers, and their sister states. Separate diplomatic activity by them and their violations of national treaties were frequent. Thus, interstate conflicts and intrastate revolts disrupted internal tranquillity,[39] while American disunity and the provocative behavior of individual states invited foreign aggression.[40] Jefferson wrote Washington early in the Philadelphia Convention about the need "to make our states as one to all foreign concerns," and Madison concluded that "[i]f we are to be one nation in any respect, it clearly ought to be in respect to other nations,"[41] and he spoke in Philadelphia of "those violations of the law of nations & of Treaties which if not prevented must involve us in the calamities of foreign wars," adding that "[t]he tendency of the States to these violations has been manifested in sundry instances": "The files of Congs. contain complaints already, from almost every nation with which treaties have been formed. Hitherto indulgence has been shewn to us. This cannot be the permanent disposition of foreign nations. A rupture with other powers is among the greatest of national calamities. It ought therefore to be effectually provided that no part of a nation shall have it in its power to bring them on the whole. The existing confederacy does (not) sufficiently provide against this evil."[42]

By the same token the Constitutional Fathers found the supremacy of national treaties over state law far more troublesome than the manner in which the federal government itself would make treaties. They were also vastly more concerned to define national war-peace authority,[43] already great in theory under the Confederation,[44] than to split the war powers between the President and Congress. And they felt it necessary to explicitly grant emergency military powers to the states rather than to the national executive, probably on the assumption that state militia would bear the first brunt of repelling sudden attack.[45]

The skimpy attention given congressional-executive war powers in 1787-88 was a by-product as well of the relatively short shrift given foreign affairs as a whole. They were rarely mentioned in direct terms in either the Philadelphia or state debates.[46] The only aspects that received real debate were war and treaty making.[47] Emphasis went to treaties, though the two merged whenever the Constitutional Fathers turned to the termination of hostilities.

Predominant attention could go to treaties, because peace was expected to be the customary state of the new nation. America would avoid aggressive war abroad and enjoy in turn "an insulated situation" from the great powers of Europe. In Alexander Hamilton's words: "Europe is at a great distance from us. Her colonies in our vicinity, will be likely to continue too much disproportioned in strength, to be able to give us any dangerous annoyance. Extensive military establishments cannot, in this position be necessary to our security."[48] This placid view of foreign relations precluded any explicit consideration of the use of American force abroad, except for defensive naval action to protect the Atlantic coast and American commerce. Only Hamilton suggested that it might be well to intervene in the Caribbean struggles of the Old World powers.[49] Commercial relations were to characterize American relations abroad. Contacts of other sorts, not much desired, would be discouraged by hobbling treaty making. Gouverneur Morris opined that "[i]n general he was not solicitous to multiply & facilitate Treaties," and James Madison believed that since Independence "it has been too easy . . . to make Treaties . . . ."[50] The isolationist mood was perhaps a reaction to the trials of the Revolution. It clearly fed on fear of great-power interference in the domestic politics of the fledgling state, especially through bribery of federal politicians.[51] Whatever the cause, a notion of peaceful retreat did grip Americans in the late 1780s —John Adams going so far as to suggest disbanding the foreign service or reducing it from its already meager proportions.[52]

Again, not surprisingly, it was the needs of domestic order,[53] not foreign intervention, that provided the incentive for an executive who could lead the national army and navy. The demons arising out of that command for the Framers and Ratifiers were those of 1787-88, not ours. Their abiding fear was that the Executive would use the military for tyrannical purposes at home, possibly to make himself a hereditary prince, not that he would use it for ill-advised foreign adventures. Controversy centered on whether it was safe to allow executive command in the field, whether standing armies might be used by the President for domestic subversion, and whether he should be allowed to pardon traitors, since their crimes could stem from efforts to help him usurp power. For some of the Constitutional Fathers, the demons lurking in military matters were not executive but congressional: The legislators were said to hold both the purse and the sword, and thus feared as incipient military despots. For these Framers and Ratifiers the remedy would have been a national military thoroughly dependent on state militia, state officers, and state military appropriations.

In short, American problems and assumptions in 1787-88 did not anticipate all of ours. They were those of a small, divided people eager for national unity but fearful of federal tyranny. Domestic rebellion and foreign invasion were their "war" concerns. More important for them were safeguards against military usurpation at home than military preparedness during peace. Greatly more than we, they valued state authority over national, legislative power over executive. They preferred peace and political isolation to a world made safe for America. The institutional arrangements developed in 1787-88 reflected these values and needs. A small, elite branch of Congress was planned as a plenary participant with the President in whatever American diplomacy might arise. State militia were to be the backbone of national defense; Congress the arbiter of military policy, by governing the existence of American armed forces and their commitment to conflict. The states and President would serve as interim defenders against sudden attack, pending opportunity for congressional decision; and the Executive would act as first general and admiral should the legislators choose to fight.

The Framers and Ratifiers did intend a more effective national executive than had previously existed in Congress, influenced by their understanding of European practice and political theory, by prior legislative excesses in America, and by the dismal executive record of Revolutionary and Confederation legislatures. They wanted presidential aid in conducting negotiations, gathering intelligence, and in framing recommendations essential to policymaking. They hoped to obtain an executive check on foolish or venal legislators, and they sought presidential execution of national policy. But with rare exception the Framers and Ratifiers did not mean to surrender congressional control over setting American policy and providing tools for its implementation. Thus, they rejected executive hegemony over foreign and military affairs, as seen in European practice and political theory. Their model was Parliament's seventeenth-century steps to curb the British king, and throughout their debates ran a persistent fear of executive despotism.

Control over Policy and Tools

More precisely, the 1787-88 debate about military action concerned only raising, organizing, and supporting the armed forces and combat. As we have seen, raising, organizing, and supporting were primarily grist for state-federal conflict, although they did help offset fears of executive usurpation—this concern was answered by congressional control over men and money. Regarding combat, the debates indicate that the country was meant to use armed force without a formal declaration of war, but not without prior authorization by majority vote of the House and Senate, unless America were suddenly attacked. It appears also that the Framers and Ratifiers meant for the country to be able to use armed force on a limited, highly selective basis, as well as for unrestricted general hostilities. They were aware that most eighteenth-century conflicts had not been formerly declared and that political theorists distinguished between general and limited conflict (between "perfect" and "imperfect" war), with marque and reprisal a means of waging the latter. Defensive or retaliatory uses of force, the sorts expected for America by the men of 1787-88, tended in that era to be limited, undeclared engagements. In addition, the word "declare" was loosely employed by the Framers in ways equating it with "begin" or "authorize." The Constitutional Fathers' grant of authority to Congress to declare war and issue letters of marque and reprisal almost certainly was intended to convey control over all involvement of American forces in combat, except in response to sudden attack.

As regards the latter, the constitutional text suggests that the Framers expected the states to bear the major burden of defense until Congress could act. The only equivalent authority for the President must be scavenged out of a brief, confused Philadelphia debate (less than two pages in Madison's notes) which ended with the substitution of "declare" for "make" war. The discussion meandered and the nature of crucial votes remains obscure. But it is not likely that the substitution signaled much gain in executive prerogative in the minds of the Constitutional Fathers. George Mason with his presidential phobias voted for the substitution, and the change later went through the ratification controversies unmentioned by the most rabid foes of the Executive. The possibility exists that the substitution was designed simply to prevent Congress from asserting control over the conduct, as well as the initiation, of conflict. Even if, as seems more probable, the change was intended to authorize emergency military action by the President, no mention was made of his defense against *imminent* attack, much less of his defense of anything *abroad*. Most happily viewed for presidential prerogative, then, the Framers' substitution of "declare" for "make" permitted executive response to ongoing physical attack on American territory—conceivably, also, pre-emptive strikes by the President against impending attack—until Congress can decide what further steps should be taken.

The commander-in-chief clause, in turn, received little from the Constitutional Fathers. It was viewed as a modest grant of authority. Hamilton's limited "first general and admiral" interpretation reflected the consensus. During hostilities the President would set strategy and tactics, and his authority would inevitably grow during military crisis. But he would not commit America to hostilities except by signing authorizing legislation; and he would not make peace except as a participant with the Senate in the treaty process. Those who fought the commander-in-chief clause did so for fear the President would turn the army to treason and usurp authority not legally his. The federalists replied with the need for single command during war, a lesson of the Revolution, and with the danger of placing it in an ambitious general rather than a civil officer with a fixed four-year tenure. They said that only the rare President would personally command the troops, and that there would be no armies, navies, or militia for him to lead unless Congress so provided.

Against this background, it is probable that had the Framers and Ratifiers dealt explicitly with all types of military action, they would have assigned control over deploying or stationing troops abroad, arming merchantmen, convoying, and so on to the legislative process, except when these uses are incident to the conduct of an authorized conflict. Several factors already seen in the constitutional text suggest this: the extensive military powers specifically given Congress, the definition of state war powers in the legislative article, the provision there for suspension of habeas corpus during invasion or rebellion, as well as the Ratifiers' understanding that suspension of habeas would be at legislative, not executive, instance. Finally, it seems clear that the declare-war and commander-in-chief clauses passed with little debate because they left Congress with authority over whether the American military would be used. Other than the President's participation in legislating military policy, his only role was to execute it.

The Framers and Ratifiers talked very little about the various types of nonmilitary action with war and peace consequences. They simply gave Congress authority over the bulk of such action when it was treated specifically in the Constitution. Debates concerned with state-federal authority indicated an awareness that congressional decisions about foreign commerce, in particular, would bear squarely on the country's foreign relations.

Had the Constitutional Fathers filled the gaps in their debate concerning nonmilitary action—the gaps about recognition and diplomatic relations, for example—they very likely would have given control either to the legislative process or to the President and Senate together. Congress received specific authority over those matters which the Framers thought would be important to American war and peace, except for the pardon power, treaty making, and diplomatic appointments. The Senate held sole responsibility over treaties and ambassadors until the last two weeks of the Philadelphia Convention, when the President was suddenly associated with their control. Strong evidence exists that the Constitutional Fathers expected the Senate, no less than the President, to govern those aspects of American foreign relations not committed to Congress as a whole. Thus the Executive's capacity to receive foreign diplomats was ignored during the Philadelphia debates and dismissed as meaningless during the ratification process, and there was no suggestion that "the executive Power" of Article II, Section 1, conveyed authority over anything, other than enumerated prerogatives.

Little hard evidence exists concerning intent about the other war-power variables. The substitution of "declare" for "make" war provides the reed on which sweeping executive claims have rested since 1789, on the untenable assumption that the Framers authorized any sort of executive action with a response-to-attack purpose. There is no evidence at all from 1787-88 suggesting an expansive law-enforcement justification for presidential action. Costs were mentioned only to say that hostilities are too perilous to be left to the control of any but *both* houses of Congress, with the President involved to the extent of his participation in the legislative process. Congress got authority over marque and reprisal, as well as war, implying control over inexpensive as well as expensive military ventures.

Direct provisions for speedy military action went to the states, and for secret action to Congress. A capacity for speed and secrecy, however, was recognized as an institutional advantage of the presidency, and to a lesser extent of the Senate, as opposed to the House. But in the Framers' and Ratifiers' discussions of the Executive, this capacity was described as an aid to senatorial or congressional policymaking and as a means to meet sudden opportunity or crisis, pending action by the legislators, not as a basis for presidential policymaking in other circumstances.

Although there was no explicit debate on the significance of the phase of action, a distinction between initiation and conduct was implicit in the Framers' and Ratifiers' efforts to separate the conduct of national affairs, an executive function, from their initiation, a legislative one. Authority over terminating hostilities was debated, with defeat for attempts to permit senatorial peacemaking despite presidential objections. It seems that the Constitutional Fathers anticipated that our conflicts would end by treaties acceptable to the President and two-thirds of the Senate.

Little attention went to the issues posed by the extent to which each branch does nor does not participate in any particular decision. One Ratifier said that if the President used false information to trick the Senate into foreign-affairs action, he should be impeached. The Framers and Ratifiers were not concerned with the form by which Congress authorizes hostilities, whether by declaration of war or some other device. There was some indication that a treaty might suffice, though it excludes House participation. Finally, it was stressed that the various branches may exercise only their own constitutional powers, and not those of another branch. But the Constitutional Fathers were just as concerned that the Senate, or Congress as a whole, might usurp executive functions as vice-versa, and they described no telltale signs of impermissible delegation.

Turning to tools, no hint came in 1787-88 that the Executive may create federal personnel, except as he participates in lawmaking and shares appointment authority with the Senate. Money was wholly committed to Congress, with the House of Representatives given first say over appropriations to guard against aggrandizement by the Senate and President. Debate on international agreements (viewed as the core stuff of foreign relations) did not dwell on the division of control between the Senate and President; it then focused on an effort to limit his say in peace treaties. The Framers and Ratifiers assumed that the Senate, though not the House, would be able to participate in transacting the country's diplomatic business. They expected it to do so. With foreign communications as with treaties, the President's unique capacity for speed and secrecy was recognized even as against the Senate. But only Hamilton implied that for these reasons the President *alone* controlled the channels of American conversation with other nations. Finally, there was no indication that regulations affecting private American conduct may arise except by legislation or treaties.

Tools, like the other war-power variables, suffer from gaps in intent—whether, for instance, the President may create special diplomatic agents, make purely executive agreements with other countries, forbid foreign diplomats to communicate with the American government except through him, or ban trade with foreign belligerents. Had these and numerous like issues been confronted, however, it is difficult to believe that many would have been resolved in favor of executive prerogative, given the temper of 1787-88.

Hazards of Extrapolating from 1787-88

Several caveats are overdue. A constant of human experience is that our conclusions about desirable allocations of power change with shifts in the basic facts on which those allocations are premised. Accordingly, we must recognize the hazards of seeking to fill gaps in the Framers' and Ratifiers' intent by extrapolation from their debates. They acted on the basis of many assumptions about reality that no longer hold, and they often seemed obsessed with ephemeral economic and security concerns.[54] What the Constitutional Fathers would have thought given late twentieth-century realities often cannot be confidently assumed from what they said amid the circumstances of the late 1780s. What if they had realized that peace and noninvolvement with the rest of the world would not be America's customary state; that the hazards, pace, and complexity of international affairs would burgeon, along with the country's capacity and need to work its will abroad; that treaties would hardly prove to be the guts of American foreign relations; that from the outset the Senate could not keep step with the President in diplomacy, and the militia could not replace federal forces; that the regular military would grow huge and stand during peace, little restrained by the need for Congress to raise and support it; and that the loyalty of naturalized citizens, the navigation of the Mississippi, and other compelling issues of the late eighteenth century would quickly fade?

There are, of course, aspects of the 1787-88 purposes not tainted by the passing assumptions and problems of those years. But any attempt to move from the specifics of the Framers' and Ratifiers' debates to resolve contemporary war-power issues must have its adequacy measured by reference to questions such as those above, and it must convincingly rebut the possibility that the extrapolation is too speculative to be meaningful.

Three other factors contribute to the hazards of extrapolating from 1787-88. First, records of the drafting and ratifying conventions come in fragments. The Framers did have an official secretary, William Jackson, but he restricted himself largely to recording motions and votes. Even these spotty notes were "carelessly kept." While his "statement of questions is probably accurate in most cases, . . . the determination of those questions and in particular the votes upon them should be accepted somewhat tentatively."[55] The Framers debated in secret, and Jackson's Journal remained undisclosed, first in the hands of George Washington and then in the Department of State, until it was published by order of Congress in 1819, following the deaths of most of the Convention delegates.[56] At that point, it was largely beyond verification or correction.

In subsequent years other accounts of the Framers' Philadelphia proceedings were published, most importantly the notes of James Madison in 1840. But Madison as an old man had dubiously revised his account after appearance of the Journal.[57] His attempt to reconstruct events of more than thirty years before was necessarily clouded by the passage of time. Similarly, Charles Pinckney, attempting in 1819 to produce a copy of the plan that he had presented the Convention, could not remember which of four or five papers in his hands was the correct version.[58]

Even when the available if checkered accounts of the Philadelphia proceedings are mustered, their overlapping discussion comes to very little for a convention that met steadily for almost four months. The standard compilation of the debates runs to less than 1,300 pages;[59] the verbatim transcript of a proceeding of similar length today could easily reach twenty times that volume. Records of most of the state ratifying conventions are even more modest than those of Philadelphia.[60] When executive and congressional prerogatives clashed in the *Steel Seizure Case*, Mr. Justice Jackson lamented the "poverty of really useful and unambiguous authority applicable to concrete problems of executive power . . . . Just what our forefathers did envision, or would have envisioned had they foreseen modern conditions," he said, "must be divined from materials almost as enigmatic as the dreams Joseph was called upon to interpret for Pharaoh."[61] The situation is not that grim, but available records are poor.

Second, though attendance varied, a total of fifty-five men participated in the four months of deliberation in Philadelphia, and many more took part in the state ratifying conventions.[62] Divergent positions had to be compromised during the drafting of the Constitution. Compromise on one provision did not prevent efforts to reassert more extreme positions in later provisions. Interpretation of specific language varied among delegates. Because the Philadelphia Convention met in secret and its participants said little about its deliberations during ratification, delegates to the state conventions were largely unaware of the previously expressed views of the Framers. Even those Framers who were also Ratifiers and chose to tell their colleagues of the Philadelphia debates did not always recall them with precision. Under the circumstances it is not likely that a majority, much less all, of those who voted in the federal and state conventions for the Constitution's war-power provisions held a finely drawn, common "intent" about their meaning.

Third, evidence of several sorts suggests that the Framers may have drafted with a measure of deliberate ambiguity. Any constitutional scheme that depends on separation of powers and on checks and balances necessarily allocates among the branches of government competing powers with vaguely defined frontiers of authority.[63] Also apparent on the face of the Constitution is a drafting technique that eschewed detail for terse statement, leaving much to be assumed. For "[c]onstitution makers, in that day at least, did not regard themselves as framers of detailed codes. To them the statement of the bare principle was sufficient . . . ."[64]

The Constitutional Fathers were practical men, and their laconic drafting technique may well have reflected awareness of the difficulty of laying down rules to govern situations whose dimensions are at best dimly grasped. James Madison in remarks to the Virginia ratifying convention was quite explicit about the need for experience, stating that "the organization of the general government of the United States was, in all its parts, very difficult. There was a peculiar difficulty in that of *the executive.* Every thing incident to it must have participated in that difficulty. That mode which was judged most expedient was adopted, till experience should point out one more eligible."[65] As Washington noted, "Time and habit are necessary to fix the true character of governments."[66] And though not a Framer, Thomas Jefferson suggested in 1816 what they "would say themselves" about the need for experience, "were they to rise from the dead."

Some men look at constitutions with sanctimonious reverence, and deem them like the ark of the covenant, too sacred to be touched. They ascribe to the men of the preceding age a wisdom more than human, and suppose what they did to be beyond amendment. I knew that age well; I belonged to it, and labored with it. It deserved well of its country. It was very like the present, but without the experience of the present; and forty years of experience in government is worth a century of book-reading; and this they would say themselves, were they to rise from the dead . . . . Let us . . . avail ourselves of our reason and experience, to correct the crude essays of our first and unexperienced, although wise, virtuous, and well-meaning councils.[67]

Deliberate ambiguity may also have been a means of producing agreement among fractious delegates. Gouverneur Morris, very influential in drafting the final version of the document, explained that "it became necessary to select phrases which, expressing my own notions, would not alarm others . . . ."[68] For men whose overriding objective was ratification of a Constitution promising a more viable union, the precise meaning to be given ambiguous but generally acceptable language could await resolution in practice.

It follows that all judgments about the Constitutional Fathers' purposes must be viewed with a cold and suspicious eye. Fragmentary evidence of the debates, the limited extent to which there is ever common purpose in any process as long, contentious, and complex as the drafting and ratifying of the Constitution, the chance that the text includes deliberately ambiguous language to be shaped by experience, the presence of gaps in intent caused by assumptions and problems peculiar to the late 1780s, and the dangers of extending what was said then about the war powers, in response to concrete problems of that era, to unforeseen issues in unforeseen times—all these call for restraint about what the Framers and Ratifiers really had in mind.

Enduring Purposes

With trepidation it can be said that there do seem to be certain long-term ends that the Constitutional Fathers sought by the way in which they divided authority over war and peace between the President and Congress. They were:

1. To ensure national defense

2. To hinder the use of the military for domestic tyranny

3. To hinder its use for aggression abroad

4. To create and maintain consensus behind American action for war and peace

5. To ensure democratic control over policy about these matters

6. To encourage rational war and peace decisions

7. To permit continuity in American policy when desirable and its revision as necessary

8. To permit emergency action for war or peace that has not yet been blessed by national consensus or democratic control

9. To ensure American capacity to move toward war and peace rapidly or secretly when necessary, and flexibly and proportionately always

10. To permit the efficient setting and executing of war-peace policy.

Substance for this list comes in later pages, especially Chapters IV, V, and VIII. Next is an undiluted look at the twists and turns in the path that led finally to the Constitution's war-power provisions. The Introduction has already prepared the way for this dalliance in 1787-88. If more detail about the Framers and Ratifiers holds no allure, skip directly to Chapter VI and its account of practice since 1789.

CHAPTER IV

Philadelphia 1787

THE FRAMERS of the Constitution deliberated from May 14 to September 17, 1787. Attendance averaged forty or less among the fifty-five delegates representing all states except Rhode Island. Of the twelve states on hand, not all voted on every motion, including some crucial to the evolution of war and peace powers. The delegates met in secret session as a Committee of the Whole, debating and acting on provisions section-by-section, each state having one vote and the majority ruling within both state delegations and the Convention itself. Most of the actual drafting was done by smaller groups of influential delegates. Not until late July did a five-man Committee of Detail produce the first version of the Constitution written at the Convention. We will look at the debates in two ways: first, a day-by-day account of the matters to which the delegates gave most attention—war and treaty making—and, second, a more summary review of other miscellaneous debates pertinent to how the war powers should be divided between the President and Congress. It will be clear from the day-by-day account that the Framers' action on war and peace tended to be episodic with heavy intermingling of distinct issues.

Little Progress from May through July

The first substantive proposals were laid before the Convention on May 29, 1787, when Edmund Randolph presented the Virginia Plan. It made no specific reference to foreign or military affairs and ducked legislative versus executive issues. The proposed national Executive was essentially a legislative agent, and policy almost certainly was expected to remain a congressional preserve, as had been the case since Independence.

The Virginia Plan was elliptical. Its sixth resolution suggested simply that "the National Legislature ought to be impowered to enjoy the Legislative Rights vested in Congress by the Confederation & moreover . . . to call forth the force of the Union agst. any member of the Union failing to fulfill its duty under the articles thereof"; and its seventh resolution suggested a national executive of unspecified number, to be elected by the legislature, who "besides a general authority to execute the National laws . . . ought to enjoy the Executive rights vested in Congress by the Confederation."[1] As debate three days later made clear, these "Executive rights" were not thought to cover war and treaty making.

Following Randolph's speech, Charles Pinckney of South Carolina presented his own, more detailed constitutional scheme. What he actually said is uncertain. The account that Pinckney produced in 1819 for publication differs in certain respects with views that he himself expressed during and immediately after the Convention, and it resembles results later reached by the delegates only after much effort.[2] Nonetheless, the Pinckney Plan, as recalled in 1819, vested in Congress power to raise, support, and organize the military; in the Senate, authority over war, treaties, and diplomatic appointments; and in the President, the executive power and military command. Articles seven and eight of the plan provided that "[t]he Senate shall have the sole & exclusive power to declare War & to make treaties & to appoint Ambassadors & other Ministers to Foreign nations," and that "[t]he Executive Power . . . shall be vested in a President," who "shall be Commander in chief of the army & navy of the United States & of the Militia of the several states . . . ."[3] Pinckney did not explain "[t]he Executive Power," but it could have had little foreign-affairs content, given the authority that he assigned the Senate. His proposals were referred to the Committee of the Whole but never debated. The Virginia Plan became the first focus of Convention discussion.

On June 1 the Framers took up the seventh, or executive, resolution of the Virginia proposals. During argument whether the Executive should be one or several persons, discussion turned to which branch ought to govern war and peace. Even those favoring a strong Executive opted for legislative control:

Mr. Pinckney was for a vigorous Executive but was afraid the Executive powers of (the existing) Congress might extend to peace & war &c which would render the Executive a Monarchy, of the worst kind, towit an elective one.

. . . .

Mr. Rutlidge . . . was for vesting the Executive power in a single person, tho' he was not for giving him the power of war and peace. A single man would feel the greatest responsibility and administer the public affairs best.

. . . .

Mr. Wilson preferred a single magistrate, as giving most energy dispatch and responsibility to the office. He did not consider the Prerogatives of the British Monarch as a proper guide in defining the Executive powers. Some of these prerogatives were of a Legislative nature. Among others that of war & peace &c. The only powers he conceived strictly Executive were those of executing the laws, and appointing officers . . . .[4]

According to the convention notes of Rufus King, Madison joined Wilson: "Mad: agrees wth. Wilson in his difinition of executive powers—executive powers ex vi termini, do not include the Rights of war & peace &c. but the powers shd. be confined and defined—if large we shall have the Evils of elective Monarchies—probably the best plan will be a single Executive of long duration wth. a Council, with liberty to depart from their Opinion at his peril."[5] Others, such as Roger Sherman, did not confront the issue because they viewed "the Executive magistracy as nothing more than an institution for carrying the will of the Legislature into effect, that the person or persons ought to be appointed by and accountable to the Legislature only, which was the depositary of the supreme will of the Society."[6]

Agreement that war and peace policy were for the legislature, however, did not mean that the Convention felt that the legislators should direct a conflict, once authorized. The need for a single Executive as commander in chief was stressed by Pierce Butler on June 2 and Elbridge Gerry two days later. Butler said that "his opinion on this point had been formed under the opportunity he had had of seeing the manner in which a plurality of military heads distracted Holland when threatened with invasion by the imperial troops. One man was for directing the force to the defence of this part, another to that part of the Country, just as he happened to be swayed by prejudice or interest."[7] As for Gerry, he "was at a loss to discover the policy of three members of the Executive. It wd. be extremely inconvenient in many instances, particularly in military matters, whether relating to the militia, an army, or a navy. It would be a general with three heads."[8]

On June 15, William Paterson presented the New Jersey Plan, the small-state reaction to the Virginia proposals. As was true with the Virginia Plan, no mention was made of foreign or military policy, though it seems clear that legislative control was assumed in light of Confederation practice favored by the small states and in light of the June 1 debate, just described, calling for legislative control of war and peace. New Jersey's second proposition left to the legislature "the powers vested in the U. States in Congress, by the present existing articles of Confederation . . . ."[9] Paterson also proposed a multiple Executive, who would be commander in chief but might not take field command of American armies: "[T]he Executives besides their general authority to execute the federal acts ought to appoint all federal officers not otherwise provided for, & to direct all military operations; provided that none of the persons composing the federal Executive shall on any occassion take command of any troops, so as personally to conduct any enterprise as General, or in other capacity."[10]

Three days after Paterson spoke, Alexander Hamilton on June 18 advanced a starkly different view of the Executive. His "Governour" would have had extensive sway over foreign and military affairs through his "sole appointment of the heads . . . of the departments of Finance, War and Foreign Affairs," and he would have made treaties "with the advice and approbation of the Senate . . . ." But even Hamilton did not propose that one "Governour" control the commitment of American forces to combat. Rather, the *Senate* was to have that power, and the Executive only the authority to wage the conflict. The fourth and sixth provisos in his plan stated:

IV. The supreme Executive authority . . . to be vested in a Governour to be elected to serve during good behaviour . . . . The . . . functions of the Executive to be as follows: . . . to have the direction of war when authorized or begun; to have with the advice and approbation of the Senate the power of making all treaties; to have the sole appointment of the heads . . . of the departments of Finance, War and Foreign Affairs . . . .

VI. The Senate to have sole power of declaring war, the power of advising and approving all Treaties, the power of approving or rejecting all appointments of officers except the heads . . . of Finance War and foreign affairs.[11]

Note the apparent interchangeability with which Hamilton used the terms "declare" and "authorized or begun." He said the Senate was to "declare" war and the Executive to direct it once "authorized or begun."

Hamilton and his Governour were ignored. There was no dissent on June 26 when James Wilson, himself an advocate of potent executive authority, said that the Senate—not the Executive—"will probably be the depositary of the powers" regarding "foreign nations." Wilson was arguing external relations to his colleagues to support a nine-year term for Senators, with trennial rotation of one-third their number. "Every nation," he said, "may be regarded in two relations 1 to its own citizens. 2 to foreign nations. It is therefore not only liable to anarchy & tyranny within but has wars to avoid and treaties to obtain from abroad. The Senate will probably be the depositary of the powers concerning the latter objects. It ought therefore to be made respectable in the eyes of foreign nations."[12]

More than two months after the Convention first met, the Framers finally found time to pass a resolution on the scope of legislative authority. It was akin to the Virginia proposal of May 29: "[T]he national Legislature ought to possess the legislative rights vested in Congress by the confederation; and moreover to legislate in all cases for the general interests of the Union, and also in those to which the States are separately incompetent, or in which the harmony of the United States may be interrupted by the exercise of individual legislation."[13] On July 26 the Convention adopted a resolution on the Executive, providing stingily that one "be instituted to consist of a Single Person to be chosen by the national Legislature . . . with power to carry into execution the national Laws [and] to appoint to Offices in cases not otherwise provided for."[14]

With these skimpy guides and the background of prior debate, a small Committee of Detail was left to work out the allocation of war and treaty powers, as part of their larger mandate to draft a proposed constitution. The Convention as a whole recessed on July 26 pending the Committee's report two weeks later. The fact that its members were able to move with ease to an allocation suggests the existence of general, if largely unspoken, consensus about the appropriate division: policy-making to the legislators and policy-implementation to the Executive.

Significant August Developments

On August 6 John Rutledge reported for the Committee of Detail. A two-house legislature was proposed, with the treaty-making authority taken from the whole and given to the more elite of the new houses. One article stated that "[t]he Senate . . . shall have power to make treaties, and to appoint Ambassadors . . . ."[15] And the Committee report gave to the legislature the power "to make war," among other military grants. Proposed Article VII provided:

Sect. 1. The Legislature of the United States shall have the power . . .
To make rules concerning captures on land and water;
To declare the law and punishment of piracies and felonies committed on the high seas, . . . and of offences against the law of nations;
To subdue a rebellion in any State, on the application of its legislature;

To make war;

To raise armies;

To build and equip fleets;

To call forth the aid of the militia, in order to execute the laws of the Union, enforce treaties, suppress insurrections, and repel invasions . . . .[16]

The Committee also proposed a single Executive who "shall be commander in chief of the Army and Navy of the United States, and of the Militia of the Several States."[17]

The Convention began consideration of the constitution as proposed, moving clause by clause. On August 11 a proviso for publication of legislative debates was reached, with some suggestion that the Senate might act in a nonlegislative capacity requiring greater secrecy than ordinary and that questions of war and peace should be considered in secret. Advocates of complete public disclosure, however, prevailed for the moment:

Mr. (Madison) & Mr. Rutlidge moved that each House shall keep a journal of its proceeding, & (shall) publish the same from time to time; except such (part) of the proceedings of the Senate, when acting not in its Legislative capacity as may (be judged by) that House (to) require secrecy.

Mr. Mercer. This implies that other powers than legislative will be given to the Senate which he hoped would not be given.[18]

The motion then failed, with Virginia alone in favor. At which point Gerry and Sherman moved "to insert after the words 'publish them' the following 'except such as relate to treaties & military operations.' Their object was to give each House a discretion in such cases." Their motion was also unsuccessful.[19]

Two days later, on August 13, foreign affairs surfaced again amid debate over the sole authority of the House of Representatives to initiate revenue measures. James Wilson joined those opposing any such prerogative for the House. "War, Commerce & Revenue were the great objects of the Genl. Government," he said. "All of them are connected with money. The restriction in favor of the H. of Represts. would exclude the Senate from originating any important bills whatever."[20] But Edmund Randolph felt strongly that money—"the means of war"—as well as actual decisions to fight, should be dominated by the House:

When the people behold in the Senate, the countenance of an aristocracy; and in the president, the form at least of a little monarch, will not their alarms be sufficiently raised without taking from their immediate representatives, a right which has been so long appropriated to them.—The Executive will have more influence over the Senate, than over the H. of Reps—Allow the Senate to originate in this case, & that influence will be sure to mix itself in their deliberations & plans. The Declaration of War he conceived ought not to be in the Senate composed of 26 men only, but rather in the other House. In the other House ought to be placed the origination of the means of war . . . . The Senate will be more likely to be corrupt than the H. of Reps and should therefore have less to do with money matters.[21]

On August 15, there was a flurry about the treaty power, again during controversy over the Representatives' fiscal prerogatives. George Mason was "extremely earnest" to prevent initiation of money bills by the Senate, "who he said could already sell the whole Country by means of Treaties." He suggested that "[i]f Spain should possess herself of Georgia therefore the Senate might by treaty dismember the Union."[22] Responding to Mason, John Francis Mercer of Maryland suddenly broke from the pack to oppose treaty making by the Senate rather than the Executive, though with the debilitating proviso that treaties required congressional ratification before becoming law. Mercer felt "that the Senate ought not to have the power of treaties. This power belonged to the Executive department; adding that Treaties would not be final so as to alter the laws of the land, till ratified by legislative authority," citing British precedent.[23] But his comment prompted no other expressions of support for executive treaty making.

On August 17 the Convention reached its most celebrated war-power moment: the substitution of "declare" for "make" in what became the congressional declaration-of-war clause. The recorded debate in its various versions, however, is anticlimax. It covers only a few pages, with conflict between the accounts of Jackson and Madison. While confusing and potentially unreliable on the crucial issue of executive authority, Madison's notes provide the only substantial coverage of the Framers' thoughts.

Charles Pinckney began the debate with an objection to placing war-commencement authority in Congress as a whole, on the ground that the House of Representatives was institutionally incapable of handling it well. He preferred the Senate alone, noting that the states are equally represented there and that the Senators, as was still the case at that stage of the Convention, had sole authority over the making of peace treaties:

Mr. Pinckney opposed the vesting this power in the Legislature. Its proceedings were too slow. It wd. meet but once a year. The Hs. of Reps. would be too numerous for such deliberations. The Senate would be the best depositary, being more acquainted with foreign affairs, and most capable of proper resolutions. If the States are equally represented in the Senate, so as to give no advantage to large States, the power will notwithstanding be safe, as the small have their all at stake in such cases as well as the large States. It would be singular for one—authority to make war, and another peace.[24]

Pierce Butler then pushed argument as to institutional advantages one step further, proposing that war commencement be left to the judgment of the most rapid, expert, and national of all, the President: "The objections agst the Legislature [noted by Pinckney] lie in a great degree agst the Senate. He was for vesting the power in the President, who will have all the requisite qualities, and will not make war but when the Nation will support it."[25]

Butler's suggestion is the only recorded proposal by either a Framer or Ratifier that the Executive control war making. Butler never formally so moved. Further, as we shall see, he claimed no credit for the proposal when describing it to the South Carolina ratification convention, and by September 7 he had harsh words for executive good faith. Several Philadelphia delegates expressly attacked his proposal, as noted below.

After Butler spoke, Madison, seconded by Gerry, made his famed "sudden attack" motion. It did not refer to executive authority to repel imminent, as well as ongoing, attack, even though authority over both was given to the states by explicit language in the August 6 draft constitution. The motion, nonetheless, did seem to intend greater emergency authority for the President than had been proposed for him to that point: "Mr. M(adison) and Mr. Gerry moved to insert *'declare'* striking out *'make'* war; leaving to the Executive the power to repel sudden attacks."[26]

What happened thereafter none can say with confidence. Both the Jackson and Madison accounts agree that the substitution of "declare" for "make" ultimately passed eight states to one; but Jackson recorded the motion as having been initially defeated five to four, while Madison reported that it first passed seven to two, and then became eight to one when Oliver Ellsworth of Connecticut "gave up his objection," thus shifting his state's vote from no to yes.[27] In Madison's version Sherman, Gerry, Ellsworth, and Mason all spoke before the first vote was taken. Their remarks as recorded did little to lessen the confusion.

Sherman seemed to think that the President already had authority to repel sudden attacks under the Committee of Detail language, and that adoption of the motion might unduly narrow congressional authority: "Mr. Sherman thought it stood very well. The Executive shd. be able to repel and not to commence war. 'Make' better than 'declare' the latter narrowing the power too much."[28]

Gerry, apparently ignoring Sherman's objection to the motion that he had just seconded, turned to attack Butler for having suggested that the President be empowered to make war: "Mr. Gerry never expected to hear in a republic a motion to empower the Executive alone to declare war."[29]

Ellsworth then gained the floor for reasons best known to him. Perhaps he wished to oppose Pinckney's view that the Senate should control war because it controlled peace: "Mr. Ellsworth. there is a material difference between the cases of making *war*, and making *peace*. It shd. be more easy to get out of war, than into it. War also is a simple and overt declaration. peace attended with intricate & secret negociations."[30] What exactly Ellsworth thought of the sudden-attack motion, on which he is recorded by Madison as having first voted no and then yes is lost to time.

Then came George Mason with warnings against executive or senatorial war making and his famed plea for "clogging" war and "facilitating" peace. The tenor of Mason's remarks would seem to place him with Sherman in opposition to the sudden-attack motion, but for reasons also lost to time he must have believed that the "make-to-declare" change would lessen the likelihood of American involvement in hostilities: "Mr. Mason was agst giving the power of war to the Executive, because not (safely) to be trusted with it; or to the Senate, because not so constructed as to be entitled to it. He was for clogging rather than facilitating war; but for facilitating peace. He preferred 'declare' to 'make.' "[31]

At this juncture Madison records a vote on the motion. It may or may not have been favorable. He then indicates that Rufus King pointed out that "make" might be read to authorize congressional conduct of hostilities, an executive function: King remarked "that 'make' war might be understood to 'conduct' it which was an Executive function . . . ."[32] According to Madison this argument led Ellsworth to drop his objection to "declare," altering Connecticut's vote and producing eight to one approval. If such was the case, it seems that a majority of the Framers voted for "declare" to create sudden-attack authority for the President, only Ellsworth going along to ensure that congressional authority not be thought to extend to conducting war. If, however, Jackson correctly noted a defeat for the sudden-attack motion on its first try, and if King's argument was the decisive factor in the changed vote, then a majority of the Framers may well have preferred "declare" to avoid suggestion that Congress controls the conduct as well as the authorization of conflict.

The inconclusive records of the Philadelphia debate on the make-to-declare change are not sharpened by available accounts of the ratification debates. The one remark made during them that was even tangentially relevant to the Framers' substitution of "declare" for "make" came from none other than Pierce Butler, the man who had suggested presidential control. On January 16, 1788, he "endeavor[ed] to recollect" for his fellow delegates to the South Carolina convention "those reasons by which [the Framers] were guided." But his explanation was only casually related to the debate as recorded by Madison and wholly ignored the sudden-attack motion. "It was first proposed," recalled Butler,

to vest the sole power of making peace or war in the Senate; but this was objected to as inimical to the genius of a republic, by destroying the necessary balance they were anxious to preserve. Some gentlemen were inclined to give this power to the President; but it was objected to, as throwing into his hands the influence of a monarch, having an opportunity of involving his country in a war whenever he wished to promote her destruction. The House of Representatives was then named; but an insurmountable objection was made to this proposition—which was, that negotiations always required the greatest secrecy, which could not be expected in a large body.[33]

Thus, despite its immense significance to post-1789 practice, the Framers' make-to-declare debate scarcely concerned the Constitutional Fathers. It went unmentioned during the ratification process. Perspective on this debate's limited utility for judgment about the Framers' war-power purposes also stems from the fact that four of the thirteen states took no part in it. Massachusetts, New Jersey, New York, and Rhode Island had no "intent" at all on the substitution.[34]

Action on war and peace continued on August 17, immediately after the substitution debate. Pinckney's effort to strike the whole declare-war clause failed, with no record of argument. Concern heard on August 15 about possible senatorial venality in peacemaking was renewed by Gerry, when Butler tried to put the power over war and peace in the same hands, those of Congress as a whole:

Mr. Butler moved to give the Legislature power of peace, as they were to have that of war.

Mr. Gerry 2ds. him. 8 Senators may possibly exercise the power if vested in that body, and 14 if all should be present; and may consequently give up part of the U. States. The Senate are more liable to be corrupted by an Enemy than the whole Legislature.

The motion "for adding 'and peace' after 'war'" then failed ten states to none, Massachusetts having returned to vote.[35]

On August 18 marque and reprisal were mentioned in passing for the first time, among a list of additional legislative powers for consideration by the Convention. Madison's notes suggest that Pinckney prepared the list, but also state that Gerry
"remarked that . . . something (ought to be) inserted concerning letters of marque, which he thought not included in the
power of war."[36] Marque and reprisal were within congressional authority under the Articles of Confederation; the Framers doubtless felt it natural that similar authority be given Congress under the Constitution. Gerry's concern, perhaps, was
rooted in the fact that the Articles permitted Congress to authorize marque and reprisal "in times of peace" as well as war.[37]
His concern suggests a desire to make absolutely clear that congressional control covered minor as well as major uses of
American armed force.

Two days later, on August 20, Gouverneur Morris struck a
blow for executive prerogative reminiscent of Hamilton's effort on June 18. Morris urged a presidential "Council of State,"
consisting of the Chief Justice and the Secretaries of Domestic
Affairs, Commerce and Finance, Foreign Affairs, War, and the
Marine. The Secretaries were to "be appointed by the President and hold office during pleasure," though subject to impeachment. The duties of the Secretary of Foreign Affairs implied executive control of American diplomacy. Significantly,
the President would not have to follow the advice given him
by the Council. Charles Pinckney, departing his heavy senatorial bias, found merit in the proposal:

Mr. Govr. Morris 2ded. by Mr. Pinkney submitted the following
propositions which were in like manner referred to the Committee
of Detail.

To assist the President in conducting the Public affairs there shall
be a Council of State composed of the following officers—
. . . .

4.   The Secretary of foreign affairs who shall also be appointed by
the President during pleasure. It shall be his duty to correspond with
all foreign Ministers, prepare plans of Treaties, & consider such as
may be transmitted from abroad; and generally to attend to the interests of the U- S- in their connections with foreign powers.

5.   The Secretary of War who shall also be appointed by the Presi-

dent during pleasure. It shall be his duty to superintend every thing relating to the war-Department, such as the raising and equipping of troops, the care of military Stores—public fortifications, arsenals & the like—also in time of war to prepare & recommend plans of offence and Defence.

. . . .

The President may from time to time submit any matter to the discussion of the Council of State, and he may require the written opinions of any one or more of the members: But he shall in all cases exercise his own judgment, and either Conform to such opinions or not as he may think proper; and every officer abovementioned shall be responsible for his opinion of the affairs relating to his particular Department.[38]

Morris's plan was submitted to the Committee of Detail, where it was shredded. His aspirations for the President, like those of Hamilton before him, were not shared by their colleagues. The Committee in its August 22 report denied constitutional status to the various secretaries, leaving their existence subject to legislation; it said nothing about their duties, again leaving their definition to statute and practice; and it took control over the appointment of these officers from the President:

The Committee report that in their opinion the following additions should be made to the report now before the Convention vizt

. . . .

"The President . . . shall have a Privy-Council which shall consist of the President of the Senate, the Speaker of the House . . . , the Chief-Justice . . . , and the principal Officer in the respective departments of foreign affairs, domestic-affairs, War, Marine, and Finance, as such departments of office shall from time to time be established—whose duty it shall be to advise him in matters respecting the execution of his Office, which he shall think proper to lay before them: But their advice shall not conclude him, nor affect his responsibility for the measures which he shall adopt."[39]

Whether the President should have a council, and the extent of its power over him, remained burning issues for the rest of the Convention. The tenor of debate was one of checking presidential prerogative through a council, not enhancing it. Ultimately, the Framers opted for no privy advisers other than the Senate and for an innocuous proviso that the Executive "may require the Opinion in writing, of the principal Officer in each of the executive Departments, upon any subject relating to the Duties of their respective Offices . . . ."[40]

On August 23 the clause giving exclusive treaty power to the Senate came up for discussion. Reaction to the heady authority proposed for the Senators set in. Madison wished to involve the President as "an agent"—not "the" agent—in treaty making, principally because the Senate represented only state interests: "Mr. (Madison) observed that the Senate represented the States alone, and that for this as well as other obvious reasons it was proper that the President should be an agent in Treaties."[41]

Gouverneur Morris was not certain that "he should agree to refer the making of Treaties to the Senate at all," but his remedy was to involve the House of Representatives by requiring that "no Treaty shall be binding on the U.S. which is not ratified by a law."[42] His motion to this end failed, eight states opposed, Pennsylvania in favor, and North Carolina divided.

Arguments on Morris's motion strikingly evidenced what was on the Framers' minds. Madison felt that convenience demanded exclusion of the House from precisely those agreements with direct bearing on the use of force. He "suggested the inconvenience of requiring a legal *ratification* of treaties of alliance for the purposes of war &c &c," and later "hinted for consideration, whether a distinction might not be made between different sorts of Treaties—Allowing the President & Senate to make Treaties eventual and of Alliance for limited terms—and requiring the concurrence of the whole Legislature in other Treaties."[43]

Nathaniel Gorham and William Johnson expected the Senate to control negotiations and worried about practical problems were the House to be able to derail the Senators' plans:

Mr. Ghorum. Many other disadvantages must be experienced if treaties of peace and all negociations are to be previously ratified—and if not previously, the Ministers would be at a loss how to proceed . . . . American Ministers must go abroad not instructed by the same Authority . . . which is to ratify their proceedings.
. . . .
Docr. Johnson thought there was something of solecism in saying

that the acts of a Minister with plenipotentiary powers from one Body, should depend for ratification on another Body . . . .[44]

Presumably when presidential involvement in treaty making was later approved unanimously by the Convention, Gorham and Johnson thought that "solecism" was avoided because the Senate and the President were to act jointly during negotiation and approval of agreements.

Morris defended his motion on a number of ephemeral grounds, and was answered by the equally transient reasoning of Gorham:

Mr. Govr. Morris. As to treaties of alliance, they will oblige foreign powers to send their Ministers here, the very thing we should wish for. Such treaties could not be otherwise made, if his amendment shd. succeed. In general he was not solicitous to multiply & facilitate Treaties. He wished none to be made with G. Britain, till she should be at war. Then a good bargain might be made with her. So with other foreign powers. The more difficulty in making treaties, the more value will be set on them.

. . . .

Mr. Ghorum in answer to Mr. Govr Morris, said that negociations on the spot were not to be desired by us, especially if the whole Legislature is to have any thing to do with Treaties. It will be generally influenced by two or three men, who will be corrupted by the Ambassadors here. In such a Government as ours, it is necessary to guard against the Government itself being seduced.[45]

Finally, James Wilson suggested that the Morris amendment simply reflected British practice: "In the most important Treaties, the King . . . being obliged to resort to Parliament for the execution of them, is under the same fetters as the amendment . . . will impose on the Senate."[46] And John Dickinson, voicing the state-federal concern that ever underlay treaty debate, said that he "concurred in the amendment, as most safe and proper, tho' he was sensible it was unfavorable to the little States; wch would otherwise have an *equal* share in making Treaties."[47] Amid this gaggle of views, the Framers decided to postpone action on treaties, except to reject Morris's motion for House ratification of Senate-made agreements.

Before returning to the treaty power, the Convention on Au-

gust 27 disposed of the commander-in-chief clause with phenomenal rapidity, in light of its fundamental importance in
later years. Recall that the Committee of Detail had proposed
that the President's command run equally over "the Army and
Navy of the United States, and of the Militia of the Several
States." The only recorded debate centered on this equality of
command, with its suggestion of an undue federal hand on state
troops: "Mr. Sherman moved to amend the clause giving the
Executive the command of the Militia, so as to read 'and of the
Militia of the several States, *when called into the actual service
of the U- S- . . . .*' " The motion and clause so altered passed
six states to two, with Massachusetts, New Jersey, New York,
and North Carolina not voting, and Rhode Island absent as always.[48]

There may also have been brief debate over whether the
President should be permitted to command in the field. One of
the Framers, Luther Martin, told the Maryland legislature on
November 29, 1787, that "[o]bjections were made to that part
of this article, by which the President is appointed Commander-in-chief . . . and it was wished to be so far restrained,
that he should not command in person; but this could not be obtained."[49] As we have seen, too, the New Jersey Plan introduced on June 15 would have forbidden an Executive on horseback.

Thus, it seems that the only commander-in-chief concerns of
the Convention were undue federal authority over the militia
and the possibility that executive field command might lead
to tyranny. It is reasonable to assume that the commander-in-
chief clause was noncontroversial because the Framers intended it to convey tightly circumscribed authority.

Quick Culmination in September

On September 4, only thirteen days before the end of the Convention, there came the first hard proposal that the President
join the Senate in making treaties. David Brearley, speaking for
the eleven-member Committee on Unfinished Business, proposed that "[t]he President by and with the advice and Consent
of the Senate, shall have power to make Treaties . . . . But

no Treaty shall be made without the consent of two thirds of the members present."[50] Brearley's copy of the proposal has interlined "except treaties of peace" after "Treaty" in the second sentence of the clause.[51] There was no further discussion of treaty making on the fourth.

On the following day, September 5, the Framers without debate unanimously accepted a further suggestion from the Committee on Unfinished Business: "To add to the clause 'to declare war' the words 'and grant letters of marque and reprisal.'"[52] This proved to be the last occasion on which the Convention allocated control between Congress and the President over the use of armed force.

All that remained were questions on treaty making, which themselves bore heavily on war and peace. A number of issues were in contention: whether the House of Representatives should be joined with the Senate in making treaties, whether the President should be joined, by what majority the Senate was to act, and whether peace treaties should be treated like other pacts as regards the size of the Senate majority needed for approval, and the possibility that the Senate might override presidential objections. In short, to what degree was senatorial prerogative over foreign affairs to be tempered?

The Framers turned first to House participation when they reached treaty making on September 7. The August 23 effort to have the Representatives included was renewed, and again decisively rejected, with scant debate. In Sherman's words, "[T]he only question that could be made was whether the power could be safely trusted to the Senate. He thought it could; and that the necessity of secrecy in the case of treaties forbade a reference of them to the whole Legislature."[53]

The language leaving treaties to the Senate and President was then approved unanimously, without further debate.[54] Discussion centered on other language in that clause concerning executive-senatorial control over federal appointments. Belated but hard consensus had formed that the Executive should be joined in treaty making with the Senate to guard the national interest. During later controversy over the size of the Senate majority required to approve treaties, Rufus King reminded his colleagues "that as the Executive was here joined in the business, there was a check which did not exist in [the Confederation] Congress where The concurrence of 2/3 was required," and Gorham echoed that "[t]here is a difference in the case, as the President's consent will also be necessary in the new Govt."[55] As Madison explained in 1831: "After the compromise which allowed an equality of votes in the Senate, that consideration, with the smaller number and longer tenure of its members, will account for the abridgment of its powers by associating the Executive in the exercise of them."[56]

Also influential, no doubt, was recognition that executive speed and secrecy could be useful during negotiations, and belief that no independent prerogative was being given the President, only association with the Senate. The Framers' prior debate leaves little doubt that they thought the Senate institutionally capable of handling the country's diplomatic business. And against the background of British and colonial use of "advice and consent," those words surely were intended to grant the Senate at least as plenary a role in treaty making as the President.

The rest of the treaty debate on September 7 went largely to the disposition of peace agreements. Madison first moved that two-thirds approval by the Senate be required for all pacts "'except treaties of peace' allowing these to be made with less difficulty than other treaties." His proposal to ease the way to peace was unanimously approved, without discussion.

Madison then sought to cut back the presidential role in peacemaking. He proposed that the Senate by two-thirds vote be allowed to make peace over the Executive's objection, lest he find war so conducive to personal power that he block its end: "Mr. Madison . . . moved to authorize a concurrence of two thirds of the Senate to make treaties of peace, without the concurrence of the President.—The President he said would necessarily derive so much power and importance from a state of war that he might be tempted, if authorized, to impede a treaty of peace."[57] Pierce Butler seconded the motion, in contrast to his August 17 suggestion that the President be allowed to commence war on his own authority because he "will not make war but when the Nation will support it."

Gorham and Morris disagreed, arguing that the President could not carry on war opposed by the legislature, since it controlled the tools of conflict, and that the Executive, in any event, was himself the defender of the national interest:

Mr. Ghorum thought the precaution unnecessary as the means of carrying on the war would not be in the hands of the President, but of the Legislature.

Mr. Govr Morris thought the power of the President in this case harmless; and that no peace ought to be made without the concurrence of the President, who was the general Guardian of the National interests.[58]

But Butler, citing the danger of avaricious Executives, said he "was strenuous for the motion, as a necessary security against ambitious & corrupt Presidents. He mentioned the late perfidious policy of the Statholder in Holland; and the artifices of the Duke of Marlbro' to prolong the war of which he had the management."[59]

Elbridge Gerry and Hugh Williamson then concluded the debate, apparently harking back to Madison's first motion regarding majority—rather than two-thirds—Senate approval of peace. These Framers saw a greater threat in ending wars on disadvantageous terms than in extending them for lack of a two-thirds vote for peace:

Mr. Gerry was of opinion that in treaties of peace a greater rather than less proportion of votes was necessary, than in other treaties. In Treaties of peace the dearest interests will be at stake, as the fisheries, territories &c. In treaties of peace also there is more danger to the extremities of the Continent, of being sacrificed, than on any other occasions.

Mr. Williamson thought Treaties of peace should be guarded at least by requiring the same concurrence as in other Treaties.[60]

The Convention voted, rejecting eight states to three, any empowering of the Senate to make peace treaties without presidential approval. But the Framers immediately thereafter approved by the same margin the two-thirds requirement for Senate approval of all treaties "amended by the exception as to Treaties of peace."[61]

The following morning, September 8, the decisions of the

prior day came unhinged. "A reconsideration of the whole [treaty] clause was agreed to."[62] King had earlier that morning moved to strike the peace-treaty exemption from the two-thirds requirement, while Wilson, to the contrary, had proposed eliminating the necessity for an extraordinary majority for any treaty. The debate centered on the peace problem. Like Gerry the previous day, the Framers showed the influence of passing economic and security problems, as well as the influence of more enduring considerations, principally the rights of the majority as against those of the minority. Wilson argued:

If the majority cannot be trusted, it was a proof, as observed by Mr. Ghorum, that we were not fit for one Society.

. . . .

Mr. Govr. Morris was agst. striking out the "exception of Treaties of peace" If two thirds of the Senate should be required for peace, the Legislature will be unwilling to make war for that reason, on account of the Fisheries or the Mississippi, the two great objects of the Union. Besides, if a Majority of the Senate be for peace, and are not allowed to make it, they will be apt to effect their purpose in the more disagreeable mode, of negativing the supplies for the war.

Mr. Williamson remarked that Treaties are to be made in the branch of the Govt. where there may be a majority of the States without a majority of the people, Eight men may be a majority of a quorum, & should not have the power to decide the conditions of peace. There would be no danger, that the exposed States, as S. Carolina or Georgia, would urge an improper war for the Western Territory.

Mr. Wilson If two thirds are necessary to make peace, the minority may perpetuate war, against the sense of the majority.

Mr. Gerry enlarged on the danger of putting the essential rights of the Union in the hands of so small a number as a majority of the Senate, representing perhaps, not one fifth of the people. The Senate will be corrupted by foreign influence.

Mr. Sherman was agst leaving the rights, established by the Treaty of Peace, to the Senate, & moved to annex a "proviso that no such rights shd be ceded without the sanction of the Legislature.["]

Mr. Govr. Morris seconded the ideas of Mr. Sherman.

Mr. Madison observed that it had been too easy in the present Congress to make Treaties altho' nine States were required for the purpose.[63]

The Convention then reversed its decision of the prior day,

and voted eight states to three to strike out "except Treaties of peace."[64] There ensued a series of votes, with little debate, on the two-thirds requirement itself, with some effort to make it more stringent by requiring two-thirds of all members of the Senate, not just of those present. At one juncture Roger Sherman's less stringent motion to require "a Majority of the whole number (of the Senate)" failed only six states to five.[65] Ultimately, however, the treaty clause as it now exists in the Constitution was adopted against the opposition of Georgia, New Jersey, and Pennsylvania.

The debates provide only fleeting indication why the Framers finally decided to exclude the House from the treaty process and to require Senate approval by two-thirds vote of the members present. Drawing on the Philadelphia and ratification records, there seem to have been three principal reasons for eliminating the House. First, an intent to maximize small-state power by excluding the element of Congress that reflected population. William R. Davie, a Framer, told the North Carolina ratifying convention that

the extreme jealousy of the little states, and between the commercial states and the non-importing states, . . . made it indispensable to give to the senators, as representatives of states, the power of making, or rather ratifying, treaties. Although it militates against every idea of just proportion that the little state of Rhode Island should have the same suffrage with Virginia, . . . yet the small states would not consent to confederate without an equal voice in the formation of treaties. Without the equality, they apprehended that their interest would be neglected or sacrificed in negotiations.[66]

Second, there apparently was serious question in many Framers' minds whether the House, as opposed to the Senate, had the institutional capacity to deal with foreign affairs. The House was thought too large and infrequently in session for the requisite speed and secrecy, too short-term and fluctuating in its membership for the development of the necessary expertise, and too prone to factions to reflect the national interest. Charles Cotesworth Pinckney, a Framer, attacked during the South Carolina convention any notion that "the diplomatic power of the Union" might be safely vested in the representatives:

Can secrecy be expected in sixty-five members? The idea is absurd.

Besides, their sessions will probably last only two or three months in the year; therefore, on that account, they would be a very unfit body for negotiation; whereas the Senate, from the smallness of its numbers, from the equality of power which each state has in it, from the length of time for which its members are elected, from the long sessions they may have without any great inconveniency to themselves or constitutents, joined with the president, who is the federal head of the United States, form together a body in whom can be best and most safely vested the diplomatic power of the Union.[67]

Third, the Representatives were too closely tied to the public —to the full play of democracy—for many of the Framers, especially as regards foreign affairs. Recall James Wilson's concern on June 26 to make Senators "respectable in the eyes of foreign nations" by nine-year terms and triennial rotation.[68] James Madison in *The Federalist, No. 62*, was more explicit: "The necessity of a senate is . . . indicated by the propensity of all single and numerous assemblies, to yield to the impulse of sudden and violent passions, and to be seduced by factious leaders into intemperate and pernicious resolutions." He added that "a body which is to correct this infirmity ought itself be free from it, and consequently ought to be less numerous. It ought moreover to possess great firmness, and consequently ought to hold its authority by a tenure of considerable duration."[69]

Reasons for the two-thirds requirement are more obscure. Confederation practice very likely had an influence, as did the desire to have fewer treaties, and thus fewer entanglements with the rest of the world, than had been the case to 1787. Perhaps the dominant motive, however, was protection of state and regional interests. There appears to have been genuine fear of treaties of peace approved by only a majority of the Senate—it could "be corrupted by foreign influence" to give away American territory, fishing rights, navigation of the Mississippi, and more.[70]

Then, too, by early September, the Framers were simply tired and ready for resolution, one way or another, of the treaty power. They had been meeting six days a week for almost four months, and had problems outstanding beyond the allocation of control over international agreements. It is probable that a part of their intent on September 8 was simply to lay treaty issues to rest, no matter how. This they did. There was no further discussion of issues concerning war and peace before the Framers concluded their labors nine days later.

Miscellaneous Debate

Beyond discussion of war and treaty making, precious little was said by the Framers that bore directly on the division of the war powers between the President and Congress. Without debate, control was given Congress over a range of nonmilitary action with war and peace consequences, in Article 1. During federal-state debate there was specific recognition that power over trade and tariffs vitally affects foreign relations, James McHenry explicitly equating embargoes with war.[71] Similarly, it was recognized that the treatment of aliens (especially immigrants and foreign economic interests) bears on external relations.[72] But in both instances, the issue was not whether Congress or the President should control policy, but whether Congress or the states.

By the same token, debate over raising, organizing, and supporting the military ran to federal-state problems. Very likely because of expectation that Congress would control policy on war and peace, the Committee of Style near the end of the Convention placed in the congressional article those provisions denying to the states certain foreign and military powers. The Committee placed there also the proviso for suspending habeas corpus during military emergency.[73]

Convention review of clauses dealing with the Executive was similarly truncated so far as the allocation of war powers is concerned. The terse treatment of the commander-in-chief clause was typical. There was brief debate about joint executive-senatorial control over appointments, with Wilson and Pinckney expressing reservations about Senate involvement. Wilson opted for executive appointments with guidance from a "Council . . . provided its advice should not be made obligatory on the President," and Pinckney, significantly, "was against joining the Senate in these appointments, except in the instances of Ambassadors who he thought ought not to be appointed by the President."[74]

Nothing was said about the purpose for the Article II, Section 1 language that "[t]he executive Power shall be vested in a President of the United States of America." There is no record of debate explaining why "herein granted" does not modify the executive power, as it does the Article I, Section 1 grant to Congress of legislative power.[75] Early in the Convention, however, it was thought crucial to enumerate executive powers to "assist the judgment in determining how far they might be safely entrusted to a single officer."[76] Throughout the Philadelphia proceedings fear was expressed over the potential for executive usurpation, with steady desire to avoid steps that might permit the potential to become real.[77] The Senate, further, was pictured by some as having equal or greater authority than the restrained Executive.[78]

Counter to this evidence that the Framers intended no undefined reservoir of presidential authority is the fact that they did finally create an independent Executive—a development by no means certain during most of the Convention. The presidency was made separate from Congress, to be held by one person with a nonlegislative source of election and a fixed term subject only to impeachment; the Executive was to be eligible for reelection and to have his own enumerated powers; and the President would not be saddled with a council to oversee his actions.[79]

Similarly, it was generally assumed that George Washington would be the first Executive, and confidence in him may have fostered intent that the President have wide powers. A year after the Convention, Pierce Butler wrote a relative in England that the powers of the President "are full great, and greater than I was disposed to make them. Nor, Entre Nous, do I believe they would have been so great had not many of the members cast their eyes toward General Washington as President; and shaped their Ideas of Powers to be given to a President, by their opinions of his Virtue."[80]

The weight of the evidence at Philadelphia does suggest that a majority of the Framers by September wished an Executive who would be more than an agent of Congress. But to conclude from that purpose that the Framers, without saying so, also intended to clothe the President with an indeterminate reservoir of foreign and military authority via the executive-power clause is difficult, given the Framers' caution concerning executive power and their expressed desire to limit it.

On September 17 the Framers came at last to the end of their labors. They committed the Journal of their debates to George Washington, "subject to the order of Congress, if ever formed under the Constitution." It was not published immediately lest "a bad use . . . be made" of the deliberations "by those who would wish to prevent the adoption of the Constitution."[81] Thirty-nine men signed the document and stated their "opinion" that Congress should begin government under it upon ratification by nine states.[82] The Framers then dissolved the Convention, and went to the states.

CHAPTER V

Ratification

DELAWARE'S RATIFYING convention met first, in December 1787, and Rhode Island's last, in 1790, after the Constitution had already gone into effect. All in all, well over a thousand Ratifiers gathered in the thirteen state conventions, most of which ended in a matter of days or weeks.[1] The Ratifiers' purposes for the Constitution are as important as those of its Framers. In fact, Madison suggested in 1796 that the desires of Ratifiers are the more crucial: "If we were to look . . . for the meaning of that instrument beyond the face of the instrument, we must look for it, not in the General Convention which proposed, but in the State Conventions which accepted and ratified it."[2]

Like the Framers, the Ratifiers gave little attention to the division of the war powers between the President and Congress. The state conventions prodigiously proposed changes in the Constitution to meet their concerns about government under it. But though amendments were seriously considered in nine states (formally advanced by seven), no more than 20 percent of the changes sought had anything to do with the war powers, and these changes made clear the Ratifiers' preoccupation with domestic tyranny rather than foreign affairs and their expectation that Congress, not the President, would control national policy. The only aspects of executive authority to attract proposed amendments were the President's power to command troops in the field and pardon traitors.

The Ratifiers, on the other hand, *were* concerned with congressional authority on many fronts. For instance, there were amendments to raise the majority by which Congress may declare war and the Senate approve commercial treaties; to require a three-fourths vote of both the Senate and House for treaties adversely affecting American territory, fishing, or river navigation; to force each house to publish its journals at least annually "except such parts thereof, relating to treaties, alliances, or military operations, as, in their judgment, require secrecy"; to hedge congressional capacity to suspend habeas corpus during military emergency; and above all to limit the legislators' control over organizing, raising, and supporting standing armies and state militia.[3]

We know significantly more about the Framers' debates at Philadelphia than most of the Ratifiers did. The Framers met in private, and the official Journal of their discussions was not made public for twenty years more. Accounts that certain Framers did offer during the state conventions were skimpy and often scrambled. Accordingly, the Ratifiers' purposes for the war-power provisions that they approved were influenced far less by the Framers' debates than by the Constitution's words themselves, by newspaper and pamphlet interpretation of them, and by the body of experience and assumptions shared by leading Americans of the era. Of the newspaper and pamphlet comment, *The Federalist Papers* most reflected the Philadelphia consensus, but it is questionable whether these papers shaped the Ratifiers' views nearly as much as they have those of later Americans.[4] Nonetheless, because of *The Federalist*'s subsequent import, its conclusions receive full play here.

War Making

"Are the people of England more secure," asked John Marshall rhetorically of the Virginia convention, "if the Commons have no voice in declaring wars? or are we less secure by having the Senate [*sic*] joined with the President?"[5] Marshall's exclusion of the House from war-commencement decisions was no doubt a momentary lapse, but it does suggest the imprecision accompanying the Ratifiers' deliberations.

Marshall notwithstanding, it seems that the Ratifiers generally equated Congress's power to declare war under the Constitution with its power to determine on war under the Articles of Confederation. Robert R. Livingston put it most directly in the New York convention: "But, say the gentlemen, our present [Confederation] Congress have not the same powers [as those proposed for Congress by the Constitution]. I answer, They have the very same . . . [including] the power of making war . . . ."[6] The declare-war clause, in any event, posed no problems for even those state delegates most allergic to the new Constitution. The first North Carolina convention found the document too defective for ratification, but allowed the clause giving Congress the power "to declare War [and] grant Letters of Marque and Reprisal" to be "read without any observation."[7]

As in Philadelphia, the inattention to this clause must have stemmed from the unanimous expectation that it left the President no independent war-making authority. James Wilson's comments in Pennsylvania say much, both in their implicit equation of declaring and commencing war and in their explicit foreclosure of unilateral executive action:

This system will not hurry us into war; it is calculated to guard against it. It will not be in the power of a single man, or a single body of men, to involve us in such distress; for the important power of declaring war is vested in the legislature at large: this declaration must be made with the concurrence of the House of Representatives: from this circumstance we may draw a certain conclusion that nothing but our national interest can draw us into a war.[8]

In North Carolina, James Iredell stated that "[t]he President has not the power of declaring war by his own authority . . . . These powers are vested in other hands."[9] As we have already seen, Pierce Butler explained to the South Carolina convention that war making by the President on his own authority "was objected to [by the Framers], as throwing into his hands the influence of a monarch, having an opportunity of involving his country in a war . . . ."[10] Charles Pinckney also told the South Carolina delegates that "the President's powers did not permit him to declare war."[11]

In similar vein Hamilton declared in *The Federalist, No. 69*, that the power "of the British king extends to the *declaring* of war . . . which by the constitution under consideration, would appertain to the legislature." And George Clinton's bitterly antifederalist *Letters of Cato* found no independent war-making authority for the Executive. Rather, in his effort to equate the President with the King, Clinton resorted to a more realistic view than Hamilton of the royal prerogative: "[T]hough it may be asserted that the king of Great Britain has the express power of making peace or war, yet he never thinks it prudent to do so without the advice of his Parliament, from whom he is to derive his support, and therefore these powers, in both president and king, are substantially the same . . . ."[12]

By the same token, the Ratifiers understood the commander-in-chief clause very narrowly. It was more discussed and opposed in the state conventions than had been the case in Philadelphia. Robert Miller in North Carolina was particularly fearful that the President had been given undue military authority and "considered it as a defect in the Constitution, that it was not expressly provided that Congress should have the direction of the motions of the army."[13] James Iredell, also in North Carolina, stated the more general view that conduct of hostilities is appropriately an executive function. He stressed the advantages of a single commander. But Iredell went on to equate presidential authority as commander in chief with that of the state governors:

I believe most of the governors of the different states have powers similar to those of the President. In almost every country, the executive has the command of the military forces. From the nature of the thing, the command of armies ought to be delegated to one person only. The secrecy, despatch, and decision, which are necessary in military operations, can only be expected from one person. The President, therefore, is to command the military forces of the United States, and this power I think a proper one; at the same time it will be found to be sufficiently guarded.[14]

Hamilton in *The Federalist, Nos. 69-70, 72, 74,* and *75* similarly construed the clause. In *No. 74* he stressed the overwhelming merit of unified command during war—a reality recognized by the state constitutions:

The propriety of this provision is so evident in itself; and it is at the same time so consonant to the precedents of the state constitutions in general, that little need be said to explain or enforce it. Even those of them, which have in other respects coupled the chief magistrate with a council have for the most part concentred the military authority in him alone. Of all the cares or concerns of government, the direction of war most peculiarly demands those qualities which distinguish the exercise of power by a single hand. The direction of war implies the direction of the common strength; and the power of directing and employing the common strength, forms an usual and essential part in the definition of the executive authority.[15]

In *No. 69*, however, Hamilton ignored the advantages of single command to hammer at the restrictive nature of the presidential military prerogative, as compared to that of the British king and even state governors. He began by reciting limits on the Executive's command of the militia and went from there:

First. The president will have only the occasional command of such part of the militia of the nation, as by legislative provision may be called into the actual service of the union. The king . . . and the governor of New-York, have at all times the entire command of all the militia within their several jurisdictions. In this article therefore the power of the president would be inferior to that of either the monarch or the governor. *Second*. The president is to be commander in chief of the army and navy of the United States. In This respect his author-ity . . . would amount to nothing more than the supreme command and direction of the military and naval forces, as first general and admiral of the confederacy; while that of the British king extends to the *declaring* of war, and to the *raising* and *regulating* of fleets and armies; all which by the constitution under consideration, would ap-pertain to the legislature . . . . [I]t may well be a question whether [the constitutions] of New-Hampshire and Massachusetts . . . do not in this instance confer larger powers upon their respective gov-ernors, than could be claimed by a president of the United States.

Evidence is compelling that the Ratifiers, like the Framers, understood the President as commander in chief to be simply "first general and admiral," a man whose "energy" could save the country during military crisis but who had authority neither to commit America to war nor to govern any but the strategic and tactical aspects of its conflicts, once begun.[16]

Some Ratifiers, nonetheless, had trouble with the com-mander-in-chief clause. They feared the base it might provide for unconstitutional seizure of power. "[T]he President, in the field, at the head of his army," warned Patrick Henry in Virginia, "can prescribe the terms on which he shall reign master . . . ."[17] James Monroe feared that the Executive could use the army to escape punishment for his crimes, thus encouraging foreign governments to bribe him to the country's ruin.[18] George Mason, also in the Virginia convention, would have had the President command, but not in person without the consent of Congress. Mason "admitted the propriety of his being commander-in-chief, so far as to give orders and have a general superintendency; but he thought it would be dangerous to let him command in person, without any restraint, as he might make a bad use of it. He was, then, clearly of opinion that the consent of a majority of both houses of Congress should be required before he could take the command in person."[19]

Concern was not limited to Virginia. We have already seen that Luther Martin reported in Maryland on his disappointment that the Framers had not restricted the President's right to personal command,[20] and the New York convention wished to amend the Constitution so "[t]hat the President, or person exercising his powers for the time being, shall not command an army in the field in person, without the previous desire of the Congress."[21]

Reluctance to have Presidents in the field was linked with fear of standing armies during peace. The failure of the Constitution to prohibit a national military establishment except during war was a frequent antifederalist objection. It was answered by assurances that the militia would provide the backbone of peacetime defense;[22] or by assurances that Congress controlled raising and supporting the army, thus precluding executive misfeasance.[23] As Hamilton argued in *Federalist No. 26*, the Constitution's two-year limit on military appropriations would ensure legislative oversight, because Congress "will be *obliged* . . . once at least every two years, to deliberate upon the propriety of keeping a military force on foot; to come to a new resolution on the point . . . . They are not at *liberty* to vest in the executive department permanent funds for the support of an army; if they were even incautious enough to be willing to repose in it so improper a confidence."

The Ratifiers' stingy concept of the Executive as commander

in chief was also reflected in concern that Congress, not the President, was the potential military despot. All agreed that Congress controlled the military purse, and there were some who believed that the legislators dominated the sword as well, thus putting the country's armies into congressional hands without check.[24]

In 1790-91 James Wilson—who had been a leading Framer, Ratifier, and proponent of executive power—gave a series of law lectures in which he termed the war powers "congressional":

The power of declaring war, and the other powers naturally connected with it, are vested in Congress. To provide and maintain a navy—to make rules for its government—to grant letters of marque and reprisal—to make rules concerning captures—to raise and support armies—to establish rules for their regulation—to provide for organizing . . . the militia, and for calling them forth in the service of the Union—all these are powers naturally connected with the power of declaring war. All these powers, therefore, are vested in Congress.[25]

The President, Wilson continued, has simply "to take care that the laws be faithfully executed; he is commander in chief of the army and navy . . . [and] he [has] authority to lead the army."[26]

Thomas Jefferson, who found the Constitution defective on other scores, was not perturbed by how it split the war powers between the President and Congress. In his celebrated "dog of war" letter to James Madison in 1789, he wrote that "[w]e have already given in example one effectual check to the Dog of war by transferring the power of letting him loose from the Executive to the Legislative body, from those who are to spend to those who are to pay."[27]

Diplomacy, Especially Treaty Making

The Ratifiers clearly did not mean for the President to make treaties on his own authority. William Davie, a Framer, complained to the North Carolina convention: "On the principle of the propriety of vesting this power in the Executive Department, it would seem that the whole power of making treaties ought to be left to the President, who, being elected by the people of the United States at large, will have their general interest at heart. But that jealousy of executive power which has shown itself so strongly in all the American governments, would not admit this improvement."[28] Francis Corbin in Virginia was more enthusiastic about the lack of executive control over treaty making: "It would be dangerous to give this power to the President alone, as the concession of such power to one individual is repugnant to republican principles. It is, therefore, given to the President and the Senate (who represent the states in their individual capacities) conjointly."[29] And among many others who sounded the theme, James Wilson said in Pennsylvania that "[n]either the President nor the Senate, solely, can complete a treaty; they are checks upon each other . . . ."[30]

While there was isolated contrary comment,[31] it was generally intended that the Senators participate with the President in *all* aspects of treaty making; further, that they jointly oversee American foreign affairs as a whole, with some expectation that the Senate was to be the dominant partner. In Massachusetts,[32] Ames felt that "[i]t need not be said that [the Senators] are principally to direct the affairs of war and treaties." King defended a six-year term for Senators because "[i]f for a shorter period, how can they be acquainted with the rights and interests of nations, so as to form advantageous treaties?" And Bowdoin described the Senate as "having not only legislative, but executive powers; being a legislating, and, at the same time, an advising body to the executive."

In the New York convention[33] G. Livingston found the Senate "a dangerous body," citing its powers as "council to the President, and in the forming of treaties," and terming it "a council of appointment, by whom ambassadors and other officers of state were to be appointed." Robert Livingston was more sanguine about the virtue of the Senate but equally free in his understanding of its diplomatic authority: "They are to form treaties with foreign nations. This requires a comprehensive knowledge of foreign politics, and an extensive acquaintance with characters, whom . . . they have to negotiate with, together with such an intimate conception of our best interests, relative to foreign powers, as can only be derived from much experience in this business." He later stated that the "Senate was to transact all foreign business . . . ." Hamilton, too, said that the Senators, "together with the President, are to manage all our concerns with foreign nations; they must understand all their interests, and their political systems."

James Wilson in Pennsylvania[34] went to great lengths to defend the President against the charge that he "is no more than the *tool* of the Senate." And McKean, finding the Senators "joined with the President in concluding treaties," indicated that "it therefore behoves them to be conversant with the politics of the nations of the world, and the dispositions of the sovereigns and their ministers . . . ."

In Virginia[35] Randolph could not "conceive" how the President's "powers can be called formidable . . . . He can do no important act without the concurrence of the Senate." "Consider the connection of the Senate with the executive," declared Monroe. "Has it not an authority over all the acts of the executive? What are the acts which the President can do without them?" And Patrick Henry, though chary of Presidents on horseback, lacked similar fear of them at the treaty table: "The honorable gentleman told you that there were two bodies, or branches, which must concur to make a treaty. Sir, the President, as distinguished from the Senate, is nothing. They will combine, and be as one."

Iredell speaking in North Carolina[36] pointed to the institutional advantages of the Senate, as against the weaknesses of the House, in public affairs and stated that "they apply much more forcibly to the case of foreign negotiations, which will form one part of the business of the Senate." He later said that the President "is to regulate all intercourse with foreign powers, and it is his duty to impart to the Senate every material intelligence he receives." "If it should appear," Iredell continued, "that he has not given them full information, but has concealed important intelligence which he ought to have communicated, and by that means induced them to enter into measures injurious to their country, and which they would not have consented to had the true state of things been disclosed to them," impeachment is appropriate. Spencer, also at the North Carolina convention, felt that by dint of the Senators' capacity to impeach the President, they "possess the chief of the executive power; they are, in effect, to form treaties, . . . and they have obviously, in effect, the appointment of all the officers of the United States," on the assumption that they could reject presidential nominations until he bends to their will. Finally, in South Carolina,[37] Charles Pinckney argued that the President "cannot appoint to an office without the Senate concurs; nor can he enter into treaties, or, in short, take a single step in his government, without their advice."

Jay and Hamilton in *The Federalist* took a broader view of the President's role in foreign affairs, but with no suggestion that he might ignore the Senate in their conduct. Madison talked only of the Senators. In *No. 62* he justified their age and period-of-citizenship requirements on the grounds that Senators must have "greater extent of information and stability of character," because they will be "participating immediately in transactions with foreign nations . . . ." He began *No. 63* with a "FIFTH desideratum illustrating the utility of a senate": "Without a select and stable member of the government, the esteem of foreign powers will not only be forfeited by an unenlightened and variable policy . . . . but the national councils will not possess that sensibility to the opinion of the world, which is perhaps not less necessary in order to merit, than it is to obtain, its respect and confidence."

Jay in *Federalist No. 64* focused on treaty making, indicating that the Senators' long and staggered terms enabled them "to become perfectly acquainted with our national concerns, and to form and introduce a system for the management of them." He then turned to institutional advantages peculiar to the Executive: "secrecy and dispatch." His unity facilitates gathering "intelligence" from those "who would rely on the secrecy of the President, but who would not confide in that of the senate," and it permits him better than the Senators to respond to changing "tides" in "the affairs of men." Jay, however, limited to "preparatory and auxiliary measures" the action which the President might take solely on his own authority, justified by a need

for speed or secrecy, and he added that "should any circumstance occur which requires the advice and consent of the senate, he may at any time convene them."[38]

Hamilton touched the allocation of diplomatic authority between the President and Senate in several papers. He made
explicit in *No. 75* their joint control over treaties. Treaty making, he said, "will be found to partake more of the legislative
than of the executive character, though it does not seem strictly
to fall within the definition of either of them . . . . The power
in question seems therefore to form a distinct department, and
to belong, properly neither to the legislative nor to the executive."[39] Thus he concluded that "the union of the Executive
with the Senate, in the article of treaties, is no infringement" of
the separation of powers.

Hamilton apparently expected the President to handle the
mechanics of American conversation with other nations. In
Federalist No. 72 he termed the "actual conduct of foreign
negotiations" an "executive function" and argued in *No. 75*:

> To have intrusted the power of making treaties to the senate alone,
> would have been to relinquish the benefits of the constitutional
> agency of the president, in the conduct of foreign negotiations. It is
> true, that the senate would in that case have the option of employing
> him in this capacity, but they would also have the option of letting it
> alone; and pique or cabal might induce the latter rather than the for-
> mer. Besides this, the ministerial servant of the senate could not be
> expected to enjoy the confidence and respect of foreign powers in the
> same degree with the constitutional representative of the nation; and
> of course would not be able to act with an equal degree of weight or
> efficacy.

But the President's "constitutional agency . . . in the conduct" of foreign affairs was to be senatorially guided. In *No.
84* Hamilton stated that "the management of foreign negotiations will naturally devolve" upon the Executive, "according to
general principles concerted with the senate, and subject to
their final concurrence." While discussing treaty making in *No.
66*, he said, "So far as might concern the misbehaviour of the
executive in perverting the instructions, or contravening the
views of the senate, we need not be apprehensive of the want

of a disposition in that body to punish the abuse of their confidence, or to vindicate their own authority." He spoke in *No. 75* of legislative "sanction in the progressive stages of a treaty" and in *No. 77* indicated that it might often be necessary to "call" the Senate "together with a view to" treaties "when it would be unnecessary and improper to convene the house of representatives."

Presidential prerogative over American diplomacy was not Hamilton's position, except perhaps as to the *channels* of foreign communication. Jay, more than Hamilton, was ambiguous even as to executive prerogative over channels. And Madison's comments in no way barred the Senate from involvement in any aspect of American diplomacy that it wished to enter.

Miscellaneous Debate

The range of congressional authority over action with indirect impact on American war and peace received some attention in *The Federalist*, but, as was true in Philadelphia, in a federal-state context. Madison and Hamilton argued foreign affairs to justify congressional power to tax and borrow, control foreign trade, define and punish piracy and other offenses against the law of nations, regulate the coining and value of domestic and foreign money, punish counterfeiters, fix weights and measures, and establish a uniform rule of naturalization.[40]

When the Ratifiers thought of executive versus legislative power over foreign affairs in terms other than war and treaty making, they turned to diplomatic appointments, thus furthering the association in their minds of the President and Senate in foreign matters. In a 1789 congressional speech, Framer and Ratifier Roger Sherman spoke of appointments and treaties when he constitutionally linked the Executive and the Senators "in every transaction which respects the business of negotiation with foreign powers":

The establishment of every treaty requires the voice of the Senate, as does the appointment of every officer for conducting the business. These two objects are expressly provided for in the Constitution, and they lead me to believe that the two bodies ought to act jointly in every transaction which respects the business of negotiation with foreign powers . . . . There is something more required than responsibility in conducting treaties. The Constitution contemplates the united wisdom of the President and Senate, in order to make treaties . . . . The more wisdom there is employed, the greater security there is that the public business will be well done.[41]

There was no hint during the ratification process that the President's constitutional authority to receive foreign diplomats conveyed any substantive power over foreign affairs. Hamilton in *Federalist No. 69* had little to say for the clause, other than that it spared Congress inconvenience:

The President is also to be authorized to receive ambassadors and other public ministers. This, though it has been a rich theme of declamation, is more a matter of dignity than of authority. It is a circumstance, which will be without consequence in the administration of the government; and it was far more convenient that it should be arranged in this manner, than that there should be a necessity of convening the legislature, or one of its branches, upon every arrival of a foreign minister; though it were merely to take the place of a departed predecessor.

Madison in *No. 42* did not mention the President while commenting on the reception of diplomats.[42]

The Executive's duty to take care that the laws be faithfully executed was thought significant. But it was not considered authority for him to enforce anything except congressional acts and treaties or for him to use military force to implement a law without explicit legislative authorization.[43]

The President's pardon power received more attention. It was seen by some as a key to executive usurpation. Luther Martin of Maryland dreaded authority to pardon even more than that of military command:

The power given to these persons [the President and Vice-President] over the Army, and Navy, is in truth formidable, but the power of Pardon is still more dangerous, as in all acts of Treason, the very offence on which the prosecution would possibly arise, would most likely be in favour of the Presidents own power.[44]

[Martin elaborated that] no treason was so likely to take place as that in which the President himself might be engaged—the attempt to assume to himself powers not given by the Constitution, and establish himself in regal authority; in which attempt a provision is made for him to secure from punishment the creatures of his ambition . . . .[45]

New York wished to pull the sting from pardon by amending the Constitution to condition executive clemency in treason cases on congressional approval.[46] Hamilton in *Federalist No. 74*, however, explained that the power was properly executive, in order to quell domestic revolt: "[I]n seasons of insurrection or rebellion, there are often critical moments, when a well-timed offer of pardon to the insurgents . . . may restore the tranquillity of the commonwealth; and which, if suffered to pass unimproved, it may never be possible afterwards to recall. The dilatory process of convening the legislature, or one of its branches, for the purpose of obtaining its sanction to the measure, would frequently be the occasion of letting slip the golden opportunity."[47]

To at least one Ratifier, the limited executive authority to summon Congress in the event of emergency and to dismiss it, should the two houses be unable to agree on a date for adjournment, smacked of incipient monarchy.[48] But none suggested that this authority might be used by Presidents to block congressional action on issues of war and peace. Similarly, none suggested that the provision for suspension of habeas corpus during military emergency posed an executive threat. Rather, the general assumption was that only Congress could suspend it.[49]

Great emphasis fell on the national government's being one of enumerated powers, wielding only authority specifically given it by the Constitution.[50] In none of the President's enumerated powers did the Ratifiers find wide-ranging authority.[51] For them, "[i]n republican government the legislative authority necessarily predominates."[52]

Nor did the Ratifiers think that the President received an undefined, nonenumerated reservoir of power in the executive clause.[53] Instead, his authority was compared with the limited powers of the state governors. James Bowdoin said in Massachusetts:

The legislative powers of the President are precisely those of the governors of this state and those of New York—rather negative than positive powers, given with a view to secure the independence of the executive, and to preserve a uniformity in the laws which are committed to them to execute.

The executive powers of the President are very similar to those of the several states, except in those points which relate more particularly to the Union, and respect ambassadors, public ministers, and consuls.[54]

And, as we have seen, the President's authority was often linked with the Senators', not always in a manner suggesting executive parity with them.

Even those at the state conventions opposed to the Constitution—because, in Patrick Henry's words, "[y]our President may easily become king"[55]—did not find monarchy lurking in the executive-power clause. George Clinton as *Cato* sought to describe the President in the most regal terms possible, but cited only *enumerated* grants of authority to that end: military command, pardon, and appointments. The Executive, said Clinton, "is the generalissimo of the nation, and of course has the command and control of the army, navy and militia; he is the general conservator of the peace of the union—he may pardon all offences, except in cases of impeachment, and [is] the principal fountain of all offices and employments. Will not the exercise of these powers therefore tend either to the establishment of a vile and arbitrary aristocracy or monarchy?"[56]

Certainly the friends of the Constitution did not speak of reservoirs of nonenumerated authority in the executive-power clause. A measure of the federalists' narrow acount of presidential authority may be discounted as ratification strategy. Undoubtedly some of them privately intended much more for the Executive. But what the Ratifiers actually said during the ratification process provides the most authoritative guide to their and their colleagues' purposes for approving the document. And that evidence shows a limited reading of the President's enumerated grants of authority and no intent to give him non-enumerated powers.

On July 2, 1788, Congress received word that, during the previous month, New Hampshire had become the ninth state to ratify the Constitution. The legislators then debated for two months an act to put the document into effect, finally providing that "the first Wednesday in March next be the time, and the present seat of Congress the place, for commencing proceedings under the said Constitution." Thus war-power practice under the present government dates from March 4, 1789.[57]

CHAPTER VI

Congressional Retreat and
Resilience since 1789

WITH GEORGE WASHINGTON's inauguration, the country confronted immediately the vague language, competing grants of authority, and outright gaps in the war-power provisions of the Constitution. Despite them, answers were demanded to a number of questions if the new government was to operate. Might the Executive wage war on threatening Indians without prior congressional approval? Which branch was to decide whether the United States would recognize the revolutionary French regime? Which was to construe the Franco-American alliance and act on whether America would remain neutral in the ongoing European conflict? How were our military and diplomatic establishments to be created, organized, and administered? And what was to be the relationship among the President, Senate, and House in treaty making, in controlling official channels of communication with other nations, and in otherwise governing American diplomacy?

No Shortage of Precedent

During succeeding years the country has continued to grapple with the question of which branch has what war powers. At times the issues have been new. Since the country lacked a floating navy while Washington was in office, whether the President might deploy warships on his own authority, and, if so, exactly how far off our coasts he might send them—indeed, whether he might risk naval combat in some circumstances— had to await later administrations, most notably those of John

Adams, Jefferson, Jackson, Lincoln, Wilson, Franklin Roosevelt, and Kennedy. Similarly, since the Central Intelligence Agency and its extensive covert operations arrived with the Cold War, it was not until then that we seriously confronted the question of how to allocate control over secret armed action by this country abroad.

At times the issues have been old, resurfacing after dormancy to be reconsidered in the light of changed national circumstances. Lyndon Johnson's 1965 intervention in the Dominican Republic and Gerald Ford's 1975 rescue of the *Mayaguez* posed kindred yet distinct questions to those raised by executive use of force in the Caribbean during the first two decades of this century and by presidential police action during the 1800s against primitive, stateless peoples (the natives of Sumatra, Fiji, and the like) and against weak nations (China and Japan, for instance). Kindred were the desires to protect American citizens and property against foreign outrage, to punish and deter aggressors, also to advance broader interests —to make the world safe for American merchants, buttress national security, or whatever. Common also was the military impotence of those struck by the American stick. Quite distinct were the contexts in which the stick fell. Primitive, stateless people passed on with the 1800s. Weak states today often have powerful foreign protectors, able to inflict quick harm on the United States. Even in the absence of such protectors, heightened distaste has arisen in this century for one nation's unilateral use of force against another. This distaste ensures greater legal and political costs for any coercion of weak states now than was true in the more Darwinesque 1800s. Further, the consequences of miscalculation, should a minor military venture escalate, are more compelling today, given international interdependence and missiles.

While many war-power issues continue on unresolved, others (whether new, old, or recurring) have been laid to rest. During the Whisky Rebellion in 1794, Washington established that the President might appear in the field, leave the seat of government to do so, and wield the pardon power to hasten peace. Whether the Executive might send the militia out of the

country lingered until Woodrow Wilson's time. According to
Congressman Hannis Taylor in 1919: "The unauthorized trans-
portation by the executive power of our conscripted National
Militia to the battle fields of Europe, in defiance of section 8,
Article I, of the Constitution, will stand out in time to come as
the most stupendous act of illegality in all history."[1] Whether
American involvement in war might end constitutionally
except by treaty lingered beyond Wilson's presidency. He said
not. Since Richard Nixon stopped the Vietnamese aspect of
our third most costly conflict by pure executive agreement, in
the manner of Eisenhower's Korean settlement, it seems that
practice has not borne Wilson out, at least as to undeclared
wars. By the same token, strenuous demands for Senate approval of treaty negotiators and other special diplomatic
agents faded at the turn of the century. Presidents have also
ignored into oblivion a congressional hope perhaps most
keenly expressed in a 1913 statute which provided that hence-
forth "[t]he Executive shall not extend or accept any invitation
to participate in any international congress, conference, or like
event, without first having specific authority of law to do so."[2]
Theodore Roosevelt had mediated the Russo-Japanese war
and participated in Europe's Algeciras negotiations without
such approval before the 1913 act. Wilson went to Versailles
without approval after it.

    Although war-power precedent is found in every administra-
tion, the country's effort to come to grips with the respective
prerogatives of its political branches has varied in intensity
from one presidency and Congress to another. During some,
new ground has been broken, often amid acute controversy.
When John Quincy Adams tried to have the United States participate in the 1826 Panama Conference of new Latin states
fearful of European attack, uproar ensued over whether the
country might constitutionally attend such an international
"congress," and if it could, pursuant to what congressional
strings (ultimately, only Senate confirmation of the American
representatives), and with what limits on executive diplomacy,
lest it constrain Congress's later freedom to shape American
response to Latin wars. New ground but much less uproar

accompanied an equally significant step during Jackson's presidency: the beginning of executive use of force in primitive places and weak states *not* contiguous to this country to safeguard American lives and property and to retaliate against their assumed attackers. During some eras, war-power practice has moved more slowly, hewing largely to well-established paths —while Hayes, Garfield, and Arthur were in office, for instance, and during Cleveland's first term. But even these presidencies were notable for the Senate's diplomatic irredentism, shown principally through efforts to narrow the Executive's role in treaty making.

So far as military action is concerned, developments were perhaps most spare during Hoover's administration and Franklin Roosevelt's first term (among Presidents who survived a full four years in office). Campaigns against pirates had ended during the 1820s, though Presidents at times thereafter found it convenient to term their armed action "antipirate." Hot pursuit into territory contiguous to the United States, preemptive invasion of such areas to ward off threatened incursions into this country, armed occupation of territory desired by the United States, landings abroad to protect American lives and property, reprisals against those who had harmed them or otherwise insulted the flag, military intervention in other states' domestic affairs pursuant to treaty, the search for naval coaling stations —all these had largely dried up by the end of Woodrow Wilson's time, if only after a rich final flowering from President Benjamin Harrison through Wilson. Outright invasion and occupation of Caribbean states for political purposes had a last flurry when Calvin Coolidge took Nicaragua, with repercussions in this country that precluded the near-term renewal of such ventures. And by 1929 there was no national resolve for the use of force abroad to promote inchoate interests, such as national security, notwithstanding Japanese, Italian, and German threats. Franklin Roosevelt's steps toward American involvement in World War II were a decade away, and the Cold War further. In short, the Hoover to early Roosevelt years contributed as little war-power precedent as any in our history. But much like the interlude between Grant and Harrison, this period was also significant for congressional resurgence, albeit of a sort designed to withdraw the country from active involvement in international affairs.[3]

Over almost two hundred years, then, the country has built up a mass of precedent on how to divide the war powers between the President and Congress. The precedent exists in chilling bulk for three main reasons. First, there are so many matters (the war-power variables described in Chapter I) about which relevant data have been gathering since 1789. Second, these data involve what Americans have *said* the division of authority should be (their expectations about its nature), as well as the extent to which the President or Congress has *actually controlled* policy and tools, notwithstanding any contrary expectations about where control should lie. As to expectations, recorded beliefs are voluminous, coming from former Framers and Ratifiers, Presidents, Secretaries of State, diplomats, field commanders, individual Senators and Representatives, their committees and staffs, the Senate, House, Congress as a whole, Supreme Court Justices, judges, scholars, students, newspaper editors and other media members, polemicists, and occasionally even citizens whose views happen to be preserved. As to actual control, there are hundreds of instances in which this country has made significant use of its military, or declined to do so. Accordingly, there are hundreds of occasions in which the President and Congress have shaped American action, each to one degree or another. The same is true of the far more numerous instances in which the United States has taken nonmilitary action with significant consequences for war or peace.

Third, as Chapter I pointed out, conflicting beliefs and conflicting degrees of control run throughout the precedent amassed since 1789. Also, expectations about the sort of control that each branch should exercise have at times run counter to the actual balance of power. Senators Taft and Douglas disagreed about the war powers when American forces were being committed to battlefields in Korea and to potential conflict in Europe. Senator Fulbright stood with Douglas in those days but became Taftian in later years, following the Dominican and Vietnam interventions. Before 1850 Congress was far more influential in the resolution of our territorial disputes with Spain and Britain than it was in the disposition of the Texas boundary controversy with Mexico. Such inconsistencies enhance the importance of the various bits and pieces of war-power evidence. These data resist easy amalgamation into a few conclusions about post-1789 practice. With this warning, we turn now to a few such conclusions, starting with several summary statements about Congress.

Although the constitutional text and 1787-88 debates tilt toward congressional authority over war and peace, Congress as a whole, and the Senate in particular, have proved inept at turning these strengths into post-1789 substance. Despite this failure to preserve, much less capitalize on, 1787-88 strengths, there have been many instances in which the legislators *have* controlled American policy or participated as the President's equal in shaping it. These occasions have usually involved areas where congressional prerogative has never been seriously threatened, even if eroded from time to time by sweeping delegations of authority to the Executive. But at times these occasions have also concerned unsettled areas, including the use of armed force. And no matter how low congressional influence has sunk, it has retained a singular capacity to rebound.

Congress and Military Action

The legislators have been the driving influence behind certain American decisions to fight. War with Britain and near war with France in 1812, as well as conflict with Spain in 1898, were congressionally inspired. But, as a rule, when the President and Congress have not been equally enthusiastic about a given use of force, the legislators have been the more reluctant. Under these circumstances some Presidents have sought *prior* congressional approval, been denied it, and foresworn armed action. Congress declined to grant prior approval to Washington in 1792 for offensive action against Indians, to Jefferson in 1805 for American occupation of West Florida, and to Jackson in 1835 and 1837 for reprisals against France and Mexico. This phenomenon peaked with President Buchanan, who made eight unsuccessful requests for authority to use force in Latin America between 1857-59.

On other occasions Executives or their subordinates have begun a use of force only to have it ended when Congress refused to vote ratification or vital implementing tools. Thus, in 1812 an overzealous field commander occupied Amelia Island in Spanish East Florida. President Madison permitted the occupation to stand pending an opportunity for Congress to ratify it. When that was not forthcoming, he withdrew the troops. As regards termination by denial of tools, recent events are seminal. Following the 1970 Cambodian incursion, the Special Foreign Assistance Act of 1971 was amended to provide that "none of the funds authorized or appropriated pursuant to this or any other Act may be used to finance the introduction of United States ground combat troops into Cambodia, or to provide United States advisers to or for Cambodian military forces in Cambodia."[4] And when America bombing continued in Cambodia after United States withdrawal from Vietnam, the 1973 Supplemental Appropriations Act was similarly amended: "Notwithstanding any other provision of law, on or after August 15, 1973, no funds herein or heretofore appropriated may be obligated or expended to finance directly or indirectly combat activities by United States military forces in or over or from off the shores of North Vietnam, South Vietnam, Laos or Cambodia."[5]

On yet other occasions Presidents have been permitted to go forward subject to congressional constraints. Congress did not ratify the 1812 occupation of Amelia Island, but it did authorize Madison to oust the Spanish from *West* Florida. And Congress did not cut off funds for American *air* operations over Cambodia until August 15, 1973, long after it had cut off monies for *ground* operations.

Presidents, too, have been deterred from attempting military action in the face of anticipated congressional opposition, or they have been forced to pursue their policy through indirection and subterfuge. During Benjamin Harrison's administration, though without his instructions, American diplomats and naval forces aided an 1893 coup against Hawaii's Queen Liliuokalani. Upon taking office, Grover Cleveland repudiated our involvement but did not use force to restore the monarchy in the wake of Senate and House resolutions warning him against it. Similarly, legislative enactment of isolationism between the two World Wars—Neutrality Act limits on preferring one European belligerent over another, Selective Service Act limits on the use of draftees outside the Western Hemisphere, and the like—drove Franklin Roosevelt to circumspection and sophistry as he brought American economic and military power to bear against the Germans before Pearl Harbor. President Nixon kept certain American bombings in Indochina secret in part to avoid congressional opposition.

We have been looking at situations in which Congress shaped policy by either urging conflict on the Executive or by restraining in one fashion or another his capacity to engage in it. More frequently the legislators have accepted presidential policy. Sometimes that acceptance has been the product of genuine interchange between the two branches; sometimes it has been congressional acquiescence to presidential initiatives.

Genuine interchange between the Executive and legislators led to the 1798 Naval War with France during John Adams's administration. He presented Congress with information and recommendations. The legislators debated in minute detail what action to take and what should be the limits on presidential control over it. This is not to say that the process was harmonious. Quite to the contrary, vilification of Adams by his political and policy opponents had a 1960s analogue in the MacBird approach to Lyndon Johnson as alleged information manipulator, warmonger, and usurper of congressional prerogatives. The point is that both political branches engaged the merits of the alternative policies open to the country and jointly worked their way to decision about the appropriate national course. Genuine interchange also characterized American response to continued Spanish presence in Florida through Monroe's presidency, the Latin American revolutions in the 1820s and 1830s, the liberal European revolts at mid-century, disarmament under the peace pacts of the 1920s, a post-Coolidge good neighbor, noninterventionist policy in Latin America, the creation of the United Nations, and communist containment via the web of alliances and foreign aid programs that came to maturity during the 1950s.

It remains true, though, that when the two branches have agreed on the use rather than the nonuse of armed force, Congress has most often simply acceded to presidential initiatives without further ado, because most legislators thought well of the policies being pursued. Such was true of certain of Washington's campaigns against the Indians, Jefferson's naval steps in the Mediterranean to curb Barbary attacks on American shipping, Polk's manifest destiny at Mexico's expense, as well as Wilson's and Franklin Roosevelt's moves to block German militarism. Similarly, steps against pirates, slavers, and other international outlaws; armed protection of American citizens abroad; reprisals against primitive peoples and weak states who transgressed American interests; military intervention in Caribbean politics in the early decades of this century; hot pursuit into Mexico over a much longer period; and the military incidents of the Cold War from the Berlin airlift of 1948 to the later stages of Indochina—these were all executive initiatives to which Congress acceded. The executive initiative may have been bitterly attacked by some legislators, even by a majority in one house or the other. But necessary implementing tools were nonetheless voted and resolutions to set aside the President's policy or censure him as an usurper defeated, because most legislators agreed with his policies. When majorities in both houses have not agreed, they have curbed him.

In those instances when Congress has chosen *explicitly* to vote its approval of armed action, it has done so variously— both before the President began military steps and after; by acceptance of a specific venture and by generic authorization of any venture falling within a particular class of action; by relatively precise indication of the steps authorized and by broad, ill-defined assents; by declaration of war, joint resolution, statute, treaty, and other means, such as voting a gold medal for the navy captain who trained his ship's guns on an Austro-Hungarian vessel at Smyrna in 1853 to recover Martin Koszta, a local revolutionary who also happened to be a partially naturalized American. Examples follow.

Sometimes congressional approval has been incontestably "prior"—the legislators' 1858 joint resolution authorizing Buchanan to "adopt such measures and use such force as, in his judgment, may be necessary and advisable, in the event of a refusal of just satisfaction by the government of Paraguay"[6] (satisfaction for the shelling by a Paraguayan fort of the U.S.S. *Water Witch*).

Sometimes prior approval has preceded most but not all of a particular use of force. Formal declarations of war in 1846 against Mexico and in 1941 against Germany followed significant provocative action by the Executive but preceded most of the fighting. All of our formal declarations, in fact, have been of the "recognizing" war kind, premised on the assumption that conflict is already ongoing, having been "thrust upon" us by the enemy. The 1917 declaration is a good example:

Whereas the Imperial German Government has committed repeated acts of war against the Government and the people of the United States of America: Therefore be it

Resolved . . . That the state of war between the United States and the Imperial German Government which has thus been thrust upon the United States is hereby formally declared; and that the President be, and he is hereby, authorized and directed to employ the entire naval and military forces of the United States and the resources of the Government to carry on war against the Imperial German Government; and to bring the conflict to a successful termination all of the resources of the country are hereby pledged by the Congress of the United States.[7]

In 1861 Congress faced its most pressing need to date either to ratify executive war-power initiatives or to let pass in silence a stunning claim of presidential prerogative. During the early months of Abraham Lincoln's presidency while Congress remained out of session, the Executive increased the size of the army and navy, called out the militia, summoned volunteers, paid monies from the Treasury to private persons to further his war effort, and blockaded Confederate ports, among other military steps. Once in session, the legislators chose to ratify rather than silently acquiesce, beginning with an act declaring the "existence of war" and concluding with a proviso that "all the acts, proclamations, and orders of the President of the

United States after [March 4, 1861] respecting the army and navy of the United States, and calling out or relating to the militia or volunteers of the States, are hereby approved and in all respects legalized and made valid, to the same intent and with the same effect as if they had been issued and done under the previous express authority and direction of the Congress of the United States."[8] Such direct ratifications have been infrequent. The absence of disapproval, buttressed by the continued supply of implementing tools, *e.g.*, money, has been more ordinary when the legislators have chosen not to end or limit presidential military initiatives.

Explicit legislative authorization has usually concerned a specific venture, though that venture may subsume many undertakings. The 1941 declaration of war against Japan is a classic example. At times, however, authorization has run generically to a category of ventures. An 1819 statute "authorized" the President "to instruct the commanders of the public armed vessels of the United States" to attack other armed vessels "which shall have attempted or committed any piratical aggression . . . upon any vessel of the United States, or of the citizens thereof, or upon any other vessel."[9] Similarly, in 1856 Congress authorized armed force to protect the claims of American citizens to any guano islands that they discovered which did not belong to another government.[10] Also in this vein was the 1957 Middle East resolution, which provided that "if the President determines the necessity thereof, the United States is prepared to use armed force to assist any such nation or group of such nations requesting assistance against armed aggression from any country controlled by international communism . . . ."[11]

The legislators have sometimes been rather precise in the sort of military action approved. In 1798 Congress authorized the Executive to instruct the navy to attack any French vessels found armed within our territorial waters or on the high seas, not elsewhere, and to commission privateers against the French.[12] A secret act of 1811 provided

that the President . . . is . . . authorized, to take possession of, and occupy [East Florida] in case an arrangement has been, or shall be, made with the local authority of the said territory, for delivering up the possession of the same, or any part thereof, to the United States, or in the event of an attempt to occupy the said territory, or any part thereof, by any foreign government; and he may, for the purpose of taking possession, and occupying the territory aforesaid, and in order to maintain therein the authority of the United States, employ any part of the army and navy of the United States which he may deem necessary.[13]

Similarly, in 1839 Congress authorized President Van Buren for a period of eighteen months "to resist any attempt on the part of Great Britain to enforce, by arms, her claim to exclusive jurisdiction over the part of Maine, which is in dispute . . . and for that purpose to employ the naval and military force of the United States."[14] Recall also the 1858 *Water Witch* joint resolution noted above: Approval ran only to steps against Paraguay for redress of a specific grievance already incurred, with no more coercion than necessary to obtain "just satisfaction."

During the period between Monroe and Lincoln, the legislators were unusually loath to let the President fight upon the happening of a specific *future* event. Ironically, the deferential Buchanan bore the brunt of this concern. In response to his 1859 request for authority to protect American lives and property in transit across the Central American isthmus if they were threatened by revolutionary activity, Senator Seward caught the prevailing mood:

[The Executive] tells us that it would not be a surrender of the war-making power; but that we should be making war ourselves. Could anything be more strange and preposterous than the idea of the President of the United States making hypothetical wars, conditional wars, without any designation of the nation against which war is to be declared; or the time, or place, or manner, or circumstances of the duration of it, the beginning or the end; and without limiting the number of nations with which war may be waged? No sir. When we pass this bill we do surrender the power of making war or preserving peace, in each of the States named, into the hands of the President of the United States.[15]

Buchanan returned later in 1859 with another plea for approval to police the isthmus and "to protect American merchant vessels, their crews and cargoes, against violent and lawless seizure and confiscation in the ports of Mexico and the Spanish American States when these countries may be in a disturbed and revolutionary condition."[16] In an effort to calm Congress, he cajoled:

But can Congress only act after the fact, after the mischief has been done? Have they no power to confer upon the President the authority in advance to furnish instant redress should such a case afterwards occur? . . . [T]o meet future cases under circumstances strictly specified is as clearly within the war-declaring power as such an authority conferred upon the President by act of Congress after the deed had been done. In the progress of a great nation many exigencies must arise imperatively requiring that Congress should authorize the President to act promptly on certain conditions . . . .[17]

The legislators were not moved.

Viewed against practice since 1789, Buchanan's formulation (much less Senator Seward's) suggests more precision in congressional authorizations than has generally been the case, whether they have been given before or after the fact. Washington was authorized in 1789 to use armed force "for the purpose of protecting the inhabitants of the frontiers of the United States from hostile incursions of Indians"[18] with no further indication of what sort of threat or what sort of response the legislators had in mind. Recall the sweeping terms in which Woodrow Wilson was authorized to fight World War I: Congress made no effort to specify the territorial limits of American involvement (important when Wilson sent troops to Russia during the war and to Trau after the armistice) or the objectives for which the United States was fighting (crucial at Versailles).

Given its notoriety once Vietnam went sour, the 1964 Gulf of Tonkin Resolution was surprisingly more precise than many of its antecedents. The resolution stated:

The Congress approves and supports the determination of the President . . . to take all necessary measures to repel any armed attack against the forces of the United States and to prevent further aggression.

Sec. 2. The United States regards as vital to its national interest and to world peace the maintenance of international peace and security in southeast Asia. Consonant with the Constitution of the United States and the Charter of the United Nations and in accordance with its obligations under the Southeast Asia Collective Defense Treaty, the United States is, therefore, prepared, as the President determines, to take all necessary steps, including the use of armed force, to assist any member or protocol state of [SEATO] requesting assistance in defense of its freedom.

Sec. 3. This resolution shall expire when the President shall determine that the peace and security of the area is reasonably assured by international conditions created by action of the United Nations or otherwise, except that it may be terminated earlier by concurrent resolution of the Congress.[19]

Thus, the Tonkin Gulf Resolution stated objectives for the use of force, put certain territorial limits on it, and set out a veto-proof mechanism for terminating it. Nonetheless, until voted away by Congress in 1971, the resolution did leave the President sweeping discretion in his direction of American involvement in the Indochina War.[20]

On infrequent occasions the legislators have also influenced military action through the passage of institutional measures not directed at any particular use of force or generic category of uses but turned rather to broader questions of the allocation of the war powers. During Washington's administration Congress confronted how best to implement its Article I power "[t]o provide for calling forth the Militia to execute the Laws of the Union, suppress Insurrections and repel Invasions." Despite concern among some legislators that the President should not be left to determine the exact time, place, and cause of calling out troops, by 1795 there was a statute vesting him with authority to summon the militia whenever in his judgment it was necessary to execute the laws, suppress insurrections, or repel actual or *imminent* invasions.[21] In 1878 Congress enacted a ban on use of the army "for the purpose of executing the laws, except in such cases and under such circumstances as such employment of said force may be expressly authorized by the Constitution or by act of Congress."[22] In 1973, over President Nixon's veto, the legislators passed the War Powers Resolution, their most vigorous attempt yet at such institutional legislation.[23]

At least as often as there have been successful attempts at

institutional acts, there have been unsuccessful ones—for instance, a move in the House of Representatives, following
General Andrew Jackson's 1818 invasion of Spanish Florida, to
bar statutorily any executive incursion into foreign territory
without prior congressional approval, unless in hot pursuit.[24]
Again, in 1864 the House became disturbed at presidential
tolerance of a French protectorate in Mexico under Maximilian.
After the administration told Paris that it, not the House, constitutionally controlled American diplomacy and that the President "does not at present contemplate any departure from the
policy which this Government has hitherto pursued in regard to
the war which exists between France and Mexico,"[25] the Representatives counterasserted:

Congress has a constitutional right to an authoritative voice in declaring and prescribing the foreign policy of the United States, as well in
the recognition of new powers as in other matters; and it is the constitutional duty of the President to respect that policy, not less in diplomatic negotiations than in the use of the national forces when authorized by law; and the propriety of any declaration of foreign policy
by Congress is sufficiently proved by the vote which pronounces it;
and such proposition while pending and undetermined is not a fit
topic of diplomatic explanation with any foreign power.[26]

This House resolution did not survive the Senate Foreign Relations Committee. Recall also the attempt by Congress as a
whole in 1913 to end presidential discretion over American
participation in international conferences. But even unsuccessful attempts at legislation, whether specific or institutional,
have often had an impact on executive policy. Well before
Congress voted its first curb on federal funds for Indochina,
rising legislative unrest had helped drive Lyndon Johnson from
office, a one-term war President, and helped lead Richard
Nixon to a policy of withdrawal.

Congressional Resilience

During American retreat from Indochina, congressional influence over war and peace came into flood tide after a period
of unprecedented ebb. As we shall see in Chapter XI, the legislators challenged the President's control over a range of action

that seemed about to become permanently his by virtue of repeated congressional acquiescence. At the core of these matters was the commitment of American forces to undeclared combat on a large or small scale, openly or covertly. The constitutional text and debates account for much of this congressional resilience. They establish certain hard-core legislative powers and give rise to procongressional expectations which, in concert, create an enduring base from which the legislators can reassert their hold over war and peace from time to time.

In areas of hard-core congressional authority, Presidents have usually felt themselves able only to recommend action, sign or veto resulting legislation, and receive any delegation of authority that Congress offered. While these areas do *not* include most types of military action, they do cover most types of nonmilitary action with consequences for war or peace, and most of the tools vital to implement policy.

The following list suggests the heavily fiscal cast of hard-core congressional authority:

Military Action

1. Changes in the size or weapons of the armed forces
2. Formal declarations of war

Nonmilitary Action

1. Aliens when neither military nor diplomatic personnel: terms of their entry and stay in this country, of their naturalization and extradition

2. American individuals, organizations, and businesses abroad: terms of their exit from and reentry to this country

3. Economic claims against the United States or its citizens: their financial disposition

4. Fiscal or monetary policy with international effect

5. Foreign aid: the provision of money, matériel, and civilian personnel

6. International organizations: American membership and financial support

7. Technology and scientific data: the terms of its flow into and out of this country

8. Territorial claims and concessions by the United States

9. Trade policy

Tools

1. Federal personnel: their creation, organization, and discharge

2. Money: its raising and authorization

3. International agreements when in the form of treaties or congressional-executive pacts

4. Regulations governing the conduct of American citizens

Beyond these hard-core powers there has also been persistent popular feeling that the Constitution requires legislative approval of American use of force. Twentieth-century Presidents (unlike their predecessors) have rarely said that explicit congressional approval is needed for most military action, but the view has been pressed with vigor by others during this century. Even during the 1950s a remnant in Congress kept the faith, Senator Taft being their leading apostle.

Appendix B surveys a number of pro-congressional expectations, beginning with those of President Washington in 1793. The survey is highly selective. It ignores the most fertile source of recorded beliefs favoring Congress, that is, the words of the Senators and Representatives themselves and those outside government who have opposed particular executive policies. The survey is limited to executive figures, principally Presidents and Secretaries of State, though it also includes an 1848 statement of Congressman Abraham Lincoln. No effort is made to place these recorded beliefs in context—to note the extent to which their proponents deferred to Congress in fact as well as in rhetoric, the degree to which a necessity for congressional approval may have been claimed in order to shield an executive preference for inaction, or the extent to which the speakers may have responded to political rather than constitutional drums. Nor has there been an attempt to include all significant executive statements that Congress constitutionally controls. The survey does show that for quite some time after 1789 Presidents and Secretaries of State conceded significant war powers to Congress. These executive statements have continuing impact as precedent during today's constitutional controversies. Indeed, their impact is greatest when they are advanced as in the appendix, without the qualifications of context.

Beyond hard-core powers and belief in congressional primacy, the legislators' resilience also reflects the fact that congressional influence can be kept alive even though Congress as a whole declines to vote on the merits of a particular policy. The power of congressional committees to investigate and oversee provides a means of sparking national debate, molding opinion, and thereby influencing presidential action, as Senator Nye's "merchants of death" hearings in 1934 on American involvement in World War I and Senator Fulbright's 1967 hearings on Vietnam made clear. Such activity by individual Senators and Representatives can focus political pressure already existing outside Congress and bring it to bear on the Executive. Legislators can work privately too, communicating quietly with the President to persuade him that his plans are ill advised or subject to great potential opposition. Legislators can also work in tandem with rebellious elements in the bureaucracy to thwart presidential policy.

Finally, the door is kept further ajar for Congress by the restraints imposed on an Executive by his own capacity to persuade others to take steps he wishes taken. Other centers of power within the country—the bureaucracy, courts, and media in particular—lessen his freedom of maneuver. And the electorate stands ready to turn against him if his policies are perceived to be unresponsive to popular needs or, worse, illegitimate. Intensifying these restraints is fear of the President as a potential despot, a fear with us since 1787-88. In Arthur Schlesinger's terms: "The theory . . . of the President as the great moloch generating its own divinity and about to swallow all power can be reproduced at every stage in our history, beginning with those who . . . complained against the presidency of General Washington."[27] Anti-Moloch pressures have as their by-product an opportunity for Congress to reassert its influence when in the mood.

To date, however, the legislators have proved unable to reassert themselves once and for all by establishing enduring channels for a congressional voice in decisions about war and peace. Like most of the rest of us, legislators tend to be result oriented. Their concern with the particulars of policy often overshadows their concern with the institutional process by which it is made. Principal interest goes to *what* we should do (whether or not to rescue the *Mayaguez*) rather than to *how we should go about deciding* what to do (whether by executive fiat announced to congressional leaders shortly before the fact, by prior congressional approval, or by some intermediate method). Accordingly, most legislators become seriously solicitous of their prerogatives only when they disagree with executive policy. Then no oar is spared to set to rights presidential "usurpation." But once the tempest over policy has passed, concern with the institutional aspects of decision making fades also, to await the next tempest. We will consider in a later chapter whether the War Powers Resolution of 1973 signals a change in congressional habits.

CHAPTER VII

Presidential Advance

THE TREND since 1789 has been rising presidential sway over war and peace, as Chapter I noted with appropriate qualifications. Doctrinally this rise has relied upon the Constitution's textual uncertainties. Abel Upshur in an 1840 essay *Federal Government* gloomily concluded:

The most defective part of the Constitution beyond all question, is that which relates to the Executive Department. It is impossible to read that instrument, without being struck by the loose and unguarded terms in which the powers and duties of the President are pointed out. . . . [I]n regard to the Executive, the Convention appears to have studiously selected such loose and general expressions as would enable the President, by implication and construction . . . to enlarge his powers.[1]

Chapter II suggested the commander-in-chief, take-care, and executive-power clauses as particularly fruitful sources of textual uncertainty. Thus Secretary of State Acheson advised in July 1950 that President Truman needed no explicit congressional approval of the Korean War because he could "rest on his constitutional authority as Commander in Chief of the armed forces."[2] The State Department explained shortly thereafter that "[t]he President, as Commander in Chief of the Armed Forces of the United States, has full control over the use thereof."[3] The Department had not changed its mind by 1966:

There can be no question . . . of the President's authority to commit United States forces to the defense of South Viet-Nam. The grant of authority to the President in article II of the Constitution extends to the actions of the United States currently undertaken in Viet-Nam. . . .
Under the Constitution, the President, in addition to being Chief

Executive, is Commander in Chief of the Army and Navy. He holds the prime responsibility for the conduct of United States foreign relations. These duties carry very broad powers, including the power to deploy American forces abroad and commit them to military operations when the President deems such action necessary to maintain the security and defense of the United States.[4]

And Solicitor General Griswold agreed in more restrained terms in 1971:

[T]he Constitution provides explicitly that "The Executive power shall be vested in a President of the United States of America." Obviously this means something; and it is not a merely passive grant. The grant of Executive power is broad and general. It is made more concrete by the further provision that "The President shall be Commander-in-Chief of the Army and Navy of the United States," and the provision that "he shall take care that the laws be faithfully executed." Our President is not, and never has been thought to be, from the time of Washington on to the present, a mere automaton, doing only what he is told; nor is he a mere moderator, standing by to carry out the directives of other officers and branches of the govenment. . . . [A]s President, he has great powers—great executive power because he is the Chief Executive—and we would not want to have it otherwise. Any political organism needs a spokeman, . . . someone to meet emergencies, someone with the capacity to act, someone to speak, and in proper situations, to make decisions. That is what we mean by Executive power; and the Constitution expressly grants "The Executive power" to the President.[5]

Executive doctrine has also stemmed from the Constitutional Convention's substitution of "declare" for "make" in the congressional declaration-of-war clause. But, above all, it has taken advantage of the war-power variables. Presidents have emphasized the "friendly" ones (*e.g.*, a need for speed or secrecy), parlaying them into control over the situation as a whole, including those of its aspects not so conducive to executive authority (*e.g.*, the possibility that a particular use of force may impose heavy costs on the country). Starting with the first variable—the type of action—the less the Constitution has said about it, the more likely an executive claim to control it. The following list suggests the range of executive ambition. Noted are matters which various Presidents have governed without obtaining explicit congressional approval before or after the fact:

Military Action

1. Deploying the military anywhere for short periods, including on the borders and within the territories of other states

2. Stationing the military in foreign territory for longer periods, sometimes as an occupying and administering force, sometimes as an allied force; similarly, using the military to govern territory newly acquired by the United States

3. Sending military personnel to train and advise foreign armed forces

4. Allowing merchant ships to arm themselves against attack by international outlaws and by the public forces of another state; providing private vessels threatened on sea, land, or air with military protection, on each vessel and by convoy; also, tracking the movements of foreign war ships thought hostile to American or other friendly vessels

5. Airlifting persons and matériel across disputed and hostile territory

6. Searching and seizing foreign citizens and property on land and sea and forcing their ships to port and aircraft to earth for search and seizure

7. Blockading foreign territory by land, sea, or air

8. Intelligence operations abroad

9. Verbal and written threats and assurances about the circumstances in which the United States will take military action to help or hurt other countries, insurgent groups, or international organizations

10. Actual combat, from a few shots to major hostilities, involving armed attack on foreign persons and property by the regular American military, our secret agents, or foreign mercenaries, and involving both open and covert action

Nonmilitary Action

1. American individuals, organizations, and businesses abroad: their treatment by foreign governments

2. Apologies whatever the affront: demands that they be made to the United States, and their offering or refusal by America to other governments

3. Economic claims whatever their basis: the definition, prosecution, or waiver of American claims, public or private, against other states and the rejection of foreign claims against America

4. Foreign officials and troops: the terms of their American entry, stay, and exit

5. Ideological and political operations by this country abroad and by other states in America: their existence and nature

6. International law: its recognition by the United States and our adherence to or violation of it

7. International conferences, summits, and ad hoc joint ventures: American political participation

8. International organizations: American political participation and acceptance or rejection of their recommendations

9. Neutrality in foreign conflicts

10. Recognition by this country of new states, new governments, and belligerents and the making or breaking of diplomatic relations with them

11. Verbal or written threats and assurances about the circumstances in which America will take nonmilitary action to help or hurt other states, international organizations, or ventures

Tools

1. Federal personnel: their day-to-day direction

2. International agreements: their negotiation and ratification and their complete control when not treaties or congressional-executive agreements

3. Channels of official communication between the United States and the rest of the world

Executive doctrine, of course, has also taken heart from the purpose behind action.

Response to Attack

Beginning with power to defend *American* territory against attack when Congress has not yet had an opportunity to respond, Presidents have moved on to the defense of (a) territory claimed by the United States, even if the claim is disputed by another nation and has not been recognized by Congress; (b) American troops, civilians, and property abroad; and (c) foreign territory, persons, and property. From presidential prerogative simply to repel *ongoing* attack on any of the above, Executives have gone on to hot pursuit of the aggressor and preemptive attack on him. Even further, a right has been claimed to take purely punitive reprisals against an erstwhile aggressor and to treat his attack as grounds for offensive action of a sort disproportionate to the attack and unnecessary to prevent its quick resumption.

Hot pursuit and preemptive attack gained some currency during Washington's administration in response to Indian attacks. Executive incursions into Spanish Florida in 1818, Mexico in 1914-17, and Cambodia in 1970 provide more robust examples. Punitive reprisal came into its own during Jackson's presidency. In an 1832 message to Congress, he reported punishing Sumatra:

An act of atrocious piracy having been committed on one of our trading ships by the inhabitants of a settlement on the west coast of Sumatra, a frigate was dispatched with orders to demand satisfaction for the injury if those who committed it should be found to be members of a regular government, capable of maintaining the usual relations with foreign nations; but if, as it was supposed and as they proved to be, they were a band of lawless pirates, to inflict such a chastisement as would deter them and others from like aggressions. This last was done, and the effect has been an increased respect for our flag in those distant seas and additional security for our commerce.[6]

McKinley's response to Boxer nationalism in China at the turn of this century, Wilson's reaction to the brief seizure of nine American sailors at Tampico, Mexico, in 1914, and Ford's bombing of mainland Cambodia during the *Mayaguez* recovery all involved elements of reprisal.

The doctrine that foreign attack justifies even *offensive* response by the President has old roots. Alexander Hamilton censured President Jefferson in 1802 for timidity against Tripolitan naval forces before congressional authorization of the First Barbary War. Writing as Lucius Crassus, Hamilton argued that

the plain meaning of . . . [the declaration-of-war clause] is, that it is the peculiar and exclusive province of Congress, *when the nation is at peace* to change that state into a state of war; whether from calculations of policy, or from provocations, or injuries received: in other words, it belongs to Congress only, *to go to War*. But when a foreign nation declares, or openly and avowedly makes war upon the United States, they are then by the very fact *already at war*, and any declaration on the part of Congress is nugatory; it is at least unnecessary.[7]

The Supreme Court agreed in 1863, while upholding Lincoln's blockade of Confederate ports:

If a war be made by invasion of a foreign nation, the President is not only authorized but bound to resist force, by force. He does not initiate the war, but is bound to accept the challenge without waiting for any special legislative authority. . . .

The battles of Palo Alto and Resaca de la Palma had been fought before the passage of the Act of Congress of May 13th, 1846, . . . which recognized "a state of war as existing by the Act of the Republic of Mexico." This Act not only provided for the future prosecution of the war, but was itself a vindication and ratification of the Act of the President in accepting the challenge without a previous formal declaration of war by Congress.[8]

By 1949 Edward Corwin believed that the substitution of "declare" for "make" in 1787 "had developed into an undefined power [for the President] to employ without Congressional authorization the armed forces in the protection of American rights and interests abroad whenever necessary."[9] In 1966 the Legal Adviser to the State Department gave explicit substance to Corwin's belief:

At the Federal Constitutional Convention in 1787, it was originally proposed that Congress have the power "to make war." . . . Madison and Gerry . . . moved to substitute "to declare war" for "to make war," "leaving to the Executive the power to repel sudden attacks." It was objected that this might make it too easy for the Executive to involve the nation in war, but the motion carried with but one dissenting vote.

In 1787 the world was a far larger place, and the framers probably had in mind attacks upon the United States. In the 20th century, the world has grown much smaller. An attack on a country far from our shores can impinge directly on the nation's security. . . .

. . . .

The Constitution leaves to the President the judgment to determine whether the circumstances of a particular armed attack are so urgent and the potential consequences so threatening to the security of the United States that he should act without formally consulting the Congress.[10]

Law Enforcement

Starting from executive power to take military steps approved by statute, Presidents have moved on to justify armed enforcement of treaties, international agreements made solely by them, general tenets of international law, and inchoate American foreign policy interests defined by them. A right has also been claimed to use force even when the provision in question says nothing about its armed enforcement. During the "great debate" in 1951 over Truman's stationing American troops in Europe under NATO, Secretary of State Acheson told Congress: "Not only has the President the authority to use the Armed Forces in carrying out the broad foreign policy of the United States and *implementing treaties*, but it is equally clear that this authority may not be interfered with by the Congress in the exercise of powers which it has under the Constitution."[11] The President committed troops in Korea "to enforce" the United Nations Charter, the June 27, 1950, Security Council request for such military action, and later requests of the same nature from the U.N. General Assembly.

The State Department in 1966 also spoke of American involvement in Vietnam as the President's execution of treaty obligations:

Under article VI of the . . . Constitution, "all Treaties made, or which shall be made, under the Authority of the United States, shall be the supreme Law of the Land." *Article IV, paragraph 1, of the SEATO treaty establishes as a matter of law that a Communist armed attack against South Viet-Nam endangers the peace and safety of the*

United States. In this same provision the United States had undertaken a commitment in the SEATO treaty to "act to meet the common danger in accordance with its constitutional processes" in the event of such an attack.

Under our Constitution it is the President who must decide when an armed attack has occurred. He has also the constitutional responsibility for determining what measures of defense are required when the peace and safety of the United States are endangered. If he considers that deployment of U.S. forces to South Viet-Nam is required, and that military measures against the source of Communist aggression in North Viet-Nam are necessary, he is constitutionally empowered to take those measures.[12]

Treaty justifications for presidential use of force were equally common in earlier days. Expeditions into Spanish Florida in 1818 and Mexico in 1836 were said to be presidential enforcement of the treaty obligations of Spain and Mexico to close their territories to Indian invaders of the United States. Numerous military ventures were conducted in Central America under the New Granada Treaty of 1846, including executive intervention in Panama's 1903 secession. Presidents also justified armed action in Cuba, Haiti, and the Dominican Republic on treaty-enforcement grounds in the early years of this century and again in 1965.

At times Executives have used the military to enforce international agreements made by themselves. As Secretary of State Rogers told the Senate Foreign Relations Committee in 1973:

At the time the Vietnamese Agreement was concluded [solely on presidential authority], the United States made clear to the North Vietnamese that the armed forces of the Khmer [Cambodian] Government would suspend all offensive operations and that the United States aircraft supporting them would do likewise. We stated that, if the other side reciprocated, a *de facto* cease-fire would thereby be brought into force in Cambodia. However, we also stated that, if the communist forces carried out attacks, government forces and United States air forces would have to take necessary counter measures and that, in that event, we would continue to carry out air strikes in Cambodia as necessary until such time as a cease-fire could be brought into effect.[13]

Defense Secretary Richardson took the same tack before a House appropriations subcommittee: "If the President had the authority to pursue the cease-fire agreements, he has the authority to secure adherence with those agreements."[14]

In similar vein Theodore Roosevelt made a pact with Santo Domingo in 1905 that the United States would take over and militarily protect the local customs houses. As he later explained: "The Constitution did not explicitly give me power to bring about the necessary agreement with Santo Domingo. But the Constitution did not forbid my doing what I did. I put the agreement into effect, and I continued its execution for two years before the Senate acted; and I would have continued it until the end of my term, if necessary, without any action by Congress."[15]

Woodrow Wilson occupied Haiti in 1915 and then coerced its senate into a treaty which held that, "[s]hould the necessity occur, the United States will lend an efficient aid for the preservation of Haytian Independence and the maintenance of a government adequate for the protection of life, property, and individual liberty."[16] In 1916 the President tried the same gambit in Santo Domingo, but the provisional government set up under American aegis refused to cooperate. Ever inventive, Wilson termed his use of force the implementation of a 1907 treaty which forbade the Dominicans to increase their debt without United States consent.

From the outset Presidents have chased pirates to enforce international law and cited it to justify armed self-defense. As President Monroe stated in 1818: "The inability . . . of Spain to maintain her authority over the territory and Indians within her limits, and in consequence to fulfill the treaty, ought not to expose the United States to other and greater injuries. When the authority of Spain ceases to exist there, the *United States have a right to pursue their enemy on a principle of self-defense.* In this instance the right is more complete and obvious because we shall perform only what Spain was bound to have performed herself."[17]

After Germany announced in early 1917 that she would sink on sight all ships in the war zone outside a small channel, President Wilson was concerned how "to protect our ships and our people in their legitimate and peaceful pursuits on the seas."[18] He concluded that he might arm and convoy American merchantmen under his own constitutional authority. Chairman Stone of the Senate Foreign Relations Committee, while rejecting this view, crystallized the law-enforcement basis advanced for it: "I can not consent that this clause [that the Executive 'shall take care that the laws be faithfully executed'] confers, or was ever intended to confer, power upon the President to determine an issue between this Nation and some other sovereignty—an issue involving questions of international law—and to proceed to employ the Army and Navy to enforce his decision. A contrary view would clearly place the war making power in the hands of the President."[19] The enforcement of international law was also among President Eisenhower's explanations for his 1958 Lebanese intervention: "I have come to the sober and clear conclusion that the action taken was essential to the welfare of the United States. It was required to support the principles of justice and international law upon which peace and a stable international order depend."[20]

As Eisenhower's "essential to the welfare of the United States" suggests, inchoate interests defined by the President have been among the laws receiving armed executive enforcement. President Truman claimed the right to send troops anywhere on earth he felt in the national interest. Recall Secretary Acheson's assertion that the President may commit troops to implement "broad foreign policy" of his making. Or as Senator Paul Douglas obscurely put it at the outbreak of the Korean War: "[U]nder the Constitution, since the power of Congress [is] limited to a declaration of war, the President can take steps to resist aggression."[21] And as Borchard's *Diplomatic Protection of Citizens Abroad* had concluded earlier in the century: "Inasmuch as the Constitution vests in Congress authority 'to declare war,' and does not empower Congress to direct the President to perform his constitutional duties of protecting American citizens on foreign soil, it is believed that the Executive has unlimited authority to use the armed forces of the

United States for protective purposes abroad in any manner and on any occasion he considers expedient."[22]

Nor is executive enforcement of inchoate interests a phenomenon of this century. The best early instance was President Tyler's 1844 dispatch of American ships and troops to protect Texas following the signing of an annexation treaty, but before the agreement's approval by the Senate. As Tyler told the bilious Senators, it is "my opinion that the United States having by the treaty of annexation acquired a title to Texas which requires only the action of the Senate to perfect it, no other power could be permitted to invade and by force of arms to possess itself of any portion of the territory of Texas pending your deliberations upon the treaty without placing itself in an hostile attitude to the United States and justifying the employment of any military means at our disposal to drive back the invasion."[23]

President Grant was more blatant. He used American forces from 1869-71 to shore up a Santo Domingo regime with which he had concocted an annexation treaty. Grant continued his military presence even after the Senate rejected the treaty, prompting Charles Sumner, Chairman of the Senate Foreign Relations Committee, to advance unsuccessfully the following resolution:

. . . That while the President, without any previous declaration of war by act of Congress, may defend the country against invasion by foreign enemies, he is not justified in exercising the same power in an outlying foreign island, which has not yet become part of the United States; that a title under an unratified treaty is at most inchoate and contingent, while it is created by the President alone, in which respect it differs from any such title created by act of Congress; and since it is created by the President alone, without the support of law, whether in legislation or a ratified treaty, the employment of the Navy in the maintenance of the Government there is without any excuse of national defense, as also without any excuse of a previous declaration of war by Congress.[24]

Costs

Limited costs—those short of "war"—have been conducive to executive prerogative. Thus Presidents have stressed immediate, not potential, burdens; direct costs (American casualties and military monies), not related physical, economic, political, and social burdens. And no available theory has been spurned to show that each military action is compatible with international law.

In 1854 an American naval force shelled and then burned Greytown, a settlement in Nicaragua sponsored by the British. Greytown competed for Central America transit business with a neighboring settlement under American patronage. Rivalry was intense, and during one of several incidents, an American diplomat was slightly injured by a local mob. President Pierce downplayed the town's destruction, describing the incident to Congress in antipirate terms:

Not standing before the world in the attitude of an organized political society, being neither competent to exercise the rights nor to discharge the obligations of a government, it was, in fact, a maurauding establishment too dangerous to be disregarded and too guilty to pass unpunished, and yet incapable of being treated in any other way than as a piratical resort of outlaws or a camp of savages depredating on emigrant trains or caravans and the frontier settlements of civilized states.[25]

In 1900 President McKinley committed 5,000 troops and naval forces to the allied expedition that suppressed the Boxers in China, ostensibly with the consent of the Chinese government. The campaign involved significant combat, casualties, and intervention in the domestic politics of another state. The Executive nonetheless described the effort to the legislators in mild terms, assuring them that it "involved no war against the Chinese nation. We adhered to the legitimate office of rescuing the imperiled legation, obtaining redress for wrongs already suffered, securing wherever possible the safety of American life and property in China, and preventing a spread of the disorders or their recurrence."[26]

Senator Root caught the essence in 1912 during his celebrated debate with Senator Bacon over presidential use of force. Root saw no constitutional bar to the Executive's sending troops outside the country "unless it be for the purpose of making war, which, of course, he can not do."[27] Root did not believe that armed landings to protect lives and property were "war." Nor did the Solicitor of the State Department, J. Reuben Clark, who distinguished that same year between "an intervention by one power in the local political affairs of another government" and nonpolitical intervention, or "interposition," designed for "the protection of citizens . . . from the acts of government itself or from the acts of persons . . . within the jurisdiction of a government which finds itself unable to afford the requisite protection, until the government concerned is willing or able to afford the protection."[28] Clark felt that the Executive may "interpose" without asking Congress.

While Presidents have at times joined action to protect lives and property with outright political intervention, it is true that most executive uses of force abroad have been to guard Americans and their belongings. These uses have generally involved scant costs, including no combat with the forces of another state or even its likelihood. The aggregate result, however, has been the growth of doctrine that so long as the overall costs to the country of a particular venture do not compel its characterization as "war," then the venture occurs at the President's discretion.

Calvin Coolidge intervened in Nicaragua in 1926, ultimately committing over 5,000 troops to suppress a guerilla war against the pro-American regime. Coolidge expressly denied that he was making war on Nicaragua. He said to Congress:

It has always been and remains the policy of the United States in such circumstances to take steps that may be necessary for the preservation and protection of the lives, the property, and the interests of its citizens and of this Government itself. In this respect I propose to follow the path of my predecessors.

Consequently, I have deemed it my duty to use the powers committed to me to insure the adequate protection of all American interests in Nicaragua, whether they be endangered by internal strife or by outside interference in the affairs of that Republic.[29]

John Bassett Moore noted with some dismay early in this century:

There can hardly be room for doubt that the framers of the constitution, when they vested in the Congress the power to declare war, never imagined that they were leaving it to the executive to use the military and naval forces of the United States all over the world for the purpose of actually coercing other nations, occupying their territory, and killing their soldiers and citizens, all according to his own notions of the fitness of things, so long as he refrained from calling his action war or persisted in calling it peace.[30]

Speed and Secrecy

A sense of emergency often runs with a need for speed or secrecy, and military emergency has posed the situations in which strong Presidents have most thought that they might act unilaterally and in which other Americans have most often agreed. "I felt," said Abraham Lincoln in April 1864, "that measures otherwise unconstitutional might become lawful by becoming indispensable to the preservation of the Constitution . . . ."[31]

The country's occasional need for military speed has supported executive prerogative since Washington's time. Writing for the Supreme Court in its 1827 *Martin v. Mott* decision, Justice Story read the militia act of 1795 accordingly:

We are all of opinion, that the authority to decide whether the exigency has arisen [the need to call out the militia to meet actual or imminent invasion], belongs exclusively to the President, and that his decision is conclusive upon all other persons. We think that this construction necessarily results from the nature of the power itself . . . . *The power itself is to be exercised upon sudden emergencies, upon great occasions of state, and under circumstances which may be vital to the existence of the Union.* A prompt and unhesitating obedience to orders is indispensable to the complete attainment of the object. The service is a military service, and the command of a military nature; and in such cases, *every delay, and every obstacle to an efficient and immediate compliance, necessarily tend to jeopard the public interests.* . . .

. . . The power itself is confided to the Executive of the Union, to him who is, by the constitution, "the commander-in-chief of the militia, when called into the actual service of the United States," whose duty it is to "take care that the laws be faithfully executed," and whose responsibility for an honest discharge of his official obligations is secured by the highest sanctions.[32]

Justice Nelson while on circuit also emphasized speed in his 1860 decision in *Durand v. Hollins,* which upheld executive action during the Greytown incident described above (albeit in reliance on the laundered facts offered Congress by President Pierce).[33] And the Supreme Court in the 1863 *Prize Cases* found presidential prerogative in the necessity for rapid response.[34]

Speed has become even more important to Presidents with recent technological advances in communications and weapons. Senator Douglas defended Truman's action in Korea by stressing the reality of quick attack, the potential for delay in congressional decision making, and the possibility that countries important to American security could be overrun if the Executive were to wait for legislative approval.[35] George Ball, an adviser to President Kennedy during the Cuban Missile Crisis, made similar arguments to the Senate Foreign Relations Committee in 1971:

> Let us suppose that during [the first week of the crisis] the following circumstances had prevailed. First, Congress was not in session. Second, several Soviet ships containing missiles were within very few hours of Cuba. Under the circumstances instead of announcing on that memorable Monday evening of October 22, that a quarantine had been instituted, the President had been compelled to say that he was calling Congress back so that within the next 2 or 3 days they might authorize a quarantine. Almost certainly the effectiveness of the action would have been far diminished, the Soviets would have felt under much less pressure, and it is at least possible that the Soviet reaction would have been very different from the reaction which indeed actually occurred.[36]

Secretary of State Rogers urged on the same Committee "the clear need to preserve the President's ability to act in emergencies in accordance with his constitutional responsibilities. . . . I believe the framers of the Constitution intended decisions regarding the initiation of hostilities to be made jointly by the Congress and the President, *except in emergency situations.*"[37]

Executive secrecy in matters of war and peace has also been with us since the beginning. Early in his presidency George Washington secretly signed a treaty with the Northwest Indians before telling the Senate that negotiations were underway, lest that fact leak to the British. In 1798 President Adams withheld from Congress details of the XYZ negotiations in Paris until he felt that disclosure would not imperil American negotiators, even though the information bore directly on the merits of war with France.[38]

The atomic bomb was developed with vast monies appropriated by Congress for ends unknown to *any* congressman until a few were taken to Oak Ridge in May 1945. Covert military ventures were frequent during Eisenhower's administration—among others, U-2 overflights of the Soviet Union, involvement in the 1954 overthrow of a left-wing regime in Guatemala, as well as the 1960 arming and training in that country of anti-Castro Cubans. Similarly, John F. Kennedy's response to Russian missiles in Cuba was prepared in the strictest secrecy so that it might be sprung with maximum effect on the unsuspecting Soviets, and Jimmy Carter launched his military effort to rescue American hostages in Iran in utter secrecy.

Phase

The phase of action has provided fertile material for executive prerogative. So long as the President stays within the "conduct" of a venture, his right to control has firm constitutional credentials. Thus executive doctrine deems the *initiation* of even major undertakings to be part of the *conduct* of a larger venture if they can be termed means to the larger end. Difficulty arises when a particular step can be viewed as the strategy or tactics of one undertaking *or* the initiation of a wholly new venture. Such was the case with the 1970 Cambodian incursion. William Rehnquist nonetheless defended it as clearly part of the conduct phase, the probity of which was heightened because the Executive was defending Americans attacked abroad:

The President's determination to authorize incursion into these Cambodian border areas is precisely the sort of tactical decision traditionally confided to the Commander-in-Chief in the conduct of armed conflict. From the time of the drafting of the Constitution it has been clear that the Commander-in-Chief has authority to take prompt action to protect American lives in situations involving hostilities

. . . . President Nixon had an obligation as Commander-in-Chief of the country's armed forces to take what steps he deemed necessary to assure their safety in the field. A decision to cross the Cambodian border . . . to destroy sanctuaries being utilized by North Vietnamese in violation of Cambodia's neutrality, is wholly consistent with that obligation. It is a decision made during the course of an armed conflict already commenced as to how that conflict shall be conducted, rather than a determination that some new and previously unauthorized military venture shall be taken.[39]

"Termination" also has potential for the President on the assumption that he may oversee the terms and timing of a venture's cessation so long as the broad aims of its beginning are honored. Presidents have shaped the ways in which all of America's declared wars have ended. Perhaps most striking were McKinley's initiatives: A war begun in 1898 simply to ensure Cuban independence from Spain ended with American occupation of that island and with our ownership of Puerto Rico and the Philippines. To settle title to the latter, from 1899 to 1901 over 126,000 troops waged a bitter struggle against Philippine nationalists. That struggle was not remotely contemplated by Congress when war was declared in 1898. It stemmed from the President's decision to fight the Spanish in the Far East, as well as in the Caribbean, and to claim the Philippines as the spoils of victory. Congressional approval, to the extent that it was explicitly given, came only in Senate approval of the treaty of peace with Spain. President Nixon, of course, resumed bombing of North Vietnam in late December 1972 to force a peace agreement on terms acceptable to him, despite acute opposition by many in Congress. Secretary Rogers later claimed an executive prerogative to bomb Cambodian communists in the hope of forcing a like end to that aspect of the Indochina War.

Tools

The notion that the President controls official channels of communications between our government and foreigners took hold early. As Washington's Secretary of State, Thomas Jefferson told a French diplomat prone to deal with Congress that the President "being the only channel of communication between this country and foreign nations, it is from him alone that foreign nations or their agents are to learn what is or has been the will of the nation; and whatever he communicates as such, they have a right, and are bound to consider as the expression of the nation, and no foreign agent can be allowed to question it . . . ."[40] Jefferson warmed to the subject: "The transaction of business with foreign nations is executive altogether; it belongs, then, to the head of that department, except as to such portions of it as are specially submitted to the senate. Exceptions are to be construed strictly."[41] Appraisal of the President as "the sole organ of the nation in its external relations and its sole representative with foreign nations" came from Congressman John Marshall a few years later, during a debate in 1800 over the executive role in implementing treaties.[42]

At times, Presidents have been truculent about the matter. In 1877 Grant vetoed two congressional joint resolutions asking the Secretary of State to thank Pretoria and Argentina for their kind words on our centennial. "Sympathizing, as I do," said the President,

in the spirit of courtesy and friendly recognition which has prompted the passage of these resolutions, I can not escape the conviction that their adoption had inadvertently involved the exercise of a power which infringes upon the constitutional rights of the Executive.

. . . .

The Constitution . . . has indicated the President as the agent to represent the national sovereignty in its intercourse with foreign powers and to receive all official communications from them . . . making him, in the language of one of the most eminent writers on constitutional law, "the constitutional organ of communication with foreign states."

. . . .

If Congress can direct the correspondence of the Secretary of State with foreign governments, a case very different from that now under consideration might arise, when that officer might be directed to present to the same foreign government entirely different and antagonistic views or statements.[43]

So far as international agreements are concerned, the Senate approved an 1882 treaty with Korea but recoiled from its negotiation by presidential agents, resolving

not [to] admit or acquiesce in any right or constitutional power in the President to authorize or empower any person to negotiate treaties or carry on diplomatic negotiations with any foreign power, unless such person shall have been appointed for such purpose or clothed with such power by and with the advice and consent of the Senate, except in the case of a Secretary of State or diplomatic officer, appointed by the President to fill a vacancy occurring during the recess of the Senate . . . .[44]

Despite this and numerous other senatorial runs at executive treaty making, the President now firmly controls all aspects of the process, except for Senators' right to reject what he sets before them or to condition their approval on various amendments.

Since President Washington's construction of the requirements of the Franco-American alliance and President Madison's termination of the 1782 Dutch treaty, Executives have also been interpreting and ending our formal agreements with other states. Executive interpretation of SEATO loomed particularly large during the last two decades. But as to termination, it is not wholly settled that the Executive may act in the face of congressional opposition. Thus Eisenhower in 1965 renounced treaty-based extraterritoriality rights in Morocco only after prompting Congress to pass a resolution asking him to. In December 1978, however, Jimmy Carter acted alone to terminate this country's Mutual Defense Treaty with the Republic of China (Taiwan), despite the strong objections of many legislators and their insistence that the President might not end the treaty without the approval of either the Senate or Congress as a whole. Litigation ensued. There was also litigation when the House of Representatives had no role in ending American control over the Panama Canal; it occurred by treaty. The Executive's authority to terminate treaties, and the President's and Senate's power to make international agreements without the House, emerged from the litigation strengthened.

Executives have not limited their international agreements to treaties. In June 1844 the Senate turned down President Tyler's annexation agreement with Texas. Two days later he took steps to have Texas acquired by a congressional joint resolution. As Tyler pragmatically argued to the House of Representatives:

[W]hile I have regarded the annexation to be accomplished by treaty as the most suitable form in which it could be effected, should Congress deem it proper to resort to any other expedient compatible with the Constitution and likely to accomplish the object I stand prepared to yield my most prompt and active cooperation.

The great question is not as to the manner in which it shall be done, but whether it shall be accomplished or not.[45]

Majorities in the House and Senate approved the necessary resolution, and the President promptly signed it into law. Such international agreements have enabled his successors at times to bypass the two-thirds majority required for treaty approval and to involve the House directly in the agreement process. That involvement can be crucial when the agreement requires significant implementing legislation or appropriations.

At times Executives have made international pacts without bothering to obtain even approval by joint resolution. The United States and England agreed to demilitarize the Great Lakes by an 1817 exchange of notes between acting Secretary of State Rush and British Ambassador Bagot. Recall also Theodore Roosevelt's arrangement in 1905 with Santo Domingo. From Franklin Roosevelt's through Nixon's administrations, Presidents were especially willing to make agreements having war and peace consequences on their own authority, sometimes secretly.

Even as to tools which Presidents have rarely claimed the right to create—federal personnel and money above all—they have often been willing to use tools already available to fashion faits accomplis for Congress. "Give Knox [the Secretary of War] his army, and he will soon have a war on hand,"[46] grumbled one disaffected Senator with some cause in 1790, when Washington asked for means to guard the country against Indians. Theodore Roosevelt started the Great White Fleet around the world in 1907 despite congressional misgivings, thereby leaving the legislators no choice but to vote new monies to bring the warships home when funds ran dry en route. Decisions during the Cold War to take military steps off Formosa, in Berlin, Korea, Lebanon, Cuba, the Dominican Republic, Congo, and Indochina were largely executive, begun by using tools on hand in such a fashion as to encourage Congress to vote additional tools as necessary. On May 4, 1965, Lyndon Johnson wasted no sublety on Congress when he sought $700,000,000 "to meet mounting military requirements in Vietnam":

I do not ask complete approval for every phrase and action for your Government. I do ask for prompt support for our basic course: resistance to aggression, moderation in the use of power, and a constant search for peace. Nothing will do more to strengthen your country in the world than the proof of national unity which an overwhelming vote for this appropriation will clearly show. To deny and delay this means to deny and to delay the fullest support of the American people and the American Congress to those brave men who are risking their lives for freedom in Vietnam.[47]

On April 24, 1980, Jimmy Carter sent aircraft and troops into Iran to try to rescue American hostages held in Tehran. Had his fait accompli unintentionally led to the movement of Soviet forces from Afghanistan into Iran or to the obstruction of the Strait of Hormuz, Congress could easily have had little choice but to support American involvement in war.

Participation in Decision Making

Presidents have cited congressional silence as tacit approval of their action. Congressional approval has also been implied from the legislators' willingness to provide implementing tools, from their refusal to enact limits on or an end to presidential initiatives, and from broad delegations of authority to the Executive. As Tyler's preference that the United States annex Texas by treaty indicates, Presidents have thought the consent of two-thirds of the Senate to be sufficient legislative approval for war-peace action. Further, they have come increasingly to treat a briefing of legislative leaders as sufficient involvement of Congress in use-of-force decisions, or, when full congressional approval is sought, to treat that approval as a matter of sound policy not constitutional necessity.

Most cases in which Presidents have made use-of-force decisions did involve action about which Congress was silent. At times this silence has resulted from the Executives' failure to call out-of-session Congresses back to Washington. Following the June 1807 attack of the British warship *Leopard* on the American *Chesapeake*, a belligerent mood was afoot in the United States. President Jefferson, however, preferred peaceable means of redressing injustice, an option that he feared might be lost if Congress were to act on the matter. Thus he set late October as the date for reconvening the legislature, explaining that Washington was too sickly a place to meet during the summer, and pursued peaceful remedies during the interim. Polk declined to call Congress into session during his months of military maneuver in Texas that triggered the Mexican War, and Lincoln did not choose to summon the legislators during the early months of the Civil War, while he raised unauthorized troops, spent unappropriated money, and blockaded hostile ports.

Congress has often remained silent even though in session. Presidents governed territory taken as a result of the Louisiana Purchase, Mexican War, Hawaiian annexation, Spanish-American War, and Panamanian independence for significant periods before the legislators got around to making their will known. Secretary of War Root counseled the military governor of Cuba in 1901 as he was shaping the Cuban constitution: "These provisions may not, it is true, prove to be in accord with the conclusions which Congress may ultimately reach when that body comes to consider the subject, but as, until Congress has acted, the Executive must necessarily within its own sphere of action be controlled by its own judgment, you should now be guided by the views above expressed."[48] And as President Eisenhower told Congress in 1955 concerning Formosa:

Authority for some of the actions which might be required would be inherent in the authority of the Commander in Chief. Until Congress can act I would not hesitate, so far as my constitutional powers extend, to take whatever emergency action might be forced upon us in order to protect the rights and security of the United States.

However, a suitable congressional resolution would clearly and publicly establish the authority of the President as Commander in Chief to employ the Armed Forces of this Nation promptly and effectively for the purposes indicated if in his judgment it became necessary.[49]

The Indochina War provided ample occasion for Executives to deem their policies approved by the legislators' willingness to delegate authority to them, to vote implementing tools, and to refuse to enact limits on, or an end to, their initiatives. In 1966 the Legal Adviser to the State Department pointed out that the "August 1964 [Tonkin Gulf] joint resolution continues in force today," though the resolution was always subject to termination by majority, nonvetoable vote in each house. "Instead," said the Legal Adviser,

Congress in May 1965 approved an appropriation of $700 million to meet the expense of mounting military requirements in Viet-Nam. . . . The President's message asking for this appropriation stated that this was "not a routine appropriation. For each Member of Congress who supports this request is also voting to persist in our efforts to halt Communist aggression in South Vietnam." The appropriation act constitutes a clear congressional endorsement and approval of the actions taken by the President.

On March 1, 1966, the Congress continued to express its support of the President's policy by approving a $4.8 billion supplemental military authorization by votes of 392-4 and 93-2. An amendment that would have limited the President's authority to commit forces to Viet-Nam was rejected in the Senate by a vote of 94-2.[50]

Congressman Gerald Ford said that it was clear "that anyone who votes for this legislation [the 1966 $4.8 billion supplemental military appropriation] is endorsing the policy currently being executed by the Commander in Chief."[51]

When Presidents want congressional involvement during the early stages of military action, they have become prone to summon select Senators and Representatives to the White House for consultation, rather than seeking the views and approval of Congress as a whole. Similarly, consultation with the summoned has come more and more to involve their learning what the President is doing rather than conferring with him about what the country should do. The ritual of congressional leaders hurriedly gathered at the White House for briefing on presidential policy has become commonplace since 1945.

Even when Presidents prefer to involve Congress as a whole, they have become accustomed to terming that involvement something less than a constitutional necessity. Recall President Eisenhower's ambiguity about his need for the 1955 Formosa Resolution. Although Lyndon Johnson sought the Tonkin Gulf Resolution in 1964, we have seen that he never premised the constitutionality of his commitment of troops to Vietnam solely on its existence. Woodrow Wilson was particularly lucid on two occasions about his desire for congressional approval as a matter of sound policy but not constitutional imperative. In April 1914 troops of the Huerta government in Mexico briefly seized a few American sailors in Tampico. The Mexicans released the sailors within the hour, apologized for the incident, but refused to fire a twenty-one-gun salute to the American flag to further memorialize their regret. Wilson, no friend of the Huerta regime, demanded the salute. He also was determined to prevent a German ship then nearing Vera Cruz from landing arms for Huerta. The President sought congressional approval for his impending resort to force, but disclaimed any constitutional need for it:

> No doubt I could do what is necessary in the circumstances to enforce respect for our Government without recourse to the Congress, and yet not exceed my constitutional powers as president; but I do not wish to act in a manner possibly of so grave consequence except in close conference and co-operation with both the Senate and House. I therefore come to ask your approval that I should use the armed forces of the United States in such ways and to such an extent as may be necessary to obtain from General Huerta and his adherents the fullest recognition of the rights and dignity of the United States, even amid the distressing conditions now unhappily obtaining in Mexico.[52]

Before Congress acted on his request, Wilson attacked and captured Vera Cruz at a cost of 400 casualties, mostly Mexican. Again in early 1917, when the President wanted to arm American merchantmen against German submarines, he sought congressional approval because he wished "to feel that the authority and the power of the Congress are behind me," but Wilson also claimed that "[n]o doubt" he might act alone "by the plain implication of my constitutional duties and powers."[53] After a "small group of willful men" in the Senate filibustered to death an authorizing resolution,[54] Wilson armed the merchantmen without congressional blessing.

With this background, it comes as no surprise that, despite some initial Jeffersonian diffidence, Presidents have assumed that they may constitutionally take any sort of action thought to fall within their prerogative, even if it risks large-scale combat or requires a response for which congressional approval is essential. J. N. Pomeroy stated it well in his 1886 *Introduction to the Constitutional Law of the United States*:

The President cannot declare war; Congress alone possesses that attribute. But the President may, without any possibility of hindrance from the legislature, so conduct the foreign intercourse, the diplomatic negotiations with other governments as to force a war, as to compel another nation to take the initiative; and that step, once taken, the challenge cannot be refused. How easily the Executive might have plunged us into a war with Great Britain by a single dispatch in answer to the affair of the Trent. How easily might he have provoked a condition of active hostilities with France by the form and character of the reclamation made in regard to the occupation of Mexico.[55]

Hans Morgenthau developed the same theme more briskly: "[The Executive] can narrow the freedom of choice which constitutionally lies with Congress to such an extent as to eliminate it for all practical purposes."[56]

There has been much reference to "executive doctrine" and to "what Presidents have done." We should be clear that there is no ark of presidential precepts sealed by George Washington and preserved for the ages. Rather, the "doctrine" has evolved since 1789. It is the product of many Americans, not just Presidents and their spokesmen. Certain democratic Senators in office during the Cold War have been among its most forceful exponents. But it is not remotely the case that this doctrine is universally accepted nor that its various tenets have equal strength. A President is always on stronger constitutional ground when he defends American rather than foreign territory against sudden attack. And obviously he will do better constitutionally when he commits troops to enforce a congressional declaration of war, rather than inchoate foreign-policy objectives of his own definition.

Similarly, any particular tenet varies in strength with the nature of the President. Some more than others have been willing to push executive doctrine for all that it is worth. Presidential opinion has ranged widely, from the modest constitutional views of Buchanan to the brash interpretations of Franklin Roosevelt. Taft aptly stated the case for executive modesty: "The true view of the Executive functions is, as I conceive it, that the President can exercise no power which cannot be fairly and reasonably traced to some specific grant of power or justly implied and included within such express grant as proper and necessary . . . ."[57] Buchanan adhered rigidly to his concept of limited presidential authority, going so far as to reject Virginia's proposal in 1860 for a conference of the states and, pending it, an agreement between the Secessionists and the President to abstain from violence. Buchanan strongly favored the plan but refused to act, because "Congress, and Congress alone, under the war-making power, can exercise the discretion of agreeing to abstain 'from any and all acts calculated to produce a collision of arms' between this and any other government. It would therefore be a usurpation for the Executive to attempt to restrain their hands by an agreement in regard to matters over which he has no constitutional control."[58]

At the other extreme, Franklin Roosevelt believed that he possessed constitutional power to act even in direct opposition to existing law, if an emergency so warranted. He approached the executive "prerogative" formulated by John Locke "as the power to act according to discretion for the public good, without the prescription of the law and *sometimes even against it* . . . ."[59] Roosevelt's activities leading to United States involvement in hostilities with Germany in the Atlantic were of dubious legality, if not clearly contrary to law upon occasion. His September 7, 1942, proclamation that either Congress repeal a certain provision of the Emergency Price Control Act, or he would, was Lockean.

Midway between Buchanan's and Franklin Roosevelt's readings of executive authority stands the "Stewardship Theory," described by Theodore Roosevelt in these terms: "My view was that every executive officer . . . was a steward of the people . . . . My belief was that it was not only his right but his duty to do anything that the needs of the Nation demanded unless such action was forbidden by the Constitution or by the laws. . . . In other words, I acted for the public welfare . . . whenever and in whatever manner was necessary, unless prevented by direct constitutional or legislative prohibition."[60] Presidents since Franklin Roosevelt have assumed, at the least, the powers of "a steward of the people."

But no matter how assertive the President, some times will be more receptive to expansive executive doctrine than others. Receptivity has been modest since the conjunction of Indochina and Watergate. Nor was it great following the administrations of Monroe, Jackson, Polk, Lincoln, or Wilson. It would be naive to assume, however, that executive doctrine was mortally wounded by Indochina and Watergate. Presidents Ford and Carter began to resound some of its basic themes.

Causative Factors

The growth of presidential authority over war and peace has stemmed largely from three factors: the evolving nature of those institutional characteristics of the presidency and Congress pertinent to the war powers; certain historical developments that have favored the Executive's characteristics over those of Congress; and, finally, the willingness of many Presidents, greater than that of Congress, to exercise their constitutional authority to the fullest and beyond. We have already explored the third factor. Attention now goes to the first two, beginning with institutional considerations.

Unity of Office

The number of people in both Congress and the Executive Branch, though not the presidency itself, has exploded since

1789. Congress had trouble with war and peace decisions in the late eighteenth century when less than a fifth its present size. Twenty-six Senators proved too many for the plenary diplomatic role meant for them by the Constitutional Fathers. These problems have intensified as the increase in Senators and Representatives has not been balanced by equivalent growth in party discipline, leadership authority, and decision-forcing rules of procedure.

Far greater growth in those parts of the Executive Branch involved in shaping policy about war and peace has not similarly hobbled the President in reaching decisions. Particularly since World War II he has had more advice and more intra-branch interests to accommodate, but as in 1789 he retains unfettered discretion to set presidential policy. Even if "the Grand Signor himself had his Divan," as George Mason protested in 1787, the Constitutional Fathers chose not to have a multi-headed Executive and not to associate an obligatory council of advisers with him. The unity of the presidency remains after almost two centuries.

Availability to Conduct Government Business

The President is always "in session." Congress even in the late twentieth century is not, and it depends on the Executive for recall if absent when a crisis breaks. Congress was not in session at the outset of the Korean War or during the Cuban Missile Crisis. Thus the War Powers Resolution of 1973 provides that after the President has reported on hostilities to the Speaker of the House and President of the Senate, then if "Congress has adjourned sine die or has adjourned for any period in excess of three calendar days, the Speaker . . . and the President . . . of the Senate, if they deem it advisable (or if petitioned by at least 30 percent of the membership of their respective Houses) shall jointly request the President to convene Congress in order that it may consider the report and take appropriate action pursuant to this section."[61]

In the past, longer congressional recesses and poorer communications often precluded even the possibility of a legislative hand in policy at crucial moments. Some nineteenth-century Presidents also declined to recall Congress during the early months of more extended emergencies. Telephones and airplanes, in addition to briefer recesses, now ensure the physical possibility of congressional influence during most crises. Congress as a whole can be quickly recalled, its leaders even more rapidly, as during the Cuban Missile Crisis.

But technology has also virtually ensured the availability of the President for government business. Though he may have been sitting in the White House in years past, significant decisions often had to be left to diplomats and commanders on the scene, for lack of quick communications. Today no matter what the hour, or where the President and the developments, he usually can take charge of the situation, as Mr. Carter did during his abortive attempt to remove American hostages from Iran.

Day-to-Day Control over Government Machinery

The chief executive and commander in chief has more effective daily control over the federal bureaucracy than Congress. The President is better able to have federal employees gather and analyze information for him, to set priorities for their work, and to order them directly to do his will. Moreover, the entire Executive Branch, particularly the Office of the President, has become far better staffed and organized in this century than ever before to control the day-to-day workings of the government.

Not so with Congress. And even were it to see to the effective institutionalization of its functions, Congress would still have little call on the day-to-day workings of the federal government. Its principal impact would remain more indirect: in creating the federal machinery, defining its basic organization and procedures, enacting the programs that it is to implement, and checking on its performance. In part, of course, the different access of the two branches to the bureaucracy is a result of their different governmental roles. As Walter Lippmann said: "The executive is the active power in the state, the asking and the proposing power. The representative assembly is the consenting power, the petitioning, the approving and the criticizing, the accepting and the refusing power."[62]

The President's hold on government machinery also reflects,

however, the tendency of Executives to occupy their sphere fully and then encroach on legislative functions through claims of outright prerogative or by pursuing and obtaining sweeping delegations of authority from Congress. The legislators have been more diffident about trying to assume executive functions.

Mode of Election, Constituency, and Term of Office

American politics focus on the selection of Presidents and on their support once elected, not on the choice and effectiveness of Congressmen (except as the Executive has become an effective *external* leader of Congress). The focus of party politics easily came to rest on the presidency, in view of its power and capacity to provide the heroes needed to cement the country.

The President, too, is the sole politician with a national constituency. That fact gives him greater freedom from special interests than the more parochially based Senators and Representatives. Also, unlike the Representatives, the President's term of office is sufficient to avoid constant campaigning. Unlike the Senators, he has had the likelihood of no more than two terms, first by tradition and then law, and thus he has been less driven by electoral passions during his second four years.

These distinctions are important to which branch is the stronger force for the *general* interest and the keener symbol of national unity. The President has historically been more successful on both scores. Edward Corwin summarized:

[T]he Constitution reflects the struggle between two conceptions of executive power: that it ought always to be subordinate to the supreme legislative power, and that it ought to be, within generous limits, autonomous and self-directing; or, in other terms, the idea that the people are *re-presented* in the Legislature *versus* the idea that they are *embodied* in the Executive. Nor has this struggle ever entirely ceased, although on the whole it is the latter theory that has prospered.[63]

President Polk captured the essence of "embodied in the Executive," when he told Congress that "[i]f it be said that the Representatives in the popular branch of Congress are chosen directly by the people, it is answered, the people elect the

President. If both Houses represent the States and the people, so does the President. The President represents in the executive department the whole people of the United States, as each member of the legislative department represents portions of them."[64] Lyndon Johnson squeezed the ultimate ounce in 1966: "There are many, many who can recommend, advise, and sometimes a few of them consent. But there is only one that has been chosen by the American people to decide."[65]

These executive institutional advantages have been enhanced by certain historical developments.

The Growing Hazard, Pace, and Complexity of America's Foreign Relations

Foreign relations were central to survival during the first generation under the Constitution. European intervention in American affairs was an armed reality through the War of 1812. At times during the balance of the nineteenth century, the United States was internationally threatened, acutely during the Civil War. But through most of the 1800s, security was an easy outgrowth of rising American strength, geographical isolation, modest military technology, and European balance of power. Security problems abroad centered on the protection of Americans from pirates, primitives, or weak states and on the consequences of manifest destiny in North America.

Times changed with the Spanish-American War. Militarily, politically, ideologically, economically, and legally the country has found itself increasingly threatened since 1900, and increasingly forced to react to developments more numerous, rapidly evolving, and complicated than before. The changed international environment has placed a new premium on informed, expert decisions made in accord with overall American objectives. It has valued rapid, flexible action and a willingness to make hard choices.[66] Institutionally, the President has been better equipped than Congress to meet these demands. Woodrow Wilson anticipated as much in the 1901 edition to his book *Congressional Government*:

Much the most important change to be noticed is the result of the war with Spain upon the lodgement and exercise of power within our federal system; and greatly increased power and opportunity for constructive statesmanship given the president, by the plunge into international politics and into the administration of distant dependencies, which has been the war's most striking and momentous consequence. When foreign affairs play a prominent part in the politics and policy of a nation, its Executive must of necessity be its guide; must utter every initial judgment, take every first step of action, supply the information upon which it is to act, suggest and in large measure control its conduct. It may be, too, that the new leadership of the executive, inasmuch as it is likely to last, will have a very far-reaching effect upon our whole method of government. It may give the heads of the executive departments a new influence upon the action of the Congress.[67]

The Growing Reach of the Federal Government

The country began with narrow views about what the federal government should do and with a national apparatus severely limited in its capacity to do anything anyway, given the minuscule federal personnel and funds—718 troops on active duty and a total federal budget of $4,269,000 in 1789. With the decline of federalism at home and isolationism abroad and with the staggering growth in national employees and revenues, the reach of the federal government has ballooned in all areas, war and peace included. As a practical matter, the Executive has benefited most, because he is the more active force in the national government. Though Congress has gained also in the expanded scope of the matters that it may legislatively govern, such legislation has often increased executive control by creating vast law-enforcement opportunities for him.

The Growing Capacity of Public Officials to Communicate with the Electorate

Beginning with an upsurge in newspaper circulation in the late 1800s and continuing with radio, films, and now television, the capacity of decision makers to go directly to the electorate has greatly increased. This development has also redounded largely in favor of the President. In any month compare the pictures of the President and his family in our newspapers with the coverage given all 535 members of Congress and their teeming relations. As a single rather than a collective decision maker, the

Executive provides an easy target for the public and the media to follow. As the country's chief initiator and implementor, rather than its leading deliberator and legislator, he provides a more exciting and thus newsworthy target. As the country's master of ceremonies and the head of its first family, he commands attention. Walter Bagehot's phrase "intelligible government"[68] describes contemporary presidential government better than it did the constitutional monarchy of Victoria about which he wrote. Bagehot argued that the great virtue of a monarchy, as opposed to a republic, was that it provided the people with a government which they could understand, one which acted, or so they thought, with a single royal will and provided a ruling family to whom they could relate. The President provides intelligible government par excellence, and, unlike Victoria, he governs as well as reigns.

Theodore Roosevelt was perhaps the first to capitalize upon the Executive's appeal to the media. The presidential press conference, special address, and grand tour have since been prime means for winning public support for executive policies. War and peace provide an Executive with unusual opportunities to "shield and enhance his authority by wrapping the flag around himself, invoking patriotism, and national unity, and claiming life-and-death crisis."[69] John Kennedy's address to the nation on October 22, 1962, ranks among the most effective uses of the media to support a presidential decision to use force abroad. More than in domestic affairs, contemporary Presidents have been willing to argue their foreign policies directly to the people. As one European commentator noted, when comparing American democracy with parliamentary systems:

[T]he American presidential system, with the separation of powers, virtual direct election of the President and his nonparticipation in congressional debates, facilitates . . . recourse to a means of disseminating information that bypasses the legislature. . . . "The President from time to time shall report to the Congress on the State of the Union." The Founding Fathers certainly did not intend this to mean only the annual message to Congress. In the Cuban crisis of October, 1962, a statement to Congress would have corresponded to the text of the Constitution, rather than a televised talk to the nation.[70]

The Growing Cult of the Presidency

Like other people, Americans need heroes. Precious few Congressmen have sufficed. Presidents have, often as a result of their control over war and peace. Clinton Rossiter describes the great Executives as "more than eminent characters and strong Presidents. They were and are luminous symbols in our history. . . . Who are the most satisfying of our folk heroes? With whom is associated a wonderful web of slogans and shrines and heroics? The answer, plainly, is the six Presidents I have pointed to most proudly."[71] Rossiter's lyrical tones may grate on Watergate nerves, but they are realistic.

Finally, there is a momentum to the President's influence. With each new function assumed, each crisis met, and each corresponding rise in prestige, popular expectations, and presidential myth, the office has become more potent. The President's varied powers have fed upon one another to produce an aggregate stronger than the sum of his individual responsibilities. Clinton Rossiter's lyricism is helpful again:

The Presidency . . . is a wonderful stew whose unique flavor cannot be accounted for simply by making a list of its ingredients. It is a whole greater than and different from the sum of its parts, an office whose power and prestige are something more than the arithmetical total of all its functions. The President is not one kind of official during one part of the day, another kind during another part—administrator in the morning, legislator at lunch, king in the afternoon, commander before dinner, and politician at odd moments that come his weary way. He is all these things all the time, and any one of his functions feeds upon and into all the others.[72]

Rossiter breaks down the various functions of the Executive into five responsibilities which he believed to stem from the President's constitutional duties (chief of state, chief executive, commander in chief, chief diplomat, chief legislator) and five additional functions that have otherwise evolved: chief of party, voice of the people, protector of the peace, manager of prosperity, and world leader.[73] Rossiter's assumption of constitutional underpinnings for much of his "wonderful stew" is overblown, but not his description of the reality of presidential power since 1945.

Presidential control over federal affairs has been matched by a decline in congressional influence. Although Congress remains a far more powerful body than the legislature of any other sizable nation, the times in which it was able to dominate public affairs have passed. The existence of two coequal houses militated against its ever being able to assert complete supremacy, thereby relegating the Executive to a ceremonial role. And unlike the institutional characteristics of the presidency, those of Congress have not attracted power during times of rapid change, complexity, and recurrent crisis. The multitudes who make up the two houses of Congress, their constitutional task of deliberation and authorization, the decision-making process when many people are engaged in legislative work, and the diversity of the legislators' constituencies inevitably have made Congress a more ponderous, public, and indecisive decision maker than the President, and one, it seems, in need of external guidance. But much of Congress's difficulty does not stem from such inexorable factors. It comes from the legislators' reluctance to adopt procedures that would enable them to wield power effectively. Far more than the President, Congress has been slow to part with old ways, even at the cost of diminishing influence.[74]

It is important to determine to what extent the present balance of war powers between the President and Congress has resulted from the tendency of each to follow the path of least resistance, carried along by their institutional characteristics and by changing times, as opposed to the extent to which today's balance exists because the national good requires presidential dominance. The more the latter is the case, the more insistence on renewed congressional influence should be avoided. But the more that post-1789 practice appears *needlessly* to have diverged from the constitutional understandings of 1787-88, the greater the incentive to bring it back into line. The remaining chapters center on these questions.

Constitutional Guidelines for Splitting the War Powers between the President and Congress

THE CONSTITUTIONAL division of the war powers between the two branches is not clear today. Many hold beliefs nurtured by post-1789 practice (events of the Cold War in particular) that the Constitution vests in the Executive broad prerogative over American war and peace. For many others, Indochina reawakened belief in a dominant congressional role, well rooted in the constitutional text and debates of the Framers and Ratifiers. As a result, interested Americans have disagreed vigorously in recent years about the constitutionality of various presidential and congressional steps regarding the use of force.

Constitutional Mechanics

By what criteria do we decide how the Constitution allocates the war powers? Four possibilities were named in the Introduction and pursued in succeeding pages: the text of the Constitution's war-power provisions, the purposes of those who wrote and ratified the text, evolving beliefs since 1789 about what the Constitution requires, and—irrespective of text, purposes, or beliefs—the *actual* allocations of control that have existed between the President and Congress since 1789.

Chief Justice Taney had no difficulty in 1857 assigning primacy to two of these criteria. He wrote in *Dred Scott* that "as long as [the Constitution] continues to exist in its present form, it speaks not only in the same words, but with the same meaning and intent with which it spoke when it came from the hands of its framers . . . ."[1] Taney's conclusion is difficult to skirt when the constitutional text is clear itself or becomes clear in light of the 1787-88 debates.

The actual language of the Constitution has unique standing. Its words alone have been formally drafted and ratified as constitutional law—a status not shared by the Framers' and Ratifiers' comments or by any aspect of subsequent practice, Supreme Court decisions included.[2] It follows that when the war-power provisions of the document do unavoidably allocate control between the two branches one way or another, the allocation has been honored. To do otherwise would risk the legitimacy of government and rule of law.[3] Accordingly, none doubt that Congress must vote to declare war *if* America is to declare it. But in most cases concrete meaning for the Constitution has to come from sources other than the words themselves. We must go beyond the text to decide which if any hostilities entered by America *must* be declared.

Evidence of the Framers' and Ratifiers' purposes for adopting particular provisions has the first claim to shape whatever concrete meaning is given to any uncertainties in these provisions. Adherence to the 1787-88 purposes guards against self-serving interpretations by passing Presidents and Congresses[4] and, akin to adherence to the letter of the text, helps preserve public confidence in the rule of law. In fact, so strong a whiff of illegitimacy surrounds any disregard of the original intent, that fealty to it is often claimed even when the claimant cannot realistically say what if anything the Framers had in mind or when he in fact seems to go against their expectations.

It is fair to say that the country has usually honored the Framers' and Ratifiers' purposes except when they were out of step with existing American circumstances. So long as the underlying objectives of 1787-88 remain responsive to contemporary realities, they are generally clothed in institutional arrangements responsive to the times.[5] While the precise ways in which the Constitutional Fathers expected Congress to be involved in matters of war and peace may not coexist with the late twentieth century, the necessity for the legislators' involvement may itself be suited and awaiting compatible means of expression.

That the deliberations of 1787-88 are entitled to deference, however, does not mean that they should mesmerize us. As the Constitutional Fathers themselves were aware, much of their debate reflected problems peculiar to America just at that moment. They and others of their generation were prone to interpret the ratified Constitution by reading its text in light not of the minutiae of their deliberations but rather of experience and the document's underlying principles. Henry Merritt Wriston, commenting on congressional deliberations in 1789 over executive control of the Department of Foreign Affairs, described interpretative custom of the day:

[A]lthough this was a debate on constitutional interpretation, and although it was participated in by men who had been members of the Convention, there is no reference to the discussions of that body or to the decisions of its committees. True, they were not yet public property, but the journal and other papers were held by Washington, "subject to the order of Congress," and the members were not without memories which might have been summoned to their aid, if any could be furnished from that source. Instead, they *took the words of the printed Constitution and interpreted them from the point of view not of the framers in 1787, but from the point of view which had been developed through nearly two years of discussion. They spoke frequently of the principles involved in the decisions of the Convention, but they spoke about as often of the criticisms and discussions which had filled the air for many months.*[6]

At times, moreover, the constitutional text has been successfully interpreted in ways contrary to the apparent intentions of its Framers and Ratifiers. A strikingly greater diplomatic role for the Senate was manifest in the 1787-88 conventions than actually developed during the first generation under the Constitution.[7] It is inescapable that beliefs about what the Constitution's war-power provisions require, as well as the nature of actual allocations of control, have evolved over the past two centuries. It is not true that their evolution has simply been a descent into unconstitutionality. Rather, from 1789 the country has struggled to give concrete meaning to the Constitution's abstract terms, mark the bounds of its competing grants of authority, and fill its gaps. Along the way we have frequently replaced old expectations about the law and old divisions of raw power with new understandings and arrangements more responsive to the changing circumstances of the country. Far more than Taney in *Dred Scott*, James Bradley Thayer described constitutional reality as the war powers have known it, when he wrote in 1889 about analogous matters:

[A]s one looks back over our history . . . he seems to see the whole region strewn with the wrecks of the Constitution,—of what people have been imagining and putting forward as the Constitution. That it was unconstitutional to buy Louisiana and Florida; that it was unconstitutional to add new states to the Union from territory not belonging originally to it . . . that these and a hundred other things were a violation of the Constitution, has been solemnly and passionately asserted by statesmen and lawyers.[8]

But, Thayer concluded, "[m]en have found, as they are finding now, when new and unlooked-for situations have presented themselves, that they were left [by the Constitution] with liberty to handle them."[9]

Practice since 1789, in other words, has a role in constitutional interpretation. Indeed, no dispute over the war powers would be complete without reference to the sayings and doings of Hamilton, Madison, and a long succession of other Executives, legislators, Secretaries of State, military officers, judges, and commentators. But practice since 1789—whether evolving *beliefs* about what the Constitution requires or shifting *balances of power* between the President and Congress—is not a compelling guide to what the Constitution means except as practice is embodied in *current* laws, executive orders, or court rulings. Practice, of course, lacks any formal association with constitution making, unlike the intentions of the Framers and Ratifiers. And even more than their intentions, it is often shaped by the transient concerns of particular times.

Admittedly, today's (as opposed to yesterday's) popular beliefs about constitutional requirements cannot safely be treated with contempt, no matter how ill founded. Public confidence in the rule of law is too fragile for that. But this problem scarcely exists today in the war-power arena. Popular beliefs amount to little more than vague intimations that Congress should have a greater role in decisions about war and peace than it has had recently, with no hard concept of *when* or *how* the legislative voice should be heard. And these beliefs are countered by others that executive primacy is essential, given the realities of our times.

An existing balance of raw power—to the extent that it is not believed to be constitutional—can always be safely shunted aside, with the caveat that its passing may produce less wise and efficient government. Restructuring American decision making to involve Congress more fully in war-peace policy can be questioned on that score. But the simple fact that a balance of power now exists says nothing about whether it can be altered at tolerable cost. And it says nothing about the constitutionality of the arrangement. At most, it amounts to a claim by the aggressive branch for heightened constitutional prerogative. Our tradition does not require that such a claim be accepted simply because it has existed for a while and been given some substance in practice. That would permit the Executive or Congress to broaden their constitutional sway by boot-strapping—by grabbing and hanging on.

It is true, though, that persistent boot-strapping for an extended period can prove persuasive. The actual balance of power usually has greater impact on constitutional development than naked rhetoric about what the balance ought constitutionally to be, sometimes because the actual pattern of control, more than the rhetoric, is involved with the business of governing and thus more quickly reflects changing national circumstances. Accordingly, patterns of actual control often provide the most natural, if not the most doctrinally sound, guideline for constitutional evolution.[10] If for another generation Presidents dominate American policy about war and peace, challenged only by congressional rhetoric, our constitutional expectations may be reshaped in the image of their control.

It is quixotic, then, to hope that the war powers can be unraveled simply by studying the language of the Constitution or merely by harking back to the 1787-88 debates or solely by looking to subsequent practice. It is also quixotic to doubt that reasonable people will disagree about the proper guidelines for reaching constitutional answers, as well as about the answers themselves. *One* reasonable approach, taken here, begins with a search for war-power guidelines that are reflected in the 1787-88 debates and constitutional text, vindicated in post-1789 practice, and still vital to the national good. These talismans were listed at the close of Chapter III.

Guidelines for Dividing the War Powers between the President and Congress

There are ten guidelines, usually called "war-power ends" from here on, or simply "ends."

First, to ensure national defense. The Constitution empowers Congress to tax to "provide for the common Defence" and to call out the militia to "suppress Insurrections and repel Invasions." Habeas corpus may be suspended "when in Cases of Rebellion or Invasion the public Safety may require it." The states are guaranteed federal protection against invasion and permitted to "engage in War" without congressional authorization if "actually invaded, or in such imminent Danger as will not admit of delay." Many congressional powers run to the care and tending of the national military, and the President is made commander in chief to ensure its effective use. The Constitution flatly seeks the physical safety of the Union. The defensive advantages of American unity proved a prime selling point for the document during its struggle for ratification.

"Defence" came very shortly after 1789 to encompass protection of territory possessed *or* claimed by this country and to cover the security of American citizens and property *abroad*. During this century our defense has been linked with that of other peoples, so that an attack on allies has been equated with one on America. Zeal for security against both subversion and overt attack characterized the Cold War, indicative that the first end sought by Americans in how they constitutionally split the war powers between the President and Congress is their own physical protection.

Second, to hinder use of the military for domestic tyranny. The Framers and Ratifiers were adamant that the war powers not encourage federal usurpation. Thus the Constitution limits the purposes for which Congress may use state militia and provides that "[a] well regulated Militia, being necessary to the security of a free State, the right of the people to keep and bear Arms, shall not be infringed." It limits congressional army appropriations to two years, makes the commander in chief a civilian, and narrowly restricts suspension of habeas corpus. Quartering troops in private homes during peace is forbidden without the owners' consent. There are numerous other guarantees of state and individual rights, all to guard against domestic tyranny.

The Framers and Ratifiers feared blatant instances of this evil: armed steps by federal politicians to oppress states and individuals, even to set aside the Constitution and replace it with congressional dictatorship or an executive prince. Today's more subtle threat stems from the influence of huge military establishments and their civilian adjuncts, and from the light regard for civil liberties of a siege mentality. Hamilton spoke to another problem in *Federalist No. 8* (the dangers of disunion), but he caught the present concern when he warned that "the continual effort and alarm attendant on a state of continual danger, will compel nations the most attached to liberty, to resort for repose and security, to institutions, which have a tendency to destroy their civil and political rights. To be more safe they, at length, become willing to run the risk of being less free."

Third, to hinder the use of the military for aggression abroad. In comment on End One we saw the defensive cast of important constitutional language on the war powers. Naively even for their own times, the Framers and Ratifiers anticipated peace as America's wont. Exhausted by the Revolution, aware of the country's weakness, and inclined toward peace in principle, they hoped to avoid the perils of conflict unless they were unavoidably thrust upon the nation. In filling out its continental borders, an increasingly robust United States did find armed force useful to remove Spanish, Mexican, and Indian obstacles. But even during the most virulent moments of Manifest Destiny, Americans tended to think of their military steps as defensive. On the heels of the Mexican War the Supreme Court had no difficulty opining that American wars "can never be presumed to be waged for the purpose of conquest or the acquisition of territory."[11]

Aggressive action, however, had greater claim to international legality and to predictable, tolerable consequences in the late eighteenth and nineteenth centuries than it does now. Nondefensive use of force today, unless part of internationally approved collective security, would violate international law and trifle with survival. In addition to endangering our external security, it could produce conditions conducive to tyranny at home or to bitter internal strife on moral and political fronts. The country's interest in avoiding aggressive use of force abroad has a new intensity.

Fourth, to create and maintain national consensus behind American action for war or peace. Very much on the Framers' and Ratifiers' minds were the burdens imposed on the country's prior military and diplomatic efforts by internal bickering and non-cooperation. They knew that if most citizens do not at least acquiesce in national policy, the country plunges into controversy, with potentially grim impact on national effectiveness at home and abroad. Versailles and Vietnam in this century witness the consequences of internal division over American initiatives abroad. The antidote was called bipartisanship during the days when foreign affairs significantly divided Republicans from Democrats. An end to acrimony between the Executive and Congress is the most pressing concern today, followed by their development of a foreign policy acceptable to the country at large.

Fifth, to ensure democratic control over war and peace policy. The consensus of End Four may or may not result from democratic control. It can stem as well from policies sold for a time by executive fait accompli or factual slight of hand. Consensus, of course, is most firm when it is the product of decision by the legislative process, responsive to the views of citizens whose interests are affected. This democratic control involves decisions made by all the federal representatives of the people—the Senate, House, and President—each on a timely and informed basis. It involves explanation of policy to constituents and openness to their judgments when clearly and persistently voiced. It requires federal officials to take clear responsibility for national action and account for it to the voters, all on the assumption that the full play of representative democracy is most likely to produce policy in the general interest.

Admittedly, many of the Constitutional Fathers felt public judgment to be uninformed, irrational, inconstant, and either too militant or not militant enough. Similar fears were advanced concerning the House as against the Senate and President. The Framers and Ratifiers deemed popular wisdom particularly abysmal in foreign affairs and took steps to commit American diplomacy to the Senate and Executive, both shielded from direct electoral contact with the voters by the 1787-88 scheme.

Nonetheless, consent of the governed was central to the Framers' and Ratifiers' polity. Many of them feared the Senate and Executive for their separation from the people and presumed susceptibility to foreign or venal influence. Accordingly, the most fundamental war-peace decision—whether to enter hostilities—was placed squarely under congressional control, and the House was awarded special prerogative over federal money: one of the most basic war-peace tools.

Admittedly, also, a recurrent fear since 1789 has been that public judgment is not adequate to foreign affairs. We have Hans Morgenthau's conclusion that "there exists an inevitable incompatibility between the requirements of good foreign policy and the preferences of democratically controlled public opinion," and Walter Lippmann's "unhappy truth . . . that the prevailing public opinion has been destructively wrong at the critical junctures."[12]

But the 1787-88 efforts to shield the President and Senate

from direct electoral contact with the voters have been abandoned, and the franchise progressively freed from restraints of race, sex, and age. Consent of the governed becomes increasingly central to our politics. It is likely that today's more educated and demanding voters will insist on growing opportunities to challenge and shape policy on war and peace, since consent of the governed has compelling appeal when the consequences of decision are heavy. Democratic control remains a proper war-power guideline pending better evidence than now exists that popular judgment is consistently either poor or impervious to persuasion by those better advised.

Sixth, to encourage rational war and peace decisions. The goals of ensuring national defense without tyranny at home and aggression abroad define policy only in broad outline. Steps toward these goals can be sound or foolish. When to negotiate or fight, what to concede or demand, present the best-intentioned politicians with difficult choices as they try to protect America. The importance of rational decision making figured in the Constitutional Fathers' opposition to Confederation government and in their concern for an institutionally elite Senate and Executive. They wanted informed, well-considered policy on war and peace. The country's excruciating experience in Indochina testifies to the difficulties of making such policy and to the necessity for it.

To obtain decisions responsive to world realities and American needs, it has become increasingly clear that authority should be in the hands of officials who are well acquainted (by dint of their own labors, magnified manyfold by staff aid) with five facets of sound decision: (a) the country's overall foreign policy priorities, (b) the basic facts of the situation at issue, (c) realistic alternatives for dealing with it, (d) expert technical and political evaluations of the costs and benefits of each alternative, and (e) forceful criticism of these evaluations, directed especially to the factual, technical, and political assumptions underlying alternatives dear to principal officials. Without decision making of this sort, honest error and incompetence fall on fertile soil.

Seventh, to permit continuity in American war-peace policy,

when desirable, and its revision as necessary. Continuity leads
to national credibility and predictability, both vital to assure
allies, deter enemies, and produce agreements with other countries. The Framers and Ratifiers worried about harm from the
states' sabotage of American foreign policy and from the inconstancy of Confederation Congresses. In matters of war and
peace they recognized that discontinuity is safer by choice than
by internal disarray or caprice and that periodic review of
action, including its timely modification, often has importance
equal to its timely initiation. Thus during the earliest years under the Constitution, the country backed away from military
alliance with France, a step traumatic but calculated to avoid
destruction of the fledgling Republic in European struggles.
Credibility and predictability became objects of passion for
many Americans during the Cold War. While continuity was
overemphasized then as a buttress for third-world dominoes
and nuclear trip-wires, prudence still dictates that discontinuity
should be the product only of informed review and revision of
existing policy.

*Eighth, to permit emergency action for war or peace that has
not yet been blessed by national consensus or democratic control.* Any attempt to absolutize the need for consensus or democratic control founders on those occasions when public opinion
has been neutral or wrong and when government advocacy or
the course of events has still to garner backing for the necessary
policies. Suspicion of public judgment, noted in End Five,
feeds on more than elitist bias. Average voters (as well as members of the House of Representatives, so far as many Framers
and Ratifiers were concerned) do lack the information and
expertise often crucial to grasp quickly the demands of emerging international situations.

Isolationist opinion during the period immediately before
American entry into World War II could not have been honored
as befit its strength without serious cost to national defense, nor
could anti-British sentiment in the North during the Civil War.
We do need emergency philosopher kings to meet pressing
needs not fully appreciated by their fellow citizens. Should
these officials misjudge the link between international reality

and America's interests, they will be stymied ultimately by lack of consensus and the workings of democratic control.

Ninth, to ensure American capacity to move toward war or peace rapidly or secretly when necessary, flexibly and proportionately always. There will often be a need for speed and secrecy in negotiations and in the *conduct* of action, occasionally also in its initiation or termination. Flexibility (the capacity to act in a manner responsive to emerging circumstances) and proportionality (the avoidance of too little or too much reaction) are always vital to matters as intolerant of error as war and peace. The constitutional text reflects concern for speed and secrecy in its provisions for anti-invasion action by states and for withholding sensitive congressional action from the public. The 1787-88 debate on the reflexes of the Senate and Executive showed a keen appreciation of the objectives in question, as did the substitution of "declare" for "make" in the declaration-of-war clause. The demands of nuclear defense have bred singular concern for speed and secrecy. Both also became highly regarded during the Cold War in conventional military circumstances, not just nuclear. Though we are returning to a more balanced view of the occasions appropriate for them, a national ability to act quickly or quietly remains crucial.

Tenth, to permit the efficient setting and executing of war-peace policy. Consistent failure on either count undermines the wisest attempts at action. Bumbling national government invited constitution making in 1787-88. Effective federal action in military and foreign affairs was a basic objective of the Constitutional Fathers. It is now even more a basic demand, its intensity grown in step with the country's problems, our desire for federal solutions, and our disgust with inept government.

Competition and Preference among the Guidelines

A strain of incompatibility runs among these ten war-power ends. Even were the national government still a one-house assembly wielding legislative and executive powers, it could not give equal attention at once to speed and secrecy, on the one hand, and consensus and democratic control, on the other. Such incompatibility becomes more pronounced since the legislative and executive branches are separate, each with different capabilities for realizing the same objectives. A bow toward Congress to serve consensus and democratic control turns the back on the President and his comparative advantage for speed and secrecy.

The war-power ends, and respective capabilities of the two branches to realize them, fall into two rough groups. On one side are Ends Two to Five, with their ban on predatory action at home and abroad and their concern for consensus and democratic control. These objectives are more likely to be obtained if policy is made by the legislative process, rather than by the President alone. On the other side are Ends Six to Ten, calling for a rational process of decision making, for continuity in policy until its timely revision, for national capacity to take unpopular action, for speed, secrecy, flexibility, and proportionality, and for efficiency in making and executing national decisions. These objectives are more likely to be realized if the Executive may act without the need for *prior* congressional approval. End One stands alone, its interest in national defense vulnerable to default on any of the other objectives.

Conflict among the ends is not inevitable. Even if the President alone controlled the war powers, he might scrupulously avoid predatory action at home and abroad. He might build consensus behind his policies, and temper them in the fire of congressional and public opinion. Conversely, even if exercise of the war powers were subject to prior congressional approval, no immutable force compels the legislators to use irrational means of decision making, to toss aside essential continuity in policy or refuse its revision when necessary. No iron law binds Congress to vote down unpopular action vital to the national good or to prove incapable of speed, secrecy, flexibility, and proportionality. Nor are the legislators fated to sit astride the efficient making and execution of American war-peace policy.

Competition between the two groups of ends does seem probable, however. In light of the nature of these objectives and the different capacities of the President and Congress to reach them, no division of authority can give equal weight to securing *both* groups at the *same* time. A division of authority designed to maximize success for the first, or legislative, set of ends necessarily places less stress on obtaining the second, or executive, set.

Which interests are to be preferred, since all cannot be sought with *equal* importance at once? None deserves absolute primacy. Preference runs by time, with some objectives favored early in the life of any action and others later. Realization of the Executive Ends, numbers Six to Ten, ought to be the first concern, with secondary attention to the Legislative Ends, numbers Two to Five. Once the action is underway, the order of preference should reverse. There is greater probability that both sets of ends can ultimately be realized if the executive group receives an initial moment in the sun. This conclusion rests on a number of interlocking judgments.

At the threshold, even if the President may act initially without prior congressional approval, he will rarely attempt tyranny at home or abroad. Similarly, his policies may mirror existing consensus or lead quickly to it. And the Executive is an integral link in the chain of democratic control. Thus, despite initial preference for Ends Six to Ten, Ends Two to Five should suffer only modestly during their time of secondary emphasis. If nonetheless the President were to embark on wayward action, his policies could be promptly curbed by the shift in preference to the Legislative Ends. The possibility that presidential faits accomplis will go unchallenged, simply because they exist, has scant basis in history before the Cold War and reduced prospects after Indochina. Accordingly, if Ends Two to Five are initially slighted, they ought thereafter to be capable of vindication.

The likelihood of ultimately realizing both sets of ends declines if the legislative set is preferred from the beginning. Were congressional approval invariably required before American action could begin, the effect could be lethal to unpopular steps vital to national security (End Eight) and to speed, secrecy, flexibility, and proportionality (End Nine).

When politically risky action for war or peace must be taken, the legislators often prefer that the President step out first. If Congress were *obliged* to move before the country could act, the legislators might more willingly seize the nettle. But the past is not reassuring on this score, and the issue is not one with which nations in troubled times safely experiment. So far as the End Nine national reflexes are concerned, they too could be lethally affected by any necessity to seek and await prior congressional approval, even if the legislators work with all feasible speed and secrecy. While there are few cases in which the initiation or termination of steps toward war or peace must be instant, secret, or supple if they are to succeed, in those cases nothing else will do, and it defies man to define them precisely in advance. In turn, continuity in policy and its timely revision (End Seven) would suffer from a failure of American will or reflexes. Finally, a rational decision-making process and government efficiency (Ends Six and Ten) are more likely to be hurt than helped by denying initiative to the Executive, so long as the respective capacities of the two branches to handle foreign affairs remain as they are.

It follows that, if the legislative objectives are preferred from the outset, Ends Six to Ten are likely to go begging in many cases. There is no historic basis for confidence that they will be realized as a matter of course by a division of the war powers insistent on consensus and democratic control before any action may begin. Moreover, while our constitutional tradition can readily accommodate presidential initiative in war and peace *before* the legislative process takes hold, it does not contemplate that the President may commit America to action *after* Congress has explicitly forbidden it, even though he believes the action vital to the national good.

Beyond the greater likelihood that all of the allocational objectives can be realized if Ends Six to Ten are initially favored, there is a second basis for the recommended order of preference. To obtain these objectives, there must be more executive freedom than seemed necessary in 1787-88. The Framers and Ratifiers misperceived the needs of even their own times; by 1815 presidential authority over war and peace was greater than they had expected. The world has also changed over the last two hundred years in ways that makes Ends Six to Ten more important to America now than they were in the late eighteenth and nineteenth centuries. For reasons already considered, during most of the nineteenth century the American government infrequently faced the prospect that an unpopular, speedy, or secret commitment of troops abroad might be vital to national security. Nor did it face the need to take action, including commitments to other countries, on whose credibility and predictability American security and world order would depend. Through most of the 1800s the timely revision of war-peace policies—indeed, their making and execution by rational, efficient processes—had second-order importance akin to the second-class status of the policies themselves. None of these happy circumstances exist today.

Beyond new threats to security from the passing of ocean moats, sailing-ship invasions, and agrarian self-sufficiency, other factors have revalued Ends Six to Ten. International events arise, progress, and alter their complexion much more rapidly in an era of missiles and communication satellites than during one linked by horses, wind, and quills. Foreign affairs are more dense today. The world's supply of humans, independent states, and international bodies has multiplied many times over. So have their ideological and political differences. Exploding wealth and technology provide these people with the means to take steps beyond imagining in less endowed ages. As a result, international life has become far more demanding of its manipulators. We do have greater interest in realizing Ends Six to Ten than the Constitutional Fathers did. Our concern with Ends Two to Five, however, also remains intense. Tyranny at home, aggression abroad, or debased democracy in the name of national defense are as unappealing today as in 1787-88.

It is well to fatten the two institutional judgments stated earlier—that the legislative process is better equipped to realize Ends Two to Five and executive initiative Ends Six to Ten. Tyranny and aggression are best prevented if each branch acts as a fail-safe against the other's error, incompetence, or venality.

Each by its independence and unique perspective is well-positioned to ward off the other's lapses, and the probability that both will take leave of their senses at once is necessarily less than that of solitary dementia. True, the separation of powers works more efficiently against action than against culpable inaction, but even the latter is less likely if there is one branch ready to prod the other. Mutual restraint and exhortation are present in the legislative process: It requires the joint approval of the President and Congress unless two-thirds of the House and Senate reject a veto, an improbable majority for tyranny or aggression.

Legislation is also the best route to national consensus behind American war or peace action. A congressional act signed by the President stamps policy with constitutional legitimacy and places behind it the whole of federal political authority. Further, both branches having assumed responsibility for the action, both have vested interests in defending it before their constitutents. Disagreement between the President and Congress, on the other hand, divides the country and cripples contested policy. The Executive can strike quickly and persuasively for popular backing. But the hosts in Congress, plugging forward in less rapid and dramatic fashion, can riddle presidential consensus and replace it with their own, or with debilitating national dispute.

Finally, democratic control inevitably involves both political branches. Each in its own way represents the people. Whether the President or Congress more embodies the national will depends on the issue and the moment. The Executive by virtue of his national constituency is freer of special interests and thus more able to focus on the general good. Congress by its 535 members, smaller electorates, biennial return of the full House and one-third of the Senate, and by its more public decision-making process has greater feel for popular passions and is more open to public revenge for failure to heed those passions. For these reasons also, the public has greater access to legislative than to executive decision makers. It seems that Congress does bear the heavier burden of ensuring policies responsive to the immediate majority will. Accordingly, the legislative process, with its heavy executive involvement but final congressional say, is well suited to achieve End Five. If Ends Two to Five stood alone, *prior* congressional approval for American action toward war or peace would be an absolute.

Chapter VII has already stated the case for the President regarding Ends Six to Ten. He has the more rational process for making decisions because of his unity, availability for federal business, control over the services and activities of most federal personnel, and term of office. Unity and time in office enable him to take account of the country's overall foreign policy objectives and priorities. And because he is everpresent at the center of the national intelligence network and assisted by countless experts, he is more able to grasp the basic facts of emerging situations, to generate alternatives for dealing with them, and to weigh the costs and benefits of each alternative. Thus, he is well equipped to appreciate the demands of both continuity in policy and its timely revision.

The President's unity and national constituency permit him greater freedom than Congress to take unpopular action when it appears vital to national security. Because he shares executive power with no one, he is not hobbled by fainthearted colleagues. Nor is he hindered by the strong preferences of one special or geographical interest. He has also come to symbolize the nation during crisis, and thus has immense capacity to preempt the media, seize the flag, and rally support for his plunge toward war or peace. And his more rational decision-making apparatus often gives him greater confidence than Congress in the necessity for politically risky initiatives.

As a single man always on the job, the President is more able to move swiftly, secretly, flexibly, and proportionately. Finally, as the leader of federal personnel and the one charged with interpreting and executing American policy, he has the greater capacity to see to efficient federal action.

Paean to presidential advantages in achieving Ends Six to Ten can be overdone, however. Growth of executive war powers to their Cold War apogee was the natural result of certain institutional and historical forces, a movement along the path of least resistance for both branches and for the country. But

not all of these forces related to national defense. To the extent
that the recent presidential hold on policy for war and peace reflects apotheosis of the Executive as a folk hero, his more skill-
ful exploitation of the media than Congress, overreaction to the
uncertainties of world leadership in a nuclear age, and simple
habit, it can be cut back without undermining the Republic.

The comparative, not absolute, nature of executive advantage in seeing to Ends Six to Ten is apparent on a number of
fronts. First, Congress is important to an element of rational
decision making: the necessity for forceful, independent criticism of alternative courses of action. The President's own
devil's advocates often fail to hold his attention. Not so, powerful Senators and Representatives who have the means to negate
executive policy. Having been involved less, if at all, in the
work of creating presidential proposals, these legislators may
be particularly able to spot their defects. And members of the
opposition party often feel little compunction about exposing
defects as they see them.

Second, Congress may be needed to ensure timely revision
of American policy. The Executive can become obsessively
fond of initiatives that he sponsored and in which he has invested much political capital. Individual legislators are subject
to similar obsessions, but since there are 535 of them, Congress
generally avoids monolithic positions and rarely lacks a few
willing to describe the emperor's nakedness. Third, Congress is
crucial to federal efficiency. Otiose as congressional procedures themselves are, legislators frequently have a keen eye for
institutional flaws in the Executive Branch, and they have the
capacity to force remedial steps. In any event, their approval
is required for most reform of the bureaucracy. Fourth, if the
President falters, the country depends on Congress to press on
toward Ends Six to Ten. It is the American institution next most
capable of realizing them. Finally, of course, the legislators
could always improve the ways in which they do business so as
to narrow the Executive's comparative advantage.

The executive and congressional capabilities just described
exist in most, not all, cases. Should abnormally wise and forceful Congressmen face abnormally foolish and weak Execu-

tives, the legislative process could become the best hope for both sets of ends. Even with normal Presidents and Congresses, there will be some times when the legislators are more capable of reaching Objectives Six to Ten and other instances in which the President alone could do the best job for Ends Two to Five. But it is *most* cases that count. To divide the war powers on the assumption of a "worst case" performance by either the Executive or Congress would require excluding the offending branch from authority. And that, obviously, would leave the country without a first line of defense against the fallibility of the favored branch. Allocational emphasis first on the Executive Ends and then on the Legislative provides a firm middle ground.

Should the middle ground satisfy devotees of presidential prerogative still shaken by what Congress might have done to Franklin Roosevelt's war against the Axis during the months preceding formal American entry into World War II? Should it satisfy devotees of congressional prerogative traumatized by how Presidents Johnson and Nixon buffeted the legislators over Indochina? Very probably not, for their positions rest on certain inescapable dilemmas. Roosevelt, had he been forced to report candidly to Congress, could easily have been directed to pull back, though his action seems to have been important to American defense. And the Johnson-Nixon manipulation of Congress made clear that the legislators can be herded by executive fait accompli. There is no avoiding the fact that given an opportunity to decide, Congress may make poor judgments, or the fact that, given an opportunity to shape events before seeking congressional approval, the President may narrow the legislators' freedom to decide. But with a cooperative war-power relationship between the two branches, and reasonably good luck, these dilemmas ought to consume only the Chicken Littles among us.

CHAPTER IX

Recommended Division of

the War Powers

WHILE MUCH remains unsettled about how war and peace powers should be split between the President and Congress, ultimate control over some sorts of action does seem clearly committed to the legislators—over formal declarations of war and foreign aid, for instance. The Executive very likely has clear title to the deployment of American forces in international seas or air, and he seems to have won an undisputed right to control whether we have formal relations with other states. But Congress must act through a legislative process in which the President wields information, recommendations, and vetoes and in which he often receives broad delegations of authority. Congress, in turn, becomes disturbed if not consulted about policy within executive prerogative, especially if its implementation requires legislation. Both branches also control tools that can be used to undo the other's policy initiatives. Without men and money voted by Congress, the President is hard pressed to begin most sorts of war-peace action, much less complete them. Denied executive channels of communication with foreign governments, Congress is equally hard pressed to make and effect international decisions. Thus, even if one branch concedes policy primacy to the other over certain types of action, it often retains the capacity to renege by withholding vital implementing tools. War-power rights and duties fall deeper into confusion, of course, when neither branch concedes authority to the other over a particular sort of action.

Confusion is especially thick around the type most important in our times: the commitment of American forces to undeclared combat abroad, as in Korea and Indochina. Establishing the lines of constitutional control over such commitment would point the way to the division of authority in other uncertain war-peace areas. It should also lessen the use of tools firmly in the hands of one branch to gut the other's policy. If presidential control is the answer for the commitment of American forces to undeclared combat, a presumption would rise in favor of more of the same for those other sorts of action that condition when and how we enter undeclared combat. And strong tides would run against congressional manipulation of men or money to sabotage presidential commitments of the country to conflict. Opposite ramifications would rise from decision in favor of congressional control over undeclared combat. Still different implications would result if both branches must agree to involvement. Taking into account the conclusions of Chapter VIII about the war-power ends, the order of preference among them, and the respective institutional capabilities of the President and Congress to realize them, what interpretation of the Constitution's war-power provisions best serves the country today?

Presidential Prerogative When Congress Is Silent

The first core issue concerns the scope of executive prerogative over the initiation, conduct, and termination of American involvement in combat when Congress as a whole enacts no legislation regarding the merits of the venture, whether to approve, limit, or end it. Given congressional silence, the President should be constitutionally free to act, limited only by (1) the necessity to inform the legislators fully of developments on a continuing basis, (2) defensive purpose, and (3) the availability of implementing tools.

When Congress is silent, the phase of action has limited practical significance to presidential prerogative, except as phase makes clear the distinction between the conduct of one conflict and the initiation of another unrelated venture. So long as the legislators do not explicitly condition or reject policy adopted by the Executive and so long as he can lawfully obtain the necessary implementing tools, he ought to control the operation from initiation through conduct to termination. This means that the legislators should not have a constitutional right to kill ongoing executive action simply by failing to ratify it; for instance, by failing to vote approval within 60 days after its beginning or by failing to vote yes at set intervals thereafter. Congressional failure to ratify (whether because no vote at all is taken or because no resolution of approval passes) cannot be automatically equated with rejection of the President's policy. Instead, it may reflect confusion, political cowardice, or minority machinations. Nor in most cases can congressional failure to ratify be thought as rational a decision on the merits as the President's affirmative judgment. Pending such time as Congress squarely votes to condition or end executive policy, we are more likely to realize the war-power ends by allowing it to stand.[1]

Along the way, however, the President ought not to be able to withhold from Congress nontactical information about the venture. He should report promptly and in detail at the outset, with supplemental statements periodically thereafter. So informed, Congress would have the necessary data and recurring opportunity to consider our participation in undeclared combat, should the legislators so desire. In this manner the reports would safeguard war-power Ends Two through Five. Further, the President's awareness that he must make full and continuing disclosure would discourage hasty, ill-considered action on his part. And faced with the necessity to report and the possibility of adverse, nonvetoable congressional judgment in return,[2] the President—as a matter of practical politics, not constitutional duty—could be expected to obtain prior assurance of congressional support except when he feels that (1) unpopular action is essential to national defense, (2) a compelling need for *initial* speed or secrecy exists, or (3) the costs to the country of the action are likely to be very slight.

To realize war-power End Three, the President should never act for aggressive purposes. But it is for him to judge at the outset where defense ends and aggression begins, subject to later review by Congress and the public. The reasons are those given in the prior chapter for initial preference of Ends Six to Ten over Ends Two to Five. Beyond this requirement of defensive intent, the purpose behind the President's action should have no bearing on his authority when Congress is silent. Attempts to frame "purpose" tests for executive prerogative quickly become lost in trackless wilds. What sorts of attacks, on whom, where, justify what kinds of action by the Executive under a response-to-attack rationale? What sorts of "laws," recognized by whom, support his resort to arms under the President's duty to take care that the laws be faithfully executed? These and other unknowns would require resolution to produce a purpose test for executive prerogative. Further, if the test were not spelled out in detail, it would risk meaningless ambiguity and bode ill for the rule of law. As a practical matter it might also have no limiting effect on presidential discretion. If the test were minutely elaborated, on the other hand, it could unduly hobble national reflexes. We lack the capacity to foresee all the circumstances in which a sudden-attack or law-enforcement rationale will call for executive speed or secrecy to protect the country.

Of course, the more "pure" the President's purpose for acting while Congress is silent, the greater the likelihood that his policy will be supported thereafter by the legislators and voters. His rapid response to sudden enemy attack on American territory seems virtually rejection-proof. In that event, outrage would greet presidential inaction pending congressional consent. Not so for presidential response to covert enemy attack on an exotic land half the world away from America. The President will also be far more certain of approval when he uses the military to enforce a congressional joint resolution than when he lands marines to enforce a United Nations resolution or a purely executive international agreement.

The costs of action, similarly, ought not to affect executive prerogative if Congress is silent. A "costs" test would pose its own definitional dilemmas. What sorts of adverse consequences, of what magnitude and immediacy, would be compatible with unilateral executive action? But again, the smaller the costs, the more likely executive initiatives are to be tolerated by Congress and the public. The dangers of ambiguity or rigidity would accompany "speed or secrecy" tests for presidential prerogative even more surely than they would travel with "purpose" criteria. It is true, nonetheless, that the more the circumstances at issue do demand speed or secrecy, the greater the likelihood that unilateral executive action will be hailed by other Americans.

Tools are another matter. The means required to begin and sustain American involvement in undeclared combat should limit the President. His right to initiate action ought to depend either upon the existence of the necessary men and money or upon prior congressional delegation to him of authority to raise them. If international agreements or domestic regulations are required, the President should be able to go only so far as his *own* tool-providing authority can take him. Draft laws, appropriations, and so forth ought not to fall to him simply because they are essential to effect his military policy. Were they to do so, the separation of powers could be irretrievably breached and Congress denied an ultimate means of restraining a President otherwise impervious to its will.

On the other hand, Congress as a matter of comity and sound decision making (though not constitutional obligation) ought rarely to deny the Executive tools that he requests, so long as the Senate and House remain silent about the policy for which he requests them. Defeat of policy by denying tools to implement it is less likely to realize the war-power ends than is debate and voting focused on the merits of the policy itself. In short, congressional use of tools to hamstring executive policy ought to be abnormal, arising only when an Executive fails to accede to direct congressional decisions about policy. A hamstringing use of tools, of course, may be more frequent during a transition in which Congress learns to deal squarely with policy and the Executive to honor its judgments.

The presidential prerogative just sketched assumes that Congress should have no constitutional right in the late twentieth century to approve *all* American involvement in undeclared combat *before* its initiation. Neither the rule of law nor

End One—national defense—would profit from an attempt to carve executive exceptions out of a general requirement of prior congressional approval. The definitional ambiguities or rigidities of purpose, costs, and speed or secrecy criteria for such exceptions have already been noted. More important, the President's comparative advantage in realizing Ends Six to Ten, and his capacity to go far toward Ends Two to Five by himself, should permit him to set policy so long as Congress acquiesces.

Congressional Prerogative When the President Is Silent

A simpler situation exists when the Executive neither recommends, signs, nor vetoes legislation regarding the commitment of American troops to undeclared combat but when he is willing to take care that the laws be faithfully enforced. Then Congress ought to be able to forbid the taking of any action or to direct that it go forward subject to specified ground rules—for example, ceilings on the number of men to be committed and on the geographical areas in which they are to fight—so long as the legislators leave the actual strategy and tactics of execution to the President—for example, how the available men are to be used within the specified geography. When the Executive is passive, Congress necessarily becomes our best hope for realizing the war-power ends, with the exception of the efficient execution of American policy. Even if Congress assumes responsibility for efficiently setting that policy, legislatures do not effectively direct military operations.

Prerogatives When the Two Branches Disagree

When the President and Congress are at odds over the proper national course, the phase of action becomes crucial to the division of the war powers between them.

Initiation

The President should be able to begin action so long as Congress has not yet voted against it, even if such a vote seems imminent. In other words, until the legislators actually take a formal position, the Executive ought to retain the prerogative that is his when Congress is silent. Under that prerogative he must promptly report his action to Congress, which can then condition or end it. Presumably the President would act despite rising congressional sentiment only to advance policies he feels vital to national defense, when speed or secrecy is crucial to their success. The Executive would hope by his fait accompli to buy time to win the legislators to his view through the persuasive force of events and his appeals to public opinion. Why allow the President this option? Because of the contemporary importance of Ends Six to Ten and his comparative advantage in realizing them.

However, if Congress does take a formal position before the President initiates action, the legislators should have the right to prevent the action's ever beginning, or to condition its nature. The prohibition or limits ought to come from an explicit vote to block or bound the action, not from simple failure to vote for a resolution authorizing it. If the President vetoes the negative legislation, two-thirds of both houses must renew the ban, or the Executive should retain his right to act unilaterally, subject thereafter to an obligation to report the action promptly to Congress and to be bound by a nonvetoable decision by Congress to limit or end the action if it so desires. But if his veto is overridden, the Executive should not commit the troops. Ends Four to Five—consensus and democratic control—then demand acceptance of the judgment of the legislative process. At that juncture the President may only attempt to have the legislators repeal their negative.

Similarly, when the President favors doing nothing at all, Congress should have the right to pass legislation directing him to cease inaction and commit troops. Beyond the qualified absolute of his veto, the President should have no prerogative to refuse to heed congressional will. He ought not to be able to block American involvement in combat simply because he opposes the idea. Were he able to ignore rejection of his veto in such cases, the legislators would have no recourse but impeachment to overcome the military default of a venal or incompetent Executive—a sluggish remedy, especially when speed may be of the essence. Far better for Congress to have the constitutional right to order military action begun. Faced with such a directive, a venal President may be moved to virtue and an incompetent to wisdom. Even if the President refuses to act, other federal officials could do so under the constitutional shelter of the congressional order.

Conduct

No matter how action is initiated, the President should control its conduct so long as he stays within any conditions laid down by Congress. Speed and secrecy when necessary, flexibility, proportionality, and efficiency always, demand one executive, not 535. The difficult question is how to separate conditions on the nature of an action, which Congress may define, from strategy and tactics, the prerogative of the commander in chief at all times. No bright line exists. Broadly, however, Congress ought to be able to state (1) the underlying objectives of any American involvement in combat, (2) an outer limit on the length of time it may continue, (3) geographical boundaries for where it is to occur, (4) ceilings on the number of men and amount of money to be committed, and (5) whether unconventional weapons may be used. How within those conditions the action is to be conducted then becomes a matter for executive discretion.

To set aside congressional conditions, the President should be required to obtain a majority vote of both houses. But to the extent that Congress has not specified ground rules for the action, he should be free to fix them under the terms of his prerogative to control policy when Congress is silent. For example, if the legislators have said nothing about the precise geography of American participation in a foreign conflict, the President should be free to expand its territorial scope so long as he reports his action to Congress and stands ready to have it conditioned or ended.

Termination

To condition or end an ongoing action, two different allocations of authority are desirable. First, if the President began the action by himself, Congress should be free to limit or terminate it *by majority vote of both houses, without the possibility of executive veto*, no matter how acute presidential distress at the passing of his policy. Why permit Congress to work its will by concurrent resolution? Because, as we have seen, concern for Ends Two to Five requires that the legislative process take conclusive hold, once Ends Six to Ten have been given initial preference by unilateral executive action. And the legislative process, after the President has in effect "signed" policy by initiating it, runs in reverse. It needs only the legislators' judgment. There is no place for executive veto, for when the legislative process operates normally, congressional failure to vote approval results in no bill, in nothing for the President to veto. In fact, when the legislative process runs normally, rather than in reverse, the lack of a majority in *either* the House or the Senate proves fatal to presidential policy. In the interests of Ends Six to Ten, however, majorities in both houses ought to be required before an executive use of the military is conditioned or ended.

Second, if the President began action only because Congress so required, he should be free to end it when he believes that the congressional objectives have been reached, unless ordered to continue by two-thirds vote of both houses, over his veto. Why permit Congress to force him to continue? Again, because it is well to have a less extreme mechanism than impeachment to move a venal or incompetent Executive and his subordinates to necessary military action. If an initially reluctant President develops a taste for action imposed on him by Congress and wishes to continue it despite a contrary majority in the Senate and House, there is no reason to deny him his veto. In this case, the legislative process has not run in reverse, and a two-thirds vote ought to be required to restrain him.

Purpose, Costs, Need for Speed or Secrecy, and Tools

The purpose for American involvement in combat ought to be irrelevant to executive-congressional prerogative when the two branches disagree. The President ought not to be free to fight on simply because he is defending American territory against enemy attack or simply because he is enforcing an order of the United Nations Security Council. In the first instance, Congress may think surrender is the best way to save what remains of the country; such a decision has proved fruitful for many enemies of the United States, including its southern states. In the second instance, Congress may believe that the costs of collective security for this country outweigh the benefits, even though among the costs is default on its international obligations.

The costs of action should also be irrelevant, as well as its need for speed or secrecy. Modest costs support executive prerogative only on the assumption that Congress is uninterested in acting on so slight a matter. And any demands of speed or secrecy will have been met by Congress, happily or unhappily, once it has acted on the pending question. In the face of the legislators' vote, the President can hardly argue that the pertinent costs are too minor to interest them, that there is too little time to seek their opinion, or that doing so might breach vital confidentiality.

Tools, to the contrary, do provide a second front on which the two branches can further wage their policy disputes. Abolition of this second front, by consolidating control over all tools in one or the other branch, would not be desirable. Tools provide bedrock checks and balances to prevent evil or foolish action by a branch holding policy authority and to prevent one branch from usurping the other's legitimate voice in decision making. Arguably, only Congress has tools available as checks and balances, since the President must use his to take care that the laws be faithfully executed, even laws enacted despite his veto. But often little practical difference exists between congressional refusal to produce tools needed by the President and the sluggish use by him of tools needed to execute congressional policy. Further, the need for executive restraint of Congress exists, as well as the obverse. It is conceivable that two-thirds of both houses could order blatantly unwise military action. But, again by custom, tools should be used to derail policy only in extremis. Their hamstringing use is not conducive to a spirit of cooperation between the President and Congress. Nor can it usually provide as informed decision making as does direct focus on the merits of the policy in question.

Prerogatives When the Two Branches Agree

At issue, first, are questions concerning the instrument of agreement, the delegation of authority from one branch to another, and the ratification by one of the other's initiative. Since 1945 especially, some have claimed that a declaration of war provides the only constitutional means by which the President and Congress may agree to commit American forces to costly combat. The language of the Constitution, the intentions of its Framers and Ratifiers, practice since 1789, and common sense offer them scant comfort. Formal declarations are one way to authorize military action, but they provide a blunt, excessive method possibly extinct after a generation in which no nation has declared its wars. A congressional joint resolution or some other form of legislation will generally be more conducive to the war-power ends, so long as the measure is approved by majorities in both houses and signed by the President. Further, if the legislators are ratifying after the fact an action already begun by the Executive, it seems clear that the House and Senate may indicate approval by simple majority vote in both houses, without the need for presidential signature.

What if the agreement in question runs only between the President and two-thirds of the Senate? As we have seen, the Framers and Ratifiers envisaged a more splendid Senate than proved to be ours—one, compared to the House, unusually capable of speedy, secret, and internationally wise action. Thus the Constitutional Fathers' debates and some post-1789 practice, including executive claims during the Indochina War, suggest that treaties may authorize American involvement in undeclared combat. This sanguine view of the constitutional force of treaties faces declining national confidence in the Senate vis-a-vis the House, as well as the growing importance of appropriations and other legislation to American military initiatives. Few would deny the President and Senate the authority to take steps that risk, but do not directly commit, the country to costly, undeclared combat. Equally appropriate, however, is rejection of any notion that the Senate may speak for Congress as a whole in agreeing to the country's direct involvement in such action.[3]

So far as delegation is concerned, if the President has discretion to commit troops so long as Congress remains silent about the matter, it follows that the legislators should be free to authorize him in advance to do so. Similarly, if Congress may forbid the President to involve the country in a particular conflict or impose conditions on our involvement, it follows that such bans or limits may usefully be included as conditions in any delegated authority voted the Executive. In the real world, delegations often provide Congress with its only means of shaping American policy *before* the President acts. They are particularly appropriate when a response-to-attack or law-enforcement purpose of high quality is involved (authority to the President to repel physical attacks on American territory or to help enforce resolutions of the United Nations Security Council), when the costs of action are not likely to be great (authority to the Executive to use the military against pirates in the open seas), or when a need for speed or secrecy is probable (delegation to deal with the imminent threat of nuclear attack). Congress in fact has frequently awarded the President broad prior approval for undeclared combat, beginning in Washington's administration.

But while permissible war-power delegations to the Executive ought to be unlimited, they should expressly approve any armed action that is meant to fall within the delegation. If it says nothing about such action, then no explicit congressional approval exists. Thus legislation calling for another state to compensate expropriated American interests does not also, without so stating, approve undeclared war against the expropriator to force compensation. At best, Congress should be deemed silent on the matter and the Executive, should he wish to take military action, must determine his prerogative against that assumption of silence.

As noted in Chapter I, an issue related to congressional delegation arises if both branches agree to American response should certain future events occur; for instance, a congressional joint resolution signed by the President providing for attacks by this country on any state that has itself attacked one of our allies. The constitutionality of such contingent agreement can be questioned on the ground that it eliminates a weighing of costs and benefits at the moment of truth, important because their balance can have altered since the time both branches chose the policy in question. But this argument ignores the capacity of the two branches to renege at the eleventh hour, as well as the earlier benefits possible from the agreement's existence. The two branches should be free to reap any international benefit available from adopting a contingent policy, in reliance on their power to fail to honor the commitment at the appointed hour, should doing so no longer serve the national interest.

Earlier pages have suggested that ratification by one branch of the other's action must be *explicit* to constitute agreement between them that America is to engage in undeclared combat. Situations in which implied approval might arguably exist have been treated here as incidents in which one branch remains silent while the other sets policy alone. Admittedly, Congress might be said to ratify executive action by implication when it votes vital implementing tools, or when it rejects resolutions to condition or end the action, or even when Congress simply does nothing, letting the venture proceed uninterrupted. Similarly, in the light of the President's historic capacity to negate congressional policy by sluggish or inept enforcement, his diligent execution of laws in whose making he took no part arguably constitutes implied approval. But the sounder constitutional position requires express approval before the active branch may cease judging its authority against the background of the other's silence. Congress can have many reasons for voting tools to service executive conflicts other than a belief on the part of most legislators that the benefits of the fighting outweigh its costs, and a passive Executive may enforce congressional war policy for reasons other than his agreement with it. Accord should not be said to exist between the two branches until both unambiguously note their agreement, subject to the caveat that broad delegations of authority are acceptable means of prior congressional approval.

Since 1789 few have quibbled about the timing of ratification, though the more promptly it comes, the less constitutionally questionable the venture. Nor have many doubted that ratification can constitutionally justify action otherwise beyond the prerogative of the active branch. And few have urged that ratification is automatically void under the Constitution if tainted by the fraud of the active party. Relief comes through other means. If sufficiently aggrieved, the deceived branch can cancel its agreement. Congress having ratified in reliance on executive misstatement could promptly vote to modify or terminate. Similarly, the aggrieved branch might retaliate by withholding necessary tools, by political attack, or, when the legislators are the aggrieved, by formal votes of censure or impeachment.

Questions of instrument, delegation, and ratification deal mainly with the initiation of action. Historically, the President's prerogative over the conduct of a venture has proved most sweeping when the legislators have agreed to its initiation but not specified its ground rules. Once Congress approves an undeclared conflict without imposing conditions on American prosecution of it, the President may justify under the aegis of conduct virtually any armed step related to engagement of the specified enemy; for instance, the invasion and occupation of a third state to prevent its shipment of munitions to the foe.

Congress and the President in their agreement to initiate undeclared war can also provide for its termination (*e.g.*, by legislating that American involvement may continue no longer than a year). The two branches, of course, can agree as well during the conduct of a venture on the terms of its conclusion, notwithstanding any prior arrangements. Somewhat more difficult is the question whether the President alone may end an undeclared but major conflict that was begun with statutory approval (or in line with treaty commitments) but without any express arrangements for termination. So long as the President remains faithful to the goals for which the venture was launched, there should be no need for the legislators expressly to agree to its end. Termination under these circumstances is a natural incident of the President's duty to take care that the laws be enforced. The more controversial the terms of peace, however, the more Ends Three and Four militate in favor of the President's obtaining legislative approval.

   The issues treated above, though not all-inclusive, are central to the division of the war powers between the President and Congress. As promised in the Introduction, the recommended constitutional allocation involves less control for Congress than the Constitutional Fathers expected, but also less control for the President than most Executives in this century and a number before have actually exercised.

CHAPTER X

Routes to the

Recommended Allocation

FORMAL AMENDMENT of the Constitution would be the shortest route to national consensus about the division of authority just described. Such amendment-based consensus would then ensure the necessary changes in the existing balance of power between the President and Congress. Formal amendment would also lessen the hazards of self-serving interpretation and of diminished public commitment to law that accompany the development of constitutional consensus by practice.

Cheerful as these advantages of formal amendment may be, they pale beside its disadvantages. The first is the improbability that the war-power text will ever be rewritten. The prospect of such amendment would not excite the public. Its complications are too numerous and its benefits too abstruse to have the ready appeal of a two-term presidency, eighteen-year-old vote, or liberated women. Formal revision is also unlikely to draw significant support from the politically potent. Supporters of unchanged executive control would oppose it, and even those in favor of a stronger congressional voice are likely to prefer its coming by the more flexible route of practice.

Rewriting the war-power text, in any event, would be risky. Once begun, a thorough job should follow, lest the new language be undone by its own generality, competing grants of authority, or gaps. A thorough job would be difficult given the array of issues to be resolved. Adrift amid the complexities, the amenders could easily produce rules unrealistic in their own times and certainly in those to come. Moreover, the new, detailed prose of a thorough job would measurably tarnish the Constitution as an unchanging symbol of national continuity. Thus, even if formal amendment were realistic, it would not be wise.

The Judicial Route

The advantages and disadvantages of using judicial decisions to confirm the recommended war-power allocation are somewhat like those of formal amendment. What courts say about constitutional law has greater initial authority than what the President or Congress says. It follows that judicial decisions—more often than the claims and concessions of the political process—can quickly create beliefs about legal requirements that are sufficiently clear and strong to alter contrary power realities. Judges are also better able than politicians to avoid the dangers accompanying constitutional evolution by practice. When ruling on the authority of the President or Congress, courts are less likely to adopt self-serving interpretations. And since the public is more accustomed to thinking of constitutional construction as a judicial, rather than a presidential or congressional, function, people's commitment to the rule of law is less unhinged when courts rather than politicians nudge the Constitution along. On the other hand, judge-made rules tend to be more rigid and difficult to change than those made by claim and concession between the political branches, and courts have been reluctant to act on the war powers.

While judicial decision does resemble formal amendment, important distinctions exist. Courts would not feel any need to try to deal comprehensively with all of the war powers at one sitting. They can take on the pertinent issues one by one in concrete cases. Nor is judicial decision all that rigid and unchanging. When courts want legal evolution, they are prone to distinguish or simply ignore inconvenient precedent. And as the Warren Court made clear, federal judges in recent years have often been more willing to respond to changing national circumstances than have the President and Congress, for example, as regards desegregation and reapportionment.

Nonetheless, judges have generally avoided war-power cases, finding them too "political" for comfort.[1] It seems that the judges have been unduly fastidious. There are two senses in which courts have termed questions "political." The first is innocuous. It arises when a judge refuses to second-guess a decision made by one of the political branches because the Constitution gives that branch discretionary authority over the matter in question. A court might hold that the Constitution authorizes Congress to declare war as it sees fit, thereby precluding judicial review of political determinations by the legislators about whether, when, or why to declare war.

The second dimension of a political question is the problem. It arises when a judge refuses to decide whether a political branch has usurped another branch's constitutional authority or has exercised its own power in an unconstitutional fashion. Despite the possibility of illegal action, the court washes its hands of the matter on the ground that it is best left to resolution by the political process. A court might decline to hear a challenge to presidential war making, even though it is alleged to infringe constitutional authority of Congress. Or a judge might duck a challenge to a congressional declaration of war, even though it is alleged to violate a constitutional ban on aggressive use of American troops.

No one can say for sure whether courts are duty-bound to allocate constitutional authority between the political branches when the issue arises in a proper case.[2] As a practical matter many courts have relied on the political-question doctrine to avoid war-power issues, indicating that they felt no constitutional obligation to decide them.

Mr. Justice Brennan, writing for the Supreme Court in its 1962 reapportionment decision, *Baker v. Carr*,[3] laid down criteria for determining when a question is to be avoided by judges as political. His initial criterion dealt with political questions in the first sense, and the following criteria with the doctrine in its second sense:

Prominent on the surface of any case held to involve a political question is found a textually demonstrable constitutional commitment of the issue to a coordinate political department; or a lack of judicially discoverable and manageable standards for resolving it; or the impossibility of deciding without an initial policy determination of a kind clearly for nonjudicial discretion; or the impossibility of a court's undertaking independent resolution without expressing lack of the respect due coordinate branches of government; or an unusual need for unquestioning adherence to a political decision already made; or the potentiality of embarrassment from multifarious pronouncements by various departments on one question.

Certain of these criteria reflect separation-of-power considerations. They assume that the courts have less information, expertise, and flexibility than the political branches as regards some problems. To replace political decision with judicial in these areas would risk less competent answers. They assume also that there are areas of national policy in which the consistency and finality of one federal voice serves America's best interests. Judicial intervention could be dangerously disruptive. Thus judges have traditionally avoided ruling on military and foreign policy. These separation-of-power considerations recognize, too, that the political branches can urge one another to obey the Constitution. Like the courts, the President and Congress may construe the Constitution and are bound by oath to protect it. Unlike private citizens, each political branch has means to curb usurpation and abuse of authority by the other. The separation-of-power factors also take into account the need for comity among the three federal branches. It is easier for the federal courts to speak from Olympus to state officials or even national bureaucrats, than to instruct the President or Congress about their constitutional limits.

Other of the political-question criteria turn on judicial reluctance to enter uncharted areas. When the nature of the issues and even more their constitutional answers remain confused, judges prefer not to meet them in politically acute cases. Such cases are more readily handled when they fit into a well-developed body of law. Judges can then take them on with reasonable confidence in their capacity to understand the problems posed and to provide sound solutions within a feasible length of time. Cases involving civil liberties, though sometimes highly charged, tend to pose familiar issues and to turn on familiar law. As prior chapters make clear, division of the war powers between the President and Congress often presents little that is legally clear or comfortable.

The political-question criteria also reflect a third concern, epitomized by *Dred Scott* and its aftermath.[4] In that 1857 decision the Supreme Court held unconstitutional the Missouri Compromise's limitation on slavery in the territories. The Justices' decision was widely flouted, and the Court's moral and political standing debased as a result. Experiences such as *Dred Scott* encourage judges to avoid cases raising divisive issues, lest their decisions be ignored by one or another of the contending factions. Judges are encouraged even more strongly to shun cases in which public opinion will tolerate only one outcome, lest their decision be rejected by nearly everyone. To take such cases risks either judicial expediency or unenforceable judgments.

Though these political-question criteria suggest caution in war-power cases, they do not compel absolute avoidance. It is true that the courts have less information, expertise, and flexibility in dealing with questions of war and peace than does the President or Congress. But in cases concerning the nature of executive or congressional prerogative, the merits of a particular policy are not at issue, though they will doubtless be influenced if the case is decided. On what *is* at issue—the constitutional authority of one or both branches to set policy—the judges are at least as competent to decide as the President or Congress. So far as the indirect effect of such decisions on war and peace is concerned, it can be tolerated on most occasions. There is nothing sacrosanct about foreign affairs, a fact borne home increasingly as our domestic and external interests become entwined.

There are moments, of course, when a consistent, uncontradicted federal voice is of the essence, both in foreign and domestic affairs. On those occasions, judges should abstain and await better cases. The height of American involvement in a major conflict is likely to be a less opportune moment for judges to define the war powers than are other times, perhaps during the latter stages of that conflict's termination or at the outset of a minor use of force. And even though there will surely be some impact on policy whenever the court rules, that impact is a one-time price to be paid for the larger continuing good: a clearer, more common understanding of the prerogative in question.

True, the President and Congress have means to restrain one another's unconstitutional activities. But the courts sometimes step in when political checks and balances fail to operate. As regards comity among the federal branches, judicial intervention can be seen not as disrespect for the President or Congress but as the restoration of that mutual regard lost when one branch exceeds its constitutional authority and the other acquiesces. Nor, when an opportune war-power case is presented the Supreme Court, need it hang back for lack of familiar issues and doctrine. Our grasp of war-power problems and answers has advanced significantly since America intervened in Indochina. And the Supreme Court, unlike lower federal tribunals, has never invoked political question to avoid ruling on these matters. It has simply refused to hear such cases, relying on its discretionary jurisdiction. The Justices, accordingly, should have little trouble in taking an appropriate case.

What of *Dred Scott*? It was just suggested that the time for judicial action be picked wisely, with a view toward creating consensus on the constitutional rules in nonmomentous cases. The authority of the Supreme Court is such, however, that its decisions should be enforceable even if handed down amid moral and political passion. Open defiance of a final judicial directive is remote, especially if it runs against only the President or Congress, as opposed to both. To take an extreme example, compare the 1952 *Steel Seizure*[5] events with a hypothetical Supreme Court decision ordering the President to withdraw hundreds of thousands of American troops from a foreign war because he committed them on his own authority and never obtained congressional approval. *Steel Seizure* required President Truman to release steel mills that he had taken over to prevent their disruption by labor troubles. He acted to ensure uninterrupted arms and munitions for troops at war in Korea and for allies elsewhere, whose determination to resist communism was thought to rest in part on American ability to provide them weapons. Nonetheless, a majority of the Justices held that Truman lacked constitutional authority to take the mills, since his action violated Congress's Taft-Hartley strike remedy. The impact on American military policy of the hypothetical ruling, of course, would be far more direct and profound: that ruling would require actual withdrawal of American troops from an ongoing conflict.

For a number of reasons, Presidents will more readily obey decisions like *Steel Seizure* than the hypothetical troop withdrawal case. First, the effect of a *Steel Seizure* on the President's policy is less severe, and, second, such a ruling may enjoy greater domestic political support than decisions such as that hypothesized. Action whose principal costs are felt in this country will usually raise more political opposition than action whose principal impact falls abroad, especially if the domestic effects impinge on steel magnates and the foreign effects on draftees. Further, there will generally be greater tolerance for executive autocracy abroad than at home and greater fear of disrupting his foreign than his domestic initiatives lest national security suffer. Thus, seizing American steel mills is likely to be more risky for the President than involving us in combat in a distant land. Third, his disregard of a court order is more difficult when compliance requires relatively simple steps wholly within the United States. It would be far easier for an Executive to subvert an order to disengage American armies from a foreign war than to ignore an order to rescind a decree seizing private property in this country.

Even so, if confronted with the hypothetical decision, the President would almost certainly obey it, (1) out of respect for American practice that the Supreme Court has final authority on constitutional questions when it chooses to speak; (2) because defiance could destroy the legitimacy of his administration, quite possibly produce his removal from office, and undermine the stability of the country; (3) because Congress would very likely refuse to vote further tools to carry on the war. Nor could he expect courts committed to the unconstitutionality of his action to assist in the prosecution of draft dodgers and the like.

Indochina Precedent

During the Indochina conflict judges did grapple with executive and congressional war powers to an extent unequaled during prior American conflicts.[6] Well over twenty courts recognized that "war" was at hand and that serious questions existed as to the boundary between the President's and Congress's constitutional control over the struggle. With one exception, however, the courts did not directly attempt to alter the prevailing balance of power between the two branches.

Despite being confronted with repeated claims that the President was unconstitutionally making war and repeated requests that he be ordered to stop doing it, the great majority of the judges so confronted simply refused to interfere with the status quo. Some courts ruled that Congress had either authorized our Indochinese involvement in advance or ratified it after the fact —citing the Tonkin Gulf Resolution and, even after its repeal, military appropriation acts, extensions of the draft, and the like. This expansive view of what constitutes congressional approval was reinforced at times by a judicial conclusion that the legislators had ample means to redirect or end any executive use of force with which they disagreed. Other courts found that the issues posed were not appropriate for judicial resolution, usually on the ground that they were political questions. As a federal court of appeals said in August 1973:

Judge Judd [whose decision was being reviewed by the court of appeals] found that the continuing bombing of Cambodia, after the removal of American forces and prisoners of war from Vietnam, represents "a basic change in the situation: which must be considered in determining the duration of prior Congressional authorization." He further found such action a tactical decision not traditionally confided to the Commander-in-Chief. These are precisely the questions of fact involving military and diplomatic expertise not vested in the judiciary, which make the issue political and thus beyond the competence of [Judge Judd's] court or this court to determine. We are not privy to the information supplied to the Executive by his professional military and diplomatic advisers and even if we were, we are hardly competent to evaluate it. . . . It is true that we have repatriated American troops and have returned American ground forces in Vietnam but we have also negotiated a cease fire and have entered into the Paris Accords which mandated a cease fire in Cambodia and Laos. The President has announced that the bombing of Cambodia will terminate on August 15, 1973 and Secretary of State Rogers has submitted an affidavit to this court providing the justification for our military presence and action until that time. The situation fluctuates daily and we cannot ascertain at any fixed time either the military or diplomatic status. We are in no position to determine whether the Cambodian insurgents are patriots or whether in fact they are inspired and manned by North Vietnam Communists. While we as men may well agonize and bewail the horror of this or any war, the sharing of Presidential and Congressional responsibility particularly at this juncture is a bluntly political and not a judicial question.[7]

Judge Judd, whose decision was the object of this language, provided the most acute exception to the general rule of judicial nonintervention. On July 25, 1973, he ordered the Executive to stop "participating in any way in military activities in or over Cambodia or releasing any bombs which may fall in Cambodia." The judge issued this cease-and-desist order because he had concluded that "there is no existing Congressional authority to order military forces into combat in Cambodia or to release bombs over Cambodia, and . . . military activities in Cambodia by American armed forces are unauthorized and unlawful . . . ."[8]

Despite bizarre machinations, Judd's order never took hold. He himself postponed its initial effectiveness for two days in order to give the defendants an opportunity to seek a stay. On July 27 the court of appeals granted one, at the Executive's hurried request. Disappointed, the plaintiffs then asked the Supreme Court for help. On August 1 Justice Marshall denied their overture, refusing to set aside the stay issued by the court of appeals. Thereupon the plaintiffs sought out a more sympathetic Justice, William O. Douglas. On August 3 he did vacate the stay, thereby putting Judd's cease-and-desist order into effect. On August 4, Justice Marshall nullified Douglas's action by granting a new stay, after getting the support of the other members of the Court.[9] The court of appeals heard oral argument on August 8 and decided the case the same day. Two of the three appellate judges voted to reverse Judge Judd's decision, and the third voted to affirm it. In April 1974, long after the Cambodian bombing had stopped, the Supreme Court decided not to review the court of appeals' two-to-one reversal of Judge Judd.[10]

Indeed, throughout the course of the Indochina conflict most members of the Supreme Court—and thus the Court itself—declined to become involved except when involvement was unavoidable, as in the battle of the stays just described. Justice Douglas dissented strongly, urging his colleagues to review the Indochina cases.[11] Justice Stewart joined at times in Douglas's concern that the Court should take the cases, if not in Douglas's clear feeling that unconstitutionality was afoot. As early as 1967 Stewart would have reviewed a case brought by reluctant draftees. According to Stewart:

> There exist in this case questions of great magnitude. . . .
>
> I.   Is the present United States military activity in Vietnam a "war" within the meaning of Article I, Section 8, Clause 11, of the Constitution?
>
> II. If so, may the Executive constitutionally order the petitioners to participate in that military activity, when no war has been declared by the Congress?
>
> III. Of what relevance to Question II are the present treaty obligations of the United States?
>
> IV. Of what relevance to Question II is the Joint Congressional ("Tonkin Gulf") Resolution of August 10, 1964?
>
>   (a) Do present United States military operations fall within the terms of the Joint Resolution?
>
>   (b) If the Joint Resolution purports to give the Chief Executive authority to commit United States forces to armed conflict limited in scope only by his own absolute discretion, is the Resolution a constitutionally impermissible delegation of all or part of Congress' power to declare war?

These are large and deeply troubling questions. Whether the Court would ultimately reach them depends, of course, upon the resolution of serious preliminary issues of justiciability. We cannot make these problems go away simply by refusing to hear the case of three obscure Army privates. I intimate not even tentative views upon any of these matters, but I think the Court should squarely face them by granting certiorari and setting this case for oral argument.[12]

As we have seen, only one cease-and-desist order did emerge from the Indochina litigation, and it proved to be inoperative. Nonetheless, as the conflict wore on, courts became increasingly willing to probe the boundary between executive and congressional authority and to make statements hostile to the status quo. In April 1971 thirteen members of the House of Representatives went to court asking for a declaration that the Executive was waging an unconstitutional war and for an injunction forbidding him to fight further unless Congress "explicitly, intentionally and discretely authorized a continuation of the war . . . ."[13] The district court dismissed the case without reaching these issues. In March 1973 the court of appeals for the District of Columbia agreed that, at least on political-question grounds, the case had no future. But in the process of dismissing it, two of the appellate judges also decided that Congress had not validly assented to the war—a conclusion squarely at odds with the bulk of the prior Indochina cases. Judge Wyzanski wrote for himself and Judge Bazelon:

> The overwhelming weight of authority, including some earlier opinions by the present writer, holds that the appropriation, draft extension, and cognate laws enacted with direct or indirect reference to the Indo-China war, . . . did constitute a constitutionally permissible form of assent. . . .
>
> But Chief Judge Bazelon and I now regard that body of authority as unsound. It is, of course, elementary that in many areas of the law appropriations by Congress have been construed by the courts as involving Congressional assent to, or ratification of, prior or continuing executive action originally undertaken without Congressional legislative approval. Without a pause to cite . . . the vast body of cases involving such construction, it is more relevant to emphasize the special problem which is presented when one seeks to spell out from military appropriation acts, extensions of selective service laws, and cognate legislation the purported Congressional approval or ratification of a war already being waged at the direction of the President alone.

This court cannot be unmindful of what every schoolboy knows: that in voting to appropriate money or to draft men a Congressman is not necessarily approving of the continuation of a war no matter how specifically the appropriation or draft act refers to that war. A Congressman wholly opposed to the war's commencement and continuation might vote for the military appropriations and for the draft measures because he was unwilling to abandon without support men already fighting. An honorable, decent, compassionate act of aiding those already in peril is no proof of consent to the actions that placed and continued them in that dangerous posture. We should not construe votes cast in pity and piety as though they were votes freely given to express consent. Hence Chief Judge Bazelon and I believe that none of the legislation drawn to the court's attention may serve as a valid assent to the Vietnam war.[14]

Judge Tamm, the third member of the court, disagreed. Three months later, in June 1973, the entire nine-man District of Columbia court of appeals considered whether to rehear the case *en banc* to deal with the passage just quoted. Four judges voted for rehearing "to correct [its] manifest error,"[15] but their five colleagues chose not to permit rehearing, very probably because they saw no such error.

Similarly, in August 1973 when Justice Marshall upheld the stay of Judge Judd's cease-and-desist order, pending the order's review by the court of appeals, the Justice simultaneously expressed severe doubt about the constitutionality of the continued bombing:

A fair reading of Congress' actions concerning the war in Cambodia may well indicate that the Legislature has authorized only "partial hostilities"—that it has never given its approval to the war except to the extent that it was necessary to extricate American troops and prisoners from Vietnam. . . . Moreover, this Court could easily conclude that after the Paris Peace Accords, the Cambodian bombing is no longer justifiable as an extension of the war which Congress did authorize and that the bombing is not required by the type of pressing emergency which necessitates immediate presidential response.

Thus, if the decision were mine alone, I might well conclude on the merits that continued American military operations in Cambodia are unconstitutional.[16]

Given such precedent, future federal courts may well be

more willing than their predecessors to alter the status quo if the judges believe the prevailing balance of war powers between the President and Congress to be unconstitutional. Such judicial intervention has been further encouraged by post-Indochina developments. When confronting constitutional issues with acutely political overtones, the Supreme Court reached the Watergate merits, even though that required rejecting the President's interpretation of his constitutional authority. In July 1974 the Court voted that certain Nixon tapes and documents must be produced, stating in part:

In the performance of assigned constitutional duties each branch of the Government must initially interpret the Constitution, and the interpretation of its powers by any branch is due great respect from the others. The President's counsel, as we have noted, reads the Constitution as providing an absolute privilege of confidentiality for all Presidential communications. Many decisions of this Court, however, have unequivocally reaffirmed the holding of *Marbury* v. *Madison* . . . that "it is emphatically the province and duty of the judicial department to say what the law is." . . .

. . . .

. . . [I]n *Baker* v. *Carr*, . . . the Court stated:

"Deciding whether a matter has in any measure been committed by the Constitution to another branch of government, or whether the action of that branch exceeds whatever authority has been committed, is itself a delicate exercise in constitutional interpretation, and is a responsibility of this Court as ultimate interpreter of the Constitution."

Notwithstanding the deference each branch must accord the others, the "judicial Power of the United States" vested in the federal courts by . . . the Constitution can no more be shared with the Executive Branch than the Chief Executive, for example, can share with the Judiciary the veto power. . . . Any other conclusion would be contrary to the basic concept of separation of powers and the checks and balances that flow from the scheme of a tripartite government. . . . We therefore reaffirm that it is the province and duty of this Court "to say what the law is" with respect to the claim of privilege presented in this case.[17]

The same rationale could obviously lead the Court to define executive and congressional war powers.

The Political Route

Constitutional evolution by claim and concession between the President and Congress has the overriding virtue of probability. Unlike formal amendment and quite possibly judicial decision, the political process *will* operate in years to come, as it has in the years past, to shape the way in which the war powers are divided between the two branches.[18]

It is not likely that Presidents will move voluntarily toward the division of authority recommended in Chapter IX, except for its executive prerogative to set policy while Congress remains silent. Nor can Congress expect much aid and comfort from the federal bureaucracy. Though legislatively created and sustained, most national officials are far more responsive to the President's influence, and just as eager as he to minimize congressional interference in their affairs. Nonfederal opinion makers (the media, major businessmen and academics, governors, and so on) are at least one step removed from a capacity to affect the balance of war-peace powers, and a significant number of them will oppose much increase in congressional influence until the legislators first show the will and capacity to handle it. The voters could move allocational mountains at the electoral and Gallup polls. But public action requires that the issues first be framed and then popularized by a reformist elite such as solid majorities in both congressional houses. Change in presidential primacy of the last generation over war and peace is up to Congress.

Step one is the development by a majority in each house of the will to create a new relationship with the President. To develop the will, as to sign on with the Alcoholics Anonymous, there must first come acceptance that all is not well and that remedies do exist. Many legislators, however, will oppose for reasons of personal power the internal reforms needed to increase Congress's capacity for systematic, rational decision about foreign affairs. Some Congressmen will always prefer to avoid voting on such politically sensitive matters as war and peace until constituent opinion has shown them how to jump. In any given case, others will support the President's policy and be unwilling for that reason to defend Congress's constitutional interest in an appropriate voice. Persuasion or coercion of a reluctant Executive will be especially difficult on the sustained basis necessary to elicit his *continuing* cooperation. And most legislators will always be hard pressed to find time amid their other commitments to nurture the recommended division of the war powers. But there can be too much gloom and doom. Congress is far less a helpless creature of its own habits than the average alcoholic. A majority in both houses can develop the necessary will, and there are remedies. If the legislators were to strike out toward them, that alone could help firm their resolve. It would also help dispel the lack of confidence in congressional competence that has kept many legislators from demanding greater war powers for themselves, the President from acquiescing, and the country from insisting on it.

Step two is agreement in Congress on how the war powers should be constitutionally divided. Until majorities in both the Senate and House have their own claims clearly in mind, they will have difficulty bringing the Executive to concede them. Expectations about what the Constitution requires are matters of the mind, and thus readily susceptible to written and oral argument. Legislators can shape the views of other legislators, using their own persuasive powers and those of outside allies. A third step is reform of congressional ways of doing business to assist legislative decision making, and a fourth is for the legislators to bite the bullet and *actually begin* systematic participation in decisions about war and peace. Finally, Congress should enact war-power legislation that gives substance to steps one to four.

The rest of this chapter offers a few thoughts on step three. Especially in this century, Presidents have done very little to promote constant, focused congressional involvement in shaping American policy on war and peace. Nor have the legislators shown much interest in self-help. The Senate forfeited its opportunity in the late 1700s to become a plenary participant in American diplomacy, and Congress has never fully pulled itself together for foreign affairs. Its institutional difficulties have mounted with growth in Senate and House memberships, the Representatives' move into areas formerly senatorial preserves, and the spread of matters affecting war and peace throughout many committees on both sides of the Capitol. While teeming literature exists about how the Executive as well as Congress could improve the government's foreign-affairs machinery,[19] the legislators bear the greater onus of reform, since the status quo favors the President. Whatever the defects in his equipment, it is more geared to today's needs than the vintage model operated by Congress.

Do the legislators make their war-peace decisions in light of overall American foreign policy objectives and priorities? Unquestionably there are individual Senators and Representatives with as much wisdom on these scores as anyone in the Executive Branch, perhaps greater wisdom because Congressmen long involved in foreign affairs have thought more about objectives and priorities than the more transient Presidents and their advisers. But these sagacious Senators and Representatives are a few among 535, though they may be more than equal by dint of seniority. A significant element in Congress has little or no feel for foreign affairs. This element votes too.

Further, the splintering of power among various groups in Congress impedes consistent, integrated action. Decisions affecting war and peace are divided among numerous committees in both houses, the respective regulators of business on each floor, the full Senate and House, and their conference committees. Jurisdictional and personal antagonisms flower at each level. All too often there results piecemeal consideration of unitary problems, with predictably inconsistent solutions, or the adoption of measures attractive in isolation but at serious odds with other American interests. Congress at present does not approach the Executive in capacity to make decisions informed by overall objectives and priorities.

A remedy? Congress ought further to concentrate its decision making about war and peace. It would be impractical to center in one committee the oversight of all potentially relevant action. The committee's jurisdiction would be untenably sweeping. The heart of that action—military and diplomatic affairs—could be feasibly united, however. Then, by congressional custom, a Foreign and Military Affairs Committee could be involved in the work of other committees when issues before them bore directly on war and peace; joint hearings and reporting of legislation are means to this end.

Ideally, the union of military and diplomatic affairs should come in a standing joint committee with full authority to sponsor legislation.[20] In this manner, cooperation between the pertinent House and Senate establishments would be institutionally forced and the relative weakness of the House International Relations Committee in its own chamber overcome. Rivalry between foreign relations and armed services establishments within each house would also be attacked at its roots.

Such a joint committee in collaboration with the Executive, perhaps in response to an annual message from him, could periodically state a congressional view of foreign policy objectives and priorities. The committee could then work to ensure the passage of legislation consistent with its statement. Presumably the jurisdiction and cross-house composition of the joint committee would win it respect from appropriations czars and floor regulators. Its views ought also to have great influence on full Senate and House judgments.

Objection can be made to a joint Foreign and Military Affairs Committee on the ground that it would be too potent a shaper of legislation, easily overriding the ideas and qualms of Congressmen not in its councils, especially those of the newer Senators and Representatives. Or that it would come to be dominated by old hawks or old doves. But the beliefs of the committee's members and the extent of their disregard of other Congressmen's views would not be cast in stone. The committee's behavior could be influenced by the party caucuses responsible for its membership. Moreover, concern that it might wield power misses the point, if the goal is a Congress competent to deal with war and peace. Should the legislators quail at delegating authority to a few of their own—as they have so freely delegated it to the President—they cannot expect to keep up with him in setting American policy.

Another objection to a Joint Foreign and Military Affairs Committee is the fragility of its chances for creation. Too many baronies would be shaken to make union within each house likely, much less union between Senators and Representatives.

Assuming no change in committee structure, progress might still be made if party leaders were to fill the respective foreign affairs committees with strong, thoughtful figures and if they were to help these committees to positions of unique influence over war-power matters. The committees, in turn, could issue and police the periodic statements on foreign policy objectives and priorities noted earlier. Without unduly straining baronial sensibilities, they might collaborate with one another as well as the President in this effort, to avoid two statements of purpose, one for the Senate and another for the House.

Do the legislators have basic information about war-peace situations? Are they aware of alternatives for dealing with them and of expert appraisals, both technical and political, of their costs and benefits? Few if any legislators are now as competent as the President in these regards. Unlike the President, most Congressmen depend on the media for data about breaking developments. But emerging situations often elude either prediction by television and the press or comprehensive, accurate accounts as they unfold. A few Senators and Representatives do receive intelligence reports from the Executive, but often of a spotty, selective nature. Congress itself has established no reliable system to ensure that certain of its number are, in fact, systematically informed of imminent and ongoing events crucial to war and peace.

Once emerged, most facts essential to informed decision appear in readily accessible sources, such as the *New York Times*. But even then the information must be laboriously gathered and organized before it becomes useful. Alternative courses of action rarely leap full-blown from raw data. Defining them and evaluating their costs and benefits require significant thought and skill. As a rule, Presidents and Congressmen are expert in the political aspects of decision; they can realistically judge proposed action in terms of American values and needs. But they are usually less expert in technical matters; for example, the intricacies of military hardware or the governmental preferences of southeast Asians. Of course, even experts need their assumptions and judgments tested by their peers. Congressional staff capacity in these regards pales beside presidential.

For the legislators to be meaningfully involved with foreign affairs, the data and expertise available to them need not approach the gross tonnage of each in the Executive Branch. All the legislators need is enough information and skill to evaluate presidential proposals and cure their defects. That point is reached when congressional committees no longer lack the facts or expertise to judge executive policies, and thus when they no longer must either accept them on faith or mindlessly tamper with them. A few good people can evaluate and cure programs that legions have been required to formulate.

Several means are open by which Congress can get the necessary information and skill: (1) more people and computers for existing committee staffs; (2) greater reliance on consultants (*e.g.*, the Office of Technology Assessment or private experts) for gathering and evaluating data; (3) more systematic aid on both scores from elements in the bureaucracy, such as the Central Intelligence Agency, which can be directed by law to report fully to Congress as well as the President; and (4) heightened cooperation from persons high in the Executive Branch, above all, from the upper State and Defense Departments and the National Security Council. The extent to which route (1) must be taken depends on how extensively the other three are traveled. If they prove inadequate, then Congress must develop in-house means of filling the gap. It seems, however, that most information problems could be solved by executive production of the data, whether voluntarily or under congressional pressure. Expertise, in turn, could come from small, elite congressional staffs skilled in evaluating and curing proposals obtained from others.

Assuming available data and expert evaluation, are the Senators and Representatives as likely as the Executive to take them into account in their decisions? Comments made about awareness of foreign policy objectives and priorities apply here too. Some Congressmen are at least as competent as the President, but most are not, and all of them vote. The immense press of business bearing on Senators and Representatives, coupled with their varied interests and abilities, ensures that most will come to grips with very few issues concerning war and peace.

A similar remedy applies: delegation within Congress to the

pertinent committee or committees, with a heavy presumption in favor of their recommendations. For that delegation to work, congressional party leaders must become more willing to see that the committee members themselves have the interest, ability and time to do their jobs. They could then lead Congress toward necessary continuity or revision in policy, even toward open support of vital but unpopular action. Speedy recommendations could be expected from such Senators and Representatives if they began from a base of information and expertise like that from which the Executive moves to rapid decision. It is also credible that these legislators, if not the full House and Senate, could guard classified data and act in secret as necessary. Congress, moreover, could authorize a Joint Committee on Foreign and Military Affairs or, failing that, the leaders of existing committees with similar jurisdiction to advise the President during crises, especially those involving an American response before any resort to Congress itself is realistic.

In May 1975 Defense Secretary James Schlesinger suggested that NATO must stand ready to repel Soviet invasion of Western Europe with nuclear counterattack: "[T]he attack should be delivered with sufficient shock and decisiveness to forcibly change the perceptions of the Warsaw Pact leaders and create a situation conducive to negotiations."[21] Without a congressional "crisis" committee,[22] it is probable that only an executive hand would significantly shape American decisions whether to make nuclear war in Europe or elsewhere—despite the elemental impact of any such decisions on America.

CHAPTER XI

The War Powers
Resolution of 1973

IN THE spring of 1965 the United States sent troops a short distance into the Dominican Republic. Although desiring to protect Americans threatened there by civil strife, President Johnson also feared that the Dominicans might be about to go the way of Castro's Cubans. His prophylactic intervention in Dominican affairs provided the catalyst for recent struggles between the Executive and Congress over the war powers—Chairman J. William Fulbright of the Senate Foreign Relations Committee ended 1965 actively disillusioned with presidential direction of American foreign policy. The Indochina War massively spread his disillusionment. Spurred especially by the Fulbright Committee, many legislators began to reconsider Cold War assumptions about the proper roles of the President and Congress in controlling American use of force abroad. That reconsideration peaked only when President Nixon resigned.

Although attention focused on military action in Vietnam, Laos, and Cambodia, Congress was busy on related fronts as well. Legislators demanded that the President disclose all existing executive agreements with other states, and they moved to enlarge congressional control over future American commitments abroad, especially those with war and peace consequences. Efforts were made to cut foreign aid radically, including grants for military purposes, and to reduce spending by the Defense Department for weapons and overseas bases. Steps were taken to winnow the huge emergency authority delegated to the Executive by statutes passed and left standing over the prior forty years (for instance, authority over the economy and the size of the armed forces). Legislators also tried to prevent the President from either impounding congressional appropriations, on the one hand, or spending monies not appropriated (particularly for military ends), on the other. Congress sought to pry information from the Executive branch on a timely and comprehensive basis, vigorously rejecting claims of executive privilege even as to matters said to involve national defense. There were attempts to ensure congressional oversight of covert actions, whether intelligence and military operations abroad or security measures at home. Senate confirmation was demanded for appointees to a number of newly crucial executive posts, and Senate review of nominees was taken as an opportunity to scrutinize and limit executive policy. Then, too, the legislators moved to lessen presidential influence by improving their own decision-making procedures, especially committee and budgetary practices.

All of this ferment was important to the division of the war powers between the two branches. Most telling were two of its aspects. First, Congress ended American involvement in the Indochina War by refusing to fund it any longer. The final in a series of fiscal restraints came in the Church-Case Amendment to the Continuing Appropriations Resolution of 1974, which banned outright the use of federal funds for any "military or paramilitary operations" "in," "over" or "off the shores of" the whole of Vietnam, Laos, and Cambodia.[1] Never before had Congress used its appropriations power to withdraw the United States from a major conflict. Equally novel was the War Powers Resolution of 1973. Again, never before had Congress set out procedures for how the President and legislators are to go about deciding whether to fight. Together, these unprecedented developments offer Congress the best chance it has had since 1789 for an assured voice in war and peace decisions. Of the two, the appropriations ban suggests that the legislators will command the Executive's attention whenever they become restless, but the War Powers Resolution has the greater potential for long-term legislative influence. Cutting off funds is a drastic remedy not easily adopted even in extreme circumstances and one rarely conducive to thorough debate about policy. Systematic legislative influence is more likely to flow from procedures which cover mild as well as severe cases, which direct debate to the policy merits without fiscal distractions, and which provide unavoidable channels for communication between the Executive and Congress.

The Constitution's necessary-and-proper clause permits Congress to adopt measures such as the War Powers Resolution, which reiterate constitutional requirements and define procedures for their implementation.[2] Section 2(b) of the Resolution duly recites: "Under article I, section 8, of the Constitution, it is specifically provided that the Congress shall have the power to make all laws necessary and proper for carrying into execution, not only its own powers but also all other powers vested by the Constitution in the Government of the United States, or in any department or officer hereof."[3]

Congress's authority to reiterate constitutional requirements, however, is far narrower than its power to define how they are to be implemented. No congressional discretion exists concerning the *nature* of the constitutional requirements (for example, under what circumstances the President may commit troops without prior legislative approval). So far as the necessary-and-proper clause is concerned, Congress's only option is to reiterate the Constitution, elaborating perhaps but not changing it. Wide legislative discretion exists, on the other hand, over the choice of means: The President can be ordered to give up old methods of implementation (for instance, episodic, often untimely reporting of troop commitments) and adopt new ones (complete, prompt reporting).

As a practical matter, of course, the legislators do have some leeway with respect to the nature of the constitutional requirements. It comes from the same source as the President's— uncertainty as to what the Constitution means. The greater the ambiguity, the greater the difficulty in separating a definition of constitutional requirements from the adoption of means to implement the Constitution. War-power legislation simply requiring the President to report his commitment of troops to combat seems to involve "means" alone. But such legislation moves toward constitutional "definition" if it requires prior congressional approval for American use of force except on certain occasions defined in the statute; or if it puts a deadline on any use of force begun by the President alone unless Congress subsequently approves the venture; or if it permits Congress to end an executive use of force by concurrent resolution, that is, by a measure not subject to veto.

Once war-power legislation moves beyond means to definition, it has no more right to automatic acceptance by the President than his constitutional claims have to automatic acceptance by Congress. If the President signs the act, he concedes its claims, opening the way to consensus. If he vetoes it and is upheld, then no law formally exists, but prudence may lead the Executive to accept many of the measure's would-be requirements, and the legislators will have a concrete notion of the war powers that they think are constitutionally theirs. If the President's veto is overridden, he may still refuse to acknowledge the legislation, unless the courts tell him to do so. Prudence, however, will dictate even more strongly his acquiescence in the act's requirements, and Congress will be even more confident of its war-power role. Still, if the legislation strongly offends the President's understanding of his constitutional powers or of the national good, he may defy it. And he almost surely will obey only the narrow letter of the law. In other words, a war-power statute is most likely to foster a clear, enforceable division of authority between the two branches if it is signed by the President. Thus, if there are a few basics on which the two branches can agree, the legislation ought to stick to them, leaving other aspects of the division of authority to evolve from these basics.

It comes as no surprise, then, that the War Powers Resolution of 1973 and its proponents took care to stress that they were *not* engaged in constitutional definition. As Section 2(a) of the measure chastely states: "It is the purpose of this joint resolution to fulfill the intent of the framers of the Constitution . . . ." Or in the words of Senator Muskie:

The bill does not undertake to impose on the President a modification of his constitutional powers. It does not undertake to assert a restatement of Congress' view as to the President's role with respect to the warmaking power.

What it undertakes to do is to establish a procedure for comity as to different views in the future, so that Congress can be brought in from the periphery of the warmaking power to its center in order to exercise its proper role.[4]

The Executive disagreed. President Nixon felt that "the restrictions which this resolution would impose upon the authority of the President are . . . unconstitutional," adding that "[t]he only way in which the constitutional powers of a branch of the Government can be altered is by amending the Constitution—and any attempt to make such alterations by legislation alone is clearly without force."[5] While it grates to hear a President say that constitutional change may come only by formal amendment in light of our Executives' historic taste for amendment by practice, it was seemly for Mr. Nixon to point out that the War Powers Resolution does attempt a bit of constitutional definition in Congress's image. That fact has lessened the generosity with which the White House has implemented the measure.

The steps leading to its enactment were complex and contentious.[6] They began with efforts by Senator Fulbright in the late 1960s to reduce presidential freedom in foreign affairs. On June 25, 1969, the Senate by vote of 70 to 16 adopted the following proviso, a modified version of one that the Senator had introduced almost two years earlier:

Resolved, That (1) a national commitment for the purpose of this resolution means the use of the armed forces of the United States on foreign territory, or a promise to assist a foreign country, government or people by the use of the armed forces or financial resources of the United States, either immediately or upon the happening of certain events, and (2) it is the sense of the Senate that a national commitment by the United States results only from affirmative action taken by the executive and legislative branches of the United States Government by means of a treaty, statute, or concurrent resolution of both Houses of Congress specifically providing for such a commitment.[7]

On November 16, 1970, by a vote of 289 to 39, the House of Representatives took its initial step, passing a measure requiring the President to report quickly to Congress, in writing, concerning the legal basis, circumstances, and anticipated scope of any commitment of American troops abroad, whether to enlarge forces already there, make new deployments, or fight. Later House resolutions leading to ultimate agreement with the Senate in the fall of 1973 became progressively more severe in their limits on presidential freedom, but the Representatives continued to hinge their scheme on after-the-fact reporting by the Executive.

The Senate, to the contrary, was more interested in preventing the President from acting in the first place without prior congressional approval, except in a few carefully defined circumstances. Thus Section 3 of the Senators' 1973 bill provided that

[i]n the absence of a declaration of war by the Congress, the Armed Forces of the United States may be introduced in hostilities, or in situations where imminent involvement in hostilities is clearly indicated by the circumstances, only—

(1) to repel an armed attack upon the United States, its territories and possessions; to take necessary and appropriate retaliatory actions in the event of such an attack; and to forestall the direct and imminent threat of such an attack;

(2) to repel an armed attack against the Armed Forces of the United States located outside of the United States, its territories and possessions, and to forestall the direct and imminent threat of such an attack;

(3) to protect while evacuating citizens and nationals of the United States, as rapidly as possible, from (A) any situation on the high seas involving a direct and imminent threat to the lives of such citizens and nationals, or (B) any country in which such citizens and nationals are present with the express or tacit consent of the government of such country and are being subjected to a direct and imminent threat to their lives, either sponsored by such government or beyond the power of such government to control; but the President shall make every effort to terminate such a threat without using the Armed Forces of the United States, and shall, where possible, obtain the consent of the government of such country before using the Armed Forces of the United States to protect citizens and nationals of the United States being evacuated from such country; or

(4) pursuant to specific statutory authorization . . . .[8]

As majorities in the House and Senate struggled toward compromise, the dominant issue remained whether to try to define the occasions on which the President might use force without prior congressional approval, and if he might, whether the President had independent constitutional authority to act under those circumstances or merely delegated authority from Congress. Crucial also was the issue whether to impose time limits on any presidential action, and if so, what deadlines (30 days? 120?), measured from which tripwire (from the time of an executive order committing the troops? from the moment Congress receives the President's report? and if that, how long to submit the report after the order?). Also hotly debated was whether Congress should be able to end an executive initiative by inaction—by simply failing to vote one way or another on it, as opposed to explicitly voting no.[9] Similarly contested was whether Congress might stop executive action by concurrent resolution or whether it should do so only by a vote subject to presidential veto. Finally, the nature of presidential consultation with Congress was the subject of much concern. While the House would not touch the Senate's definitional approach, it did warm to the notions of a deadline on presidential initiatives and their termination either by congressional inaction or concurrent resolution. The growing militancy of the House is epitomized by evolution in the consultation language included in the various House resolutions. The first urged the President to consult with Congress "when feasible." The fourth and last demanded that "the President in every possible instance shall consult with the leadership and appropriate committees of the Congress . . . ."[10]

On October 10, 1973, the Senate agreed by a vote of 75 to 20 to a compromise based on the House version. The Representatives concurred two days later, 238 to 123. On October 24 President Nixon vetoed the legislation, finding it "both unconstitutional and dangerous to the best interest of our Nation." On November 7 Congress overrode the veto. The text of the Resolution and veto appear in Appendix C. They are prime examples of conflicting congressional and executive claims regarding the war powers.

Congressional opinion was not monolithic. Though the War Powers Resolution as adopted did not include the constitutional definition that Senator Jacob Javits had championed, he nonetheless liked it: "The fact is that never in the history of this country has an effort been made to restrain the war powers in the hands of the President . . . . [I]t will make history in this country as has never been made before."[11] But some other supporters of the Senate's definitional approach viewed the Resolution "as a historic surrender," not "a historic recapture."[12] Thomas F. Eagleton and Gaylord Nelson, cosponsors of the Senate bill, bitterly opposed the final act. In Eagleton's terms:

If we are reluctant to deal with the constitutional issue of prior authority, then we will continue to be confronted in years to come with the prospect of desperately trying to stop misbegotten wars.

War powers legislation that is meaningful has to deal with the fundamental causes of the constitutional impasse that plagued the Nation for the past decade. It must . . . in the most precise legal language, carefully spell out those powers which adhere to the Executive by reason of his status as Commander in Chief and his obligation to act in emergencies to repel attacks upon the Nation, its forces, and its citizens abroad. For the rest, such legislation must make clear that all remaining decisions involved in taking the Nation to war are reserved to the elected representatives of the people—as the Constitution so says, the Congress.[13]

But others equally devoted to congressional prerogative feared precisely such a spelling out of presidential authority. Senator Fulbright had cautioned:

I am apprehensive that the very comprehensiveness and precision of the contingencies listed . . . may be drawn upon by future Presidents to explain or justify military initiatives which would otherwise be difficult to explain or justify. A future President might, for instance, cite "secret" or "classified" data to justify almost any conceivable foreign military initiative as essential to "forestall the direct and imminent threat" of an attack on the United States or its armed forces abroad.[14]

And, of course, a significant number of legislators saw even the House approach, embodied in the adopted Resolution, as an unconstitutional or unwise restriction on presidential power. These people made up most of the 18 Senators and 135 Representatives who voted to sustain the President's veto.

Why after almost two hundred years did Congress bring itself to institutional legislation on the war powers? A variety of factors were at work, some rooted in the Constitution and others in passing political exigencies—as is usually the case with great constitutional issues. Majorities in Congress felt a need to reassert themselves in decisions about war and peace. President Nixon's 1970 Cambodian incursion, sprung as suddenly on Congress as on the North Vietnamese, his Christmas bombing of North Vietnam in 1972, carried out in the teeth of profound congressional disquiet, and his continued bombing of Cambodia in the summer of 1973, after Congress had forced an end to American fighting in Vietnam, all against a background of presidential sway during the Cold War, had created serious constitutional imbalance, so far as most Senators and Representatives were concerned.

Further, it was presidential prerogative's bad luck that the gestation of the War Powers Resolution coincided with Watergate. The latter led most Congressmen to see constitutional imbalance in many aspects of executive power, not just those involving foreign affairs. Final action on the Resolution coalesced with the dismissal of Special Prosecutor Archibald Cox and the ensuing resignation of Attorney General Elliot Richardson, as well as with the mushrooming White House tapes controversy.

More mundane factors were also at work. Before the vote on Nixon's veto of the Resolution, the House in 1973 had sustained five successive executive vetoes. Its Democratic majority was eager to override for the sake of the party. Similarly, the 1972 election had produced numerous new members of Congress, most of them Democrats eager to vote against anything Nixonian. There was also a successful lobbying effort to win for the override a number of Representatives who had voted against the Resolution on the ground that it was too weak. Five such votes were turned around; the override margin in the House was four votes. Finally, majority sentiment in both Congress and the country had decisively rejected continued American involvement in Indochina, thereby removing the inhibitions on votes against a President and his policy that exist when the country is at war. Conditions were prime for Congress to stake an unparalleled claim to the war powers.

Constitutional Definition

In the War Powers Resolution, two-thirds of the Senate and House defined the Constitution as subjecting to legislative control all American involvement in imminent or actual combat, except perhaps for hostilities on American territory. Thus under Section 5(b) of the measure, the absence of congressional approval for such involvement compels its end after sixty days, unless Congress extends the deadline, is unable to meet in the wake of armed attack on America, or the President obtains an extra thirty days of grace by certifying in writing that our troops' safety requires their continued use during the withdrawal process. And under Section 5(c), "at any time that United States Armed Forces are engaged in hostilities outside the territory of the United States, its possessions and territories without a declaration of war or specific statutory authorization, such forces shall be removed by the President if the Congress so directs by concurrent resolution." In short, Congress claims that the President may not constitutionally commit our forces to foreign hostilities unless the legislators either explicitly authorize combat in advance or ratify it within a set time after its beginning. Further, Congress asserts that no veto is constitutionally permissible when the legislative process runs in reverse, that is, when the President commits troops without prior congressional authorization. In that event, Section 5(b) permits either the House or Senate to terminate the executive initiative simply by failing to ratify it before the statutory deadline, and Section 5(c) permits majorities in both houses to abrogate it at any time by concurrent resolution.

The principal parent of the Resolution, Representative Clement J. Zablocki, described its potential in these terms:

Our purpose . . . was to provide Congress with a two-barrel approach . . . to ending a commitment of troops ordered by the President. The first of that so-called two-barrel approach involves the 60-day period at the end of which the President would have to end the commitment of troops unless Congress, in effect, exercises its exclusive warmaking powers by endorsing or approving the action through a declaration of war or a specific authorization. . . .

The second barrel . . . involves the concurrent resolution which we regard as a statutorily legal method of ending the commitment of troops. The thought behind the desirability of the concurrent resolution route is obvious: since the Constitution gives Congress—and only Congress—the power to declare war, Congress had to have a nonvetoable method of demonstrating, if it so chose, that it did not wish to declare war, even before the expiration of the 60-day period. We recognized that the Constitution clearly states that the President is Commander in Chief but it also states with even greater clarity that only Congress can declare war.

Granted, Congress may have abdicated that power over the last few decades through inaction; as a result, Presidents began to assume the power. In time, this assumption of power by Presidents led to the erroneous idea that it was an inherent or implied Presidential power.[15]

Having claimed legislative control over American involvement in combat, Congress went on in the Resolution to read the Constitution as requiring *prior* legislative approval for such involvement except on two occasions. Thus Section 2(c): "The constitutional powers of the President as Commander-in-Chief to introduce United States Armed Forces into hostilities, or into situations where imminent involvement in hostilities is clearly indicated by the circumstances, are exercised only pursuant to (1) a declaration of war, (2) specific statutory authorization, or (3) a national emergency created by attack upon the United States, its territories or possessions, or its armed forces." In the legislators' view, the President on his own authority may *constitutionally* commit us to combat simply to repel an attack on American territory or on our troops abroad.[16] Ironically, this reading of executive prerogative is narrower even than the definition in the Senate bill, quoted previously.

Congress nailed Section 2(c)'s constitutional position tighter in Section 8(d) (2): "Nothing in this joint resolution . . . shall be construed as granting any authority to the President with respect to the introduction of United States Armed Forces into

hostilities or into situations wherein an involvement in hostilities is clearly indicated by the circumstances which authority
he would not have had in the absence of this joint resolution."
And the legislators apparently hoped to force the President
either to accept their reading of the Constitution in Section 2(c),
openly defy it, or to plead mea culpa, because Section 4(a) (B)
demands that he explain to Congress "the constitutional . . .
authority" for any commitment of troops to combat, should he
do so without prior legislative approval.

How do the constitutional conclusions of the War Powers
Resolution stand in relation to those reached in Chapters VIII
and IX? The judgment that American involvement in combat is
ultimately subject to congressional control seems sound for reasons developed there. Equally sound is the act's provision that
Congress may end presidential initiatives by concurrent resolution, again for reasons already noted.[17]

But the legislation's apparent distinction between combat on
American territory and abroad lacks merit. In both instances,
as suggested previously, Congress should have authority to
curb executive war making.[18] Nor does the Resolution indicate
with sufficient clarity that Congress may *condition*, as well as
terminate, executive policy. The distinction between an absolute congressional ban on American involvement in combat
and the imposition of congressional conditions on it has already
been noted. Explicit recognition of the distinction is important
to avoid presidential pretense that such conditions are the same
as strategy or tactics and therefore wholly within executive
control.

The act's assumption that Congress must explicitly approve
executive use of force, if the use is to be constitutional, does
not seem ultimately sound. Defects in such a notion, especially
one buttressed by a deadline for ratification, have already been
detailed. Similarly, Section 2(c)'s severe limits on presidential
discretion to commit troops have scant merit. Under this section's constitutional definition, Presidents could never on their
own authority direct American troops to confront those of
another state in order to protect American civilians or property
attacked abroad, to assist international peace keeping or

humanitarian rescue, to defend the territorial integrity of Mexico against foreign attack, and the like.

While the union of Sections 2(c), 4(a) (B), and 8(d) (2), described earlier, suggests that the legislators meant their niggardly reading of presidential war powers to govern American practice,[19] other evidence exists that this was not really congressional intent. The October 4, 1973, "Joint Explanatory Statement of the Committee of Conference" hedged: "Section 2(c) is a statement of the authority of the Commander-in-Chief respecting the introduction of United States Armed Forces into hostilities or into situations where imminent involvement in hostilities is clearly indicated by the circumstances. Subsequent sections of the joint resolution are not dependent upon the language of this subsection, as was the case with a similar provision of the Senate bill . . . ."[20] Senator Eagleton dismissed the section as "the pious pronouncement of nothing."[21] Senator Muskie attempted an explanation that seems as cogent as any, other than that the provision was included to placate backers of the Senate bill:[22]

> It is true . . . that this language is not operative language.
>
> Why was it put into the bill?
>
> It was put into the bill as an indication that, in enacting a bill, Congress did not intend to surrender any of its constitutional powers with respect to the making of war.
>
> The remainder of the bill is a procedural bill, undertaken to insure consultation by the President with Congress and undertaking to put in the hands of Congress the procedure for terminating any hostilities into which the President may have plunged us, whether or not his action in so doing conformed with our view as to what his constitutional powers might be.[23]

Presidents Ford and Carter ignored the limits of Section 2(c),[24] and their successors are likely to ignore them. The State Department has concluded that the proviso "does not constitute a legally binding definition of the President's Constitutional power as Commander-in-Chief."[25] And while modest as such definitions go, the June 1975 formulation of that power by the Department's Legal Adviser offered no comfort to the provision:

Besides the three situations listed in subsection 2(c) . . . , it appears that the President has the constitutional authority to use the Armed Forces to rescue American citizens abroad, to rescue foreign nationals where such action directly facilitates the rescue of U.S. citizens abroad, to protect U.S. Embassies and Legations abroad, to suppress civil insurrection, to implement and administer the terms of an armistice or cease-fire designed to terminate hostilities involving the United States, and to carry out the terms of security commitments contained in treaties. We do not, however, believe that any such list can be a complete one, just as we do not believe that any single definitional statement can clearly encompass every conceivable situation in which the President's Commander in Chief authority could be exercised.[26]

To the extent that Section 2(c) does lack binding effect, its unduly restrictive view of presidential authority is softened. But, to precisely that same extent, the legislation takes on a quixotic air, detrimental to the rule of law. Clear, enforceable constitutional rules, as well as the war-power ends discussed earlier, would have been better served had Congress foregone the section.

Implementing Procedures

How does the War Powers Resolution implement the legislators' definition of the constitutional requirements? As just noted, it provides very few means to enforce Section 2(c). The legislation is far more thorough about obtaining information from, and consultation with, the President and about focused, expedited congressional action on the particulars of any use of force. President Nixon's veto message did not attack these aspects of the act. As the State and Defense Departments pointed out in June 1975, the message "indicated that portions of the War Powers Resolution, including sections 5(b) and 5(c), are unconstitutional. No such position was expressed as to section 4," concerning presidential reports to Congress.[27] In fact, one of the few provisions of the Resolution singled out for praise in the veto message was the third, or consultation, section:

The responsible and effective exercise of the war powers requires the fullest cooperation between the Congress and the Executive and the prudent fulfillment by each branch of its constitutional responsibilities. [The Resolution] includes certain constructive measures which would foster this process by enhancing the flow of information from the executive branch to the Congress. Section 3, for example, calls for consultations with the Congress before and during the involvement of United States forces in hostilities abroad. This provision is consistent with the desire of this Administration for regularized consultations with the Congress in an even wider range of circumstances.

Ironically, after the act went into effect, the most bitter congressional charges that "the executive branch proclivity is toward evasive and selective interpretation" of the Resolution have concerned consultation.[28]

Information

Legislative decisions about the use of force depend on the timely receipt by Congress of pertinent information, much of it from the President. Matters relevant to his reporting include what sorts of circumstances require a report, how rapidly it must be made, its content, whether it is to be periodically updated, and the mechanics for laying it before the various legislators. Sections 4 and 5(a) of the Resolution deal with these questions:

Sec. 4(a)   In the absence of a declaration of war, in any case in which United States Armed Forces are introduced—

(1)   into hostilities or into situations where imminent involvement in hostilities is clearly indicated by the circumstances;

(2)   into the territory, airspace or waters of a foreign nation, while equipped for combat, except for deployments which relate solely to supply, replacement, repair, or training of such forces; or

(3)   in numbers which substantially enlarge United States Armed Forces equipped for combat already located in a foreign nation:

the President shall submit within 48 hours to the Speaker of the House . . . and to the President pro tempore of the Senate a report, in writing, setting forth—

(A)   the circumstances necessitating the introduction of United States Armed Forces;

(B)   the constitutional and legislative authority under which such introduction took place; and

(C)   the estimated scope and duration of the hostilities or involvement.

(b)   The President shall provide such other information as the Congress may request in the fulfillment of its constitutional responsibilities with respect to committing the Nation to war and to the use of United States Armed Forces abroad.

(c)   . . . [T]he President shall, so long as such armed forces continue to be engaged in such hostilities or situation, report to the Congress periodically on the status of such hostilities or situation as well as on the scope and duration of such hostilities or situation, but in no event shall he report to the Congress less often than once every six months.

Sec. 5(a)   Each report submitted pursuant to section 4(a) (1) shall be transmitted to the Speaker . . . and to the President pro tempore . . . on the same calendar day. Each report so transmitted shall be referred to the Committee on [International Relations] of the House of Representatives and to the Committee on Foreign Relations of the Senate for appropriate action. If, when the report is transmitted, the Congress has adjourned sine die or has adjourned for any period in excess of three calendar days, the Speaker . . . and the President pro tempore . . . if they deem it advisable (or if petitioned by at least 30 percent of the membership of their respective Houses) shall jointly request the President to convene Congress in order that it may consider the report and take appropriate action . . . .

Sections 4 and 5(a) are basically sound, with several reservations. There is no reason for Section 4(a) to dispense with a presidential report if Congress has declared war, while requiring one if Congress has *previously* authorized the use of force by legislation other than a formal declaration.[29] Since Section 8(a) of the Resolution indicates that the President is to assume authority to use force only from the most explicit congressional statements to that effect, all prior legislative approvals should be regarded as the same, whether they are clothed in a declaration of war or some other form.

There is some ambiguity in the terms used by Section 4(a) (1) to (3) to describe what sorts of circumstances require a report. The first answer to this ambiguity must come in the Executive's appraisal of the facts of each case. In October 1974 Secretary of State Kissinger explained that several months ago the Office of the Secretary of Defense instituted an arrangement whereby the Legal Adviser to the Chairman of the Joint Chiefs of Staff informs the Department of Defense General Counsel of all troop deployment actions routed through the Chairman's office which could raise a question as to whether a report to the Congress is required. In implementation of that arrangement a written instruction was promulgated establishing a War Powers Reporting System within the Operations Directorate of the JCS. Arrangements have been made for this Department's Legal Adviser to receive the same information as is supplied to the DOD General Counsel. Consultations between the two departments' legal counsels will be arranged as needed.[30]

Especially open to disagreement are the meaning of "hostilities" and "imminent involvement." Legislative history of the Resolution indicates that Congress meant for these words to cast a broad net: "In addition to a situation in which fighting actually has begun, *hostilities* also encompasses a state of confrontation in which no shots have been fired but where there is a clear and present danger of armed conflict. *'Imminent hostilities'* denotes a situation in which there is a clear potential either for such a state of confrontation or for actual armed conflict."[31] The State and Defense Departments adopted more restrictive "working definitions" of these terms:

"[H]ostilities" . . . mean a situation in which units of the U.S. armed forces are actively engaged in exchanges of fire with opposing units of hostile forces, and "imminent hostilities" . . . mean a situation in which there is a serious risk from hostile fire to the safety of United States forces. In our view, neither term necessarily encompasses irregular or infrequent violence which may occur in a particular area.

. . . .

. . . Whether or not . . . rifle fire constitute[s] hostilities would seem to us to depend upon the nature of the source of this rifle fire—i.e., whether it came from a single individual or from a battalion of troops, the intensity of the fire, the proximity of hostile weapons and troops to the helicopter landing zone, and other evidence that might indicate an intent and ability to confront U.S. forces in armed combat.[32]

These interpretative issues matter, of course, because they

determine whether the President should report at all and, if so, whether under Section 4(a) (1), rather than under Section 4(a) (2) or (3). Recall that under Section 5 of the act, *only* Section 4(a) (1) circumstances give Congress the power to end an executive initiative by inaction or concurrent resolution.

This does not mean that a President can count on avoiding the Resolution by flatly refusing to report or by declining to report under Section 4(a) (1) even though hostilities are at hand. Senator Javits has felt "it . . . timely to remind the Executive Branch—as was made clear during the floor debate on the Conference Report—failure properly to label a report required . . . under Section 4, or even a failure to submit a required report, will in no way delay or frustrate the triggering of the 60-day clock and the provisions of Sections 4 through 7 of the law."[33] In 1975 the Legal Adviser to the State Department did not quarrel with this view, though he noted that the Executive is just as entitled as Congress to interpret what the Resolution requires: "[I]t is perfectly within the power of Congress to decide even if we reported under 4(a) (2) that it was really 4(a) (1) and treat that as the beginning of the 60-day or 90-day period trigger. I don't agree that the competency is absolute. . . . [T]he Executive can have an interpretation just as the Congress can have an interpretation and in the last analysis it would arise on some sort of lawsuit which the courts would probably decide."[34]

Section 4(a) directs that the President report to Congress "within 48 hours" after "any case [listed in Sections 4(a) (1) to (3)] in which United States Armed Forces are introduced."[35] It is not likely that the Executive can both manage a crisis and prepare a report in much less time. The *Mayaguez* report anticipated the deadline by four hours. It reached the offices of the Speaker and President pro tempore in the middle of the night, after the President "had to be awakened at 2 o'clock in the morning in order to read and sign his report . . . ."[36] But it is also true that many American uses of forces will be over before a 48-hour report makes its way to the legislators. Thus, to the extent that the Resolution depends on congressional reaction to formal executive reports, it concedes control over short-term military crises to the President.

As regards Section 4(a) (A&C), a more particularized statement of content would be desirable (since Presidents will be prone to say as little as possible):[37] for instance, requirements that the Executive set forth (1) the precise objectives of his action, (2) the American personnel, money, and other resources committed to it, (3) the geographical areas affected by the action, (4) the length of time that particular resources have been committed to particular areas, and (5) his projection of future developments regarding each of the above. If any of this information might aid the enemy, procedures could be developed to make reasonably likely its submission and receipt in confidence. Section 4(a) (B) poses other problems. As already suggested, its requirement that the President state "the constitutional . . . authority" under which he acted seems designed either to force him to accept the stingy reading of his authority in Section 2(c), to defy it openly, or to admit guilt for having transgressed it. The Section 4(a) (B) requirement that he state "the legislative authority" under which he acted, if any, presumably refers to statutory approval other than declarations of war, since no report is required under the latter. This proviso renews the needless dichotomy between the two just mentioned. There would be merit, however, in requesting the President to justify his action under international law, including treaties. The degree to which the action is or is not legal under that law is an element Congress must weigh in determining whether the action's costs to the country outweigh its benefits.

Section 4(b) is little more than hortatory, since it fails to deal with the extent to which the President in the exercise of *his* constitutional war powers is entitled to withhold information from the legislators. If the act means to suggest that the President has no such right, even as to strategic and tactical data, it strays. Section 4(c) has greater merit. Periodic reporting by the President during any ongoing use of force is essential to ensure that Congress remains capable of informed decision making and that it is presented with recurrent, unavoidable occasions to take a position. Whatever the content requirements for the initial presidential report, supplemental reports should update all pertinent categories. Section 5(a) provides apt means for laying the facts of American involvement in combat before those congressional committees most competent to deal with them, as well as apt means for bringing the legislators as a whole together if they are out of session when crisis develops and the circumstances warrant their immediate consideration of the President's action.

The Resolution does not deal with secret reporting, but its terms implicitly accommodate it. Nothing is said, for instance, about automatic disclosure of the President's report in whole to all members of Congress, and certainly nothing is said about its automatic disclosure to the public. If the President is, in fact, to report meaningfully in all the circumstances covered by Section 4(a), he must have reasonable confidence that secrets told Congress will remain secret. On the other hand, the legislators must be assured that vital information is not withheld from them simply because it undercuts executive desires; and Congress cannot be bound to keep presidential secrets when it believes public awareness of them is crucial to the national interest. Most of these difficulties could be met by a constructive relationship between the Executive, on the one hand, and the Speaker, President pro tempore, and the Senate and House foreign affairs committees, on the other. It ought to be possible for these legislators to receive and keep information in confidence until the President agrees to its disclosure to the rest of Congress or until a majority of both committees so vote.[38]

Consultation

In addition to calling for formal presidential reports, the Resolution seeks to obtain a legislative voice in war and peace decisions by demanding that the President exchange views with the legislators and seek their advice about *all* American moves into or toward hostilities, except when circumstances utterly preclude consultation. Section 3 states: "The President in every possible instance shall consult with Congress before introducing United States Armed Forces into hostilities or into situations where imminent involvement in hostilities is clearly indicated by the circumstances, and after every such introduction shall consult regularly with the Congress until United States Armed Forces are no longer engaged in hostilities or have been removed from such situations." According to the

Resolution's legislative history, this "consultation" is to be a meaty process:

The use of the word "every" reflects the committee's belief that such consultation *prior* to the commitment of armed forces should be inclusive. In other words, it should apply in extraordinary and emergency circumstances—even when it is not possible to get formal congressional approval in the form of a declaration of war or other specific authorization.

At the same time, through use of the word "possible" it recognizes that a situation may be so dire, e.g. hostile missile attack underway, and require such instantaneous action that no prior consultation will be possible. It is therefore simultaneously *firm* in its expression of Congressional authority yet *flexible* in recognizing the possible need for swift action by the President which would not allow him time to consult first with Congress.

The second element of section [3] relates to situations *after* a commitment of forces has been made (with or without prior consultation). In that instance, it imposes upon the President, through use of the word "shall," the obligation to "*consult regularly with such Members and committees until such United States Armed Forces are no longer engaged in hostilities or have been removed from areas where hostilities may be imminent.*"

A considerable amount of attention was given to the definition of *consultation.* Rejected was the notion that the consultation should be synonymous with merely being informed. Rather, consultation in this provision means that a decision is pending on a problem and that Members of Congress are being asked by the President for their advice and opinions and, in appropriate circumstances, their approval of action contemplated. Furthermore, for consultation to be meaningful, the President himself must participate and all information relevant to the situation must be made available.[39]

Two defects in Section 3 are somewhat troublesome. First, it does not require consultation in Section 4(a) (2) and (3) circumstances, only 4(a) (1). The Executive has carefully noted this distinction, disclaiming any statutory duty to consult about new deployments or substantial increases in old ones. But as the State Department told a House subcommittee, "The President has not made anything of that; he intends to consult irrespective of which of these paragraphs an action may fall under."[40] From a "policy viewpoint" influential legislators have urged the

Executive to continue to make nothing of the distinction.[41] Nonetheless, it is alive and well as a matter of law.

Second, Section 3 leaves the President significant discretion to choose which Senators and Representatives he will consult and when to talk with them. Obviously, the less often they meet during a crisis, and the less the chosen legislators know about foreign affairs, the more trivial the consultation is likely to be. Triviality is probable when the President inserts into a continuous process of executive decision making a few episodic gatherings with congressional leaders, chosen without regard to their foreign affairs expertise and responsibilities.

By way of remedy, one Representative has suggested that

[t]o have a really meaningful advise and counsel procedure involving legislative action, I would think that it would be almost essential that [the congressional consultees] drop everything else they are doing and stay with the NSC during this 2½-day period in this instance or any other unfolding crisis to be there to consider and evaluate the facts as they are perceived and as they may change during this period of time.

Otherwise, if they are brought in for advi[c]e and consultation at the time of the first meeting of the NSC with the President, all of that might be totally outdated by what happens a few hours later. It might really be well for the President in the future to do his best to insist that the Speaker of the House and the minority leader as well as the majority and minority leaders in the Senate come and stay there with him and consider this crisis as it unfolds.[42]

And one Senator has argued that consultation should draw on "the expertise of the members of the committee that are pertinent to the issue":

If you call in the leadership, they don't know what they are being called in for—some general subject dealing with the war in Southeast Asia or the seizure of the *Mayaguez*. Then you consult with them and then they have to go back and find out what their particular constituent body thinks, whereas if he consults the substantive legislative standing committees he is getting the view of that body which is charged with making recommendations on that subject to its own House.

So I respectfully submit first and foremost that that should be the established method of consultation, that is with the Senate Foreign

Relations Committee and the House International Relations Committee. If the President would also like to consult with the leadership—that is fine and that is icing on the cake.[43]

Recall the remedy proposed in Chapter X: more delegation of foreign-affairs authority by Congress to a few members who would be expected to work with the Executive throughout the course of a crisis.

Meaningful collaboration between the President and Congress, from the first through the eleventh hours, constitutes the war-power millennium. Section 3 of the Resolution seeks it. The section by itself, however, does little more than exhort, unless it is backed by a growing congressional capacity for coordinated, informed, timely decision making, by greater congressional will to take and assume responsibility for decisions about war and peace, and by heightened congressional zeal to cajole and coerce the President into consultation. As Senator Javits said, "If Congress sits back passively and merely awaits Executive fulfillment of the reporting requirements of the law, the key policy decisions will continue to be monopolized by the Executive Branch, as they were in the decades leading up to enactment of the War Powers Resolution."[44]

Improved Procedures for Congressional Action
We have already seen how Section 5 ends a presidential initiative when (1) the House or Senate fails to ratify it within 60 days, subject to certain exceptions, or (2) Congress at any point votes it down by concurrent resolution. As is true of much of the other implementing detail in the act, there is nothing magic about the 60 days. They were born of the House's preference for 120 and the Senate's for 30, and many have disagreed about the likely effect of any particular time period. Devotees of congressional prerogative differ, for example, some finding 30 days essential lest the President have time to lock Congress into his policy by fait accompli, others fearing 30 days would allow the President to win rally-round-the-flag support. But whatever the time period, it does encourage focused, expedited congressional attention to the policy at hand.

The 60-day deadline, however, does more harm than good, for reasons already discussed. Indeed, the purpose of a series of complex procedures in Section 6 of the Resolution seems to be to lessen the possibility that the deadline will arrive without the legislators' having voted yea or nay. The provisions of Section 6 do not guarantee a definitive vote, nonetheless, because it can be blocked if either house "shall otherwise determine by the yeas and nays." It is also well to be clear that the 60-day proviso is not the only means to focused, expedited congressional action. Section 5(c), coupled with the presidential reporting requirements just considered, unavoidably focuses the legislators on the pertinent executive action. And Section 7 deals with expediting procedures not tied to the 60-day deadline but related rather to congressional decision by concurrent resolution at any time.

The Section 7 provisions "against filibuster, or committees pigeon-holing,"[45] are a significant step toward rationalizing Congress's handling of war and peace issues. These provisions ensure prompt but not precipitate action in the respective foreign affairs committees, on the floor of each house, and in congressional conference deliberations, so long as majorities in each house believe that rapid action is desirable. When a majority in either house does not find it necessary, the pace slows. Thus, Section 7 is likely to achieve an element essential to a responsible role for Congress in war-peace decisions: an end to obstruction of legislative judgment on presidential initiatives.

Early Life

The War Powers Resolution did not get off to a brisk start. More than 17 months passed before the first presidential report was filed under it. During the interim there was at least one executive initiative that might well have been reported under Section 4(a) (2), if not 4(a) (1). While Greece and Turkey were struggling over Cyprus in 1974, the American Ambassador to that island requested on July 21 the evacuation of local Americans. President Nixon responded the next day by sending five naval vessels to the area and by permitting 22 helicopter sorties from the U.S.S. *Inchon* to a British base in Cyprus in order to remove roughly 400 Americans and 80 foreign nationals. On July 23 a joint British-American effort rescued another 135 Americans and foreign nationals. In Senator Eagleton's view, the Executive's failure to report any of this activity violated the Resolution. The Senator was unable, however, to bring others in Congress to take a similar view of the matter—perhaps because no hostilities resulted, American armed forces did not land on any part of Cyprus where they were unwelcome, and the President traditionally has had a prerogative to rescue Americans threatened abroad. The fact remains that the Resolution could have been read to require a report on the operation. The President's refusal to do so, and Congress's disinclination to remonstrate with him, did nothing for a generous view of the legislation.

Content of sorts for it came during the last spasms of American military involvement in Indochina. President Ford sent three reports to Congress regarding the evacuation of Americans and foreign nationals. The first report on April 4, 1975, concerned the removal of thousands of refugees from Danang, Vietnam, to safer points south. The second on April 12 reported rescuing Americans and foreign nationals trapped in Phnom Penh, Cambodia. The third followed on April 30, about the evacuation from Saigon. No hostilities were involved in the Danang operation; limited enemy fire seems to have been received during the Cambodian venture, with no American response or casualties; some combat was involved at Saigon and there were American losses. The Saigon operation was the most taxing of the three. A naval task force participated offshore, 70 helicopters and assorted fighters flew numerous sorties, and 865 marines landed in an undertaking that lasted 19 hours. Approximately 1,400 Americans, 5,600 Vietnamese and 85 others were removed by helicopter while 30,000 Vietnamese were picked up at sea. There was a palpable possibility of heavy fighting with either communist forces or South Vietnamese troops desperate for rescue.

The reports submitted by President Ford to Congress concerning these operations were striking in several respects. First, none was expressly submitted pursuant to Section 4(a) (1). The Danang and Phnom Penh reports cited 4(a) (2), and the Saigon

report simply "section 4."[46] Thus the President did not come to
Congress under the only provision in Section 4 that activates
the deadline on executive action and creates the possibility that
Congress may end the venture at any time by concurrent resolution.

Second, the President was careful to claim independent
power to act. The first report was the most cautious, mixing
constitutional prerogative with statutory authority: "This effort
is being undertaken pursuant to the President's constitutional
authority as Commander-in-Chief and Chief Executive in the
conduct of foreign relations and pursuant to the Foreign Assistance Act of 1961 . . . which authorizes humanitarian assistance to refugees, civilian war casualties and other persons
disadvantaged by hostilities . . . in South Vietnam." The next
two reports were more aggressive: "The operation was ordered
and conducted pursuant to the President's Constitutional executive power and authority as Commander-in-Chief of U.S.
Armed Forces." Third, the reports were exceptionally terse,
involving little of the detail contemplated by the reporting provisions of the Resolution. Their texts appear in Appendix C.
Fourth, by the time the President reported, each of the operations was over. The Resolution did receive its first substance in
the April 1975 reports, but not much.

It is significant, however, that President Ford reported,
despite the Nixon precedent on Cyprus and despite a long tradition of Executives' rescuing Americans threatened abroad.
Ford was encouraged to report because Congress had previously banned the use of federal funds for any military activities in Indochina. While it was not clear that the ban covered the
evacuation of Americans and foreigners inextricably mixed
with them, it could be read to do so (particularly if hostilities
resulted), and the ban did seem clearly to cover foreigners not
entwined with Americans.[47] Certainly the evacuation operations involved decisions with "hostilities" implications—for
instance, what nationalities were to be rescued, how many
people should be brought out, by what means, over what
period of time, to what extent reliance should be placed on
diplomacy rather than military operations, and to what degree

combat would be accepted to achieve the predetermined objectives. With these considerations in mind, the President addressed the Senate and House in joint session on April 10, 1975: "And now I ask the Congress to clarify immediately its restrictions on the use of U.S. military forces in Southeast Asia for the limited purposes of protecting American lives by ensuring their evacuation if this should be necessary, and I also ask prompt revision of the law to cover those Vietnamese to whom we have a very special obligation, and whose lives may be in danger, should the worst come to pass."[48]

In response to the President's request, both houses passed bills, each referring to the War Powers Resolution. On April 25 a conference committee reconciled the two bills as the Vietnam Humanitarian Assistance and Evacuation Act of 1975. The Senate promptly agreed to the conference report and sent it to the House, where it was to be considered on April 29. But before it reached the floor, the evacuation of Saigon was well underway. Calling from the White House,[49] Speaker Carl Albert requested that the measure be withdrawn. It was considered by the House on May 1 and rejected. In short, the President sought explicit authority to use the military—authority which Congress might have provided and tied to the War Powers Resolution. When he had not received prior congressional approval nineteen days after asking for it, he acted nonetheless. And he acted despite a legislative ban on military operations in Indochina, which covered at least part of his initiative. The House then declined to take a position on the matter, forfeiting the opportunity at least to ratify what the President had done and to explicitly involve Congress in its authorization.

Some in the House had feared that the measure might authorize American reentry into Indochina. By May 1 others viewed the matter as moot or wished to avoid too close association with South Vietnamese refugees. There was strong sentiment among the foreign affairs leadership of the House and Senate, however, that the measure be adopted, whether before or after the fact, to associate Congress with the President in the use of military force under the War Powers Resolution. Senator

Eagleton's postmortem was characteristically dismal, but more realistic than not:

Congress fumbled the ball. When the President was forced by events to order the evacuation from South Vietnam on April 29, the House of Representatives had not yet completed the final stage in enacting the necessary legislation. Two days later, when the House finally had the opportunity to express Congressional will and intent, the House voted overwhelmingly not to act.

This unfortunate decision raises grave questions about the willingness of Congress to fulfill its constitutional responsibilities. The President obviously had no authority to use the United States forces to rescue foreign nationals in Vietnam. Yet our forces evacuated thousands of Vietnamese. Asked to explain, President Ford tried to justify his action on "moral" rather than legal grounds. Yet Congress let the precedent stand. Future Presidents might now conclude that the Commander in Chief had an inherent right to do what Mr. Ford did.[50]

And as the *Milwaukee Journal* said in a May 23 editorial:

In the spirit of partnership, Ford asked Congress to provide both money and clear authority to evacuate endangered Vietnamese along with Americans. While South Vietnam crumbled, Congress wrangled. Dozens of amendments filled the air. Many a lawmaker played general, trying to link certain kinds of aid to certain military maneuvers under certain conditions. Finally, Ford was forced to rely on inherent presidential power and order evacuation without companion action by Congress.

From all this, a pointed lesson emerges. On urgent foreign policy issues, the presidency is still the government's decision making center —if only because it can move with a crisp singularity that a congressional multitude cannot hope to match.[51]

There was some congressional feeling that the President failed to consult with the legislators during the April crises.[52] The emergencies began while Congress was in Easter recess. Nonetheless, the Executive tried to notify the congressional leadership about the Danang operation. The President spoke to Congress about the crisis that evolved into the Saigon evacuation. Four days after Mr. Ford's message to the House and Senate, he, along with the Secretaries of State and Defense and the Army Chief of Staff, met with the Senate Foreign Relations Committee to discuss the situation in Southeast Asia. Other high administration officials testified before several other congressional committees regarding the impending evacuation.[53] While the full objectives of Section 3 of the Resolution may not have been met in April 1975, neither were they wholly ignored.

Hardly had the Indochina evacuations ended when the new Cambodian regime seized an American merchant ship, the *Mayaguez*, on May 12, 1975. To recover the ship and its crew, protect the rescuers, and retaliate against the aggressors, President Ford sent American troops into Thailand, used that country as a staging area, and fought the Cambodians. Eight ships, 11 helicopters, 25 planes, and 300 marines were involved in the Cambodian hostilities, with the loss of 15 Americans dead, 3 missing, and 50 wounded. During the hostilities the United States dropped the largest bomb in its nonnuclear arsenal on the island of Koh Tang, to support marines in battle there. American forces bombed a military airfield and an oil storage depot in Cambodia, shortly after the crew of the *Mayaguez* had been released.[54]

Since hostilities were clearly involved, the President reported to Congress on May 15 under Section 4(a) (1) of the Resolution. But the President chose not to report also under 4(a) (3), although his operations in Thailand were protested by its government.[55] And as in April, he claimed an independent prerogative to use force. Like the Indochina reports, the *Mayaguez* account was terse, including, for instance, no explanation of the basis in international law for the operation. Its text is in Appendix C. And like the Indochina report, the *Mayaguez* account came after the fact. Finally, the President was not slowed by the statutory ban on military ventures in Indochina, apparently because he did not read it to preclude his armed rescue of Americans attacked abroad.

According to the State Department, "[A]lthough the *Mayaguez* incident was a rapidly unfolding emergency situation, four separate sets of communications took place between the executive branch and the congressional leadership."[56] These "communications" did not amount to much. Senator Javits accurately complained that "[t]he consultation of the Congress prior to the *Mayaguez* incident resembled to me the old and discredited practice of informing selected Members of Congress a few hours in advance of the implementation of the decision already taken within the executive branch."[57] Still, on May 14 the Senate Foreign Relations Committee announced: "[W]e support the President in the exercise of his constitutional powers within the framework of the War Powers Resolution to secure the release of the ship and its men."[58] Congress as a whole acquiesced in the level of consultation offered it. So ended an eight-week period that has been by far the most important in the Resolution's implementation to date.

Post *Mayaguez*

Several months after leaving the White House, former President Ford frontally attacked the Resolution on both legal and practical grounds. In an April 1977 speech he said that there had been six military crises during his presidency: the four discussed already and two June 1976 evacuations of American citizens from Lebanon's civil war. No reports under the War Powers Resolution were submitted on the Lebanese ventures. Mr. Ford concluded that no reports were legally required either for them or for his initiatives in Indochina, although reports were in fact filed on the Indochina and *Mayaguez* rescues: "In none of those instances did I believe the War Powers Resolution applied, and many members of Congress also questioned its applicability in cases of protection and evacuation of American citizens. Furthermore, I did not concede that the resolution itself was legally binding on the President on constitutional grounds."[59]

Mr. Ford assessed the act even more grimly from "a practical standpoint." He focused first on the difficulties of consultation during the early stages of a crisis:

When the evacuation of DaNang was forced upon us during the Congress's Easter recess, not one of the key bipartisan leaders of the Congress was in Washington.

. . . [H]ere is where we found the leaders of Congress: two were in Mexico, three were in Greece, one was in the Middle East, one was in Europe, and two were in the People's Republic of China. The rest we found in twelve widely scattered states of the Union.

This, one might say, is an unfair example, since the Congress was in recess. But it must be remembered that critical world events, especially military operations, seldom wait for the Congress to meet. In fact, most of what goes on in the world happens in the middle of the night, Washington time.

On June 18, 1976, we began the first evacuation of American citizens from the civil war in Lebanon. The Congress was not in recess, but it had adjourned for the day.

As telephone calls were made, we discovered, among other things, that one member of Congress had an unlisted number which his press secretary refused to divulge. After trying and failing to reach another member of Congress, we were told by his assistant that the congressman did not need to be reached.

We tried so hard to reach a third member of Congress that our resourceful White House operators had the local police leave a note on the congressman's beach cottage door: "Please call the White House."[60]

The former President then went into "several reasons" why, "[w]hen a crisis breaks, it is impossible to draw the Congress into the decision-making process in an effective way . . . ." His reasons constitute a classic statement of executive distaste for measures such as the Resolution. Legislators are not suited for crisis management, in Mr. Ford's judgment, for a number of reasons:

First, they have so many other concerns: legislation in committee and on the floor, constituents to serve, and a thousand other things. It is impractical to ask them to be as well-versed in fast-breaking developments as the President, the National Security Council, the Joint Chiefs of Staff, and others who deal with foreign policy and national security situations every hour of every day.

Second, it is also impossible to wait for a consensus to form among those congressional leaders as to the proper course of action, especially when they are scattered literally around the world and when time is the one thing we cannot spare. Again, we should ask what the outcome would be if the leaders consulted do not agree among themselves or disagree collectively with the President on an action he considers essential.

Third, there is the risk of disclosure of sensitive information through insecure means of communication, particularly by telephone. Members of Congress with a great many things on their minds might also confuse what they hear on the radio news in this day of instant communication with what they are told on a highly classified basis by the White House.

Fourth, the potential legal consequences of taking executive action before mandated congressional consultation can be completed may cause a costly delay. The consequences to the President, if he does not wait for Congress, could be as severe as impeachment. But the consequences to the nation, if he does wait, could be much worse.

Fifth, there is a question of how consultations with a handful of congressional leaders can bind the entire Congress to support a course of action—especially when younger members of Congress are becoming increasingly independent.

. . . .

Sixth, the Congress has little to gain and much to lose politically by involving itself deeply in crisis management.

If the crisis is successfully resolved, it is the President who will get credit for the success. If his efforts are not successful, if the objectives are not met or if casualties are too high, the Congress will have seriously compromised its right to criticize the decisions and actions of the President.

Finally, there is absolutely no way American foreign policy can be conducted or military operations commanded by 535 members of Congress on Capitol Hill, even if they all happen to be on Capitol Hill when they are needed.

Domestic policy—for housing, health, education or energy—can and should be advanced in the calm deliberation and spirited debate I loved so much as a congressman.

The broad outlines and goals of foreign policy also benefit immensely from this kind of meticulous congressional consideration.

But in times of crisis, decisiveness is everything—and the Constitution plainly puts the responsibility for such decisions on the shoulders of the President of the United States.

There are institutional limitations on the Congress which cannot be legislated away.[61]

Mr. Ford's assessment did not move Congress to repeal or otherwise limit the Resolution. To the contrary, in July 1977 the Senate Foreign Relations Committee considered amendments whose aggregate effect would have been to tighten the act's restraints on presidential use of force.[62] Three days of hearings were held on these proposals as well as on other aspects of the Resolution's "operation and effectiveness." No amendments resulted.

Unlike Presidents Nixon and Ford, Jimmy Carter had kind words for the war-powers legislation. Early in his presidency he described it as an "appropriate reduction" in the sort of control enjoyed by some Executives before Indochina. Similarly, Secretary of State Vance indicated during his confirmation hearings that the Resolution was compatible with the President's constitutional authority and that he anticipated no problems with its "good faith observance."[63] By the same token, during the Senate Foreign Relations Committee's July 1977 hearings, just mentioned, the Legal Adviser to the State Department repeated anew: "We believe that conscientious observance of the procedures set forth in the Resolution, including effective consultation and timely reporting, will assure that both the Executive and Legislative Branches possess the means to exercise their full and proper constitutional responsibilities."[64] A year later, in August 1978, the Legal Adviser assured the House International Relations Committee of Mr. Carter's continued "strong support of the War Powers Resolution."[65]

Congress constrained Jimmy Carter in matters of war and peace less than it did Presidents Nixon and Ford when Indochina and Watergate coalesced, but more than has been customary in the twentieth century. Mr. Carter was required to provide significant secret information to Congress, especially its intelligence committees. These committees and others concerned with foreign affairs and the armed forces have been frequently informed and consulted, often heeded, by the Executive. Despite presidential objections, the legislators have insisted on the use of concurrent resolutions to disapprove major arms sales abroad. They have cut off or curbed both military and economic aid to certain countries that the President very much wished to help. Individual Congressmen have dealt directly with foreign representatives—members of the Senate Foreign Relations Committee conferring with Moshe Dayan in a Washington hotel about proposed F-15 sales to Saudi Arabia and Egypt, for instance, and the House of Representatives threatening to cut off economic aid to South Korea unless its former ambassador to this country were returned to testify about South Korean influence buying in Congress. The Senate has coldly scrutinized the President's treaty initiatives, especially those involving the Panama Canal and SALT II, and many Congressmen reacted severely when the President alone terminated this country's Mutual Defense Treaty with the Republic of China.

Influenced by such constraints and by his own predilections, Mr. Carter used armed force very sparingly until late 1979, even when nothing more than deployment on the high seas was at stake. He had no need to report to Congress under the War Powers Resolution until spring 1980. Some legislators did feel that the administration's May 1978 activities in Zaire were reportable. At that time American, Belgian, and French citizens were threatened by Katangan forces in southern Zaire. Upon the request of Zaire, as well as Belgium and France, President Carter ordered U.S. transport aircraft to support rescue operations by Belgian and French troops. From May 19 to 23 the Air Force flew approximately thirty missions in Zaire, transporting matériel and some French troops to staging areas more than 100 miles from the site of the fighting. In June, after the Katangans had been repulsed, the Air Force flew the Belgians and French out while also transporting into Zaire elements of an African peace-keeping force. At one point during the June flights, as French legionnaires were loading a Peugeot onto a C-141, Zairian troops threatened to fire if the car departed with the French. The Peugeot was left on the runway without further incident. The American pilots and their support personnel took no weapons into Zaire. Nor did any American infantry or fighter aircraft accompany them.[66]

Under the circumstances, most Congressmen who paid any attention to the matter concluded that American forces had not been introduced either into a situation "where imminent involvement in hostilities is clearly indicated by the circumstances" or "into the territory . . . of a foreign nation, while equipped for combat." Thus, no presidential report to Congress was obligatory under Sections 4(a) (1) or 4(a) (2) of the Resolution. A few Congressmen emphatically disagreed. Their disquiet led to the August 1978 House hearings mentioned above.

Events in the Middle East proved to be more trying. Oil from that area became increasingly central to Western economies during the late 1970s. As the decade neared its end, Iran spun from being a force for tranquility in the area to a source of acute instability. In November 1979 the Iranians took American diplomats hostage. After the hostages had been captive for almost a year, Iraq invaded Iran, heightening the threat to Western oil. Meanwhile the Soviets invaded Afghanistan, putting Russian troops on Iran's border and within striking distance of the Persian Gulf.

In response, President Carter became more active militarily. He deployed powerful naval forces in the vicinity of Iran, sent radar command aircraft to Saudi Arabia as well as several hundred military personnel to operate and maintain equipment and train the Saudis, established an American military presence in Egypt, created a Rapid Deployment Force for the Middle East, and declared the United States would keep the oil flowing one way or another. Carter also suggested that armed action might be necessary to recover the hostages, and sent six C-130 transports, eight RH-53 helicopters, and roughly ninety combat troops into Iran on April 24, 1980, in an abortive effort to bring the captives out. American fighter aircraft from carriers off Iran were prepared to defend the rescuers against Iranian attack had that proved necessary.

Amid this activity, the President reported under the War Powers Resolution only once, on April 26, 1980. See Appendix C. He rejected claims that other reports were necessary when, for instance, the American military presence in Saudi Arabia and the Persian Gulf increased during the Iraqi-Iranian War; Senator Javits agreed with him, as Appendix C indicates.

The April 26, 1980, report was seriously flawed. It said little and made no mention of Sections 4(a) (1) and (2) of the Resolution, under which it should have been submitted. Terming the rescue effort a "humanitarian mission," Jimmy Carter simply ignored the fact that the mission, while "humanitarian" in purpose, nonetheless "introduced" American armed forces into a situation "where imminent involvement in hostilities [was] clearly indicated by the circumstances." Combat with the Iranians was likely had the rescuers reached Tehran. Combat with others such as the Soviets was possible had the rescue degenerated into a prolonged struggle between American and Iranian forces. Moreover, the rescue effort obviously introduced U.S. forces "into the territory . . . of a foreign nation . . . while equipped for combat."

The April 26 report also claimed that Carter acted "pursuant to the President's powers under the Constitution as Chief Executive and as Commander-in-Chief of the United States Armed Forces, expressly recognized in Section 8(d) (1) of the War Powers Resolution," as well as pursuant to Article 51 of the United Nations Charter. The report was certainly free to argue that the President acted pursuant to his constitutional authority and international law, but it was wrong to suggest that he acted pursuant to Section 8(d) (1). In the context of the entire Resolution, especially Sections 2(c) and 4, it is clear that Section 8(d) (1) did not authorize the rescue attempt. Within the terms of the Resolution, the April 26 report was misleading and inadequate —at least as flawed as any report submitted by Gerald Ford. In practice, though not rhetoric, Jimmy Carter gave the Resolution's reporting requirements short shrift.

He also disregarded its consultation provisions. No one in Congress was informed, much less consulted, before the rescue effort began. Ironically, on the afternoon of April 24, Senators Church and Javits wrote Secretary of State Vance on behalf of the Senate Foreign Relations Committee, insisting under Section 3 of the Resolution that the President consult Congress before using force against Iran. "We write this letter to you in the context of the grave international crisis which has been developing for some months in the region of the Persian Gulf, precipitated by the seizure of the United States Embassy in Tehran and the holding of American hostages there, and by the brutal military occupation of Afghanistan by the Soviet Union," said Church and Javits. They noted that Carter had refused to exclude force as means of reclaiming the hostages from Iran and had threatened to fight if the Soviet Union moved into the Persian Gulf. They argued that the legislative history of the Resolution "makes it clear that the consultations called for do not necessarily signify at all that a decision has been made" to use force, but rather "the advance consultation provisions of the War Powers Resolution are intended to come into play *before* any such decision has been made, in order to ensure that any such decision, if made, is a national decision jointly entered into by the President and the Congress. . . . Accordingly, Mr. Secretary, we hereby request that you inform this Committee at an early date when consultations can begin . . . ."[67] The Senators' invocation of Section 3 was too little, too late.[68] Subsequent congressional unhappiness with Carter's failure to consult, however, did not lead to steps to strengthen Section 3.[69]

Inertia

A prior page suggested that it is up to Congress to break the gravitational pull of executive hegemony over American war and peace. The War Powers Resolution provided the necessary initial thrust. But since the legislation has been on the books, Congress has done little to generate any sustained thrust. Most members of Congress remain very much result oriented.[70] Their concern with the particulars of any specific policy still overshadows their concern with the institutional process by which that policy is made. So long as they and their constituents applaud an executive initiative, they do not seriously dispute their exclusion from its development.

Congress lost a singular opportunity to give the Resolution substance in the congressional mold when the legislators failed to participate in shaping the Saigon evacuation. Consultation under the Resolution has been minimal, largely because Congress has not insisted that the President meaningfully implement Section 3. Executives will rarely pay much attention to that section, especially during crises that arise suddenly, require constant, rapid, flexible response, and end quickly, unless the legislators designate a small committee of Senators and Representatives, primed to share the command headquarters with the Executive and made acceptable to him by a capacity for informed, responsible advice and by a willingness to keep tactical secrets. Similarly, there is little reason to imagine that Presidents will accept Section 2(c)'s view of their authority to enter hostilities without prior congressional approval. As with many of their predecessors, Presidents in the future will very probably construe the Constitution to permit them to commit troops whenever they believe it essential to the national welfare.

Even so, the War Powers Resolution retains a potent bite. Following President Ford's example, his successors will doubtless report their military initiatives to Congress, usually having told congressional leaders about their plans and given them a moment to object. It is also probable that future Presidents will either accept an end to their military initiatives by the Section 5(b) deadlines or by the 5(c) concurrent resolutions, or ask the Supreme Court to rule on the constitutionality of these sections.[71] Equally important, future legislators will have guaranteed opportunities to participate in deciding whether America fights, if the combat lasts more than forty-eight hours. While the Resolution may have slight impact on quick, surgical applications of armed force by the President, it should ensure legislative approval of any long-term commitment of the country to war.

Secretary of State Haig promised more for Congress during his January 1981 confirmation hearings. He committed the Reagan administration to compliance with both the letter and the spirit of the Resolution. Shortly thereafter several Senators charged the President with skirting the act while increasing the flow of American arms and advisers to El Salvador's civil strife. *Plus ça change* . . . .

CHAPTER XII

Why Not a More
Direct Approach?

WE HAVE assumed to this point that the Constitution appropriately deals with control over the war powers by the way in
which it divides authority between the President and Congress.
This approach is an indirect means of achieving the war-power
ends set out in Chapter VIII. Would it be preferable to have the
Constitution expressly state that the war powers are to be used
only to provide for national defense while avoiding foreign
aggression, ensuring democratic control, and so on, rather than
simply trusting that these ends will be achieved by the way in
which authority is split between the two branches? Generally
not.

Development of the war powers is best left on indirect paths.
The language of the Constitution and long-standing beliefs
about its requirements are more inclined to these ways than to
the more direct. Any attempt to change could produce more
controversy than consensus. Objectives acceptable in broad
outline as guidelines for constitutional development might
easily become bones of contention if finely drawn and proposed themselves for constitutional status. Moreover, the
reasons behind a rule—here, the war-power ends sought by the
division of authority between the President and Congress—do
not have to be actually written into the rule to be effective.
They simply need to be understood.

Possible Exception for
End Three's Ban on Aggression Abroad

Chapter I suggested the possibility of international obligations
as a constitutional restraint on the exercise of the war powers.

With such a limit, even if the allocational restraints failed (for instance, both branches favored war for the acquisition of another nation's territory, or the President embarked on conquest while Congress sat supinely), international law could make the action unconstitutional. The notion is intriguing. Certainly, the national interest in End Three has never been stronger.

The international rules on war and peace have become progressively more stringent since the turn of the century. Severe limits now exist on the armed prerogatives of both nations and individuals, stemming principally from the Hague Conventions of 1907, League of Nations Covenant, Kellogg-Briand Pact of 1928, Nuremberg and United Nations Charters, and the 1949 Geneva Prisoner of War Convention. The primary restraint on national action is Article 2(4) of the United Nations Charter, which requires that "[a]ll Members shall refrain in their international relations from the threat or use of force against the territorial integrity or political independence of any state, or in any other manner inconsistent with the Purposes of the United Nations." The liability of any President, Congressman, or soldier guilty of waging war in violation of Article 2(4), or of using forbidden means to wage otherwise legal hostilities, stems from the prosecution of Germans and Japanese after World War II and from 1946 United Nations approval of the Nuremberg and Tokyo proceedings.

Admittedly, the international law of war and peace suffers from the same sorts of uncertainties as do the war-power provisions of the Constitution. Terms like "threat or use of force" and "political independence" in Article 2(4) are no more self-defining than "declare war" and "commander in chief." The United Nations General Assembly ran through a number of special committees on the question of defining aggression before reaching modest results. The vagaries of abstract language are compounded when competing provisions come into play. Thus Article 2(4) is countered by Article 51, which provides that "[n]othing in the present Charter shall impair the inherent right of individual or collective self-defense if an armed attack occurs against a Member of the United Nations, until the Security Council has taken the measures necessary to maintain international peace and security." Articles 2(4) and 51, like many of the constitutional grants to the President and Congress, stand ready to support opposite sides of most arguments. Gaps exist particularly in the international rules on one state's intervention in another's internal strife, an area of particular concern during the Cold War. It comes as no surprise that the legality of American involvement in Vietnam split the international lawyers, as well as the constitutional.

Ambiguous though they may be, the existing international restraints on armed coercion are preferable to no limits at all. Nations have become too interdependent and their weapons too telling to permit the old regime of relatively free use of force. Moreover, content for vague legal rules can evolve out of a process of claim and concession among those affected by them, assuming common interests, a modicum of good faith, and time. The United States has an unusually well-developed stake in this matter. Siege mentality, born of a threatening world, is hostile to our institutions. In 1922 Quincy Wright thought essential the "[d]evelopment by treaty of international organization and arbitration so as to bring as large a portion of diplomacy as possible under the control of recognized principles of international law, an atmosphere in which democratic institutions, and particularly American institutions, have always thriven."[1] By 1969 he was more emphatic that "the reconciliation of democracy with an efficient foreign policy requiring concentration of the foreign relations and war powers in the Executive [has] to be effected by creating a less dangerous and more law-governed world in which the deliberate processes of democracy [can] function without danger to national security."[2]

One means to hasten international consensus on the rules of war and peace would be incorporation of international use-of-force restraints into the Constitution. Richard Falk urged this course in 1967:

The condemnation of aggressive war and the United States' endorsement of the Principles of the Nuremberg Judgment seem to make adherence to international law a matter of Constitutional necessity.

True, there is no established legal doctrine to this effect, but the question is open enough that it seems reasonable to contend that this is the way the Constitution ought to be authoritatively construed. As in domestic affairs, so in foreign affairs, we should remember that it is a Constitution that we are expounding; as the organic law of the society it must be constantly readapted to the needs of nation and its citizenry. . . . To insist on Constitutional sources of legal restraint is a part of the wider global need to erode the prerogatives of the sovereign state in the area of war and peace. So long as international society remains decentralized the most effective legal restraints are likely to be self-restraints, those that are applied from *within* rather than from *without* the sovereign state.[3]

Falk, however, accurately said that "there is no established doctrine" making adherence to international law a matter of constitutional necessity, even adherence to the law of war and peace. The Constitution does recognize international obligations on a more limited basis. Congress is "[t]o define and punish Piracies and Felonies committed on the high Seas, and Offences against the Law of Nations." Treaties are the "supreme Law of the Land," and the President's duty to "take Care that the Laws be faithfully executed" has traditionally been read to cover international as well as domestic rules. In 1796 Mr. Justice Wilson stated that "[w]hen the United States declared their independence, they were bound to receive the law of nations in its modern state of purity and refinement," and in 1900 the Supreme Court reiterated that "[i]nternational law is part of our law . . . ."[4] The courts do try to construe the Constitution to avoid conflict with international law, and the political branches do generally exercise their constitutional discretion in ways consistent with the country's foreign obligations.[5] But there is little question that the Constitution overrides any international provision opposed to it.[6]

Serious line-drawing problems would dog any effort to read international law into the Constitution. Should all international obligations be given constitutional status, or only certain ones, and if so, which? More to the point, a move toward incorporation would founder on fear that it might conflict with American government or personal rights—as well as on the affront to nationalism of blocking U.S. action, otherwise constitutional, because it would violate international law. International rules will do well to make more concrete their present theoretical parity with federal legislation. It is not likely that international norms on war and peace can go further and be read into the Constitution.

There is another direct route to realization of End Three that lies wholly within our constitutional tradition. The road is surprisingly open. We have already seen the defensive cast of important constitutional language on the war powers. Congress may tax for the "common Defence," and provisions on the militia, habeas corpus, and state military action contemplate defense against rebellion and invasion, not conquest. As we have also seen, the Framers and Ratifiers expected nonaggressive use of American force and anticipated peace as the customary state of the nation. With few exceptions, most of our conflicts, large and small, have been thought defensive by the people at home. "[T]he genius and character of our institutions are peaceful," said the Supreme Court in 1850, "and the power to declare war was not conferred upon congress for the purposes of aggression or aggrandizement, but to enable the general government to vindicate by arms, if it should become necessary, its own rights and the rights of its citizens. A war, therefore, declared by congress, can never be presumed to be waged for the purpose of conquest or the acquisition of territory."[7] Relying on this language, one war-power scholar in 1921 found a "doctrine laid down by the Supreme Court that wars of conquest and aggrandizement by the United States are unconstitutional."[8] Credible support for a ban on American involvement in such conflicts, then, can be found in the constitutional language, the debates of its Framers and Ratifiers, American practice since 1789, and in the present values and needs of the country.

Recognition of the ban, however, has yet to come. The Supreme Court in its 1850 language was concerned with executive authority over captured territory, not with whether American force must be stamped nonaggressive before becoming constitutional. When speaking directly to that question, the Court has been circumspent. As Mr. Justice Field stated in 1889:

When once it is established that Congress possesses the power to pass an act, our province ends with its construction, and its application to cases as they are presented for determination. Congress has the power under the Constitution to declare war, and in two instances where the power has been exercised—in the war of 1812 against Great Britain, and in 1846 against Mexico—the propriety and wisdom and justice of its action were vehemently assailed by some of the ablest and best men in the country, but no one doubted the legality of the proceeding . . . .[9]

But the "legality of the proceeding" can be doubted, for reasons just noted. The time does seem ripe for the President and Congress, or the courts, to develop constitutional limits on the power of the political branches to commit troops as aggressively as they please.

A Parting Bow to the Constitution

The war powers, it is often said, are creatures of politics, not law: They are defined by the play of power, scarcely touched by beliefs about what the Constitution requires. Under this notion, the Constitution is useful principally to rationalize the workings of realpolitik. Thus, whenever the President or Congress has the political strength to preempt one war power or another, the seizure is termed a constitutional prerogative. Whenever a President's diplomatic or military policy suits us, we find its making "plainly" committed to him by the Constitution. When his policy goes sour, we brazenly conclude that Congress after all is the constitutional arbiter. History provides some support for this tawdry view of the war powers, but also evidence of its limitations.

These powers have traditionally been shaped by more than politics. Beliefs about what the Constitution requires have also proved crucial—beliefs drawn largely from the language of the document, its Framers' and Ratifiers' debates, and the country's evolving values and needs. The behavior of the President and Congress, like that of most other Americans, has been strongly influenced by what they have understood to be their legal obligations, not just by the political strength at their disposal.

Any notion of politics as the sole key to the war powers ignores a second reality as well. Particular relations between the President and Congress can come into being by legislative fiat, responsive to beliefs about what the Constitution requires. These relations can then shape the future play of politics. Through war-power legislation the President can be encouraged to inform Congress in detail of his initiatives for war or peace. The legislators can be similarly encouraged to state their views if the statute provides them with unavoidable occasions for so doing. And both branches can be driven to build broader collaborative bridges to one another by just such an executive necessity to report and congressional necessity to assume responsibility.

Who holds the arrows and who the olive branch? In no small part, answers do spring from our beliefs about the Constitution's requirements. That understanding has often been clouded, never more than during the past generation. But given the experience of the past forty years with intense American involvement abroad and prior experience with isolation and nonintervention, we have within grasp a mature hold on how to divide authority between the President and Congress over war and peace.

Appendixes

Notes

Bibliography

Index

Appendix A

Text of Constitutional Provisions
Important to the War Powers

Article I

Section 1 All legislative Powers herein granted shall be vested in a Congress of the United States . . . .

Section 5 (3) Each House shall keep a Journal of its Proceedings, and from time to time publish the same, excepting such Parts as may in their Judgment require Secrecy . . . .

Section 6 (2) [N]o Person holding any Office under the United States, shall be a Member of either House during his Continuance in Office.

Section 7 (1) All Bills for raising Revenue shall originate in the House of Representatives; but the Senate may propose or concur with Amendments as on other Bills.

(2) Every Bill which shall have passed the House of Representatives and the Senate, shall, before it become a Law, be presented to the President of the United States; If he approve he shall sign it, but if not he shall return it, with his Objections to that House in which it shall have originated . . . . If after . . . Reconsideration two thirds of that House shall agree to pass the Bill, it shall be sent . . . to the other House . . . and if approved by two thirds of that House, it shall become a Law.

(3) Every Order, Resolution, or Vote to which the Concurrence of the Senate and House of Representatives may be necessary (except on a question of Adjournment) shall be presented to the President of the United States; and before

LIBRARY OF CONGRESS LEGISLATIVE REFERENCE SERVICE, THE CONSTITUTION OF THE UNITED STATES OF AMERICA (1964 ed.).

the Same shall take Effect, shall be approved by him, or being disapproved by him, shall be repassed by two thirds of the Senate and House of Representatives . . . .

Section 8   (1) The Congress shall have Power To lay and collect Taxes, Duties, Imposts and Excises, to pay the Debts and provide for the common Defence . . . of the United States;

(2) To borrow Money on the credit of the United States;

(3) To regulate Commerce with foreign Nations . . . and with the Indian Tribes;

(4) To establish an uniform Rule of Naturalization . . .;

(5) To coin Money, regulate the Value thereof, and of foreign Coin . . .;

(10) To define and punish Piracies and Felonies committed on the high Seas, and Offences against the Law of Nations;

(11) To declare War, grant Letters of Marque and Reprisal, and make Rules concerning Captures on Land and Water;

(12) To raise and support Armies, but no Appropriation of Money to that Use shall be for a longer Term than two Years;

(13) To provide and maintain a Navy;

(14) To make Rules for the Government and Regulation of the land and naval Forces;

(15) To provide for calling forth the Militia to execute the Laws of the Union, suppress Insurrections and repel Invasions;

(16) To provide for organizing, arming, and disciplining, the Militia, and for governing such Part of them as may be employed in the Service of the United States, reserving to the States . . . the Appointment of the Officers, and the Authority of training the Militia according to the discipline prescribed by Congress;

(17) [T]o exercise [exclusive] Authority over all Places purchased . . . for the Erection of Forts, Magazines, Arsenals, dock-Yards, and other needful Buildings;—And

(18) To make all Laws which shall be necessary and proper for carrying into Execution the foregoing Powers, and all other Powers vested by this Constitution in the Government of the United States, or in any Department or Officer thereof.

Section 9 (2) The Privilege of the Writ of Habeas Corpus shall not be suspended, unless when in Cases of Rebellion or Invasion the public Safety may require it.

(7) No Money shall be drawn from the Treasury, but in Consequence of Appropriations made by Law . . . .

Section 10 (1) No State shall enter into any Treaty, Alliance, or Confederation; grant Letters of Marque and Reprisal; coin Money; emit Bills of Credit, make any Thing but gold and silver Coin a Tender in Payment of Debts . . . .

(2) No State shall, without the Consent of the Congress, lay any Imposts or Duties on Imports or Exports . . . .

(3) No State shall, without the Consent of Congress, lay any Duty of Tonnage, keep Troops, or Ships of War in time of Peace, enter into any Agreement or Compact . . . with a foreign Power, or engage in War, unless actually invaded, or in such imminent Danger as will not admit of delay.

Article II

Section 1 (1) The executive Power shall be vested in a President of the United States of America.

Section 2 (1) The President shall be Commander in Chief of the Army and Navy of the United States, and of the Militia of the several States, when called into the actual Service of the United States; he may require the Opinion, in writing, of the principal Officer in each of the executive Departments, upon any Subject relating to the Duties of their respective Offices, and he shall have Power to grant Reprieves and Pardons for Offences against the United States, except in Cases of Impeachment.

(2) He shall have Power, by and with the Advice and Consent of the Senate, to make Treaties, provided two thirds of the Senators present concur; and he shall nominate, and by and with the Advice and Consent of the Senate, shall

appoint Ambassadors . . . and all other Officers of the United States, whose Appointments are not herein otherwise provided for, and which shall be established by Law: but the Congress may by Law vest the Appointment of such inferior Officers, as they think proper, in the President alone . . . or in the Heads of Departments.

The President shall have Power to fill up all Vacancies that may happen during the Recess of the Senate, by granting Commissions which shall expire at the End of their next Session.

Section 3 He shall from time to time give to the Congress Information of the State of the Union, and recommend to their Consideration such Measures as he shall judge necessary and expedient; he may, on extraordinary Occasions, convene both Houses, or either of them . . . ; he shall receive Ambassadors and other public Ministers; he shall take Care that the Laws be faithfully executed, and shall Commission all the Officers of the United States.

Section 4 The President, Vice President and all Civil Officers of the United States, shall be removed from Office on Impeachment for, and Conviction of, Treason, Bribery, or other high Crimes and Misdemeanors.

Article IV

Section 3 (1) New States may be admitted by the Congress into this Union; but no new State shall be formed or erected within the Jurisdiction of any other State; nor any State be formed by the Junction of two or more States, or Parts of States, without the Consent of the Legislatures of the States concerned as well as of the Congress.

(2) The Congress shall have Power to dispose of and make all needful Rules and Regulations respecting the Territory or other Property belonging to the United States. . . .

Section 4 The United States shall guarantee to every State in this Union a Republican Form of Government, and shall protect each of them against Invasion; and on Application of the Legislature, or of the Executive (when the Legislature cannot be convened) against domestic Violence.

Appendix B

A Sampler of Executive
Statements Supporting Congressional Control

According to George Washington in 1793, offensive action against the Creek Indians could begin "whenever Congress should decide that measure to be proper and necessary. The constitution vests the power of declaring war in Congress; therefore no offensive expedition of importance can be undertaken until after they shall have deliberated upon the subject, and authorized such a measure." 10 THE WRITINGS OF GEORGE WASHINGTON 367 (J. Sparks ed. 1836).

That same year, Washington's Secretary of State, Thomas Jefferson, said that reprisals were up to Congress: "The making a reprisal on a nation is a very serious thing. Remonstrance and refusal of satisfaction ought to precede; and when reprisal follows, it is considered an act of war, and never failed to produce it in the case of a nation able to make war; besides, if the case were important and ripe for that step, Congress must be called upon to take it; the right of reprisal being expressly lodged with them by the Constitution, and not with the Executive." 7 J. MOORE, A DIGEST OF INTERNATIONAL LAW 123 (1906) (hereafter cited as MOORE).

In 1790 Jefferson had referred to Congress the problem of Barbary attacks on American commerce in the Mediterranean: "Upon the whole, it rests with Congress to decide between war, tribute, and ransom, as the means of re-establishing our Mediterranean commerce. If war, they will consider how far our own resources shall be called forth, and how far they will enable the Executive to engage, in the forms of the constitution, the co-operation of other powers." 1 AMERICAN STATE PAPERS, FOREIGN RELATIONS 105 (W. Lowrie and M. Clarke eds. 1832).

President John Adams called Congress into special session in May 1797 to denounce French harassment of American shipping and to state: "It remains for Congress to prescribe such regulations as will enable our seafaring citizens to defend themselves against violations of the law of nations, and at the same time restrain them from committing acts of hostility against the powers at war." 1 MESSAGES AND PAPERS OF THE PRESIDENTS 1789-1897, at 237 (J. Richardson ed. 1897) (hereafter cited as RICHARDSON).

In May of the next year, shortly before Congress voted the naval war with France, Alexander Hamilton instructed the Secretary of War concerning the use of a few newly available naval vessels. Hamilton advised that the Executive could do remarkably little with them, only

employ the Ships as Convoys [of American merchantmen] with authority to *repel* force by *force*, (but not to capture) and to repress hostilities within our waters including a marine league from our coasts—

Any thing beyond this must fall under the idea of *reprisals* & requires the sanction of that department which is to declare or make war.

In so delicate a case, in one which involves so important a consequence as that of War—my opinion is that no doubtful authority ought to be exercised by the President.
1 NAVAL DOCUMENTS RELATED TO THE QUASI-WAR BETWEEN THE UNITED STATES AND FRANCE 75-76 (1935).

When President himself, Jefferson in 1801 sent a squadron to the Mediterranean to defend American shipping against Barbary piracy. The *Enterprise* captured a Tripolitan cruiser after being attacked by it. Though Jefferson had not asked legislative authorization for dispatch of the squadron, he turned to Congress for support in meek terms: "The Legislature will doubtless consider whether, by authorizing measures of offense also, they will place our force on an equal footing with that of its adversaries. I communicate all material information on this subject, that in the exercise of this important function confided by the Constitution to the Legislature exclusively their judgment may form itself on a knowledge and consideration of every circumstance of weight." 1 RICHARDSON 327.

In 1805 President Jefferson sent a special message to Congress seeking its blessing for the removal of the Spanish from West Florida, which the United States believed it had obtained under the Louisiana Purchase. The President was typically deferential:

Considering that Congress alone is constitutionally invested with the power of changing our condition from peace to war, I have thought it my duty to await their authority for using force in any degree which could be avoided. I have barely instructed the officers stationed in the neighborhood of the aggressions [alleged Spanish attacks on American lives and property] to protect our citizens from violence, to patrol within the borders actually delivered to us, and not to go out of them but when necessary to repel an inroad or to rescue a citizen or his property . . . .
1 RICHARDSON 389.

Jefferson did urge on the legislators a judicious application of force to speed the Spanish on their way:

The present crisis in Europe is favorable for pressing . . . a settlement, and not a moment should be lost in availing ourselves of it. . . . Formal war is not necessary . . . but the protection of our citizens, the spirit and honor of our country require that force should be interposed to a certain degree. . . .

But the course to be pursued will require the command of means which it belongs to Congress exclusively to yield or to deny. To them I communicate every fact material for their information and the documents necessary to engage them to judge for themselves. To their wisdom, then, I look for the course I am to pursue, and will pursue with sincere zeal that which they shall approve.
1 RICHARDSON 390.

President Madison delivered an inflammatory 1812 war message to Congress but intoned nonetheless that final decision lay "wisely" with the legislators: "Whether the United States shall continue passive under these progressive usurpations and these accumulating wrongs, or, opposing force to force in defense of

their national rights, shall commit a just cause into the hands of
the Almighty Disposer of Events . . . is a solemn question
which the Constitution wisely confides to the legislative department of the Government." 1 RICHARDSON 504-05.

John Quincy Adams, Secretary of State under Monroe and
President in his own right, affirmed in later life his belief in the
constitutional primacy of Congress over war and peace—but
lamented it as an "absurdity." He termed the 1811 secret act for
executive occupation of East Florida as one of "those singular
anomalies of our system which have grown out of that error in
our Constitution which confers upon the legislative assemblies
the power of declaring war, which, in the theory of government, according to Montesquieu and Rousseau, is strictly an
Executive act." 4 MEMOIRS OF JOHN QUINCY ADAMS 32 (C. F.
Adams ed. 1875).

In late 1836, during troubles caused by the secession of Texas
from Mexico, President Andrew Jackson accorded Congress a
large voice in decisions whether the United States should
recognize other nations when recognition courts war:

It is to be presumed that on no future occasion will a dispute arise, as
none has heretofore occurred, between the Executive and Legislature in the exercise of the power of recognition. It will always be
considered consistent with the spirit of the Constitution, and most
safe, that it should be exercised, when probably leading to war, with
a previous understanding with that body by whom war can alone be
declared, and by whom all the provisions for sustaining its perils must
be furnished. Its submission to Congress, which represents in one of
its branches the States of this Union and in the other the people of
the United States, where there may be reasonable ground to appre-
hend so grave a consequence, would certainly afford the fullest satisfaction to our own country and a perfect guaranty to all other nations
of the justice and prudence of the measures which might be adopted.
3 RICHARDSON 267.

Abraham Lincoln shared none of John Quincy Adams's distaste for congressional prerogative when he defended his 1848
vote for a House resolution censuring James K. Polk on the
ground that the Mexican War had been "unnecessarily and un-

constitutionally begun by the President of the United States."
CONG. GLOBE, 30th Cong., 1st Sess. 95 (1848). Congressman
Lincoln explained to his correspondent:

Let me first state what I understand to be your position. It is that if it
shall become necessary to repel invasion, the President may, without
violation of the Constitution, cross the line and invade the territory of
another country, and that whether such necessity exists in any given
case the President is the sole judge. . . .

. . . Allow the President to invade a neighboring nation whenever
he shall deem it necessary to repel an invasion, and you allow him to
do so whenever he may choose to say he deems it necessary for such
purpose, and you allow him to make war at pleasure. Study to see if
you can fix any limit to his power in this respect, after having given
him so much as you propose. If to-day he should choose to say he
thinks it necessary to invade Canada to prevent the British from in-
vading us, how could you stop him? . . .

The provision of the Constitution giving the war-making power to
Congress was dictated, as I understand it, by the following reasons:
Kings had always been involving and impoverishing their people in
wars, pretending generally, if not always, that the good of the people
was the object. This our convention understood to be the most op-
pressive of all kingly oppressions, and they resolved to so frame the
Constitution that no one man should hold the power of bringing
oppression upon us. But your view destroys the whole matter, and
places our President where kings have always stood.

2 THE WRITINGS OF ABRAHAM LINCOLN 51-52 (A. Lapsley ed. 1905).

During Polk's administration, Secretary of State Buchanan
rebuffed a diplomat's 1848 call for the Executive to force the
Hawaiians to satisfy an economic obligation: "But if the claim
were never so just, if it had been a case in which this Government were bound officially to interfere and if the amount due
the claimant had been acknowledged by the Hawaiian Government, the President could not employ the naval force of the
United States to enforce its payment without the authority of
an act of Congress. The war-making power alone can authorize
such a measure." 7 MOORE 163.

While Tyler's Secretary of State in 1851, Daniel Webster
rejected, in turn, an appeal by the Hawaiians for assistance

against French territorial ambitions, stating that the Executive lacked constitutional authority to act:

In the first place, I have to say that the war-making power in this Government rests entirely with Congress; and that the President can authorize belligerent operations only in the cases expressly provided for by the Constitution and the laws. By these no power is given to the Executive to oppose an attack by one independent nation on the possessions of another. We are bound to regard both France and Hawaii as independent states, and equally independent, and though the general policy of the Government might lead it to take part with either in a controversy with the other, still, if this interference be an act of hostile force, it is not within the constitutional power of the President; and still less is it within the power of any subordinate agent of government, civil or military.
7 MOORE 163-64.

In 1857 Secretary of State Lewis Cass similarly declined British invitations for the United States to join in an expedition against China:

This proposition, looking to a participation by the United States in the existing hostilities against China, makes it proper to remind your lordship that, under the Constitution of the United States, the executive branch of this Government is not the war-making power. The exercise of that great attribute of sovereignty is vested in Congress, and the President has no authority to order aggressive hostilities to be undertaken.

Our naval officers have the right—it is their duty, indeed—to employ the forces under their command, not only in self-defense, but for the protection of the persons and property of our citizens when exposed to acts of lawless outrage, and this they have done both in China and elsewhere, and will do again when necessary. But military expeditions into the Chinese territory can not be undertaken without the authority of the National Legislature.
7 MOORE 164.

Cass spoke for President Buchanan, whose administration is unsurpassed in executive declarations that Congress controls war and peace. In one of his many requests to the legislators for armed authorization, the President seemed to rule out on constitutional grounds even executive action to protect American lives and property against ongoing attack, despite the 1857 opinion of his Secretary of State just quoted. Thus, in 1859 Buchanan told Congress:

If the President orders a vessel of war to any of these [Latin] ports to demand prompt redress for outrages committed, the offending parties are well aware that in case of refusal the commander can do no more than remonstrate. He can resort to no hostile act. . . . The remedy for this state of things can only be supplied by Congress, since the Constitution has confided to that body alone the power to make war. Without the authority of Congress the Executive can not lawfully direct any force, however near it may be to the scene of difficulty, to enter the territory . . . for the purpose of defending the persons and property . . . .
5 RICHARDSON 539.

Grover Cleveland in a special 1893 message to Congress deplored American involvement in the overthrow of the Hawaiian government, noting as one of the event's defects an absence of legislative approval: "By an act of war, committed with the participation of a diplomatic representative of the United States and without authority of Congress, the Government of a feeble but friendly and confiding people has been overthrown. A substantial wrong has thus been done which a due regard for our national character as well as the rights of the injured people requires we should endeavor to repair." 9 RICHARDSON 470.

In 1898 President McKinley left to Congress the final disposition of American policy toward Cuba:

. . . I ask the Congress to authorize and empower the President to take measures to secure a full and final termination of hostilities between the Government of Spain and the people of Cuba, and to secure in the island the establishment of a stable government . . . and to use the military and naval forces of the United States as may be necessary for these purposes.

. . . .
The issue is now with the Congress. It is a solemn responsibility . . . . Prepared to execute every obligation imposed upon me by the Constitution and the law, I await your action.

10 RICHARDSON 150.

Similarly, in 1911 President Taft said that it was for Congress to decide whether troops should enter Mexico to safeguard American lives and property threatened by an ongoing revolution:

It seems my duty as Commander in Chief to place troops in sufficient number where, if Congress shall direct that they enter Mexico to save American lives and property, an effective movement may be promptly made. The assumption by the press that I contemplate intervention in Mexico soil to protect American lives is of course gratuitous, because I seriously doubt whether I have such authority under any circumstances, and if I had I would not exercise it without congressional approval.
16 RICHARDSON 264 (rev. ed. 1917).

Before acceding in 1918 to Allied requests that the United States send troops to Russia, President Wilson first refused, relying in part on constitutional scruple. As he wrote Marshal Foch: "To send troops, would be to create a state of War, into which the United States could not enter without a formal declaration, by Congress, so I could not send a man, even if I wanted to, which I do not." W. GRAVES, AMERICA'S SIBERIAN ADVENTURE 93 (1931).

Franklin Roosevelt relied on like scruple when he wrote Premier Reynaud as France was falling in 1940:

In these hours which are so heart-rending to the French people and yourself, I send you the assurances of my utmost sympathy and I can further assure you that so long as the French people continue in defense of their liberty . . . so long will they rest assured that matériel and supplies will be sent to them from the United States . . . .

I know that you will understand that these statements carry with them no implication of military commitments. Only the Congress can make such commitments.
Hearings on War Powers Legislation Before the Senate Comm. on Foreign Relations, 92d Cong., 1st Sess. 266 (1971).

Among post–World War II Presidents, only Eisenhower and Carter have conceded much verbally to congressional war powers. When the United States was pressed to come to

France's aid in Indochina at the time of Dienbienphu, the President said that congressional authorization would be required. He stated at a news conference on March 10, 1954, that "there is going to be no involvement of America in war unless it is a result of the constitutional process that is placed upon Congress to declare it. Now, let us have that clear." PUBLIC PAPERS OF THE PRESIDENTS: EISENHOWER, 1954, at 306. In the same vein, Anthony Eden's 1956 efforts to have the United States assist in defusing that year's Middle East crisis came to nothing for alleged constitutional reasons. According to Eden's memoirs: "The Americans, though sympathetic in general terms, laid stress on their constitutional difficulties, which, they said, prevented them from giving commitments to use force without Congressional approval. They could not even concentrate forces as a precaution." A. EDEN, THE MEMOIRS OF ANTHONY EDEN: FULL CIRCLE 372 (1960). Eden doubted that Eisenhower's difficulties were constitutional. As to President Carter, he found the 1973 War Powers Resolution "an appropriate reduction" in executive prerogative. *See* Chapter XI, notes 63 to 65, 68 and accompanying text.

Appendix C

Text of the War Powers Resolution of 1973 and Related Documents

The War Powers Resolution

SECTION 1. This joint resolution may be cited as the "War Powers Resolution."

SEC. 2. (a) It is the purpose of this joint resolution to fulfill the intent of the framers of the Constitution of the United States and insure that the collective judgment of both the Congress and the President will apply to the introduction of United States Armed Forces into hostilities, or into situations where imminent involvement in hostilities is clearly indicated by the circumstances, and to the continued use of such forces in hostilities or in such situations.

(b) Under article I, section 8, of the Constitution, it is specifically provided that the Congress shall have the power to make all laws necessary and proper for carrying into execution, not only its own powers but also all other powers vested by the Constitution in the Government of the United States, or in any department or officer thereof.

(c) The constitutional powers of the President as Commander-in-Chief to introduce United States Armed Forces into hostilities, or into situations where imminent involvement in hostilities is clearly indicated by the circumstances, are exercised only pursuant to (1) a declaration of war, (2) specific statutory authorization, or (3) a national emergency created by

50 U.S.C. §§ 1541-48 (Supp. 1975). Inconsequential changes have been made in the Resolution since its passage. See 50 U.S.C.A. §§ 1541-48 (Supp. 1980).

attack upon the United States, its territories or possessions, or its armed forces.

SEC. 3.   The President in every possible instance shall consult with Congress before introducing United States Armed Forces into hostilities or into situations where imminent involvement in hostilities is clearly indicated by the circumstances, and after every such introduction shall consult regularly with the Congress until United States Armed Forces are no longer engaged in hostilities or have been removed from such situations.

SEC. 4.   (a)   In the absence of a declaration of war, in any case in which United States Armed Forces are introduced—

(1)   into hostilities or into situations where imminent involvement in hostilities is clearly indicated by the circumstances;
(2)   into the territory, airspace or waters of a foreign nation, while equipped for combat, except for deployments which relate solely to supply, replacement, repair, or training of such forces; or
(3)   in numbers which substantially enlarge United States Armed Forces equipped for combat already located in a foreign nation;

the President shall submit within 48 hours to the Speaker of the House of Representatives and to the President pro tempore of the Senate a report, in writing, setting forth—

(A)   the circumstances necessitating the introduction of United States Armed Forces;
(B)   the constitutional and legislative authority under which such introduction took place; and
(C)   the estimated scope and duration of the hostilities or involvement.

(b)   The President shall provide such other information as the Congress may request in the fulfillment of its constitutional responsibilities with respect to committing the Nation to war and to the use of United States Armed Forces abroad.

(c)   Whenever United States Armed Forces are introduced into hostilities or into any situation described in subsection (a) of this section, the President shall, so long as such armed forces continue to be engaged in such hostilities or situation, report to the Congress periodically on the status of such hostilities or situation as well as on the scope and duration of such hostilities or situation, but in no event shall he report to the Congress less often than once every six months.

SEC. 5.   (a)   Each report submitted pursuant to section 4(a) (1) of this title shall be transmitted to the Speaker of the House of Representatives and to the President pro tempore of the Senate on the same calendar day. Each report so transmitted shall be referred to the Committee on Foreign Affairs [now the Committee on International Relations] of the House of Representatives and to the Committee on Foreign Relations of the Senate for appropriate action. If, when the report is transmitted, the Congress has adjourned sine die or has adjourned for any period in excess of three calendar days, the Speaker of the House of Representatives and the President pro tempore of the Senate, if they deem it advisable (or if petitioned by at least 30 percent of the membership of their respective Houses) shall jointly request the President to convene Congress in order that it may consider the report and take appropriate action pursuant to this section.

(b)   Within sixty calendar days after a report is submitted or is required to be submitted pursuant to section 4(a) (1) of this title, whichever is earlier, the President shall terminate any use of United States Armed Forces with respect to which such report was submitted (or required to be submitted), unless the Congress (1) has declared war or has enacted a specific authorization for such use of United States Armed Forces, (2) has extended by law such sixty-day period, or (3) is physically unable to meet as a result of an armed attack upon the United States. Such sixty-day period shall be extended for not more than an additional thirty days if the President determines and certifies to the Congress in writing that unavoidable military necessity respecting the safety of United States Armed Forces requires the continued use of such armed forces in the course of bringing about a prompt removal of such forces.

(c)   Notwithstanding subsection (b) of this section, at any time that United States Armed Forces are engaged in hostilities outside the territory of the United States, its possessions and territories without a declaration of war or specific statutory authorization, such forces shall be removed by the President if the Congress so directs by concurrent resolution.

SEC. 6.   (a)   Any joint resolution or bill introduced pursuant to section 5(b) of this title at least thirty calendar days before the expiration of the sixty-day period specified in such section shall be referred to the Committee on Foreign Affairs of the House of Representatives or the Committee on Foreign Relations of the Senate, as the case may be, and such committee shall report one such joint resolution or bill, together with its recommendations, not later than twenty-four calendar days before the expiration of the sixty-day period specified in such section, unless such House shall otherwise determine by the yeas and nays.

(b)   Any joint resolution or bill so reported shall become the pending business of the House in question (in the case of the Senate the time for debate shall be equally divided between the proponents and the opponents), and shall be voted on within three calendar days thereafter, unless such House shall otherwise determine by yeas and nays.

(c)   Such a joint resolution or bill passed by one House shall be referred to the committee of the other House named in subsection (a) of this section and shall be reported out not later than fourteen calendar days before the expiration of the sixty-day period specified in section 5(b) of this title. The joint resolution or bill so reported shall become the pending business of the House in question and shall be voted on within three calendar days after it has been reported, unless such House shall otherwise determine by yeas and nays.

(d)   In the case of any disagreement between the two Houses of Congress with respect to a joint resolution or bill passed by both Houses, conferees shall be promptly appointed and the committee of conference shall make and file a report with respect to such resolution or bill not later than four calendar days before the expiration of the sixty-day period specified in section 5(b) of this title. In the event the conferees are unable to agree within 48 hours, they shall report back to their respective Houses in disagreement. Notwithstanding any rule in either House concerning the printing of conference reports in the Record or concerning any delay in the consideration of such reports, such report shall be acted on by both Houses not later than the expiration of such sixty-day period.

SEC. 7. (a) Any concurrent resolution introduced pursuant to section 5(c) of this title shall be referred to the Committee on Foreign Affairs of the House of Representatives or the Committee on Foreign Relations of the Senate, as the case may be, and one such concurrent resolution shall be reported out by such committee together with its recommendations within fifteen calendar days, unless such House shall otherwise determine by the yeas and nays.

(b) Any concurrent resolution so reported shall become the pending business of the House in question (in the case of the Senate the time for debate shall be equally divided between the proponents and the opponents) and shall be voted on within three calendar days thereafter, unless such House shall otherwise determine by yeas and nays.

(c) Such a concurrent resolution passed by one House shall be referred to the committee of the other House named in subsection (a) of this section and shall be reported out by such committee together with its recommendations within fifteen calendar days and shall thereupon become the pending business of such House and shall be voted upon within three calendar days, unless such House shall otherwise determine by yeas and nays.

(d) In the case of any disagreement between the two Houses of Congress with respect to a concurrent resolution passed by both Houses, conferees shall be promptly appointed and the committee of conference shall make and file a report with respect to such concurrent resolution within six calendar days after the legislation is referred to the committee of conference. Notwithstanding any rule in either House concerning the printing of conference reports in the Record or concerning any delay in the consideration of such reports, such report shall be acted on by both Houses not later than six calendar days after the conference report is filed. In the event the conferees are unable to agree within 48 hours, they shall report back to their respective Houses in disagreement.

SEC. 8. (a) Authority to introduce United States Armed Forces into hostilities or into situations wherein involvement in hostilities is clearly indicated by the circumstances shall not be inferred—

(1) from any provision of law (whether or not in effect before the date of the enactment of this joint resolution), including any provision contained in any appropriation Act, unless such provision specifically authorizes the introduction of United States Armed Forces into hostilities or into such situations and states that it is intended to constitute specific statutory authorization within the meaning of this joint resolution; or

(2) from any treaty heretofore or hereafter ratified unless such treaty is implemented by legislation specifically authorizing the introduction of United States Armed Forces into hostilities or into such situations and stating that it is intended to constitute specific statutory authorization within the meaning of this joint resolution.

(b) Nothing in this joint resolution shall be construed to require any further specific statutory authorization to permit members of United States Armed Forces to participate jointly with members of the armed forces of one or more foreign countries in the headquarters operations of high-level military commands which were established prior to the date of enactment of this joint resolution and pursuant to the United Nations Charter or any treaty ratified by the United States prior to such date.

(c) For purposes of this joint resolution, the term "introduction of United States Armed Forces" includes the assignment of members of such armed forces to command, coordinate, participate in the movement of, or accompany the regular or irregular military forces of any foreign country or government when such military forces are engaged, or there exists an imminent threat that such forces will become engaged, in hostilities.

(d) Nothing in this joint resolution—

(1) is intended to alter the constitutional authority of the Congress or of the President, or the provisions of existing treaties; or

(2) shall be construed as granting any authority to the President with respect to the introduction of United States Armed Forces into

hostilities or into situations wherein involvement in hostilities is clearly indicated by the circumstances which authority he would not have had in the absence of this joint resolution.

SEC. 9.   If any provision of this joint resolution or the application thereof to any person or circumstance is held invalid, the remainder of the joint resolution and the application of such provision to any other person or circumstance shall not be affected thereby.

SEC. 10.   This joint resolution shall take effect on the date of its enactment.

Text of President Nixon's Message
Vetoing the War Powers Resolution

I hereby return without my approval . . . the War Powers Resolution. While I am in accord with the desire of the Congress to assert its proper role in the conduct of our foreign affairs, the restrictions which this resolution would impose upon the authority of the President are both unconstitutional and dangerous to the best interests of our Nation.

The proper roles of the Congress and the Executive in the conduct of foreign affairs have been debated since the founding of our country. Only recently, however, has there been a serious challenge to the wisdom of the Founding Fathers in choosing not to draw a precise and detailed line of demarcation between the foreign policy powers of the two branches.

The Founding Fathers understood the impossibility of foreseeing every contingency that might arise in this complex area. They acknowledged the need for flexibility in responding to changing circumstances. They recognized that foreign policy decisions must be made through close cooperation between the two branches and not through rigidly codified procedures.

These principles remain as valid today as they were when our Constitution was written. Yet [the Resolution] would violate those principles by defining the President's powers in ways which would strictly limit his constitutional authority.

9 WEEKLY COMPILATION OF PRESIDENTIAL DOCUMENTS 1285-87 (1973).

[The Resolution] would attempt to take away, by a mere legislative act, authorities which the President has properly exercised under the Constitution for almost 200 years. One of its provisions would automatically cut off certain authorities after sixty days unless the Congress extended them. Another would allow the Congress to eliminate certain authorities merely by the passage of a concurrent resolution—an action which does not normally have the force of law, since it denies the President his constitutional role in approving legislation.

I believe that both these provisions are unconstitutional. The only way in which the constitutional powers of a branch of the Government can be altered is by amending the Constitution— and any attempt to make such alterations by legislation alone is clearly without force.

While I firmly believe that a veto of [the Resolution] is warranted solely on constitutional grounds, I am also deeply disturbed by the practical consequences of this resolution. For it would seriously undermine this Nation's ability to act decisively and convincingly in times of international crisis. As a result, the confidence of our allies in our ability to assist them could be diminished and the respect of our adversaries for our deterrent posture could decline. A permanent and substantial element of unpredictability would be injected into the world's assessment of American behavior, further increasing the likelihood of miscalculation and war.

If this resolution had been in operation, America's effective response to a variety of challenges in recent years would have been vastly complicated or even made impossible. We may well have been unable to respond in the way we did during the Berlin crisis of 1961, the Cuban missile crisis of 1962, the Congo rescue operation in 1964, and the Jordanian crisis of 1970—to mention just a few examples. In addition, our recent actions to bring about a peaceful settlement of the hostilities in the Middle East would have been seriously impaired if this resolution had been in force.

While all the specific consequences of [the Resolution] cannot yet be predicted, it is clear that it would undercut the ability of the United States to act as an effective influence for peace.

For example, the provision automatically cutting off certain authorities after 60 days unless they are extended by the Congress could work to prolong or intensify a crisis. Until the Congress suspended the deadline, there would be at least a chance of United States withdrawal and an adversary would be tempted therefore to postpone serious negotiations until the 60 days were up. Only after the Congress acted would there be a strong incentive for an adversary to negotiate. In addition, the very existence of a deadline could lead to an escalation of hostilities in order to achieve certain objectives before the 60 days expired.

The measure would jeopardize our role as a force for peace in other ways as well. It would, for example, strike from the President's hand a wide range of important peace-keeping tools by eliminating his ability to exercise quiet diplomacy backed by subtle shifts in our military deployments. It would also cast into doubt authorities which Presidents have used to undertake certain humanitarian relief missions in conflict areas, to protect fishing boats from seizure, to deal with ship or aircraft hijackings, and to respond to threats of attack. Not the least of the adverse consequences of this resolution would be the prohibition contained in section 8 against fulfilling our obligations under the NATO treaty as ratified by the Senate. Finally, since the bill is somewhat vague as to when the 60 day rule would apply, it could lead to extreme confusion and dangerous disagreements concerning the prerogatives of the two branches, seriously damaging our ability to respond to international crises.

I am particularly disturbed by the fact that certain of the President's constitutional powers as Commander in Chief of the Armed Forces would terminate automatically under this resolution 60 days after they were invoked. No overt Congressional action would be required to cut off these powers—they would disappear automatically unless the Congress extended them. In effect, the Congress is here attempting to increase its policy-making role through a provision which requires it to take absolutely no action at all.

In my view, the proper way for the Congress to make known

its will on such foreign policy questions is through a positive
action, with full debate on the merits of the issue and with each
member taking the responsibility of casting a yes or no vote
after considering those merits. The authorization and appropriations process represents one of the ways in which such influence can be exercised. I do not, however, believe that the
Congress can responsibly contribute its considered, collective
judgment on such grave questions without full debate and
without a yes or no vote. Yet this is precisely what the joint
resolution would allow. It would give every future Congress
the ability to handcuff every future President merely by doing
nothing and sitting still. In my view, one cannot become a responsible partner unless one is prepared to take responsible
action.

The responsible and effective exercise of the war powers
requires the fullest cooperation between the Congress and the
Executive and the prudent fulfillment by each branch of its
constitutional responsibilities. [The Resolution] includes certain constructive measures which would foster this process by
enhancing the flow of information from the executive branch
to the Congress. Section 3, for example, calls for consultations
with the Congress before and during the involvement of
United States forces in hostilities abroad. This provision is
consistent with the desire of this Administration for regularized consultations with the Congress in an even wider range of
circumstances.

I believe that full and cooperative participation in foreign
policy matters by both the executive and the legislative
branches could be enhanced by a careful and dispassionate
study of their constitutional roles. Helpful proposals for such a
study have already been made in the Congress. I would wel-
come the establishment of a non-partisan commission on the
constitutional roles of the Congress and the President in the
conduct of foreign affairs. This commission could make a
thorough review of the principal constitutional issues in Executive-Congressional relations, including the war powers, the
international agreement powers, and the question of Executive privilege, and then submit its recommendations to the

President and the Congress. The members of such a commission could be drawn from both parties—and could represent many perspectives including those of the Congress, the executive branch, the legal profession, and the academic community.

This Administration is dedicated to strengthening cooperation between the Congress and the President in the conduct of foreign affairs and to preserving the constitutional prerogatives of both branches of our Government. I know that the Congress shares that goal. A commission on the constitutional roles of the Congress and the President would provide a useful opportunity for both branches to work together toward that common objective.

Text of President Ford's Reports
Pursuant to the War Powers Resolution

Danang Report of April 4, 1975

As you know, last Saturday I directed United States participation in an international humanitarian relief effort to transport refugees from Danang and other seaports to safer areas farther south in Vietnam. The United States has been joined in this humanitarian effort by a number of other countries who are offering people, supplies and vessels to assist in this effort. This effort was undertaken in response to urgent appeals from the Government of the Republic of Vietnam because of the extremely grave nature of the circumstances involving the lives of hundreds of thousands of refugees. This situation has been brought about by large-scale violations of the Agreement Ending the War and Restoring the Peace in Vietnam by the North Vietnamese who have been conducting massive attacks on the northern and central provinces of South Vietnam.

In accordance with my desire to keep the Congress fully informed on this matter, and taking note of the provision of section 4(a) (2) of the War Powers Resolution (Public Law 93-148), I wish to report to you concerning one aspect of United

121 CONG. REC. 9079 (Danang), 10065 (Phnom Penh), 12803-04 (Saigon), 14452 (Mayaguez) (1975).

States participation in the refugee evacuation effort. Because of the large number of refugees and the overwhelming dimensions of the task, I have ordered U.S. Naval vessels to assist in this effort, including Amphibious Task Group 76.8 with 12 embarked helicopters and approximately 700 Marines. These naval vessels have been authorized to approach the coast of South Vietnam to pick up refugees and U.S. nationals, and transport them to safety. Marines are being detailed to vessels participating in the rescue mission. The first vessel entered South Vietnam territorial waters at 0400 a.m. EDT on April 3, 1975.

Although these forces are equipped for combat within the meaning of section 4(a) (2) of Public Law 93-148, their sole mission is to assist in the evacuation including the maintenance of order on board the vessels engaged in that task.

As stated above, the purpose of the introduction of United States Naval vessels into Vietnamese waters is to assist in an international humanitarian effort involving vessels of several nations, including both military and civilian craft. The United States participation in this effort includes the charter of commercial vessels, the use of Military Sealift Command vessels with civilian crews, as well as United States naval vessels with military crews. This effort is being undertaken pursuant to the President's constitutional authority as Commander-in-Chief and Chief Executive in the conduct of foreign relations and pursuant to the Foreign Assistance Act of 1961, as amended, which authorizes humanitarian assistance to refugees, civilian war casualties and other persons disadvantaged by hostilities or conditions relating to hostilities in South Vietnam.

You will appreciate, I am sure, my difficulty in telling you precisely how long United States forces may be needed in this effort. Our present estimate, however, is that this operation may involve the presence of United States Naval vessels in Vietnamese waters for a period of at least several weeks.

Phnom Penh Report of April 12, 1975

As you and other members of Congress were advised, in view of circumstances in Cambodia, the United States had certain contingency plans to utilize United States Armed Forces to assure the safe evacuation of U.S. Nationals from that country. On Friday, 11 April 1975, the Khmer Communists forces had ruptured Government of the Khmer Republic (GKR) defensive lines to the north, northwest and east of Phnom Penh and were within mortar range of Pochentong Airfield and the outskirts of Phnom Penh. In view of this deteriorating military situation, and on the recommendations of the American Ambassador there, I ordered U.S. military forces to proceed with the planned evacuation out of consideration for the safety of U.S. citizens.

In accordance with my desire that the Congress be fully informed on this matter, and taking note of Section 4 of the War Powers Resolution (P.L. 93-148), I wish to report to you that the first elements of the U.S. forces entered Cambodian airspace at 8:34 P.M. EDT on 11 April. Military forces included 350 ground combat troops of the U.S. Marines, 36 helicopters, and supporting tactical air and command and control elements. The Marines were deployed from helicopters to assure the security of [a] helicopter landing zone within the city of Phnom Penh. The first helicopter landed at approximately 10:00 P.M. EDT 11 April 1975, and the last evacuees and ground security force Marines departed the Cambodian landing zone at approximately 12:20 A.M. on 12 April 1975. The last elements of the force to leave received hostile recoilless rifle fire. There was no firing by U.S. forces at any time during the operation. No U.S. Armed Forces personnel were killed, wounded or missing, and there were no casualties among the American evacuees.

Although these forces were equipped for combat within the meaning of Section 4(a) (2) of Public Law 93-148, their mission was to effect the evacuation of U.S. Nationals. Present information indicates that a total of 82 U.S. citizens were evacuated and that the task force was also able to accommodate 35 third country nationals and 159 Cambodians including employees of the U.S. Government.

The operation was ordered and conducted pursuant to the President's Constitutional executive power and authority as Commander-in-Chief of U.S. Armed Forces.

I am sure you share with me my pride in the Armed Forces of the United States and my thankfulness that the operation was conducted without incident.

Saigon Report of April 30, 1975

On April 4, 1975, I reported that U.S. naval vessels had been ordered to participate in an international humanitarian relief effort to transport refugees and U.S. nationals to safety from Danang and other seaports in South Vietnam. This effort was undertaken in response to urgent appeals from the Government of South Vietnam and in recognition of the large-scale violations by the North Vietnamese of the Agreement Ending the War and Restoring the Peace in Vietnam.

In the days and weeks that followed, the massive North Vietnamese attacks continued. As the forces of the Government of South Vietnam were pushed further back toward Saigon, we began a progressive withdrawal of U.S. citizens and their dependents in South Vietnam, together with foreign nationals whose lives were in jeopardy.

On April 28, the defensive lines to the northwest and south of Saigon were breached. Tan Son Nhut Airfield and Saigon came under increased rocket attack and for the first time received artillery fire. NVA forces were approaching within mortar and anti-aircraft missile range. The situation at Tan Son Nhut Airfield deteriorated to the extent that it became unusable. Crowd control on the airfield was breaking down and the collapse of the Government forces within Saigon appeared imminent. The situation presented a direct and imminent threat to the remaining U.S. citizens and their dependents in and around Saigon.

On the recommendation of the American Ambassador there, I ordered U.S. military forces to proceed by means of rotary wing aircraft with an emergency final evacuation out of consideration for the safety of U.S. citizens.

In accordance with my desire to keep the Congress fully informed on this matter, and taking note of the provision of section 4 of the War Powers Resolution (Public Law 93-148), I wish to report to you that at about 1:00 A.M. EDT, April 29, 1975, U.S. forces entered South Vietnam airspace.

A force of 70 evacuation helicopters and 865 Marines evacuated about 1400 U.S. citizens, together with approximately 5500 third country nationals and South Vietnamese, from landing zones in the vicinity of the U.S. Embassy, Saigon, and the Defense Attaché Office at Tan Son Nhut Airfield. The last elements of the ground security force departed Saigon at 7:46 P.M. EDT April 29, 1975. Two crew members of a Navy search and rescue helicopter are missing at sea. There are no other known U.S. casualties from this operation, although two U.S. Marines on regular duty in the compound of the Defense Attaché Office at Tan Son Nhut Airfield had been killed on the afternoon (EDT) of April 28, 1975, by rocket attacks into a refugee staging area. U.S. fighter aircraft provided protective air cover for this operation, and for the withdrawal by water of a few Americans from Can Tho, and in one instance suppressed North Vietnamese anti-aircraft artillery firing upon evacuation helicopters as they departed. The ground security forces on occasion returned fire during the course of the evacuation operation.

The operation was ordered and conducted pursuant to the President's Constitutional executive power and his authority as Commander-in-Chief of U.S. Armed Forces.

The United States Armed Forces performed a very difficult mission most successfully. Their exemplary courage and discipline are deserving of the nation's highest gratitude.

Mayaguez Report of May 15, 1975

On 12 May 1975, I was advised that the SS *Mayaguez*, a merchant vessel of U.S. registry enroute from Hong Kong to Thailand with a U.S. citizen crew, was fired upon, stopped, boarded, and scized by Cambodian naval patrol boats of the Armed Forces of Cambodia in international waters in the vicinity of Poulo Wai Island. The seized vessel was then forced to proceed to Koh Tang Island where it was required to anchor. This hostile act was in clear violation of international law.

In view of this illegal and dangerous act, I ordered, as you have been previously advised, United States military forces to conduct the necessary reconnaissance and to be ready to respond if diplomatic efforts to secure the return of the vessel

and its personnel were not successful. Two United States reconnaissance aircraft in the course of locating the *Mayaguez*
sustained minimal damage from small firearms. Appropriate
demands for the return of the *Mayaguez* and its crew were
made, both publicly and privately, without success.

In accordance with my desire that the Congress be informed
on this matter and taking note of Section 4(a) (1) of the War
Powers Resolution, I wish to report to you that at about 6:20
A.M., 13 May, pursuant to my instructions to prevent the movement of the *Mayaguez* into a mainland port, U.S. aircraft fired
warning shots across the bow of the ship and gave visual signals
to small craft approaching the ship. Subsequently, in order to
stabilize the situation and in an attempt to preclude removal of
the American crew of the *Mayaguez* to the mainland, where
their rescue would be more difficult, I directed the United
States Armed Forces to isolate the island and interdict any
movement between the ship or the island and the mainland,
and to prevent movement of the ship itself, while still taking
all possible care to prevent loss of life or injury to the U.S. captives. During the evening of 13 May, a Cambodian patrol boat
attempting to leave the island disregarded aircraft warnings
and was sunk. Thereafter, two other Cambodian patrol craft
were destroyed and four others were damaged and immobil-
ized. One boat, suspected of having some U.S. captives
aboard, succeeded in reaching Kompong Som after efforts to
turn it around without injury to the passengers failed.

Our continued objective in this operation was the rescue of
the captured American crew along with the retaking of the ship
Mayaguez. For that purpose, I ordered late this afternoon
[May 14] an assault by United States Marines on the island of
Koh Tang to search out and rescue such Americans as might still
be held there, and I ordered retaking of the *Mayaguez* by other
marines boarding from the destroyer escort *Holt*. In addition to
continued fighter and gunship coverage of the Koh Tang area,
these marine activities were supported by tactical aircraft
from the *Coral Sea*, striking the military airfield at Ream and
other military targets in the area of Kompong Som in order to
prevent reinforcement or support from the mainland of the
Cambodian forces detaining the American vessel and crew.

At approximately 9:00 P.M. EDT on 14 May, the *Mayaguez* was retaken by United States forces. At approximately 11:30 P.M., the entire crew of the *Mayaguez* was taken aboard the *Wilson*. U.S. forces have begun the process of disengagement and withdrawal.

This operation was ordered and conducted pursuant to the President's constitutional Executive power and his authority as Commander-in-Chief of the United States Armed Forces.

Text of President Carter's Iran Report of April 26, 1980, Pursuant to the War Powers Resolution

Because of my desire that Congress be informed on this matter and consistent with the reporting provisions of the War Powers Resolution of 1973 (Public Law 93-148), I submit this report.

On April 24, 1980, elements of the United States Armed Forces under my direction commenced the positioning stage of a rescue operation which was designed, if the subsequent stages had been executed, to effect the rescue of the American hostages who have been held captive in Iran since November 4, 1979, in clear violation of international law and the norms of civilized conduct among nations. The subsequent phases of the operation were not executed. Instead, for the reasons described below, all these elements were withdrawn from Iran and no hostilities occurred.

The sole objective of the operation that actually occurred was to position the rescue team for the subsequent effort to withdraw the American hostages. The rescue team was under my overall command and control and required my approval before executing the subsequent phases of the operation designed to effect the rescue itself. No such approval was requested or given because, as described below, the mission was aborted.

Beginning approximately 10:30 AM EST on April 24, six U.S. C-130 transport aircraft and eight RH-53 helicopters entered

126 CONG. REC. H2991 (daily ed. April 28, 1980).

Iran airspace. Their crews were not equipped for combat. Some of the C-130 aircraft carried a force of approximately 90 members of the rescue team equipped for combat, plus various support personnel.

From approximately 2 to 4 PM EST the six transport and six of the eight helicopters landed at a remote desert site in Iran approximately 200 miles from Tehran where they disembarked the rescue team, commenced refueling operations and began to prepare for the subsequent phases.

During the flight to the remote desert site, two of the eight helicopters developed operating difficulties. One was forced to return to the carrier *Nimitz*; the second was forced to land in the desert, but its crew was taken aboard another of the helicopters and proceeded on to the landing site. Of the six helicopters which landed at the remote desert site, one developed a serious hydraulic problem and was unable to continue with the mission. The operational plans called for a minimum of six helicopters in good operational condition able to proceed from the desert site. Eight helicopters had been included in the force to provide sufficient redundancy without imposing excessive strains on the refueling and exit requirements of the operation. When the number of helicopters available to continue dropped to five, it was determined that the operation could not proceed as planned. Therefore, on the recommendation of the force commander and my military advisers, I decided to cancel the mission and ordered the United States Armed Forces involved to return from Iran.

During the process of withdrawal, one of the helicopters accidentally collided with one of the C-130 aircraft, which was preparing to take off, resulting in the death of eight personnel and the injury of several others. At this point, the decision was made to load all surviving personnel aboard the remaining C-130 aircraft and to abandon the remaining helicopters at the landing site. Altogether, the United States Armed Forces remained on the ground for a total of approximately three hours. The five remaining aircraft took off about 5:45 PM EST and departed from Iran airspace without further incident at about 8:00 PM EST on April 24. No United States Armed Forces remain in Iran.

The remote desert area was selected to conceal this phase of the mission from discovery. At no time during the temporary presence of United States Armed Forces in Iran did they encounter Iranian forces of any type. We believe, in fact, that no Iranian military forces were in the desert area, and that the Iranian forces were unaware of the presence of United States Armed Forces until after their departure from Iran. As planned, no hostilities occurred during this phase of the mission —the only phase that was executed.

At one point during the period in which United States Armed Forces elements were on the ground at the desert landing site a bus containing forty-four Iranian civilians happened to pass along a nearby road. The bus was stopped and then disabled. Its occupants were detained by United States Armed Forces until their departure, and then released unharmed. One truck closely followed by a second vehicle also passed by while United States Armed Forces elements were on the ground. These elements stopped the truck by a shot into its headlights. The driver ran to the second vehicle which then escaped across the desert. Neither of these incidents affected the subsequent decision to terminate the mission.

Our rescue team knew, and I knew, that the operation was certain to be dangerous. We were all convinced that if and when the rescue phase of the operation had been commenced, it had an excellent chance of success. They were all volunteers; they were all highly trained. I met with their leaders before they went on this operation. They knew then what hopes of mine and of all Americans they carried with them. I share with the nation the highest respect and appreciation for the ability and bravery of all who participated in the mission.

To the families of those who died and who were injured, I have expressed the admiration I feel for the courage of their loved ones and the sorrow that I feel personally for their sacrifice.

The mission on which they were embarked was a humanitarian mission. It was not directed against Iran. It was not directed against the people of Iran. It caused no Iranian casualties.

This operation was ordered and conducted pursuant to the President's powers under the Constitution as Chief Executive and as Commander-in-Chief of the United States Armed Forces, expressly recognized in Section 8(d)(1) of the War Powers Resolution. In carrying out this operation, the United States was acting wholly within its right in accordance with Article 51 of the United Nations Charter, to protect and rescue its citizens where the government of the territory in which they are located is unable or unwilling to protect them.

Text of Church-Javits Letter of April 24, 1980, to Secretary Vance Invoking Section 3 of the War Powers Resolution

We write this letter to you in the context of the grave international crisis which has been developing for some months in the region of the Persian Gulf, precipitated by the seizure of the United States Embassy in Tehran and the holding of American hostages there, and by the brutal military occupation of Afghanistan by the Soviet Union.

The President has recently spoken again of not ruling out the use of military force if the release of the hostages being held in Iran is not effected by peaceful means in the proximate future and other comparable statements have come on the Presidential level. Also, the issue was discussed on the Senate floor yesterday.

Moreover, the President has stated: "An attempt by any outside force to gain control of the Persian Gulf region will be regarded as an ass[a]ult on the vital interest of the United States of America, and such an ass[a]ult will be repelled by any means necessary, including military force."

In this context, we believe that the time has come to commence the consultation procedures contained in Public Law 93-148—the War Powers Resolution. The legislative history of that law makes it clear that the consultations called for do not necessarily signify at all that a decision has been made to introduce United States Armed Forces into hostilities or into situations where imminent involvement in hostilities is clearly indicated by the circumstances. On the contrary, the advance con-

Senate Comm. on Foreign Relations, *Application of the War Powers Resolution to the Iranian Crisis*, Media Notice, April 24, 1980.

sultation provisions of the War Powers Resolution are intended to come into play *before* any such decision has been made, in order to ensure that any such decision, if made, is a national decision jointly entered into by the President and the Congress.

The legislative history of the law also makes it clear that advance consultations are to be conducted with the established Committees of the Congress having legislative jurisdiction over Public Law 93-148 and over the question of declarations of war by the Congress in accordance with the Constitution. The appropriate committee of the Senate in this respect is the Committee on Foreign Relations. It is our view that additional consultations with the leadership, other committees or with individual members are, of course, not precluded but would be supplementary to the consultations with the Foreign Relations Committee under the law.

Accordingly, Mr. Secretary, we hereby request that you inform this Committee at an early date when consultations can begin with this Committee in accordance with Section 3 and any other pr[o]visions of Public Law 93-148. The Committee stands ready to commence these advance consultations and wishes to assure the President that it will take all necessary measures to assure that such consultations will be conducted in circumstances which insure the strictest confidentiality of the proceedings.

Partial Text of Javits Letter of December 11, 1980 to the *New York Times*

. . . I regret to say that in my judgment Mr. Landau [to whose letter the Senator was replying] has misread certain provisions of the law. Specifically, he cites the deployment of U.S. naval forces in the Persian Gulf region and the temporary posting of unarmed Awacs planes in Saudi Arabia as "violations" of the War Powers Resolution. A careful reading of Section 4(a) of the law shows that this is not in fact the case.

. . . .

Mr. Landau suggests that the provisions of Section 4(a)— which trigger the requirements for Congressional approval

N. Y. Times, Dec. 16, 1980, at A22.

within 60 days if the President deploys U.S. forces and does not pull them out before—are set in motion when U.S. forces are introduced into "an area engaged in hostilities or situations of imminent hostilities." This paraphrase of the law's actual requirements is inaccurate and misleading.

The actual language of Section 4(a)(1) specifies the introduction of U.S. armed forces "into hostilities or into situations where imminent involvement in hostilities is clearly indicated by the circumstances."

In my judgment, neither the current deployment of U.S. naval forces in and around the Persian Gulf waters nor the dispatch of Awacs aircraft constitutes the introduction of U.S. forces "into hostilities or into situations where imminent involvement in hostilities is clearly indicated by the circumstances."

Both deployments were reviewed in a War Powers context by Administration lawyers and have been discussed with my staff. Although the triggering line has been approached, I agree with the Administration's lawyers that the line has not yet been crossed. Nonetheless, consultations under Section 3 of the law are a prudent and useful step at this time, given the continuing volatility of the situation in the area.

One additional point requires comment. Section 4(a)(2) of the War Powers Resolution requires the President to *report* to the Congress whenever U.S. armed forces are introduced "into the territory, airspace or waters of a foreign nation, while equipped for combat, except for deployments which relate solely to supply, replacement, repair or training of such forces." The reports to Congress required under this subsection *do not*, however, trigger the requirement for Congressional approval. Moreover, the Awacs aircraft are unarmed communications and tracking aircraft, and U.S. naval deployments in and around the Persian Gulf have been in international waters removed from the scene of Iraq-Iran hostilities.

In summation, therefore, the President has in my judgment acted in accordance with his authority and responsibility, and the War Powers Resolution remains very much in force.

Notes

Introduction: Road Map and Résumé

1. K. Llewellyn, The Bramble Bush 10 (1960).

Chapter II: The Constitutional Text

1. Towne v. Eisner, 245 U.S. 418, 425 (1918).

2. Competition between the Article I and Article II grants began with ratification of the Constitution. Whether the President or Congress controls American neutrality in foreign conflicts occupied the country in 1793, producing our most celebrated contrary constructions of the war-power language. The Constitution says nothing whatsoever about which branch controls neutrality. Hamilton and Madison, at the interpretative barricades as Pacificus and Helvidius, bridged the textual gap in utterly opposed fashions, Hamilton awarding power to the Executive and Madison to Congress. Each expansively read provisions going his way, while ignoring or denigrating competing language going the other. See E. Corwin, The President's Control of Foreign Relations 7-28 (1917).

At times an interpreter can define provisions in his camp in such a manner that the chosen meaning focuses squarely on and resolves the issue—for instance, a definition of Article II, Section 1 "executive power" to cover the precise action that the President wishes to take. Usually the interpreter must advance more cautiously, drawing inferences from related provisions, often after resolving their own ambiguities to bring them closer to home. Whichever route is taken, the interpreter must deal as consistency demands with other language suggesting a contrary result—if the congressional power to declare war is to be broadly drawn, then that of the commander in chief must not.

3. E. Corwin, The President: Office and Powers 1787-1957, at 171 (4th rev. ed. 1957); *cf.* Chapter III, note 61, and accompanying text.

4. To bridge the gaps, there has been resort at times to extratextual sources, principally the sovereignty of the United States as an independent nation. Perhaps despairing of the Constitution's foreign-affairs lacunae, the Supreme Court has struck a number of the most telling blows for sovereignty as a source of federal authority. *E.g.*, Chinese Exclusion Case, 130 U.S. 581, 603-04 (1889).

The notion of gap-bridging by sovereignty has split the commentators. Some have found it unclean. *E.g.*, Berger, *The Presidential Monopoly of*

Foreign Relations, 71 MICH. L. REV. 1, 26-33 (1972); Levitan, *The Foreign Relations Power: An Analysis of Mr. Justice Sutherland's Theory,* 55 YALE L. J. 467 (1946); Wormuth, *The Nixon Theory of the War Power: A Critique,* 60 CALIF. L. REV. 623, 694-97 (1972). Others have been more receptive, *e.g.,* M. McDOUGAL & ASSOCIATES, STUDIES IN WORLD PUBLIC ORDER 496-503 (1960); *cf.* L. HENKIN, FOREIGN AFFAIRS AND THE CONSTITUTION 17-27 (1972). The extra-constitutional theory interests us for its indication of yawning textual gaps—gaps so wide that attempts to bridge them with emanations from language in the Constitution have sometimes been abandoned.

But how sovereignty allocates control over the war powers between the two branches is at least as obscure as how the division is made by the constitutional text. Unlike the text, however, sovereignty has no bias toward legislative power. It has proved even more conducive to bridging gaps with executive prerogative than has the ill-defined, competitive constitutional language, with one significant exception: Sovereignty eliminates the President's sharpest textual sword, the presence of "herein granted" in the legislative clause and its absence from the executive. There is no such bar to the plenary flow of congressional authority over foreign affairs when the source of power is American statehood, rather than the constitutional text.

5.   As we have seen, if the "take care" language is read with imagination, it includes inchoate foreign policy objectives among the laws to be executed by the President and allows him to identify these interests and vouchsafe them militarily. But when the text is not pushed to *extremis,* its justification of executive action by law-enforcement purpose diminishes. The language then offers no support for armed enforcement of congressional acts unless Congress *explicitly* authorizes it as a means of implementation. The text can also be understood to provide no basis for armed enforcement of treaties because their making does not involve the House of Representatives, which shares with the Senate the power to declare war. And textual ground can be thought lacking for armed enforcement of the requests of an international organization in the absence of explicit approval by the legislators. Equally tenuous is any reading of the language that permits the President to commit troops to combat to enforce customary international law without congressional participation in identifying that law and deciding that its implementation is worth combat.

6.   Whether the text supports a broader response-to-attack prerogative for the President is typically vague. The language can be read to cover only executive reaction to *ongoing* attack or, more generously, preemptive strikes against *imminent* enemy attack or anticipatory rescue of a potential victim, with various understandings of when a threat becomes imminent for constitutional purposes. Different interpretations are possible also about what or who must be beset in order for executive action to be vindicated by response-to-attack purpose. As we have already seen, the possibilities are numerous, involving territory, persons and property (either American or foreign), and locales within the United States or its possessions, areas claimed by this and another country, international air, space, sea, or a foreign state. Each possible object of attack occasions four more rounds of interpretative dispute: whether the President may attempt recapture of captive territory, persons,

or property; strike preemptively to prevent *renewal* of attack; take reprisals against, or otherwise chastise, the aggressor; and whether he may embark on sustained offensive action against an erstwhile attacker.

7. Unclear though the details may be, the text does explicitly establish a President and Congress, each with its own powers to exercise. This separation of powers may be read to require that each branch fully exercise its authority, but not one iota more. Suspect, then, are agreements by which Congress gives the President blank-check authorization to take action as he sees fit, because authorization without guiding standards can be seen as the complete transfer of legislative authority from its Article I home in Congress to the Executive. Also suspect is agreement between the two branches that, should certain future events occur, a preordained American reaction will follow, for contingent arrangements of this sort surrender decision-making authority to the dictate of future events.

On the other hand, the text does not insist on so inflexible a reading of separation of powers, especially given its own uncertainties about the nature of the powers being separated. There are degrees of relaxation. So far as congressional delegation of its decision-making authority to the President is concerned, the text can be thought satisfied so long as a few loose standards are stated, for instance, concerning the objectives of an American use of force and its geographical bounds. So far as contingent action is concerned, the text seems amenable that the President and Congress agree to consult immediately about the appropriate American response should an ally be invaded. The text is more reluctant about agreement that, following invasion of the ally, the Executive may commit troops to its defense if he finds intervention vital to American security. Even more questionable is agreement that, given the attack on the ally, the United States will automatically be at war with the aggressor.

8. Twentieth-century practice also shows the immense importance of rule making by the Executive under authority delegated by Congress.

9. Textual ambiguities have not been laid to rest by constitutional amendment. During the state conventions that ratified the Constitution, warpower amendments were proposed. But most were designed to protect state and individual interests against federal tyranny and most were rejected. *See* Chapter V, note 3. A few made their way into the 1791 Bill of Rights. The second amendment to the Constitution provides that "[a] well regulated Militia, being necessary to the security of a free State, the right of the people to keep and bear Arms, shall not be infringed." The third amendment states that "[n]o Soldier shall, in time of peace be quartered in any house, without the consent of the Owner, nor in time of war, but in a manner to be prescribed by law." And the fifth amendment limits criminal prosecutions to "a presentment or indictment of a Grand Jury, except in cases arising in the land or naval forces, or in the Militia, when in actual service in time of War or public danger." The ninth and tenth amendments seek to hold the federal government to its enumerated powers, among which the military especially worried the Revolutionary generation: "The enumeration in the Constitution, of certain rights, shall not be construed to deny or disparage others retained by the people," and "The powers not delegated to the United States by the Con-

stitution, nor prohibited by it to the States, are reserved to the States respectively, or to the people." None of these provisions, however, deals with the
allocation of war powers *within* the federal government.

Chapter III: The Framers and Ratifiers

1. *E.g.*, THE FEDERALIST PAPERS, NOS. 14, 38, 52, 63 (Madison); but *No. 14*
indicates that, though Americans have "paid a decent regard to the opinions
of former times and other nations, they have not suffered a blind veneration
for antiquity, for custom, or for names to overrule the suggestions of their
own good sense, the knowledge of their own situation, and the lessons of their
own experience." See the discussion in THE FEDERALIST PAPERS xix-xx, 292
n.25 (R. Fairfield ed. 1966); Lofgren, *War-Making Under the Constitution:
The Original Understanding*, 81 YALE L. J. 672, 689-90 (1972). Quotations
here and elsewhere to THE FEDERALIST PAPERS come from THE FEDERALIST:
A COLLECTION OF ESSAYS WRITTEN IN FAVOUR OF THE NEW CONSTITUTION (J. &
A. M'Lean 1788) (hereafter cited as FEDERALIST).
Research for the discussion in Chapters III-V about the Constitutional
Fathers was completed during the spring of 1973. It was first published in
1974 in somewhat different form. *See* Reveley, *Constitutional Allocation of
the War Powers Between the President and Congress: 1787-1788*, 15 VA. J.
INT'L LAW 73 (1974). A number of other inquiries into the events of 1787-88
were ongoing contemporaneously with this one and have resulted in signifi-
cant products. *See, e.g.*, J. JAVITS, WHO MAKES WAR: THE PRESIDENT VERSUS
CONGRESS 1-15 (1973); F. MARKS III, INDEPENDENCE ON TRIAL: FOREIGN AFFAIRS
AND THE MAKING OF THE CONSTITUTION (1973); A. SCHLESINGER, JR., THE
IMPERIAL PRESIDENCY 1-35 (1973); A. SOFAER, WAR, FOREIGN AFFAIRS AND
CONSTITUTIONAL POWER: THE ORIGINS 1-60 (1976); Bestor, *Separation of
Powers in the Domain of Foreign Affairs: The Intent of the Constitution
Historically Examined*, 5 SETON HALL L. REV. 527 (1974).
2. FEDERALIST No. 29 (Hamilton): "In reading many of the publications
against the constitution, a man is apt to imagine that he is perusing some ill
written tale or romance; which instead of natural and agreeable images
exhibits to the mind nothing but frightful and distorted shapes—'Gorgons,
Hydras and Chimeras dire'—discoloring and disfiguring whatever it represents, and transforming every thing it touches into a monster."
3. A. MCLAUGHLIN, A CONSTITUTIONAL HISTORY OF THE UNITED STATES
208-09 (1935). *See also* THE FEDERALIST PAPERS, *supra* note 1, at ix-xi, 280-81
n.20. Fairfield states that "[s]ince some of the most controversial points in the
Constitution were not discussed until most of the state conventions had been
held, the probability is that the *Federalist* was not too influential." But he also
notes that the extent of its influence has been controversial and cites representative opinion. *See also* Chapter V, note 4.
4. 11 BENTON'S ABRIDGEMENT 221-22 (1859).
5. FEDERALIST No. 26. Reference to British practice was legion during the
Philadelphia and state conventions and in *The Federalist. E.g.*, 1 RECORDS OF
THE FEDERAL CONVENTION OF 1787, at 65-66, 97, 289, 391, 398-404 (M. Farrand
ed. 1911) (hereafter cited as FARRAND); 2 *id.* 104, 274, 392-93, 395; 3 DEBATES IN
THE SEVERAL STATE CONVENTIONS ON THE ADOPTION OF THE FEDERAL CONSTITU-
TION 16-17, 172, 379, 393, 611 (J. Elliot ed. 1859 & 1861) (hereafter cited as

ELLIOT); FEDERALIST NOS. 37, 56 (Madison), 70, 84 (Hamilton) (references to the British constitution and laws).

   6.   *See generally* the discussion and authorities in E. MAY, THE ULTIMATE DECISION: THE PRESIDENT AS COMMANDER IN CHIEF 13-19 (1960); Q. WRIGHT, THE CONTROL OF AMERICAN FOREIGN RELATIONS 143-44 (1922); Berger, *The Presidential Monopoly of Foreign Relations*, 71 MICH. L. REV. 1, 7-9 (1972); Berger, *War-Making by the President*, 121 U. PA. L. REV. 29, 32, 78 n.315, 79 (1972); Chayes & Michelman, *Legal Memorandum on the Constitutionality of the Amendment to End the War, Hearings on Congress, the President and the War Powers Before the Subcomm. on National Security Policy and Scientific Developments of the House Foreign Affairs Comm.*, 91st Cong., 2d Sess., at 513-15 (1970); Lofgren, *supra* note 1, at 689-90, 697-99 (1972); Note, *The War-Making Powers: The Intentions of the Framers in the Light of Parliamentary History*, 50 B.U.L. REV. 5-10 (1970).

   7.   *See* H. WRISTON, EXECUTIVE AGENTS IN AMERICAN FOREIGN RELATIONS 63-71 (1929).

   8.   Gouverneur Morris, for instance, spoke in Philadelphia of the real British executive's removal by party intrigue: "Some leader of party will always covet his seat, will perplex his administration, will cabal with the Legislature, till he succeeds in supplanting him. This was the way in which the King of England was got out, he meant the real King, the Minister." 2 FARRAND 104. And James Wilson argued that "The people of Amer. did not oppose the British King but the parliament—the opposition was not agt. an Unity but a corrupt multitude." 1 *id.* 71. *See also* W. BINKLEY, THE MAN IN THE WHITE HOUSE, HIS POWERS & DUTIES 290-91 (1959), regarding colonial loyalty to the king but opposition to "ministerial policies."

   9.   In 1789 James Madison said in Congress that "if there is a principle in our constitution . . . more sacred than another, it is that which separates the legislative, executive, and judicial powers." 1 ANNALS OF CONGRESS 604 (1789). The necessity for separation was a frequent theme during the federal and state conventions, *e.g.*, 2 FARRAND 537 (Mason), 538-39 (Wilson); 4 ELLIOT 116 (Spencer), with Montesquieu seen as its greatest prophet, *e.g.*, 2 FARRAND 34; FEDERALIST No. 47 (Madison); THE FEDERALIST PAPERS 297-98 n.60 (R. Fairfield ed. 1966). The Constitutional Fathers stressed on other occasions, however, the overlapping nature of legislative, executive, and judicial powers, a necessary concomitant of checks and balances.

   10.   *See* B. BAILYN, THE IDEOLOGICAL ORIGINS OF THE AMERICAN REVOLUTION (1967).

   11.   *E.g.*, 2 Farrand 616-17, 635, 640. Jay in *Federalist No. 4* warned that "absolute monarchs will often make war when their nations are to get nothing by it, but for purposes and objects merely personal, such as, a thirst for military glory, revenge for personal affronts, ambition or private compacts to aggrandise or support their particular families, or partisans. These and a variety of motives, which affect only the mind of the sovereign, often lead him to engage in wars not sanctified by justice, or the voice and interests of his people." *Cf.* Hamilton in *Federalist No. 6* saying of the duke of Marlborough that "the ambition, or rather the avarice of a favourite leader, protracted the war beyond the limits marked out by sound policy and for a considerable time in opposition to the views of the court." *Accord*, 2 FARRAND 541 (Butler).

   12.   *E.g.*, 2 FARRAND 393; 3 *id.* 302; 4 ELLIOT 107-08, 269-70, 277-79; FED-

ERALIST Nos. 67, 69 (Hamilton). These protestations of regal might, however, were somewhat inconsistent with the Constitutional Fathers' view that Parliament had gone far toward curbing the king, *e.g.*, 2 FARRAND 279, 326-27; 3 ELLIOT 16-17. No doubt there was an element of gamesmanship in aggrandizing the king. Those in favor of the Constitution could then show how pallid and unthreatening the President was in comparison. Those opposed could argue that under the proposed government, Congress would be dangerously powerful, lacking the executive check on the legislature provided in Britain by the king, *e.g.*, 3 ELLIOT 379.

13. *See* Lofgren, *supra* note 1, at 698-99.

14. *See* E. CORWIN, THE PRESIDENT: OFFICE AND POWERS 1787-1957, at 416-18 n.1 (4th rev. ed. 1957); L. HENKIN, FOREIGN AFFAIRS AND THE CONSTITUTION 297 n.10 (1972); Q. WRIGHT, *supra* note 6, at 141-43, 363-65. On the other hand, James Wilson said in Philadelphia that "[m]aking peace and war are generally determined by Writers on the Laws of Nations to be legislative powers." 1 FARRAND 73-74. And, as we shall see, none save William R. Davie and John Francis Mercer suggested that treaty making should be left to the Executive, and only Pierce Butler in a momentary aberration argued that war making should be presidential. Also, as will become apparent, executive speed and secrecy were cited as grounds for presidential conduct of war and involvement in negotiations with other states, not as grounds for presidential prerogative to set policy.

15. See the discussion and authorities in Lofgren, *supra* note 1, at 689-93. In the early 1780s, the Federal Court of Appeals, established under the Articles of Confederation to deal with prize cases, explained that "[t]he writers upon the law of nations, speaking of the different kinds of war, distinguish them into perfect and imperfect: A perfect war is that which destroys the national peace and tranquility, and lays the foundation of every possible act of hostility. The imperfect war is that which does not entirely destroy the public tranquillity, but interrupts it only in some particulars, as in the case of reprisals." Miller v. The Ship Resolution, 2 U.S. (2 Dall.) 1, 21 (Ct. App. in Cases of Capture 1781).

16. *See* Lofgren, *supra* note 1, at 693; M. McDOUGAL & ASSOCIATES, STUDIES IN WORLD PUBLIC ORDER 715 n.135 (1960); *cf.* Hamilton in *Federalist No. 25* that "the ceremony of a formal denunciation of war has of late fallen into disuse . . . ."

17. E. CORWIN, *supra* note 14, at 5-6. But, as indicated in note 8, above, aversion to the Executive was mixed with some awareness that America's difficulties with Britain had parliamentary origins as well.

18. C. WARREN, THE MAKING OF THE CONSTITUTION 173 (1937).

19. 1 J. WILSON, THE WORKS OF JAMES WILSON 292-93 (R. McCloskey ed. 1967); *see* Berger, *War-Making by the President, supra* note 6, at 32.

20. Before the Declaration of Independence, the first Continental Congress attacked the stationing of British armies in America during peace and voted that "the keeping a standing army in these colonies, in times of peace, without the consent of the legislature of that colony in which such army is kept, is against the law." 2 JOURNALS OF THE CONTINENTAL CONGRESS 96 (1905). The Virginia constitution of 1776 included among the fundamental rights of man: "That a well-regulated militia composed of the body of the people,

trained to arms, is the proper, natural and safe defense of a free State; that standing armies in time of peace should be avoided as dangerous to liberty; and that in all cases the military should be under strict subordination to, and governed by, the civil power." *Quoted in* C. Rossiter, Seedtime of the Republic 400 (1953). *See also* Donahoe & Smelser, *The Congressional Power to Raise Armies: The Constitutional and Ratifying Conventions, 1787-1788,* 33 Rev. of Politics 202 (1971).

21. *See* E. Burnett, The Continental Congress 34 (1941); J. Guggenheimer, *The Development of the Executive Departments, 1775-1789, in* Essays in the Constitutional History of the United States in the Formative Period 1775-1789, at 116-85 (J. Jameson ed. 1889); H. Wriston, *supra* note 7, at 3-26.

22. See the accounts in R. Russell, The United States Congress and the Power to Use Military Force Abroad 11-15 (unpublished thesis, Fletcher School 1967); *Hearings on War Powers Legislation Before the Senate Comm. on Foreign Relations,* 92d Cong., 1st Sess., at 77-78 (1971) (Richard B. Morris); Wormuth, *The Nixon Theory of the War Power: A Critique,* 60 Calif. L. Rev. 623, 638-39 (1972).

23. J. Guggenheimer, *supra* note 21, at 146, 153-85.

24. Articles 6 and 9, quoted in note 43 below.

25. *Compare* Article 9 *with* Article 6, both quoted in note 43 below.

26. Delaware in its post-Independence constitution, for instance, even conditioned executive command of the militia on the concurrence of a council: "The President, with the advice and consent of the privy council, may embody the militia, and act as captain-general and commander-in-chief of them, and the other military force of this State, under the laws of the same." 1 F. Thorpe, The Federal and State Constitutions 564 (1909). *See also* Federalist No. 70 (Hamilton); A. Nevins, The American States During and After the Revolution, 1775-1789, at 117-205 (1924); H. Wriston, *supra* note 7, at 65-68.

27. The Virginia constitution of 1776 is quoted, 2 B. Poore, The Federal and State Constitutions, Colonial Charters, and Other Organic Laws of the United States 1910-11 (1878); *see* Federalist No. 47 (Madison); Berger, *War-Making by the President, supra* note 6, at 32-33.

28. 2 Farrand 35. Madison continued in similar vein in *Federalist No. 48.*

29. 1 B. Poore, *supra* note 27, at 965-66; *see* Berger, *War-Making by the President, supra* note 6, at 37.

30. Especially via the purse. *See* W. Binkley, *supra* note 8, at 3-4; E. May, *supra* note 6, at 9-10; R. Russell, *supra* note 22, at 2-11, 22.

31. On arbitrary action by the new legislatures, see R. Berger, Congress v. The Supreme Court 10-11 (1969).

32. 2 Journals of the Continental Congress 101 (1905).

33. Randolph in the Virginia ratifying convention closed his "catalogue of the evils of the dissolution of the Union by recalling . . . what passed in the year 1781. Such was the situation of our affairs then, that the power of dictator was given to the commander-in-chief, to save us from destruction." 3 Elliot 79; *see* C. Berdahl, War Powers of the Executive in the United States 18 (1921); *cf.* 2 Elliot 359-60.

34. *See* H. Wriston, *supra* note 7, at 17-26, and on the general executive

incompetence of Congress, J. Guggenheimer, *supra* note 21, at 120-26, 136-37, 142-52.

35.   The pertinent provisions were in Articles of Confederation 5 and 9. Further assurance that the Confederation Congresses would be executive incompetents came from limitations on the terms of office of congressional delegates, on the tenure of their presiding officers, from state control over delegates' salaries, and from the feeble Confederation mechanism for conduct of national affairs during congressional recesses. As quoted in 1 Elliot 80, 83:

"*Article* 5. For the more convenient management of the general interests of the United States, delegates shall be annually appointed in such manner as the legislature of each state shall direct, to meet in Congress on the first Monday in November, in every year, with a power reserved to each state, to recall its delegates, or any of them, at any time within the year, and to send others in their stead . . . .

"[N]o person shall be capable of being a delegate for more than three years in any term of six years . . . .

"Each state shall maintain its own delegates . . . .

"In determining questions in . . . Congress . . . each state shall have one vote.

"*Article* 9 . . . .

"The United States in Congress assembled shall have authority to appoint a committee to sit in the recess of Congress, to be denominated 'a committee of the states,' and to consist of one delegate from each state; and to appoint such other committees and civil officers as may be necessary for managing the general affairs of the United States under their direction—to appoint one of their number to preside, provided that no person be allowed to serve in the office of president more than one year in any term of three years— . . . .

"The United States in Congress assembled shall never engage in a war; nor grant letters of marque and reprisal in time of peace; nor enter into any treaties or alliances; . . . nor ascertain the sums and expenses necessary for the defence . . . of the United States; nor appropriate money; nor agree upon the number of vessels of war to be built or purchased, or the number of land or sea forces to be raised; nor appoint a commander-in-chief of the army or navy,—unless nine states assent to the same . . . ."

36.   M. McDougal & Associates, *supra* note 16, at 620. In Max Farrand's words, the country was run by "a congress of states." The Framing of the Constitution 3-4 (1913). Hamilton in *Federalist No. 22* had savage words for Confederation practice: "Congress from the nonattendance of a few states have been frequently in the situation of a Polish diet, where a single veto has been sufficient to put a stop to all their movements. A sixtieth part of the union, which is about the proportion of Delaware and Rhode-Island, has several times been able to oppose an entire bar to its operations."

37.   *E.g.*, Madison in Federalist No. 63: "The proper remedy for this defect [lack of national officials responsible for American policy] must be an additional body in the legislative department, which having sufficient permanency to provide for such objects as require a continued attention, and a train of measures, may be justly and effectually answerable for the attainment of those objects." *See also* note 35 above.

38.   M. McDougal & Associates, *supra* note 16, at 631. *See also id.* at 628

n.55; C. WARREN, *supra* note 18, at 3-54. The evils of confederations were very much on the nationalists' minds, *e.g., Federalist Nos. 17* (Hamilton), *18-20* (Hamilton and Madison).

39. *See, e.g.,* 1 FARRAND 316-18; 2 *id.* 455, 463; 2 ELLIOT 212; 3 *id.* 180, 424-25; FEDERALIST Nos. 3 (Jay), 6-8, 21 (Hamilton).

40. Other than as competitors for virgin reaches of North America, Britain was feared for its forts in territory officially ours, and Britain and Spain for their control over navigation on the Saint Lawrence and Mississippi. *See, e.g.,* FEDERALIST No. 15 (Hamilton). As suggested in note 44 below, the specter of European aggression was raised by nationalists in part to sell federal hegemony over foreign affairs. State authority in diplomatic and military matters, it was said, led to violations of international law and to just cause for foreign attack. *E.g.,* FEDERALIST Nos. 3 (Jay), 80-81 (Hamilton). Too, such state authority also bred national disarray rather than the "union and a good national government" essential "to put and keep" the American people "in *such a situation* as instead of *inviting war,* will tend to repress and discourage it." FEDERALIST No. 4 (Jay); *accord, id.* Nos. 3, 5 (Jay), 8, 15, 24 (Hamilton), 41 (Madison). *See also* Lofgren, *supra* note 1, at 687.

Concern over foreign attack also had deeper roots. Many of the Framers and Ratifiers recognized the passing quality of peace. As George Nicholas urged during the Virginia ratifying convention in response to argument that America would enjoy eternal peace: "Is not this deceiving ourselves? Is it not fallacious? Did there ever exist a nation which, at some period or other, was not exposed to war?" 3 ELLIOT 358. *See also, e.g.,* 2 *id.* 143, 212, 218, 379; FEDERALIST No. 34 (Hamilton).

41. Jefferson is quoted in C. WARREN, *supra* note 18, at 451, and Madison spoke in FEDERALIST No. 42.

42. 1 FARRAND 316. *See also, e.g.,* 1 *id.* 164, 171, 316-18, 426; 3 *id.* 113, 539-51, especially 547-48; FEDERALIST Nos. 3-8, 15, 22, 25, 42; L. HENKIN, *supra* note 14, at 290-91 n.10, 295 n.8, 373 n.3; M. McDOUGAL & ASSOCIATES, *supra* note 16, at 466-620.

43. State-federal struggle for control of American armed forces dominated military controversy during the drafting and ratifying conventions. *E.g.,* Donahoe & Smelser, *supra* note 20, at 202.

44. Articles of Confederation 3 and 6-9 dealt directly with diplomatic and military affairs. Much of their detail concerned raising, organizing, and supporting the military, leaving significant control to the states. *E.g.,* under Article 7 they named all army officers under the rank of colonel, and under Article 8 they were to supply the funds voted by Congress for national defense. War and treaty making, however, were largely preserves of the central government. Attention here centers on these provisions, *quoted in* 1 ELLIOT 79-82:

"*Article 3.* The said states hereby severally enter into a firm league of friendship with each other for their common defence . . . .

"*Article 6.* No state, without the consent of . . . Congress . . .shall send any embassy to, or receive any embassy from, or enter into any conference, agreement, alliance, or treaty, with any king, prince, or state . . . .

". . . .

"No state shall engage in any war without the consent of the United States

Notes to pages 60 to 61

in Congress . . . unless such state be actually invaded by enemies, or shall have received certain advice of a resolution being formed by some nation of Indians to invade such state, and the danger is so imminent as not to admit of a delay till . . . Congress . . . can be consulted; nor shall any state grant commissions to any ships or vessels of war, nor letters of marque or reprisal, except it be after a declaration of war by . . . Congress . . . and then only against the . . . state . . . against which war has been so declared, and under such regulations as shall be established by . . . Congress . . . unless such state be infested by pirates; in which case, vessels of war may be fitted out for that occasion, and kept so long as the danger shall continue or until . . . Congress . . . shall determine otherwise.

"*Article 9.* The United States in Congress assembled shall have the sole and exclusive right and power of determining on peace and war, except in the cases mentioned in the sixth article—of sending and receiving ambassadors—entering into treaties and alliances; . . . of granting letters of marque and reprisal in times of peace . . . .

" . . . .

"The United States in Congress assembled shall also have the sole and exclusive right and power of . . . making rules for the government and regulation of the [national] land and naval forces, and directing their operations."

Those favoring ratification of the Constitution argued that these powers were barren, since the national government remained dependent on the states for the means of their execution. *See* FEDERALIST Nos. 15, 22-23, 25 (Hamilton), 38, 45 (Madison).

45. *Cf.* Madison's remarks on state emergency powers during the Virginia convention, 3 ELLIOT 424-25.

46. America's external relations would figure more prominently in *The Federalist*. Hamilton in *No. 17* described the federal government's concerns as principally "[c]ommerce, finance, negotiation and war," and spoke in *No. 23* of Union to provide for "the common defence of the members—the preservation of the public peace as well against internal convulsions as external attacks—the regulation of commerce with other nations and between the states—the superintendence of our intercourse political and commercial with foreign countries." In *No. 34* he predicted the central government's "chief sources of expense" would be "wars and rebellions."

Madison in *No. 45* followed suit, describing federal powers as "few and defined" to be "exercised principally on external objects, as war, peace, negotiation, and foreign commerce" and to be "most extensive and important in times of war and danger." In *No. 41* he listed six "classes" of federal powers, including "1. Security against foreign danger; 2. Regulation of the intercourse with foreign nations"; and "5. Restraint of the states from certain injurious acts," chiefly of a diplomatic and military nature. *See also id.* Nos. 42, 45 (Madison).

As these and other papers of *The Federalist* suggest, foreign affairs were stressed to sell the Constitution. Disunited, the states were clearly less efficient in diplomatic and military affairs. And their inefficiency invited foreign aggression. Moreover, if wars and treaties were to be the main diet of the federal government, it would not impinge on other public affairs dear to state and local officials, and its operations would usually be slight, since major military and diplomatic undertakings were rarely expected.

47. "For the Framers . . . foreign relations seemed to consist wholly of making or not-making war and making or not-making treaties." L. HENKIN, *supra* note 14, at 129, 372 n.1 (1972). Henry Merritt Wriston has suggested that "The overemphasis upon treaties was . . . natural, considering the time. In the nature of the case, the problem of a new nation is to negotiate treaties, either to gain recognition thereby, or to regularize its contact, commercial and political, with older nations. The routine relations of an established nation are of a different sort. The making of treaties occupies much less time and attention, proportionately, and the interpretation of treaties, their application to particular cases, and dealing with matters outside treaty relations bulk larger." EXECUTIVE AGENTS IN AMERICAN FOREIGN RELATIONS 60 (1929).

48. FEDERALIST No. 8. Hamilton, however, felt that geography would protect only a *unified* country. *See also id.* Nos. 4 (Jay), 41 (Madison).

Richard B. Morris has noted that "[o]ur Nation's independence was achieved in the first anticolonial war of modern times, but it was at its inception dedicated to peace not war. Only a peaceful climate, it was believed, would guarantee the American people life, liberty, and the pursuit of happiness." *Hearings on War Powers Legislation Before the Senate Comm. on Foreign Relations*, 92d Cong., 1st Sess., at 76 (1971); *see, e.g., id.* at 86 (Alfred H. Kelly); Lofgren, *supra* note 1, at 682 & n.36, 694.

49. Hamilton wrote in *Federalist No. 24* that a navy was crucial "[i]f we mean to be a commercial people or even to be secure on our Atlantic side." *See also, e.g., id.* Nos. 11, 34 (Hamilton), 41 (Madison); 2 FARRAND 450; 2 ELLIOT 143, 218.

Hamilton in *No. 11* also trafficked with a more offensive use of naval power in local waters: "A further resource for influencing the conduct of European nations towards us, in this respect [trade,] would arise from the establishment of a federal navy. There can be no doubt, that the continuance of the union, under an efficient government, would put it in our power . . . to create a navy, which . . . would at least be of respectable weight if thrown into the scale of either of two contending parties. This would be more peculiarly the case in relation to operations in the West-Indies. A few ships of the line sent opportunely to the reinforcement of either side, would often be sufficient to decide the fate of a campaign, on the event of which interests of the greatest magnitude were suspended . . . . And if to this consideration we add that of the usefulness of supplies from this country, in the prosecution of military operations in the West-Indies, it will readily be perceived, that a situation so favourable would enable us to bargain with the great advantage for commercial privileges. A price would be set not only upon our friendship, but upon our neutrality. By a steady adherance to the union we may hope ere long to become the arbiter of Europe in America; and to be able to incline the balance of European competitions in this part of the world as our interest may dictate."

Hamilton in *No. 34*, however, talked no longer of even so humble realpolitik, but asked only for effective defense. "Admitting that we ought to try the novel and absurd experiment in politics, of tying up the hands of government from offensive war founded upon reasons of state," he said, "[y]et, certainly we ought not to disable it from guarding the community against the ambition or enmity of other nations."

50. 2 FARRAND 393 (Morris), 548 (Madison). James Wilson during the Pennsylvania ratifying convention went even further to denigrate treaty making. "With regard to [the Senators'] power in making treaties," he said, "it is of importance that it should be very seldom exercised. We are happily removed from the vortex of European politics, and the fewer and the more simple our negotiations with European powers, the better they will be. If such be the case, it will be but once in a number of years that a single treaty will come before the Senate. I think, therefore, that on this account it will be unnecessary to sit constantly." 2 ELLIOT 513; *see* L. HENKIN, *supra* note 14, at 372 n.2; M. McDOUGAL & ASSOCIATES, *supra* note 16, at 627-28; Q. WRIGHT, *supra* note 6, at 246.

51. *E.g.*, 2 FARRAND 268-72, 319, 389, 393, 452; 3 ELLIOT 220; FEDERALIST Nos. 5 (Jay), 16, 22, 59, 68 (Hamilton).

52. 8 WORKS OF JOHN ADAMS 37 (C. F. Adams ed. 1853). Elbridge Gerry argued during the Constitutional Convention that "[a]s to Ministers & Ambassadors few of them were necessary. It is the opinion of a great many that they ought to be discontinued, on our part; that none may be sent among us, & that source of influence be shut up. If the Senate were to appoint Ambassadors as seemed to be intended, they will multiply embassies for their own sakes. He was not so fond of those productions as to wish to establish nurseries for them." 2 FARRAND 285. And J. William Fulbright in 1961 bemoaned the fact that "[o]ur institutional arrangements for foreign affairs were drafted in the late 18th century by men who assumed that these affairs would be few and insignificant. The Founding Fathers considered, for instance, that the Department of State would quite possibly wither away from disuse." *American Foreign Policy in the Twentieth Century Under an Eighteenth-Century Constitution*, 47 CORNELL L. Q. 1, 2 (1961).

53. FEDERALIST No. 25. *See also id.* Nos. 21, 28, 70 (Hamilton). "In the late 1780's . . . the trend toward weaker executives was reversed. The reversal, however, resulted from domestic considerations—stronger and more independent leadership seemed necessary to insure liberty and stability *within* the country—and it had little or no connection with external problems of warmaking." Lofgren, *supra* note 1, at 697. *See also* G. WOOD, THE CREATION OF THE AMERICAN REPUBLIC 1776-1787, at 393-564 (1969).

54. *See, e.g.*, 2 FARRAND 268-72, 359-63, 499-503.

55. 1 FARRAND xiii-xiv.

56. *See* Chapter IV, note 81.

57. Madison changed his notes in places to correspond with the questionable records of Jackson and Robert Yates. *See* 1 FARRAND xvi-xix.

58. As Pinckney wrote John Quincy Adams, who was readying the Journal for publication, "[A]t the distance of nearly thirty two Years it is impossible for me now to say which of the 4 or 5 draughts I have was the one but enclosed I send you the one I believe was it." 3 FARRAND 595. *See* Chapter IV, notes 2, 24, and accompanying text.

59. The debates, redundantly described by different men, appear in the first two volumes of *Farrand*, covering, respectively, 606 and 667 pages.

60. *See* 2-4 ELLIOT. These records were first compiled by Jonathan Elliot in 1830 and range from a 663-page account of the Virginia debates to a 17-page fragment on the Connecticut proceedings.

61. Youngstown Sheet & Tube Co. v. Sawyer, 343 U.S. 579, 634 (1952) (Jackson, J., concurring).

62. Average attendance in Philadelphia was forty. 3 FARRAND 586 n.2. Over 1,000 delegates attended the state ratifying conventions, Massachusetts the most endowed with 364 Ratifiers and Delaware the least with thirty. *See* C. WARREN, *supra* note 18, at 819-20 (1937).

63. *See, e.g.,* 1 FARRAND 86; 2 *id.* 34-35; 4 ELLIOT 120-22; FEDERALIST NOS. 37, 47-48, 51 (Madison); 5 ANNALS OF CONG. 487 (1796) (Madison).

64. L. LEVY, ORIGINS OF THE FIFTH AMENDMENT 430 (1968), *quoted in* Lofgren, *supra* note 1, at 696 n.104.

65. 3 ELLIOT 531. *See also* FEDERALIST NOS. 38, 43, 47 (Madison), 81 (Hamilton). It may well be, however, that the Framers and Ratifiers expected experience to be taken into account by formal amendment of the Constitution and not by its informal adaptation through court decisions and a process of claim and concession between the President and Congress. *See* Chapter VIII, note 3.

66. *Quoted in* W. MUNRO, THE MAKERS OF THE UNWRITTEN CONSTITUTION 14 (1930). The Framers and Ratifiers were not unworldly men. *See* R. HOFSTADTER, THE AMERICAN POLITICAL TRADITION AND THE MEN WHO MADE IT 3-17 (1948).

67. Letter to Samuel Kercheval of July 12, 1816, 15 WRITINGS OF THOMAS JEFFERSON 40-42 (Library ed. 1903).

68. Letter to Timothy Pickering of December 22, 1814, 1 ELLIOT 506-07. Morris was speaking of language on the judiciary; the rest of the Constitution he thought clear enough but not likely by itself to restrain legislative aggrandizement. He also told Pickering that the Constitutional Fathers' debates were of little moment in interpreting the document.

"What [Morris asked] can a history of the Constitution avail towards interpreting its provisions? This must be done by comparing the plain import of the words with the general tenor and object of the instrument. That instrument was written by the fingers which write this letter. Having rejected redundant and equivocal terms, I believe it to be as clear as our language would permit; excepting . . . a part of what relates to the judiciary . . . .

"But, after all, what does it signify that men should have a written constitution, containing unequivocal provisions and limitations? The legislative lion will not be entangled in the meshes of a logical net. The legislature will always make the power which it wishes to exercise, unless it be so organized as to contain within itself the sufficient check . . . . The idea of binding legislators by oaths is puerile. Having sworn to exercise the powers granted, accordingly to their true intent and meaning, they will, when they feel a desire to go farther, avoid the shame, if not the guilt, of perjury, by swearing the true intent and meaning to be, according to their comprehension, that which suits their purpose."

Chapter IV: Philadelphia 1787

1. 1 RECORDS OF THE FEDERAL CONVENTION OF 1787, at 21 (M. Farrand ed. 1911) (hereafter cited as FARRAND). *See also* 3 *id.* 593-94. The spelling, capitalization, and punctuation are those of 1787. Precise quotation of the Philadelphia records (and of the 1787-88 state records in Chapter V) lets everyone

see for himself the somewhat obscure fragments from which the Constitutional Fathers' debates must be pieced together.

2.   *See also* note 81 below. As "reconstructed" by Max Farrand, Pinckney's May 29 proposals dealt very little with executive-legislative relations, centering rather on federal-state problems. It appears that Pinckney gave war and treaty making to the legislature, because he called for "[t]he Assent of Two-Thirds of both Houses, where the present Confederation had made the assent of Nine States necessary . . . ." He named the President "Commander in chief of the Land Forces of U.S. and Admiral of their Navy," authorized him "to inspect the Departments of foreign Affairs—War—Treasury," to "suspend Officers, civil and military," and "to advise with the Heads of the different Departments as his Council." The legislature, however, was to "institute offices and appoint officers for the Departments of for. Affairs, War, Treasury and Admiralty" and to control raising, supporting, and organizing the military. 3 FARRAND 604-09 (emphasis omitted).

3.   1 FARRAND 23; 3 *id.* 599-600.

4.   1 FARRAND 64-66. *See also id.* 73-74. Randolph "strenuously opposed a unity in the Executive magistracy." He regarded it as "the foetus of monarchy . . . . He could not see why the great requisites for the Executive department, vigor, despatch & responsibility could not be found in three men, as well as in one man." *Id.* 66.

5.   1 FARRAND 70. Madison's own account focused on the need to define the nature of executive power before settling on a single or plural Executive. *Id.* 66-67.

6.   1 FARRAND 65.

7.   1 FARRAND 89.

8.   1 FARRAND 97.

9.   1 FARRAND 243.

10.   1 FARRAND 244. Though several copies of the New Jersey Plan exist, with significant differences among them, none of the variations bears on the war powers. *See* 3 *id.* 611.

11.   1 FARRAND 292. Robert Yates's account of Hamilton's proposal states that "[t]he executive to have the power of negativing all laws—to make war or peace, with the advice of the senate—to make treaties with their advice, but to have the sole direction of all military operations, and to send ambassadors and appoint all military officers, and to pardon all offenders, treason excepted, unless by advice of the senate." *Id.* 300. It appears, however, that Yates erroneously included the Executive with the Senate in war-making decisions. The proposal that Hamilton submitted to Madison near the end of the Convention, like Madison's notes of Hamilton's June 18 speech, left these decisions to the Senate. *See* 3 Farrand 622, 624-25.

12.   1 FARRAND 426.

13.   2 FARRAND 14, 21. *See also* 2 *id.* 131-32.

14.   2 FARRAND 116. *See also* 2 *id.* 132.

15.   2 FARRAND 183.

16.   2 FARRAND 181-82.

17.   2 FARRAND 185.

18.   2 FARRAND 259.

19.   2 FARRAND 260. As we have seen, the Framers ultimately provided

in Article I of the Constitution that "[e]ach House shall keep a Journal of its Proceedings, and from time to time publish the same, excepting such Parts as may in their Judgment require Secrecy . . . ." Concern over congressional secrecy, however, remained at high pitch, and three states—New York, Rhode Island, and Virginia—ratified the Constitution with a request that it be amended to permit only the withholding of sensitive diplomatic and military information. Had the first North Carolina convention agreed to the Constitution, it very likely would have sought the same amendment. *See* 1 DEBATES IN THE SEVERAL STATE CONVENTIONS ON THE ADOPTION OF THE FEDERAL CONSTITUTION (J. Elliot ed. 1859 & 1861) 330 (New York), 336 (Rhode Island), 3 *id.* 659-60 (Virginia), 4 *id.* 245 (North Carolina) (hereafter cited as ELLIOT); Chapter V, note 3.

20. 2 FARRAND 275.

21. 2 FARRAND 278-79. Randolph said that he opposed Senate involvement as much to help win ratification of the Constitution as to ensure sound government. "His principal object," he said, "was to prevent popular objections against the plan, and to secure its adoption." *Id.* 279.

22. 2 FARRAND 297, 298.

23. 2 FARRAND 297.

24. 2 FARRAND 318. Compare Pinckney's memory in 1818 of his position on senatorial war making at Philadelphia: "It may be necessary to remark that very soon after the Convention met I changed & avowed candidly the change of my opinion . . . in giving the exclusive Power to the Senate to declare War thinking it safer . . . to vest [war making] in Congress." 3 *Id.* 428. *See also* note 2 above and accompanying text.

25. 2 FARRAND 318. Butler's commitment of war to the Executive seems to have been a passing fancy. *Compare* his comments at 2 *id.* 541 and 4 Elliot 263. *See* notes 33, 57, 59 below and accompanying text.

26. 2 FARRAND 318.

27. *Compare* 2 Farrand 313 (Jackson) *with* 2 *id.* 319 (Madison). The only other extant notes on the make-to-declare shift, those of James McHenry, add little. They tersely state: "Debated the difference between a power to declare war, and to make war—amended by substituting declare—adjourned without a question on the clause." *Id.* 320. According to Jackson, however, there was a vote on the clause, and the Convention did not again consider the declaration-of-war language.

28. 2 FARRAND 318.

29. 2 FARRAND 318. Though Gerry referred to an executive war-making "motion," neither Jackson, Madison, nor McHenry cited one. Conceivably the motion was made and the first vote mentioned by Jackson was devoted to its defeat. Such, however, is sheer speculation. And given the Framers' fear of executive power, it borders on the inconceivable that an executive war-making motion could have failed only five states to four—the vote recorded by Jackson for the first motion—or that Madison could have failed to notice both the making of so explosive a motion and its rejection by only a razor's edge.

30. 2 FARRAND 319.

31. 2 FARRAND 319. Perhaps Mason believed that heightened national capacity to repel sudden attack, via executive emergency authority, would

deter foreign aggressors. Judging by his distaste for executive military power, it is reasonable to assume that Mason did not understand the change from make to declare as granting sweeping presidential prerogative. *See, e.g.,* 3 ELLIOT 496-98.

32.   2 FARRAND 319. Madison's notes state only that "[o]n the remark by Mr. King that '*make*' war might be understood to '*conduct*' it which was an Executive function, Mr. Elseworth gave up his objection (and the vote of Cont was changed to—ay.)."

33.   4 ELLIOT 263. Note that Butler spoke of the "power of making peace or war," despite the make-to-declare substitution. Ezra Stiles marked his diary for December 21, 1787, in the same vein: "Mr. Baldwin was one of the Continental Convention at Philada last Summer. He gave me an Acct of the whole Progress in Convention. It appeared that they were pretty unanimous in the followg Ideas, viz. . . . 10. They vested Congress . . . with the Army, Navy & makg War & Peace." 3 FARRAND 168-69.

It is significant, further, that Butler's remarks did not occur during debate on the executive-legislative allocation of war powers or even during consideration of congressional authority to declare war. He was responding, instead, to fear that the Senate would be overweeningly powerful, because its members could not be impeached. Judge Pendleton had just "read a paragraph in the Constitution, which says 'the Senate shall have the sole power of impeachment,'" and said: "In the British government, and all governments where power is given to make treaties of peace, or declare war, there had been found necessity to annex responsibility. In England, particularly, ministers that advised illegal measures were liable to impeachment, for advising the king. Now, if justice called for punishment of treachery in the Senate, on account of giving bad advice, before what tribunal could they be arraigned? Not surely before their house; that was absurd to suppose. Nor could the President be impeached for making treaties, he acting only under advice of the Senate, without a power of negativing." 4 ELLIOT 263.

34.   Madison recorded: "On the Motion to insert *declare*—in place of *Make,* (it was agreed to). N.H. no. Mas. abst. Cont. no. Pa ay. Del. ay. Md. ay. Va. ay. N.C. ay. S.C. ay. Geo. ay." 2 FARRAND 319. He also asterisked the Connecticut vote, indicating in the footnote quoted in note 32 above that, with Ellsworth's change of heart, "the vote of Cont was changed to—ay."

35.   2 FARRAND 319.

36.   2 FARRAND 325-26. *See also id.* 322.

37.   Though the Articles did not explicitly state that Congress might grant letters of marque and reprisal during war, the grant to Congress of broad authority over hostilities and the proviso for state marque and reprisal during war under congressional supervision indicate the existence of the power. *See* Articles 6 and 9, *quoted in* Chapter III, note 44.

Madison similarly understood congressional power over marque under the Articles: "The prohibition of letters of marque is another part of the old system, but is somewhat extended in the new. According to the former, letters of marque could be granted by the states after a declaration of war. According to the latter, these licences must be obtained as well during war as previous to its declaration, from the government of the United States. This alteration is fully justified by the advantage of uniformity in all points which relate to foreign powers; and of immediate responsibility to the nation in all those, for whose conduct the nation itself is to be responsible." THE FEDERALIST PAPERS, No. 44 (hereafter cited as FEDERALIST).

38.   2 FARRAND 342-44; *cf.* Morris's earlier comment that "[t]here must be certain great officers of State; a minister of finance, of war, of foreign affairs &c. These he presumes will exercise their functions in subordination to the Executive, and will be amenable by impeachment to the public Justice. Without these ministers the Executive can do nothing of consequence." *Id.* 53-54.

39.   2 FARRAND 366-67.

40.   Discussion of an executive council recurred periodically, often with a foreign-affairs cast and even more frequently with an aura of executive restraint. As George Mason said when it became clear that there would be no nonsenatorial advisers, "[I]n rejecting a Council to the President we were about to try an experiment on which the most despotic Governments had never ventured—The Grand Signor himself had his Divan." 2 FARRAND 541. *See generally* 1 *id.* 21, 74, 97; 2 *id.* 328-29, 342-44, 367, 537, 539, 541-42; 3 *id.* 158, 606. *See also* the long comment by James Iredell in the North Carolina convention, 4 ELLIOT 108-10. It appears that the Framers viewed the Senate in certain of its functions as a potent executive council, *e.g.*, 2 FARRAND 537-39. On the other hand, in Luther Martin's view the Senate would provide a spineless set of advisers to the President. "The impeachment can rarely come from the Second branch," he said, "who are his Council and will be under his influence." 3 *Id.* 158.

41.   2 FARRAND 392.

42.   2 FARRAND 392.

43.   2 FARRAND 392, 394.

44.   2 FARRAND 392, 393.

45.   2 FARRAND 392-93.

46.   2 FARRAND 393.

47.   2 FARRAND 393.

48.   2 FARRAND 426-27.

49.   3 FARRAND 217-18; 1 ELLIOT 378.

50.   2 FARRAND 498-99.

51.   2 FARRAND 499 n.14, in light of *id.* 496-97 n.8.

52.   2 FARRAND 508 (Committee's proposal) & 509 (its unanimous acceptance).

53.   2 FARRAND 538.

54.   Madison recorded simply that "[t]he first sentence as to making treaties, was then Agreed to: nem: con." 2 FARRAND 538. As New York and Rhode Island did not vote, unanimity ran among only the ten states then participating in the Convention. Max Farrand has suggested: "It was evident that the convention was growing tired. The committee had recommended that the power of appointment and the making of treaties be taken from the senate and vested in the president 'by and with the advice and consent of the senate.' With surprising unanimity and surprisingly little debate, these important changes were agreed to." THE FRAMING OF THE CONSTITUTION 171 (1913). *No* debate is recorded so far as the President's involvement in treaty making was concerned, and "surprisingly little" on his linkage with the Senate in making appointments. *See* 2 FARRAND 538-41.

55. 2 FARRAND 540 (King) & 549 (Gorham).

56. 3 FARRAND 503. In Pinckney's letter of December 30, 1818, to John Quincy Adams on the Philadelphia proceedings, he described association of the President with the Senate as a rash, eleventh-hour act: "[T]he great power given to the President was never intended to have been given to him while the Convention continued in that patient & coolly deliberative situation in which they had been for nearly the whole of the preceding five months of their session, nor was it until within the last week or ten days that almost the whole of the Executive Department was altered—I can assure you as a fact that for more than Four months & a half out of Five The power of exclusively making treaties, appointing public Ministers & judges of the supreme Court was given to the Senate after numerous debates & considerations of the subject both in Committee of the whole & in the house . . . ." 3 *Id.* 427. In an 1831 letter James Madison took strong issue with Pinckney's memory and explained presidential involvement in treaties and appointments, as noted in the text. *See id.* 502-03.

57. 2 FARRAND 540.

58. 2 FARRAND 540-41.

59. 2 FARRAND 541.

60. 2 FARRAND 541. Another harbinger of hard times for the peace-treaty exception came immediately before adjournment on September 7:

"Mr. Williamson & Mr. Spaight moved 'that no Treaty of Peace affecting Territorial rights shd be made without the concurrence of two thirds of the (members of the Senate present).'

"Mr. King—It will be necessary to look out for securities for some other rights, if this principle be established; he moved to extend the motion to—'all present rights of the U. States.' " *Id.* 543. *See also* 4 *id.* 58.

61. 2 FARRAND 541.

62. 2 FARRAND 548.

63. 2 FARRAND 548.

64. 2 FARRAND 548-49.

65. 2 FARRAND 549. Sherman's purpose may have been to bar treaty making by less than an absolute majority of the Senate's membership, since two-thirds of the Senators present at any time could fall short of that mark. His purpose may also have been to reduce the majority required as a practical matter for most treaties. *See* D. FLEMING, THE TREATY VETO OF THE AMERICAN SENATE 306 (1930), regarding the narrow demise of Sherman's motion: "The change of one state delegation, probably of one man in a divided delegation, would have given us this provision instead of the two-thirds vote, and we should have revered that arrangement as an expression of the Convention's great wisdom instead of looking up to its inspired action in fixing the higher majority." *See also* M. McDOUGAL & ASSOCIATES, STUDIES IN WORLD PUBLIC ORDER 624 (1960).

66. 4 ELLIOT 120. *See also, e.g.,* 2 FARRAND 393 (Dickinson); 3 *id.* 371 (Washington), 502-03 (Madison); 4 ELLIOT 27 (Spaight).

67. 4 ELLIOT 280-81. Pinckney had spoken in the same vein earlier, *id.* 263-65. *See also, e.g.,* 1 FARRAND 426 (Wilson); 2 *id.* 318 (Pinckney), 538 (Sherman); 2 ELLIOT 306-07 (Hamilton), 506-07 (Wilson); 3 *id.* 509 (Corbin); 4 *id.* 263 (Butler); FEDERALIST Nos. 62-63 (Madison), 64 (Jay), 75, 77 (Hamilton).

Hamilton in *No. 75* minced no words in excluding the House from "a share in the formation of treaties": "The fluctuating and . . . multitudinous composition of that body forbid us to expect in it those qualities which are essential to the proper execution of such a trust. Accurate and comprehensive knowledge of foreign politics; a steady and systematic adherence to the same views; a nice and uniform sensibility to national character; decision, *secrecy*, and dispatch; are incompatible with the genius of a body so variable and so numerous . . . . The greater frequency of the calls upon the house of representatives, and the greater length of time which it would often be necessary to keep them together when convened, to obtain their sanction in the progressive stages of a treaty, would be source of so great inconvenience and expence as alone ought to condemn the project."

68.   1 FARRAND 426. Madison in the same debate opposed having the states pay the salaries of their respective senators lest it make them creatures of the states. He explained: "One great end of the [Senate] was, that being a firm, wise and impartial body, it might (not) only give stability to the Genl. Govt. in its operations on individuals, but hold an even balance among different States." *Id.* 427-28. Hamilton had previously vented his contempt for the political wisdom of the general public, especially regarding foreign affairs: "All communities divide themselves into the few and the many. The first are the rich and well born, the other the mass of the people. The voice of the people has been said to be the voice of God; and however generally this maxim has been quoted and believed, it is not true in fact. The people are turbulent and changing; they seldom judge or determine right. Give therefore to the first class a distinct, permanent share in the government. They will check the unsteadiness of the second, and as they cannot receive any advantage by a change, they therefore will ever maintain good government. Can a democratic assembly, who annually revolve in the mass of the people, be supposed steadily to pursue the common good? Nothing but a permanent body can check the imprudence of democracy. Their turbulent and uncontrouling disposition requires checks . . . . The weak side of a republican govenment is the danger of foreign influence. This is unavoidable, unless it is so constructed as to bring forward its first characters in its support." Hamilton's solutions were a permanent executive and "one body of the legislature . . . constituted during good behaviour or life." *Id.* 299-300.

In less extreme tones James Iredell argued to the North Carolina convention the need for a Senate sheltered from the full play of public opinion: "As the representatives of the people may probably be more popular, and it may be sometimes necessary for the Senate to prevent factious measures taking place, which may be highly injurious to the real interests of the public, the Senate should not be at the mercy of every popular clamor . . . . These observations apply even to acts of legislation concerning domestic policy: they apply much more forcibly to the case of foreign negotiations, which will form one part of the business of the Senate . . . ."

Iredell then elaborated on the need for long senatorial tenure: "A certain permanency in office is . . . useful for another reason. Nothing is more unfortunate for a nation than to have its affairs conducted in an irregular manner. Consistency and stability are necessary to render the laws of any society convenient for the people. If they were to be entirely conducted by men liable to be called away soon, we might be deprived, in a great measure, of their utility; their measures might be abandoned before they were fully executed, and others, of a less beneficial tendency, substituted in their stead. The public also would be deprived of that experience which adds so much weight to the greatest abilities.

"The business of a senator will require a great deal of knowledge, and more extensive information than can be acquired in a short time. . . . The acquisition of full information [on the real state of the Union] must employ a great deal of time; since a general knowledge of the affairs of all the states, and of the relative situation of foreign nations, would be indispensable. Responsibility, also, would be lessened by short duration; for many useful measures require a good deal of time, and continued operations, and no man should be answerable for the ill success of a scheme which was taken out of his hands by others." 4 ELLIOT 40-41.

69.   *See also* FEDERALIST Nos. 10, 39, 49 (Madison), 68, 71, 73 (Hamilton); THE FEDERALIST PAPERS 289-90 nn.12, 17 (R. Fairfield ed. 1966).

70.   2 FARRAND 548. *See also* Chapter III, note 49, and accompanying text.

71.   "Mr. McHenry conceived that [embargo] power to be included in the power of war." 2 FARRAND 362. *See generally* the international cast of the debate at *id.* 359-63 on export duties. And the even more heavily international tone of subsequent debate on commercial regulation at *id.* 448-53, including Pinckney's proposal that no legislation affecting American foreign trade be adopted except by two-thirds vote of both houses of Congress. *See also* Chapter V, note 3.

72.   *See, e.g.*, 2 FARRAND 268-72; 3 *id.* 100.

73.   The provisions on state war powers were moved from their prior place with other language on the states, and the proviso on habeas corpus from among language on the judiciary. *Compare* 2 FARRAND 576 (habeas corpus) & 577 (state war powers) *with id.* 596-97.

74.   2 FARRAND 538-39.

75.   *See* page 35 above.

76.   1 FARRAND 66-67. William Pierce recorded in his notes a similar statement by another Framer: "Mr. Dickinson was of opinion that the powers of the Executive ought to be defined before we say in whom the power shall vest." *Id.* 74. *See also* note 5 above.

77.   *E.g.*, 1 FARRAND 66, 74, 83, 86-87, 101-103, 119, 152, 425; 2 *id.* 35-36, 101; 3 *id.* 158, 169; *cf.* fear of the President and Senate together, *e.g.*, 2 *id.* 278-79, 512, 554. Bagehot caught the Framers' mood regarding executive, if not congressional, authority when he reported that they "shrank from placing sovereign powers anywhere. They feared it would generate tyranny; George III had been a tyrant to them, and come what might, they would not make a George III." THE ENGLISH CONSTITUTION 218 (1964). *See also* Berger, *War-Making by the President*, 121 U. PA. L. REV. 29, 33, 35 (1972).

78.   *E.g.*, 2 FARRAND 513, 522-23. During the ratifying conventions, this notion was particularly prevalent. *See* Chapter V, notes 28-37 and accompanying text.

79.   See the discussion in E. CORWIN, THE PRESIDENT: OFFICE AND POWERS 1787-1957, at 3-16 (4th rev. ed. 1957); C. ROSSITER, THE AMERICAN PRESIDENCY 74-81, 87 (2d ed. 1960); C. ROSSITER, 1787: THE GRAND CONVENTION 221-22 (1966).

80.   Letter to Weedon Butler of May 5, 1788, at 3 FARRAND 302. Butler in that letter, however, also went to lengths to describe the "material difference" between the powers of the British king and the American president, picturing the latter as far the weaker. He detailed the President's authority in a manner that suggested "full great" powers only as against the possibility that the Executive might have been a minion of Congress. *See id.* 301-02; *cf.* Thomas Hartley's remark in 1789 in Congress that presidential "powers, taken together, are not very numerous . . . ." 1 ANNALS OF CONGRESS 500 (1789).

Butler's letter does suggest that Washington as the president-apparent soothed Whiggish fears. Clinton Rossiter has concluded: "We cannot measure even crudely the influence of the commanding presence of the most famous and trusted of Americans, yet we may be sure that it was sizable, that it pointed (as we know from Washington's recorded votes) toward unity, strength, and independence in the executive, and that the doubts of some old-fashioned Whigs were soothed, if never entirely laid to rest, by the expectation that he would be chosen as first occupant of the proposed Presidency, and chosen and chosen again until claimed by the grave." 1787: THE GRAND CONVENTION 222 (1966). Rossiter cited as evidence of Washingtonian reassurance that "when Dr. Franklin predicted on June 4 that 'the first man put at the helm will be a good one,' every delegate knew perfectly well who that first good man would be." *Id.* Omitted by Rossiter, however, was the balance— and less cheery point—of Franklin's remark. He said in whole, after a dark account of the takeover of Holland by the House of Orange: "The first man, put at the helm will be a good one. No body knows what sort may come afterwards. The Executive will be always increasing here, as elsewhere, till it ends in a monarchy." 1 FARRAND 103. Others also looked beyond Washington, *e.g.,* 3 ELLIOT 160; 4 *id.* 288.

81.   According to Madison's notes:

"Mr. King suggested that the Journals of the Convention should be either destroyed, or deposited in the custody of the President [of the Convention]. He thought if suffered to be made public, a bad use would be made of them by those who would wish to prevent the adoption of the Constitution—

"Mr. Wilson prefered the second expedient. he had at one time liked the first best; but as false suggestions may be propagated it should not be made impossible to contradict them." 2 FARRAND 648.

McHenry's notes report "Injunction of secrecy taken off," *id.* 650, an indication perhaps that the Framers might speak of their debates. Some in fact did talk about them before publication of the Journal in 1819. Others, however, apparently felt that confidentiality remained in effect. For example, Madison's complaint to Jefferson in 1796, after President Washington argued the intent of the Framers during his controversy with the House of Representatives over its treaty-making role: "According to my memory & that of others, the Journal of the Convention was, by a vote deposited with the P., to be kept sacred until called for by some competent authority. How can this be reconciled with the use he has made of it?" 3 FARRAND 372. *See also* Pinckney's reference in 1818 to "the Veil of secrecy from the Proceedings of the Convention being removed by Congress . . . ." *Id.* 427.

82.   2 FARRAND 664-65. Article VII of the Constitution provides that "[t]he Ratification of the Conventions of nine States, shall be sufficient for the Establishment of this Constitution between the States so ratifying the Same."

Chapter V: Ratification

1. *See* C. WARREN, THE MAKING OF THE CONSTITUTION 819-20 (1937); 1 DEBATES IN THE SEVERAL STATE CONVENTIONS ON THE ADOPTION OF THE FEDERAL CONSTITUTION 318-38 (J. Elliot ed. 1859 & 1861) (hereafter cited as ELLIOT).

2. *Quoted in* C. WARREN, *supra* note 1, at 794.

3. Amendments were sought by Massachusetts (1 ELLIOT 322-23), Maryland (2 *id*. 547-56), New Hampshire (1 *id*. 325-27), New York (1 *id*. 327-31), Rhode Island (1 *id*. 334-37), South Carolina (1 *id*. 325), and Virginia (3 *id*. 657-63). Other revisions proposed during the Maryland convention were voted down (2 *id*. 552-53). Amendments suggested during the first North Carolina convention died when the delegates rejected the Constitution in whole (4 *id*. 242-47). And the Pennsylvania proposals were offered by a rump group that gathered after the state convention to demand changes in the Constitution (2 *id*. 542-46). Whether officially advanced or not, however, all of these proposals point to the Ratifiers' principal concerns.

Some of the revisions were labeled "bills of rights" and others simply "amendments." Counting them as they were defined by the conventions tends to understate the number of proposals actually made, since several matters were often grouped together in a single right or amendment. Nonetheless, a gross measure will suffice to suggest what was on the Ratifiers' minds. So counted, almost 250 rights or amendments were advanced.

Of these, at most 50 dealt with the war powers, only 3 with the President. New York moved to require congressional consent for executive command in the field and clemency for traitors. One of the amendments rejected in Maryland would have similarly limited executive field command.

The remaining revisions concerned Congress. New York and Rhode Island wanted a two-thirds vote of both houses for declaration of war. *Cf*. Thomas Jefferson's belief after ratification that such a majority was needed. 7 T. JEFFERSON, WRITINGS 220, 222, 243-44 (Ford ed. 1896).

Among the would-be amendments of the abortive North Carolina convention was one that Congress "not introduce foreign troops" into America without a two-thirds vote of both houses (4 ELLIOT 247). North Carolina also shared Virginia's concerns that two-thirds of all the Senators, not just those present, be required for commercial treaties and that the Constitution virtually prohibit treaties adversely affecting American territorial, fishing, or navigational interests. And North Carolina wished no treaties opposed to the Constitution or to any United States law until repealed by Congress. Among the rejected Maryland amendments was a prohibition on treaties contrary to state constitutions or bills of rights (2 *id*. 553).

New York, North Carolina, Rhode Island, and Virginia all sought to prevent congressional secrecy, except when necessary for diplomatic or military reasons. Such a prohibition had bound the Confederation Congresses. *See* 1 *id*. 83 (Article 9). New York even insisted "that both houses of Congress shall always keep their doors open during their sessions, unless the business may, in their opinion, require secrecy" (*id*. 330). And that state wanted severe time restraints on congressional power to end habeas corpus during military emergency.

The rest, and great majority, of the pertinent amendments went to limit congressional capacity to raise standing armies and to control the militia; to ensure civil rule and guarantee citizens' rights to bear arms and have no troops quartered in their homes during peace. The dominant theme of these revisions was the need to protect state and individual interests against overweening federal authority, most manifest to the Ratifiers in Congress.

4. In 1825 Jefferson named *The Federalist* as the source "to which appeal is habitually made by all, and rarely declined or denied by any as evidence of the general opinion of those who framed and of those who accepted the Constitution of the United States, on questions as to its genuine meaning." Charles Beard studied each Philadelphia delegate and concluded "that the authors of *The Federalist* generalized the political doctrines of the members of the Convention with a high degree of precision, in spite of the great diversity of opinion which prevailed on many matters." For the Jefferson and Beard quotations, *see* THE FEDERALIST PAPERS xi, 281 n.28 (R. Fairfield ed. 1966). *See also* E. CORWIN, THE DOCTRINE OF JUDICIAL REVIEW 44 (1914): "It cannot reasonably be doubted that Hamilton was here, as at other points, endeavoring to reproduce the matured conclusions of the Convention itself." So far as *The Federalist's* impact on the Ratifiers was concerned, see Chapter III, note 3, and accompanying text.

5. 3 ELLIOT 233.

6. 2 ELLIOT 278. *See also, e.g.,* 2 *id.* 284, 528; 3 *id.* 259; THE FEDERALIST PAPERS, Nos. 23 (Hamilton), 41 (Madison) (hereafter cited as FEDERALIST); Lofgren, *War-Making Under the Constitution: The Original Understanding,* 81 YALE L. J. 672, 683-84 (1972).

7. 4 ELLIOT 94.

8. 2 ELLIOT 528.

9. 4 ELLIOT 107. Iredell went on: "The power of declaring war is expressly given to Congress, that is, to the two branches of the legislature—the Senate, composed of representatives of the state legislatures, the House of Representatives, deputed by the people at large. They have also expressly delegated to them the powers of raising and supporting armies, and of providing and maintaining a navy." *Id.* 107-08.

10. 4 ELLIOT 263. For Butler's full remarks, *see* page 85 above.

11. 4 ELLIOT 287. *See also, e.g.,* 2 *id.* 195; 3 *id.* 201.

12. *Cato IV, in* ESSAYS ON THE CONSTITUTION OF THE UNITED STATES 263-64 (P. Ford ed. 1892).

13. 4 ELLIOT 114. No other participant in the ratification debates went to Miller's lengths in ignoring the lesson of the Revolution concerning the need for single command.

14. 4 ELLIOT 107. *See also, e.g.,* 3 *id.* 497 (Nicholas). George Mason disagreed "because the governor did not possess such extensive powers as the President, and had no influence over the navy." *Id.* 497.

15. In *Federalist No. 70,* Hamilton stated: "That unity is conducive to energy will not be disputed. Decision, activity, secrecy and dispatch, will generally characterise the proceedings of one man in a much more eminent degree than the proceedings of any greater number." He had just noted that "[e]nergy in the executive is a leading character in the definition of good government. It is essential to the protection of the community against foreign attacks." "In the conduct of war," he continued, "the energy of the executive is the bulwark of the national security . . . ." In *No.* 72 Hamilton described

as executive functions "the arrangement of the army and navy and the direction of the operations of war," and in *No. 75* he said that "the execution of the laws, and the employment of the common strength, either for this purpose or for the common defence, seem to comprise all the functions of the executive magistrate." *Cf.* FEDERALIST No. 64 (Jay).

16.   Speaking of executive "energy" in *Federalist No. 70*, Hamilton noted: "Every man the least conversant in Roman story, knows how often that republic was obliged to take refuge in the absolute power of a single man, under the formidable title of dictator, as well against the intrigues of ambitious individuals, who aspired to the tyranny, and the seditions of whole classes of the community, whose conduct threatened the existence of all government, as against the invasions of external enemies, who menaced the conquest and destruction of Rome."

In *No. 72* he went on: "Without supposing the personal essentiality of the man, it is evident that a change of the chief magistrate, at the breaking out of a war, or any similar crisis, for another even of equal merit, would at all times be detrimental to the community; inasmuch as it would substitute inexperience to experience, and would tend to unhinge and set afloat the already settled train of the administration."

Hamilton spoke of executive energy, however, to rebut arguments that the President should have been plural, saddled with a council or limited to a fixed number of terms. He said in *No. 70* that the "ingredients which constitute energy in the executive, are, unity—duration—an adequate provision for its support—competent powers." Nothing in his discussion of "competent powers" suggested that the President would ever have dictatorial authority, even during crisis. *But cf.* 2 ELLIOT 359-60; 3 *id.* 79, 160; Chapter IV, note 29.

In *Federalist Nos. 23, 26* and *34*, Hamilton did urge unlimited *federal* capacity to meet military threats, but with emphasis more on congressional than executive authority. "Nothing . . . can be more fallacious, than to infer the extent of any power proper to be lodged in the national government, from an estimate of its immediate necessities," he wrote in *No. 34*. "There ought to be a CAPACITY to provide for future contingencies, as they may happen; and as these are illimitable in their nature, so it is impossible safely to limit that capacity." Again, in *No. 26*: "The idea of restraining the legislative authority, in the means of providing for the national defence, is one of those refinements, which owe their origin to a zeal for liberty more ardent than enlightened." And finally in *No. 23*: "The authorities essential to the care of the common defence are these—to raise armies—to build and equip fleets—to prescribe rules for the government of both—to direct their operations—to provide for their support. These powers ought to exist without limitation: Because it is impossible to foresee or to define the extent and variety of the means which may be necessary to satisfy them. The circumstances that endanger the safety of nations are infinite; and for this reason, no constitutional shackles can wisely be imposed on the power to which the care of it is committed. This power ought to be coextensive with all the possible combinations of such circumstances; and ought to be under the direction of the same councils, which are appointed to preside over the common defence." *See also* FEDERALIST No. 41 (Madison).

17.   3 ELLIOT 59; *see* Wormuth, *The Nixon Theory of the War Power: A Critique*, 60 CALIF. L. REV. 623, 635 (1972); *cf.* in *Federalist No. 31*, Hamilton's

remark that the antifederalist "mode of reasoning appears some times to turn upon the supposition of usurpation in the national government."

18. 3 ELLIOT 220.

19. 3 ELLIOT 496. Mason's concern that the President's military power dangerously exceeded state governors' was just mentioned, note 14 above. His great distrust of armed Executives, though, may have been surpassed by his fear of militant Congresses controlling both declarations and tools of war: "How is this compared to the British constitution?" he asked. "Though the king may declare war, the Parliament has the means of carrying it on. It is not so here. Congress can do both. Were it not for that check in the British government, the monarch would be a despot." 3 *Id.* 379.

20. 1 ELLIOT 378. An unsuccessful effort was made in the Maryland convention to propose a constitutional amendment forbidding the President to "command the army in person, without the consent of Congress." 2 *Id.* 553.

21. 1 ELLIOT 330. *See also* 2 *id.* 408. The federalists' response to these fears centered on the necessity for single command and on the need for command by a civilian with a limited term of office. *E.g.*, Spaight in North Carolina: "He was surprised that any objection should be made to giving the command of the army to one man; that it was well known that the direction of an army could not be properly exercised by a numerous body of men; that Congress had, in the last war, given the exclusive command of the army to the commander-in-chief, and that if they had not done so, perhaps the independence of America would not have been established." 4 *Id.* 114-15.

In Virginia, Lee pointed out "that it did not follow, of necessity, that the President should command in person; that he was to command as a civil officer, and might only take the command when he was a man of military talents, and the public safety required it." 3 *Id.* 497. And Nicholas: "As to possible danger, any commander might attempt to pervert what was intended for the common defence of the community to its destruction. The President, at the end of four years, was to relinquish all his offices. But if any other person was to have the command, the time would not be limited." *Id.*

22. *E.g.*, Randolph during the Virginia convention: "With respect to a standing army, I believe there was not a member in the federal Convention, who did not feel indignation at such an institution. What remedy, then, could be provided? Leave the country defenceless? In order to provide for our defence, and exclude the dangers of a standing army, the general defence is left to those who are the objects of defence. It is left to the militia, who will suffer if they become instruments of tyranny." 3 ELLIOT 401. For somewhat less hopeful views of the militia, see, *e.g.*, 3 *id.* 177-78, 378, 381; FEDERALIST No. 25 (Hamilton).

23. "[T]rue," said Spaight in the North Carolina Convention, "that the command of the army and navy was given to the President; but . . . Congress, who had the power of raising armies, could certainly prevent any abuse of that authority in the President—that they alone had the means of supporting armies, and that the President was impeachable if he in any manner abused his trust." 4 ELLIOT 114. *See also, e.g.*, 2 *id.* 348-49; 3 *id.* 393-94; 4 *id.* 258; FEDERALIST No. 24 (Hamilton).

George Mason was not impressed: "Although Congress are to raise the army, . . . no security arises from that; for, in time of war, they must and ought to raise an army, which will be numerous, or otherwise, according to the nature of the war, and then the President is to command without any control." 3 ELLIOT 498.

24. During the Philadelphia Convention, George Mason had warned that "[t]he purse and sword must not be in the same hands, if this is true, and the Legislature are able to raise revenues and make & direct a war, I shall agree to a restraining power of the Legislature either in the Executive or a council of Revision." 1 THE RECORDS OF THE FEDERAL CONVENTION OF 1787, at 144 (M. Farrand ed. 1911). As we have seen, Mason's concern on this score was not met by the Constitution, and he argued during the Virginia ratifying convention that Congress held both purse and sword, 3 ELLIOT 378-81; note 19 above. Others shared his fear, *e.g.*, 2 *id.* 376-77, 552; 3 *id.* 172; *cf.* FEDERALIST No. 24 (Hamilton).

Recall that the bulk of the constitutional amendments proposed by the Ratifiers in the war-peace area sought to lessen congressional control over the military. *See* note 3 above. Federalist rebuttal to the purse-and-sword specter was mixed, some arguing that their union was acceptable in legislative hands and to be dreaded only in executive, *e.g.*, 2 *id.* 195; others that Congress would act wisely and with restraint, *e.g.*, 2 *id.* 536-37; and a few that the sword was not in congressional hands, *e.g.*, 2 *id.* 348-49; FEDERALIST No. 78 (Hamilton).

25. 1 THE WORKS OF JAMES WILSON 433 (R. McCloskey ed. 1967).

26. *Id.* 440.

27. 15 THE PAPERS OF THOMAS JEFFERSON 397 (J. Boyd ed. 1958).

28. 4 ELLIOT 120; *see* Berger, *The Presidential Monopoly of Foreign Relations*, 71 MICH. L. REV. 1, 37-42 (1972).

29. 3 ELLIOT 509-10.

30. 2 ELLIOT 507. *See also, e.g.*, 2 *id.* 533; 3 *id.* 240, 347; 4 *id.* 115-16, 280-81.

31. James Wilson, while attempting to convince the Pennsylvania convention that the Senate would not "swallow up every thing," stated that the Senators "can make no treaties: they can approve of none, unless the President . . . lays it before them." 2 ELLIOT 465-66. Still engaged in the same effort, he "beg[ged] leave to repeat, that this Senate can do nothing without the concurrence of some other branch of the government . . . . With regard to their power in forming treaties, they can make none; they are only auxiliaries to the President." *Id.* 476-77. Charles Cotesworth Pinckney, in turn, told the South Carolina Ratifiers that "[a]t last it was agreed to give the President a power of proposing treaties, as he was the ostensible head of the Union, and to vest the Senate (where each state had an equal voice) with the power of agreeing or disagreeing to the terms proposed." 4 *id.* 265. But Pinckney a few sentences later reported that the Framers had vested in the "President and Senate joined . . . the diplomatic authority of the Union." *Id.*

32. 2 ELLIOT 46 (Ames), 47-48 (King), 127 (Bowdoin).

33. 2 ELLIOT 286-87 (G. Livingston), 291 & 323 (R. Livingston), 306-07 (Hamilton).

34. 2 ELLIOT 510-14 (Wilson), 533 (McKean).

35. 3 ELLIOT 201 (Randolph), 221 (Monroe), 353 (Henry).

36. 4 ELLIOT 41 & 127 (Iredell), 116 (Spencer). Recall the Iredell statement quoted in Chapter IV, note 68.

37. 4 ELLIOT 258 (Pinckney). *See also* the remarks of Judge Pendleton, quoted in Chapter IV, note 33.

38. Jay argued in *Federalist No. 64*: "So often and so essentially have we heretofore suffered, from the want of secrecy and dispatch, that the constitution would have been inexcusibly defective if no attention had been paid to those objects. Those matters which in negotiations usually require the most secrecy and the most dispatch, are those preparatory and auxiliary measures which are no otherways important in a national view, than as they tend to facilitate the attainment of the objects of the negotiation. For these the president will find no difficulty to provide, and should any circumstance occur which requires the advice and consent of the senate, he may at any time convene them. Thus we see that the constitution provides that our negotiations for treaties shall have every advantage which can be derived from talents, information, integrity and deliberate investigations on the one hand, and from secrecy and dispatch on the other."

39. Hamilton continued: "The qualities elsewhere detailed, as indispensable in the management of foreign negotiations, point out the executive as the most fit agent in those transactions; while the vast importance of the trust, and the operation of treaties as laws, plead strongly for the participation of the whole or a part of the legislative body in the office of making them." FEDERALIST No. 75.

40. On foreign trade *see, e.g.,* FEDERALIST Nos. 11, 22 (Hamilton), 42 (Madison); on federal revenue, *e.g.,* Nos. 31 (Hamilton), 41 (Madison); on coining and valuing money, Nos. 42, 44 (Madison); on the other powers noted in the text, No. 42 (Madison).

41. 1 ANNALS OF CONG. 1122-23 (1790). During the ratification process some feared the appointment power as a source of overweening executive authority, *e.g.,* 1 ELLIOT 379 (Martin: "the person who *nominates* will always in reality *appoint*"), while others took the opposite tack and found it a font of dangerous senatorial prerogative, *e.g.,* 4 *id.* 116 (Spencer: the Senators "have a negative upon" the executive's nominations, "till he has exhausted the number of those he wishes to be appointed," and is "obliged, finally, to acquiesce in the appointment of those whom the Senate shall nominate, or else no appointment will take place"). Still others, often to support argument that the Senate would not be unduly powerful, described the joint control over appointments in more equal terms, *e.g.,* 2 *id.* 323, 476-77. Finally, there was some favorable comment on the President's power to make interim appointments during senatorial recess, *e.g.,* 2 *id.* 513-14; 4 *id.* 135 (Maclaine: "[T]he executive ought to make temporary appointments, as well as receive ambassadors and other public ministers. This power can be vested nowhere but in the executive, because he is perpetually acting for the public; for, though the Senate is to advise him in the appointment of officers, &c., yet, during the recess, the President must do this business, or else it will be neglected; and such neglect may occasion public inconveniences").

See generally Hamilton's comments on the appointment power in *Federalist Nos. 65-67, 69,* and *76-77*. Though a man imbued with Executive-first notions, he favored in *No. 77* the Senate's consent to the removal of officials appointed with its blessing. Hamilton stated: "It has been mentioned as one of the advantages to be expected from the co-operation of the senate, in the business of appointments, that it would contribute to the stability of the administration. The consent of that body would be necessary to displace as well as to appoint . . . . Those who can best estimate the value of a steady administration will be most disposed to prize a provision, which connects the official existence of public men with the approbation or disapprobation of that body, which from the greater permanency of its own composition, will in all probability be less subject to inconstancy, than any other member of the government."

42. Madison stated:

"The *second* class of powers lodged in the general government, consist of those which regulate the intercourse with foreign nations, to wit, to make treaties; to send and receive ambassadors, other public ministers and consuls; to define and punish piracies and felonies committed on the high seas, and offences against the law of nations; to regulate foreign commerce . . . .

"This class of powers forms an obvious and essential branch of the federal administration. If we are to be one nation in any respect, it clearly ought to be in respect to other nations.

"The powers to make treaties and to send and receive ambassadors, speak of their own propriety.—Both are comprised in the articles of confederation; with this difference only, that the former is disembarrassed by the plan of the convention of an exception, under which treaties might be substantially frustrated by regulations of the states; and that a power of appointing and receiving 'other public ministers and consuls,' is expressly and very properly added to the former provision concerning ambassadors." FEDERALIST No. 42.

43. *E.g.*, 2 ELLIOT 512-13.

44. 3 THE RECORDS OF THE FEDERAL CONVENTION OF 1787, *supra* note 24, at 158.

45. 1 ELLIOT 378-79; *accord, e.g.*, 3 *id*. 497 (Mason).

46. The proposed amendment stated "[t]hat the executive shall not grant pardons for treason, unless with the consent of Congress; but may, at his discretion, grant reprieves to persons convicted of treason, until their cases can be laid before the Congress." 1 ELLIOT 330.

47. During the Constitutional Convention, however, Hamilton had been willing to have the President pardon traitors only with "approbation of the Senate." 1 THE RECORDS OF THE FEDERAL CONVENTION OF 1787, *supra* note 24, at 292. *See also* James Iredell on the benefits of executive pardon power during hostilities, 4 ELLIOT 112-13.

48. Rawlins Lowndes of South Carolina, 4 ELLIOT 310-11. But Maclaine pointed out in the North Carolina convention that "Congress must meet at *least once* in every year," 4 *id*. 135, and Hamilton denigrated executive authority to summon and adjourn in *Federalist No. 77*.

49. *E.g.*, the constitutional amendment proposed by the New York convention "[t]hat the privilege of the *habeas corpus* shall not, by any law, be suspended for a longer term than six months, or until twenty days after the meeting of the Congress next following the passing the act for such suspension." 1 ELLIOT 330.

50. *E.g.*, 2 ELLIOT 436, 533; 4 *id*. 179. As Madison said in *Federalist No. 14*, national "jurisdiction is limited to certain enumerated objects," and, in *No. 45*, "The powers delegated by the proposed constitution to the federal government, are few and defined." *See also* FEDERALIST No. 41 (Madison); Chapter IV, note 76; Berger, *supra* note 28, at 20-22, 27, 32-33.

51. *See* FEDERALIST Nos. 67-77 (Hamilton), especially 69, 73-77; *cf*. No. 42

(Madison). Quite to the contrary, concern ran to expansive readings by Congress of its enumerated grants. *See id.* Nos. 33 (Hamilton), 44 (Madison) (necessary-and-proper clause); No. 41 (Madison) (congressional power to tax to "provide for the common defence and general welfare of the United States").

52. FEDERALIST No. 51 (Madison). See the third paragraph of note 53, below.

53. In *Federalist No. 77*, Hamilton reached what he termed "[t]he only remaining powers of the executive." Neither they nor those previously covered involved the executive-power clause. It went unmentioned.

Madison, however, while defending congressional power to tax, asked, "For what purpose could the enumeration of particular powers be inserted, if these and all others were meant to be included in the preceding general power? Nothing is more natural or common than first to use a general phrase, and then to explain and qualify it by a recital of particulars." FEDERALIST No. 41. Applying Madison's remarks to the President, the "preceding general power" is the executive-power clause, and the recital of explanatory and qualifying particulars occurs in the grants to the President that appear principally in Article II, Sections 2 and 3.

Finally, it was always legislative authority—never executive—that Hamilton and Madison described as plastic and aggressive. *See* FEDERALIST Nos. 48-51 (Madison), 71, 73 (Hamilton). As Madison said in *No. 48*:

"[I]n a representative republic, where the executive magistracy is carefully limited both in the extent and the duration of its power; and where the legislative power is exercised by an assembly, which is inspired by a supposed influence over the people with an intrepid confidence in its own strength . . . it is against the enterprising ambition of this department, that the people ought to indulge all their jealousy and exhaust all their precautions.

"The legislative department derives a superiority in our governments from other circumstances. Its constitutional powers being at once more extensive and less susceptible of precise limits, it can with the greater facility, mask under complicated and indirect measures, the encroachments which it makes, on the co-ordinate departments . . . . On the other side, the executive power being restrained within a narrower compass, and being more simple in its nature, and the judiciary being described by land marks, still less uncertain, projects of usurpation by either of these departments, would immediately betray and defeat themselves."

Recall Gouverneur Morris's assertion in 1814 that the "legislative" not the executive "lion will not be entangled in the meshes of a logical net," referring to the Constitution's "unequivocal provisions and limitations." Chapter III, note 68. Twenty-seven years earlier, during the Constitutional Convention, Morris had warned that "[t]he Legislature will continually seek to aggrandize & perpetuate themselves; and will seize those critical moments produced by war, invasion or convulsion for that purpose." 2 THE RECORDS OF THE FEDERAL CONVENTION OF 1787, *supra* note 24, at 52. *See also* the discussion of executive power in Chapter IV, notes 75-80 and accompanying text.

Significantly, for Hamilton the Executive's veto power existed above all else to provide him a shield against congressional usurpation. FEDERALIST No. 73.

54. 2 ELLIOT 128.

55. 3 ELLIOT 58, 43-64. *See also, e.g.,* 1 *id.* 377-80; 4 *id.* 496-97.
56. *Cato IV, supra* note 12, at 264.
57. 1 ELLIOT 332-33.

Chapter VI: Congressional Retreat and Resilience since 1789

1. 57 CONG. REC. 1729 (1919). *See* C. BERDAHL, WAR POWERS OF THE EXECUTIVE IN THE UNITED STATES 121-22 (1921). Similar complaints were raised by a few opponents of American involvement in the Indochina War.
2. 22 U.S.C. § 262 (1976). *See* L. HENKIN, FOREIGN AFFAIRS AND THE CONSTITUTION 112-13, 360 n.71 (1972).
3. The following table attempts a division of administrations by the intensity of war-power practice during them. Intensity has been measured by two principal criteria: (1) the extent to which new war-power issues, or old issues in new circumstances, were at hand and (2) the degree to which the country *consciously* confronted them. As earlier noted, these criteria have not always traveled in parallel. Significant war-power events have occasionally occurred without controversy, and uproar has sometimes been prompted by trivia. While the slots awarded particular presidencies can be debated, the instruction of the table's overall effect is clear. The country has been actively engaged with war-power issues in far more administrations than not since 1789.

Intensity of War-Power Practice

I Acute	II Strong	III Noticeable	IV Negligible
1789-1825 Washington Adams Jefferson Madison Monroe			
		1825-29 Adams	
	1829-37 Jackson		
		1837-41 Van Buren	
1841-49 Tyler Polk			1841 Harrison
			1849-50 Taylor
		1850-53 Fillmore	
	1853-57 Pierce		
1857-65 Buchanan Lincoln			

I Acute	II Strong	III Noticeable	IV Negligible
	1865-77 Johnson Grant		
		1877-81 Hayes	
			1881 Garfield
		1881-93 Arthur Cleveland Harrison	
	1893-97 Cleveland		
1897-1909 McKinley Roosevelt			
	1909-13 Taft		
1913-21 Wilson			
		1921-23 Harding	
	1923-29 Coolidge		
		1929-37 Hoover Roosevelt	
1937-53 Roosevelt Truman			
	1953-63 Eisenhower Kennedy		
1963-74 Johnson Nixon			
	1974-77 Ford		
		1977-1981 Carter	

4. The "Cooper-Church amendment," § 7(a), 84 Stat. 1943 (1971).
5. 87 Stat. 134 (1973).
6. 11 Stat. 370 (1858).
7. 40 Stat. 1 (1917).
8. 12 Stat. 326 (1861).
9. 3 Stat. 512-13 (1819).
10. 11 Stat. 119 (1856).

11.   Pub. L. No. 85-7, 71 Stat. 5 (1957).
12.   1 Stat. 578 (1798).
13.   3 Stat. 471 (1811). Though passed in secret by Congress on January 15, 1811, this measure was not published until April 29, 1818. *See generally* Rostow, *Great Cases Make Bad Law: The War Powers Act*, 50 TEXAS L. REV. 833, 857-62 (1972).
14.   5 Stat. 355 (1839).
15.   CONG. GLOBE, 35th Cong., 2d Sess. 1120 (1859).
16.   5 MESSAGES AND PAPERS OF THE PRESIDENTS 1789-1897, at 569 (J. D. Richardson ed. 1897) (hereafter cited as RICHARDSON).
17.   5 RICHARDSON 570.
18.   1 Stat. 96 (1789).
19.   Pub. L. No. 88-408, 78 Stat. 384 (1964).
20.   Pub. L. No. 91-672, 84 Stat. 2053 (1971). Rather than end the Tonkin Gulf authorization by concurrent resolution, Congress used an amendment to the Foreign Military Sales Act of 1971. That gave the Executive an opportunity to veto the repealer, which President Nixon chose not to take. But while signing he claimed a prerogative as commander in chief to wind down the war as he thought best. Despite the repealer, Congress in turn continued to fund our war effort and to reject resolutions calling for its end. Six months before the repeal, John Norton Moore questioned its wisdom during testimony given to a House subcommittee the day after the Senate first voted to abrogate Tonkin Gulf:

"MR. MOORE. The Southeast Asia resolution is the principal constitutional authority for the Vietnam war. To withdraw that authority while the war continues is to unnecessarily undercut the Presidential role in pursuing a negotiated settlement. Even if the resolution were repealed the President may continue to have constitutional authority to pursue objectives which were initially authorized by Congress. Repeal, however, would leave the extent of that authority in doubt. . . .

"Repeal . . . would also seem a step backward in the exercise of congressional responsibility for the use of Armed Forces abroad. At a time when Congress is increasingly concerned with the congressional role, repeal . . . would erode congressional responsibility by implying Presidential authority to continue the war even in the absence of congressional authorization. Congress has the principal constitutional authority to authorize the commitment of the Armed Forces to sustained hostilities abroad. It also has the authority to terminate such hostilities. The exercise of that responsibility, whether of commitment or termination, should be undertaken carefully after full debate on the merits and should clearly indicate the scope and purpose of the congressional action. The hurried and confused repeal of the Southeast Asia resolution fails in each of these respects.

"Fortunately, the House of Representatives shares the Congressional war power on an equal basis with the Senate. As such it has an important opportunity to carefully consider whether repeal of the principal constitutional authority for the Vietnam war, while the war continues, will either contribute to settlement of the conflict or clarify the proper role of Congress with respect to the use of the armed forces abroad. It seems likely that repeal at this time would be detrimental to both goals."

"[REP.] FRASER. If it is repealed does the President have to get out?"

"MR. MOORE. If Congress repeals the Southeast Asia resolution, the President's powers under the Constitution become very hazy with respect to staying in Vietnam longer than necessary to withdraw American troops and to protect them adequately during withdrawal."

"[REP.] FRASER. Then why is it not a good idea to repeal it if it leaves him with that individual power?"

"MR. MOORE. If it is the congressional intent to terminate the Vietnam war, Congress has that constitutional power. I do not feel that it is at all clear, however, that that was the intent of the Senate. There is a great deal of ambiguity and confusion evident in the Senate debate as to just what the vote means. As such I don't feel that the Senate action was a reasonable exercise which meets my earlier criteria as to well considered and precise congressional action. It seems to me also that if Congress is concerned with securing its role in the commitment of troops abroad, repeal of the Tonkin Gulf resolution is the worst possible thing that it can do, because repeal suggests that the President has continuing authority to stay in Vietnam even though Congress has withdrawn its authorization." *Hearings on Congress, the President, and the War Powers Before the Subcomm. on Nat'l Security Policy and Scientific Developments of the House Comm. on Foreign Affairs,* 91st Cong., 2d Sess. 157-58 (1970).

21. 1 Stat. 424 (1795); 10 U.S.C. § 334 (1970).

22. 20 Stat. 152 (1878). *See* Wormuth, *The Nixon Theory of the War Power: A Critique,* 60 CALIF. L. REV. 623, 639 & 639-40 n.83 (1972).

23. 50 U.S.C. §§ 1541-48 (Supp. 1975). *See* Chapter XI. Institutional proposals are not always aimed at the President alone. *E.g.,* the abortive Bricker amendment to the Constitution would have made the effectiveness of treaties dependent upon their first having been implemented by legislation that, in turn, had to concern a matter subject to congressional control in the absence of the treaty. Bricker meant to "reverse" *Missouri v. Holland,* 252 U.S. 416 (1920). If the amendment had succeeded, it would have reduced both the President's and Senate's treaty power and Congress's legislative authority.

24. 2 J. PARTON, LIFE OF ANDREW JACKSON 549-50 (1860).

25. McPHERSON, HISTORY OF THE REBELLION 349-50, *quoted in* E. CORWIN, THE PRESIDENT'S CONTROL OF FOREIGN RELATIONS 42 (1917).

26. McPHERSON, *supra* note 25, at 354, *quoted in* E. CORWIN, *supra* note 25, at 42-43.

27. A. SCHLESINGER, JR. & A. DE GRAZIA, CONGRESS AND THE PRESIDENCY: THEIR ROLE IN MODERN TIMES 91 (1967).

Chapter VII: Presidential Advance

1. A. UPSHUR, A BRIEF INQUIRY INTO THE TRUE NATURE AND CHARACTER OF OUR FEDERAL GOVERNMENT 116-17 (1840), *quoted in* E. CORWIN, THE PRESIDENT: OFFICE AND POWERS 1787-1957, at 22 (4th rev. ed. 1957); *cf.* Corwin's appraisal: "[W]hereas 'legislative power' and 'judicial power' today denote fairly definable *functions* of government as well as fairly constant *methods* for their discharge, 'executive power' is still indefinite as to *function* and retains, particularly when it is exercised by a single individual, much of its origi-

nal plasticity as to *method*. It is consequently the power of government that is the most spontaneously responsive to emergency conditions; conditions, that is, which have not attained enough of stability or recurrency to admit of their being dealt with according to rule." *Id.* 3. Recall, however, that from the perspective of the late 1700s Gouverneur Morris predicted plasticity for legislative, not executive power. *See* Chapter III, note 68.

2.   D. ACHESON, PRESENT AT THE CREATION 414 (1969). Acheson elaborated: "There has never, I believe, been any serious doubt—in the sense of nonpolitically inspired doubt—of the President's constitutional authority to do what he did. The basis for this conclusion in legal theory and historical precedent was fully set out in the State Department's memorandum of July 3, 1950, extensively published." *Id.*

3.   23 DEP'T STATE BULL. 173 (1950).

4.   54 DEP'T STATE BULL. 474, 484 (1966).

5.   117 CONG. REC. 28,977 (1971). *See also* Reveley, *Presidential War-Making: Constitutional Prerogative or Usurpation?* 55 VA. L. REV. 1243, 1291 (1969): "[T]he President's powers have been rolled into one ill-defined, mutually supportive bundle and used to justify presidential authority to do virtually 'anything, anywhere, that can be done with an army or navy,' " *quoting* Youngstown Sheet & Tube Co. v. Sawyer, 343 U.S. 579, 642 (1952) (Jackson, J., concurring). *See* 55 VA. L. REV. at 1291-92 n.159, 1257-65.

6.   2 MESSAGES AND PAPERS OF THE PRESIDENTS 1789-1897, at 596 (J. Richardson ed. 1897) (hereafter cited as RICHARDSON).

7.   7 THE WORKS OF ALEXANDER HAMILTON 746-47 (J. C. Hamilton ed. 1851). Secretary of State Adams expressed similar views in 1818: "There is no doubt that *defensive* acts of hostility may be authorized by the Executive; . . . Jackson was authorized to cross the Spanish line in pursuit of the Indian enemy. My argument is that the question of the constitutional authority of the Executive is precisely there; that all the rest, even as to the order for taking the [Spanish] Fort of Barrancas by storm, was incidental, deriving its character from the object, which was . . . the termination of the Indian War." 4 MEMOIRS OF JOHN QUINCY ADAMS 108 (C.F. Adams ed. 1875).

8.   67 U.S. (2 Black) 635, 668 (1863).

9.   Corwin, *Who Has the Power to Make War?* N.Y. Times Magazine 14 (July 31, 1949).

10.   54 DEP'T STATE BULL. 474, 484-85 (1966).

11.   *Hearings on Assignment of Ground Forces of the U.S. to Duty in the European Area Before Senate Comms. on Foreign Relations and Armed Services,* 82d Cong., 1st Sess. 92 (1951) (emphasis added).

12.   54 DEP'T STATE BULL. 474, 485 (1966) (emphasis added).

13.   *Hearings on Department of State Appropriations Authorization, Fiscal Year 1974 Before Senate Comm. on Foreign Relations,* 93d Cong., 1st Sess. 452-53 (1973).

14.   Marder, *Cease Fire and Bombing: Rationale Is Sought,* Washington Post, April 4, 1973, at A9, col. 2; *cf. Hearings on Department of Defense Appropriations for 1974 Before a Subcomm. of the House Comm. on Appropriations,* 93d Cong., 1st Sess. 153, 171-73 (1973).

15.   T. ROOSEVELT, AN AUTOBIOGRAPHY 510 (1922).

16.   Art. XIV of the Haitian Treaty, ratified February 28, 1916, *quoted in* E. Corwin, The President's Control of Foreign Relations 163 n.34 (1917).

17.   2 Richardson 31-32 (emphasis added).

18.   The quotation is from an address by President Wilson to a joint session of Congress on February 26, 1917, in which he requested the following authority to arm American merchant vessels against German submarine attacks: "[T]he President . . . is . . . authorized and empowered to supply [American] merchant ships . . . with defensive arms, should it in his judgment become necessary for him to do so . . . ; and . . . he is authorized and empowered to employ such other instrumentalities and methods as may in his judgment and discretion seem necessary and adequate to protect such ships and the citizens of the United States in their lawful and peaceful pursuits on the high seas." 54 Cong. Rec. 4273 (1917).

19.   54 Cong. Rec. 4878-79 (1917).

20.   104 Cong. Rec. 13,903 (1958).

21.   97 Cong. Rec. 61 (1951).

22.   E. Borchard, The Diplomatic Protection of Citizens Abroad 452 (1927 ed.).

23.   4 Richardson 317.

24.   Cong. Globe, 42d Cong., 1st Sess. 294 (1871).

25.   5 Richardson 282.

26.   Message to Congress, Dec. 3, 1900, *quoted in* C. Berdahl, War Powers of the Executive in the United States 52 (1921).

27.   48 Cong. Rec. 10,929 (1912).

28.   U.S. Dep't of State, The Right to Protect Citizens in Foreign Countries by Landing Forces 23 (rev. ed. 1913).

29.   Message to Congress, Jan. 10, 1927, *quoted in* Putney, *Executive Assumption of the War Making Power*, 7 Nat'l Univ. L. Rev. 1, 39-40 (1927).

30.   5 The Collected Papers of John Bassett Moore 196 (1944). *See also* B. Blechman & S. Kaplan, Force Without War (1978): "[S]ince the Second World War U.S. authorities have alerted or deployed military units on more than two hundred occasions to achieve specific objectives . . . ." *Id.* ix. Though Blechman and Kaplan do not deal with how the Constitution divides the war powers between the President and Congress, their richly detailed study makes clear that Executives have, in fact, governed American use of force during the occasions in question. Their introductory examples are apt:

"On November 11, 1944, the Turkish ambassador to the United States, Mehmet Munir Ertegün, died in Washington; not a very important event at a time when Allied forces were sweeping across France and Eastern Europe toward Germany, and Berlin and Tokyo were approaching *Götterdämmerung*. Sixteen months later, however, the ambassador's remains were the focus of world attention as the curtain went up on a classic act in the use of armed forces as a political instrument. On March 6, 1946, the U.S. Department of State announced that the late Ambassador Ertegün's remains would be sent home to Turkey aboard the U.S.S. *Missouri*, visibly the most powerful warship in the U.S. Navy and the ship on board which General Douglas MacArthur had recently accepted Japan's surrender.

"Between the ambassador's death and this announcement, not only had

World War II ended, the cold war—as yet untitled—had begun. In addition to conflicts between the United States and the Soviet Union over Poland, Germany, Iran, and other areas, the Soviet Union had demanded the concession of two Turkish provinces in the east and, in the west, a base in the area of the Dardanelles.

"On March 22 the *Missouri* began a slow journey from New York harbor to Turkey. At Gibraltar the British governor had a wreath placed on board. Accompanied by the destroyer *Power*, the great battleship was met on April 3 in the eastern Mediterranean by the light cruiser *Providence*. Finally, on the morning of April 5, the *Missouri* and her escorts anchored in the harbor at Istanbul.

"The meaning of this event was missed by no one; Washington had not so subtly reminded the Soviet Union and others that the United States was a great military power and that it could project this power abroad, even to shores far distant. Whether the visit of the *Missouri*, or it together with other U.S. actions that followed, deterred the Soviet Union from implementing any further planned or potential hostile acts toward Turkey will probably never be known. What is clear is that no forceful Soviet actions followed the visit. Moreover, as a symbol of American support for Turkey vis-a-vis the Soviet Union, the visit of the *Missouri* was well received and deeply appreciated by the govenment of Turkey, the Turkish press, and presumably by the Turkish citizenry at large. The American ambassador stated that to the Turks the visit indicated that 'the United States has now decided to oppose any effort by [the] USSR to destroy Turk[ey's] independence and integrity.'

"Three decades later, on August 18, 1976, two American officers supervising the pruning of a tree in the Korean demilitarized zone were attacked by North Korean soldiers and killed. The U.S. response was prompt. The UN military commander in Korea . . . accused North Korea of 'deliberate murder' and demanded an apology and punishment of the North Koreans involved. Secretary of State Henry A. Kissinger termed the attack 'premeditated murder,' demanded 'amends,' and warned that such attacks would not be tolerated.

"At the same time certain military preparations were taken: U.S. forces in Korea were placed on increased alert, U.S. tactical aircraft squadrons flew to Korea from bases in the United States and Okinawa, and the aircraft carrier *Midway* and accompanying vessels sailed from Yokosuka, Japan, for Korean waters. Finally, a few days after the initial incident, a large force of American and South Korean soldiers entered the demilitarized zone and cut down the offending tree while armed helicopters circled overhead and B-52 bombers flew near the border.

"North Korea never did apologize for the incident nor did it announce (publicly at least) any punishment for the North Korean soldiers involved in the incident. A North Korean representative at the Military Armistice Commission did, however, describe the incident as 'regretful'—a marked departure from previous behavior. And at a subsequent meeting North Korea submitted several businesslike proposals for avoiding such incidents in the future.

"Earlier in the summer of 1976 the United States was involved, albeit less directly, in another international incident. Following the July raid by Israeli commandos on Entebbe airport in Uganda to free passengers of a hijacked aircraft held hostage by a Palestinian group, longstanding tensions between Uganda and Kenya intensified markedly. The two states had not gotten along for some time, but when the Israeli raiders landed at the Nairobi airport on their way back to Israel with the freed hostages, Uganda's President Idi Amin threatened military retaliation.

"As the war of words between Ugandan and Kenyan leaders continued, a U.S. P-3C maritime patrol aircraft landed at the Nairobi airport, apparently the first sign of what was to become a routine operation. A day later the U.S. frigate *Beary* entered the Kenyan port of Mombasa for what was termed a 'courtesy port call.' And at the same time the U.S. aircraft carrier *Ranger* entered the Indian Ocean from the Pacific for a 'routine periodic deployment.' Although U.S. officials refused to publicly link any of these military operations to the Uganda-Kenya tension, U.S. reporters were told privately that they were meant as a show of support for Kenya.

"In each of these three incidents, as in hundreds of others since 1945, U.S. military forces were used without significant violence to underscore verbal and diplomatic expressions of American foreign policy. . . . " *Id.* 1-3 (footnotes omitted).

31. Letter to A. G. Hodges of April 4, 1864, 2 COMPLETE WORKS OF ABRAHAM LINCOLN 508 (J. Nicolay & J. Hay eds. 1907).

32. 25 U.S. (12 Wheat.) 19, 30-31 (1827) (emphasis added).

33. 8 Fed. Cas. 111 (No. 4186) (C.C.S.D.N.Y. 1860). According to Nelson:

"It is to [the Executive] . . . the citizens abroad must look for protection of person and of property, and for the faithful execution of the laws existing and intended for their protection. For this purpose, the whole executive power of the country is placed in his hands, under the Constitution, and the laws passed in pursuance thereof; and different departments of government have been organized, through which this power may be most conveniently executed, whether by negotiation *or by force*—a department of state *and a department of the navy.*

"Now, as it respects the interposition of the executive abroad, for the protection of the lives or property of the citizen, the duty must, of necessity, rest in the discretion of the president. *Acts of lawless violence, or of threatened violence to the citizen or his property, cannot be anticipated or provided for; and the protection, to be effectual or of any avail, may, not infrequently, require the most prompt and decided action.*" *Id.* 112 (emphasis added).

34. 67 U.S. (2 Black) 635, 668-69 (1863):

"This greatest of civil wars was not gradually developed by popular commotion, tumultuous assemblies, or local unorganized insurrections. However long may have been its previous conception, it nevertheless sprung forth suddenly from the parent brain, a Minerva in the full panoply of war. The President was bound to meet it in the shape it presented itself, without waiting for Congress to baptize it with a name . . . .

" . . . .

" . . . He must determine what degree of force the crisis demands. The proclamation of blockade is, itself, official and conclusive evidence to the court that a state of war existed which demanded and authorized a recourse to such a measure, under the circumstances peculiar to the case."

35.   96 Cong. Rec. 9647-49 (1950).

36.   *Hearings on War Powers Legislation Before the Senate Comm. on Foreign Relations*, 92d Cong., 1st Sess. 624 (1971).

37.   *Hearings on War Powers Legislation, supra* note 36, at 501 (emphasis added).

38.   It seems that the President may constitutionally withhold certain diplomatic and military information from Congress (even more so the public) on the ground that disclosure would hurt the nation. John Adams's delayed report to the legislators on the XYZ affair very likely fell within such "executive privilege." Details about military tactics and strategy come under the same shelter, especially if they describe imminent American steps during hostilities. *Cf.* United States v. Nixon, 418 U.S. 683, 706-07 (1974) (dictum):

"Absent a claim of need to protect military, diplomatic, or sensitive national security secrets, we find it difficult to accept the argument that even the very important interest in confidentiality of Presidential communications is significantly diminished by production of such material for *in camera* inspection with all the protection that a district court will be obliged to provide.

". . . To read the Art. II powers of the President as providing an absolute privilege as against a subpoena essential to enforcement of criminal statutes on no more than a generalized claim of the public interest in confidentiality of nonmilitary and nondiplomatic discussions would upset the constitutional balance of 'a workable government' and gravely impair the role of the courts under Art. III."

In short, the *Nixon* Court might have upheld executive privilege if the confidentiality of vital diplomatic or military secrets had been at stake. *See also* Chapter XI, note 38.

39.   Remarks to the Ass'n of the Bar of the City of New York, May 28, 1970, *quoted in Hearings on Congress, the President and the War Powers Before the Subcomm. on Nat'l Security Policy and Scientific Developments of the House Comm. on Foreign Affairs*, 91st Cong., 2d Sess. 544 (1970).

40.   6 T. Jefferson, Writings 451 (Ford ed. 1895).

41.   5 T. Jefferson, *supra* note 40, at 161. *See also* E. Corwin, *supra* note 16, at 203.

42.   According to Marshall:

"The President is the sole organ of the nation in its external relations, and its sole representative with foreign nations. Of consequence, the demand of a foreign nation can only be made on him.

"He possesses the whole Executive power. He holds and directs the force of the nation. Of consequence, any act to be performed by the force of the nation is to be performed through him.

"He is charged to execute the laws. A treaty is declared to be a law. He must then execute a treaty, where he, and he alone, possesses the means of executing it." 6 Annals of Cong. 613 (1800).

The "sole organ" metaphor has served executive doctrine generously, without regard for the limited context in which Marshall used it. *See, e.g.,* United States v. Curtiss-Wright Export Corp., 299 U.S. 304, 319-21 (1936) (dictum). *See also* the 1860 *Durand* decision: "As the executive head of the nation, the president is made the only legitimate organ of the general government, to open and carry on correspondence or negotiations with foreign nations, in matters concerning the interests of the country or of its citizens." 8 Fed. Cas. 111, 112 (No. 4186) (C.C.S.D.N.Y. 1860).

43. 7 RICHARDSON 431.

44. W. MALLOY, TREATIES 340 (1910). *See also* Q. WRIGHT, THE CONTROL OF AMERICAN FOREIGN RELATIONS 331-32 (1922).

45. 4 RICHARDSON 327.

46. THE JOURNAL OF WILLIAM MACLAY 221, 233 (1927).

47. 111 CONG. REC. 9282, 9284 (1965).

48. E. ROOT, THE MILITARY AND COLONIAL POLICY OF THE UNITED STATES 212 (1916).

49. 101 CONG. REC. 601 (1955).

50. 54 DEP'T STATE BULL. 474, 487-88 (1966).

51. 112 CONG. REC. 5566 (1966), *quoted in* R. HULL & J. NOVOGROD, LAW AND VIETNAM 181 (1968).

52. 17 RICHARDSON 31 (rev. ed. 1917).

53. The President approached Congress in qualified terms:
"No doubt I already possess . . . authority without special warrant of law, by the plain implication of my constitutional duties and powers; but I prefer, in the present circumstances, not to act upon general implication. I wish to feel that the authority and the power of the Congress are behind me in whatever it may become necessary for me to do.
". . . .
". . . I request that you will authorize me to supply our merchant ships with defensive arms, should that become necessary, and with the means of using them, and to employ any other instrumentalities or methods that may be necessary and adequate to protect our ships and our people in their legitimate and peaceful pursuits on the seas." 54 CONG. REC. 4273 (1917).

54. 5 A. LINK, WILSON: CONFUSIONS AND CRISES, 1915-1916, at 363-65 (1964).

55. J. POMEROY, INTRODUCTION TO THE CONSTITUTIONAL LAW OF THE UNITED STATES 565 (1888).

56. H. Morgenthau, *The American Tradition in Foreign Policy*, in FOREIGN POLICY IN WORLD POLITICS 264 (3d ed. Macridis 1967). Charles A Beard developed the same theme: "[The President] may do many things that vitally affect the foreign relations of the country. He may dismiss an ambassador or public minister of a foreign power for political as well as personal reasons, and if on the former ground, he might embroil the country in war. His power to receive any foreign representative authorizes him to recognize the independence of a new state, perhaps in rebellion against its former legitimate sovereign, and thus he might incur the risk of war [for example, Mr. Roosevelt's recognition of the republic of Panama in revolt against Colombia]. He may order a fleet or ship to a foreign port under circumstances that may provoke serious difficulty; the ill-fated battleship Maine was sent to the harbor of Havana by President McKinley at a time when it was regarded by many Spaniards, though not officially, as an unfriendly act. . . . As commander-in-chief of the army he might move troops to such a position on the borders of a neighboring state as to bring about an armed conflict. A notable instance of such an action occurred in the case of the opening of the

Mexican War, when President Polk ordered out troops into the disputed territory, and, on their being attacked by the Mexicans, declared that war existed by act of Mexico. Again, in his message to Congress the President may outline a foreign policy so hostile to another nation as to precipitate diplomatic difficulties, if not more serious results. This occurred in the case of the Venezuelan controversy, when President Cleveland recommended to Congress demands which Great Britain could hardly regard as anything but unfriendly." C. BEARD, AMERICAN GOVERNMENT AND POLITICS 196-97 (3d ed. 1920) (footnote omitted).

57.   W. TAFT, OUR CHIEF MAGISTRATE AND HIS POWERS 139-40 (1916).

58.   5 RICHARDSON 662.

59.   E. CORWIN, *supra* note 1, at 8, 251.

60.   T. ROOSEVELT, *supra* note 15, at 357.

61.   50 U.S.C. § 1544 (a) (Supp. 1975).

62.   W. LIPPMANN, ESSAYS IN THE PUBLIC PHILOSOPHY 30 (1955). Lippmann went on to say: "The two powers are necessary if there is to be order and freedom. But each must be true to its own nature, each limiting and complementing the other. The government must be able to govern and the citizens must be represented in order that they shall not be oppressed. The health of the system depends upon the relationship of the two powers. If either absorbs or destroys the functions of the other power, the constitution is deranged." *Id.*

63.   E. CORWIN, *supra* note 1, at 307.

64.   4 RICHARDSON 665.

65.   A. Schlesinger, Jr., *The Limits and Excesses of Presidential Power*, SATURDAY REVIEW, May 3, 1969, at 17.

66.   Some have suggested that the complexities of American foreign relations in the late 1700s equaled today's difficulties. *E.g.*, Gerhard Casper: "One of the most frequently reiterated cliches about foreign affairs . . . is that our foreign relations are infinitely more complex now than they were at the time of the nation's founding. I wonder. At the time of the Constitutional Convention, Europe presented America with incredibly intricate foreign policy problems. The Europe of that period was a tangled skein of shifting alliances, dynastic ambitions, incipient revolution, and trade rivalries. In dealing with these problems under the Articles of Confederation, the Framers undoubtedly came to appreciate the complexity of foreign affairs in a troubled world." *Response*, 61 VA. L. REV. 777-78 (1975) (footnote omitted). Without denigrating the subtleties and threats of the late seventeenth century, they do seem to have been less imposing qualitatively and quantitatively than current difficulties. For further comment on America's changed circumstances, see pages 12-13, 177, 184-85, 265.

67.   W. WILSON, CONGRESSIONAL GOVERNMENT xi-xii (13th ed. 1901). *But cf.* the discussion in Reveley, *supra* note 5, at 1248-49 n.17, concerning Wilson's slow recognition of the importance of foreign affairs for the United States even after 1900.

68.   W. BAGEHOT, THE ENGLISH CONSTITUTION 30 (World's Classics ed. 1949): "The best reason why Monarchy is a strong government is, that it is an intelligible government. The mass of mankind understand it, and they hardly anywhere in the world understand any other. It is often said that men are ruled by their imaginations; but it would be truer to say they are governed by the weakness of their imaginations. The nature of a constitution, the action of

an assembly, the play of parties, the unseen formation of a guiding opinion, are complex facts, difficult to know, and easy to mistake. But the action of a single will, the fiat of a single mind, are easy ideas: anybody can make them out, and no one can ever forget them." Bagehot admitted that there exist an "inquiring few" for whom "intelligible government" is less important, because they can handle the "complex laws and notions" of constitutional rule. *Id.* Presumably, the "inquiring few" constitute a significant portion of the present American electorate.

69. A. Schlesinger, Jr., *supra* note 65, at 18.

70. Grosser, *The Evolution of European Parliaments*, 93 DAEDALUS 153, 159 (Winter 1964).

71. C. ROSSITER, THE AMERICAN PRESIDENCY 107 (2d ed. 1960).

72. *Id.* 41.

73. *Id.* 16-41.

74. Suggestions of congressional decline in foreign affairs find little favor in some quarters, *e.g.*, Eugene V. Rostow: "Congress today is neither a rubber stamp nor a weak member of the constitutional system of shared power. Congress is not bound to uphold all the commitments the President makes in the course of his diplomacy. We know that it does not always do so. The notion that Congress is a passive tool of the President is contrary to everything I have read on the subject, and everything I myself witnessed and experienced when I was in the government. I spent at least a third of my time, and Secretary Rusk estimated that he spent half his time, consulting with members and committees of both houses of Congress. Those consultations were friendly and courteous, but they were also intensive and searching. Our Congress is the strongest parliamentary body in the world. It is strong, in my view, precisely because the Executive and the legislative functions are separated, and because the Congress must therefore take independent and responsible positions on major problems of policy." *Response*, 61 VA. L. REV. 797, 799-800 (1975).

It is certainly true that an abiding concern of the Executive is the likely reaction of Congress to presidential proposals and actions. According to Arthur Schlesinger: "[A]s I saw the executive branch in action, [i]t was haunted by a fear and at times an exaggerated fear of congressional reaction. The notion that the executive goes his blind and arrogant way, saying damn the torpedoes, full speed ahead, is just not true. I would say a truer notion is that the executive branch cowers day and night over the fear and sometimes quite exaggerated and irrational fear of what the congressional response is going to be to the things it does." A. SCHLESINGER, JR. & A. DE GRAZIA, CONGRESS AND THE PRESIDENCY: THEIR ROLE IN MODERN TIMES 171 (1967).

Chapter VIII: Constitutional Guidelines for Splitting the War Powers between the President and Congress

1. Scott v. Sanford, 60 U.S. (19 How.) 393, 426 (1857). In similar vein, *e.g.*, The Propeller Genessee Chief v. Fitzhugh, 53 U.S. (12 How.) 443 (1851); South Carolina v. United States, 199 U.S. 437, 448-49 (1905); Home Bldg. & Loan Ass'n v. Blaisdell, 290 U.S. 398, 448-49 (1934); United States v. Butler,

297 U.S. 1, 62-63 (1936); *cf.* Youngstown Sheet & Tube Co. v. Sawyer, 343 U.S. 579, 588 (1952); Powell v. McCormack, 395 U.S. 486, 546 (1969). *See generally* Berger, *The Presidential Monopoly of Foreign Relations,* 71 MICH. L. REV. 1, 48-54 (1972). *Cf.* P. MISHKIN & C. MORRIS, ON LAW IN COURTS 78-81, 258-67 (1965), concerning the crisis of confidence caused by judicial over-ruling of well-established doctrines.

2.   In addition, the constitutional text provides the most accessible and enduring guide to the division of the war powers between the President and Congress. Available records of the Framers' and Ratifiers' intentions are dif-ficult to ferret out, and, once found, establish that the bulk of their debates have not survived. War-power practice, for its part, has turned and twisted since 1789 along innumerable paths often difficult to track. But the Constitu-tion itself is as accessible and fully preserved today as in 1787-88. Its war-power language remains unchanged and continues to influence interpreta-tion as always. This language also has a symbolic importance not possessed by intent or practice. Like other provisions of the Constitution unaltered since government began under them almost two centuries ago, it evidences national continuity. Indeed, a case can be made that the text has proved more successful as a symbol than as a concrete guide to the division of authority between the President and Congress.

3.   Legal order in this country depends ultimately on voluntary obedi-ence, not coercion. There are too many citizens and laws and too few police to permit coerced obedience. Voluntary acceptance of the law stems from many factors—habit, the desire to conform, belief that law serves morality or individual self-interest, concern for peaceful and predictable relations, awareness that stability of the system depends on willing, not forced, accept-ance of its rules, and, above all, confidence that other Americans are obeying laws applicable to them, no matter how distasteful or inconvenient they find them. Should it appear that some Americans, especially leaders of the gov-ernment, are disobeying explicit constitutional requirements that they find distasteful or inconvenient, the law-abiding proclivities of other citizens will suffer.

Senator Sam Ervin pinpointed in 1969 the link between law-abiding offi-cials and public confidence in the legitimacy of government and sanctity of law. We are not concerned at this juncture with the accuracy of the Senator's view that American involvement in Vietnam was unconstitutional but, rather, with the link he drew between popular belief that the government acted un-constitutionally and public disorder. In Senator Ervin's view:

"The consequences of this failure to observe the Constitution are all too evident. True, no Supreme Court decision has adjudged the war in Vietnam as unconstitutional on the grounds that Congress adopted no formal declara-tion of war and because the Senate gave no effective advice and consent. Instead, the declaration of unconstitutionality has come from the judgment of the people. We see the decree everywhere . . . . Young men whose fathers and brothers volunteered to serve their country now desert to Canada and Scand[i]navia rather than bear arms in the country's cause . . . . Now we have riots and violence in our university campuses . . . .

". . . I cannot shake the feeling that ultimately the reason so many are now so disrespectful and unresponsive to authority is because authority was dis-respectful and unresponsive to the Constitution in the making of our policy in

Vietnam." 115 Cong. Rec. 17,217 (June 25, 1969), *reprinted in Hearings on War Powers Legislation Before the Senate Comm. on Foreign Relations*, 92d Cong., 1st Sess., at 801-02 (1971). *See also* L. Velvel, Undeclared War and Civil Disobedience: The American System in Crisis ix-xi, xiii, 119-22, 177, 316 (1970); Levi, *Unrest and the Universities*, U. Chi. Magazine, Jan/Feb 1969, at 25.

4. A razor's edge separates construction of the Constitution in order to further personal or institutional ambition from construction responsive to the country's evolving needs and values. There is constant risk that interpretation will fall to the side of personal or institutional aggrandizement. That risk, however, has been historically offset by checks and balances within the political and judicial processes and by the restraint that each exerts on the other. Improper claims by the President or Congress can be rejected by the other branch, the courts, or the electorate; improper judicial decisions can be rejected by later courts or undermined by the political branches.

5. *Cf.* L. Fuller, The Morality of Law 84-85 (1964).

6. H. Wriston, Executive Agents in American Foreign Relations 89 (1929) (emphasis added). *See also* Chapter III, notes 3, 66, 67, Chapter IV, note 81, and accompanying text.

7. Indeed, Myres McDougal and Asher Lans have urged that "[i]n innumerable respects, the division of functions between the different branches of the government and the scope of federal authority, as clearly contemplated by the Framers, have been altered by usage and prescription . . . . This process . . . has by no means been restricted to the numerous phases of government which the draftsmen deliberately left ambiguous or unsettled; in many instances the very words and phrases of the written Constitution have been given operational meanings remote from the intentions of their original penmen." M. McDougal & Associates, Studies in World Public Order 542 (1960) (footnotes omitted).

8. Thayer, *Our New Possessions*, 12 Harv. L. Rev. 464, 468 (1899).

9. *Id.* The Constitutional Fathers expected, perhaps, that formal amendment of the Constitution—rather than its interpretation by Presidents, Congresses, and courts—would become the prime engine for resolving its ambiguities so as to accommodate changing national circumstances. But some of the Framers and Ratifiers were aware that formal amendment might not prove a panacea. "To encourage us to adopt [the Constitution]," said Patrick Henry to the Virginia ratifying convention, "they tell us that there is a plain, easy way of getting amendments." But, he continued, "[w]hen I come to contemplate this part, I suppose that I am mad, or that my countrymen are so. The way to amendment is, in my conception, shut." Henry then detailed obstacles on the various paths to formal revision, ending with judgment that "[a] bare majority in . . . four small states may hinder the adoption of amendments; so that we may fairly and justly conclude that one twentieth part of the American people may prevent the removal of the most grievous inconveniences and oppression, by refusing to accede to amendments. A trifling minority may reject the most salutary amendments." 3 Debates in the Several State Conventions on the Adoption of the Federal Constitution 48-50 (J. Elliot ed. 1859 & 1861).

James Iredell in North Carolina, however, thought formal revision viable: "The Constitution before us . . . can be altered with as much regularity, and as little confusion, as any act of Assembly; not, indeed, quite so easily, which would be extremely impolitic; but it is a most happy circumstance, that there is a remedy in the system itself for its own fallibility, so that alterations can without difficulty be made, agreeable to the general sense of the people." 4 *id.* 177. Iredell more than Henry reflected his colleagues' amendment views, *e.g.*, 2 *id.* 116-17 (Jarvis); 2 THE RECORDS OF THE FEDERAL CONVENTION 558 (M. Farrand ed. 1911) (Hamilton); FEDERALIST No. 43 (Madison). *See also* the accounts in M. McDOUGAL & ASSOCIATES, *supra* note 7, at 544-45 (1960); Berger, *supra* note 1, at 51-52.

10.   Patterns of actual control are not wholly without doctrinal underpinnings, however. In United States v. Midwest Oil Co., 236 U.S. 459, 472-73 (1915), *e.g.*, the Justices stated: "It may be argued that while these facts and rulings prove a usage they do not establish its validity. But government is a practical affair intended for practical men. Both officers, law-makers and citizens naturally adjust themselves to any long-continued action of the Executive Department—on the presumption that any unauthorized acts would not have been allowed to be so often repeated as to crystallize into a regular practice. That presumption is not reasoning in a circle but the basis of a wise and quieting rule that in determining the meaning of a statute or the existence of a power, weight shall be given to the usage itself—even when the validity of the practice is the subject of investigation."

11.   Fleming v. Page, 50 U.S. (9 How.) 603, 614 (1850).

12.   Morgenthau, *The American Tradition in Foreign Policy, in* FOREIGN POLICY IN WORLD POLITICS 261 (3d ed. Macridis 1967); W. LIPPMANN, ESSAYS IN THE PUBLIC PHILOSOPHY 20 (1955).

Chapter IX: Recommended Division of the War Powers

1.   This conclusion is reinforced by other potential costs of a fixed period for ratification, with automatic termination if Congress fails to vote yes. American adversaries could have their resistance on the field and at the negotiating table strengthened by hope that the period would end with American withdrawal. Conceivably, the President might push events more vigorously than necessary if he believed national defense at stake and Congress loath to meet its demands. It would not be a wholly satisfactory counter to these possibilities to have Congress quickly take a position or extend its period for decision. The objective is informed, focused action by the legislators as soon as, but not before, they are prepared to vote their independent judgment on American policy.

But of course there is also merit in the opposing view that automatic termination should occur unless Congress expressly votes for the use of force. If the President begins armed action and wishes to continue for more than two months, a strong case can be made that it should be incumbent upon him to persuade Congress to approve the action formally; that if he cannot do so his use of force is very likely unwise, since Congress can usually be expected to avoid endangering vital American interests through inaction or untimely action; that automatic termination is necessary both to prevent Presidents from co-opting Congresses, as has happened so often in the past, and to ensure backing from the President *and* Congress for any sustained use of American force, lest it be undermined by lack of public support. In short, while automatic termination does seem the less wise approach, there is still much to be said for it.

2. Such a congressional prerogative is part of the division of the war powers recommended here. *See* pages 197-98 below.

3. Obviously, though, if the President is acting under the prerogative that is his when Congress is silent, the blessing of the Senate is better than nothing.

Chapter X: Routes to the Recommended Allocation

1. Any party who wishes to challenge the constitutionality of war-power action by either the President or Congress must first have standing: He must allege harm to himself from the challenged action. Courts want plaintiffs with sufficient interest in their cases to present the facts and law fully and sharply. While concerned citizens and taxpayers still have difficulty establishing their standing in war-power controversies, few courts now turn down draftees or others with an unavoidable interest in the proceeding. A proper plaintiff must then persuade the judge that his controversy is neither unripe nor moot: neither premature nor already resolved. And he must find a proper defendant. Occasionally cases against federal officials are thrown out on the ground of sovereign immunity, that is, refusal by the government to consent to suit against it. Rarely is the President himself a proper defendant. These hurdles, however, pose few problems to most war-power plaintiffs. The real obstacle has been the tendency of lower federal courts to find war-power questions political and the Supreme Court's refusal to hear such cases, relying on its discretionary jurisdiction.

2. Commentators have split over the justiciability of challenges to the constitutionality of American involvement in Indochina. *See, e.g.,* L. Henkin, Foreign Affairs and the Constitution 208-16 (1972); L. Velvel, Undeclared War and Civil Disobedience: The American System in Crisis 113-80 (1970); Moore, *The Justiciability of Challenges to the Use of Military Forces Abroad,* 10 Va. J. Int'l L. 85 (1969); Ratner, *The Coordinated Warmaking Power—Legislative, Executive, and Judicial Roles,* 44 S. Cal. L. Rev. 461, 480-87 (1971); Rostow, *Great Cases Make Bad Law: The War Powers Act,* 50 Texas L. Rev. 833, 892-95 (1972); Schwartz & McCormack, *The Justiciability of Legal Objections to the American Military Effort in Vietnam,* 46 Texas L. Rev. 1033 (1968); Wallace, *The War-Making Powers: A Constitutional Flaw?* 57 Cornell L. Rev. 719, 760-67 (1972); Wormuth, *The Nixon Theory of the War Power: A Critique,* 60 Calif. L. Rev. 623, 678-88 (1972); Note, *The Supreme Court as Arbitrator in the Conflict Between Presidential and Congressional War-Making Powers,* 50 B.U.L. Rev. 78 (1970); *cf.* the discussion of Powell v. McCormack, 395 U.S. 486 (1969), in Note, *The Supreme Court, 1968 Term,* 83 Harv. L. Rev. 62 (1969).

3. 369 U.S. 186, 217 (1962).

4. Scott v. Sanford, 60 U.S. (19 How.) 393 (1857).

5. Youngstown Sheet & Tube Co. v. Sawyer, 343 U.S. 579 (1952).

6. *See, e.g.,* the cases cited in Holtzman v. Schlesinger, 484 F.2d 1307, 1312-13 n.3 (2d Cir. 1973), *cert. denied,* 416 U.S. 936 (1974); Mitchell v. Laird, 488 F.2d 611 (D.C. Cir. 1973).

7. Holtzman v. Schlesinger, *supra* note 6, 484 F.2d at 1310-11 (footnote omitted).

8.   *Id.* 1308.
9.   *See* the following opinions in chambers: Holtzman v. Schlesinger, 414 U.S. 1304 (Marshall, J.) (application to vacate stay), 1316 (Douglas, J.) (reapplication to vacate stay), 1321 (Marshall, J.) (application for stay), 1322 (Douglas, J., dissenting) (Aug. 1-4, 1973).
10.   Holtzman v. Schlesinger, 416 U.S. 936 (1974).
11.   *See* Justice Douglas's dissents in Sarnoff v. Shultz, 409 U.S. 929 (1972); DeCosta v. Laird, 405 U.S. 979 (1972); Massachusetts v. Laird, 400 U.S. 886 (1970); McArthur v. Clifford, 393 U.S. 1002 (1968); Hart v. United States, 391 U.S. 956 (1968); Holmes v. United States, 391 U.S. 936 (1968); Mora v. McNamara, 389 U.S. 935 (1967); Mitchell v. United States, 386 U.S. 972 (1967).
12.   Mora v. McNamara, 389 U.S. 934-35 (1967) (Stewart, J., dissenting).
13.   Mitchell v. Laird, 488 F.2d 611, 613 (D.C. Cir. 1973).
14.   *Id.* 615.
15.   Mitchell v. Laird, 488 F.2d 616 (D.C. Cir. 1973) (separate statement by MacKinnon, J., with whom Tamm, Robb, and Wilkey, J. J., join, as to why they would grant rehearing *en banc sua sponte*).
16.   Holtzman v. Schlesinger, 414 U.S. 1304, 1312-13 (1973) (Marshall, J., in chambers).
17.   United States v. Nixon, 418 U.S. 683, 703-05 (1974); *accord, e.g.,* Nixon v. Administrator of Gen'l Serv., 433 U.S. 425, 442-43 (1977).
18.   Attempts to settle most of the controversies sketched in Chapter I have infrequently involved judicial decision. Interpretation of the Constitution has never been limited to the courts. The most compelling constitutional questions yet confronted by this country concerned states' rights, and they were settled at Appomattox in 1865. Constitutional interpretation regarding the war powers has also come mainly through the words and acts of Presidents and Congresses. The judicial role has been slight, and perhaps as influential for its potential impact (should either the President or Congress go too far) as for its actual impact.

The political branches have dealt with war-power issues in much the same manner that nation-states shape international law. Formal legislation in either sphere is rare. There has been no rewriting of the Constitution's text to clarify uncertainties about the war powers. Similarly, legislation by international organizations remains rare. Largely lacking in both spheres are courts that can, or will, resolve disputes. And there is little prospect of police action to curb the President or Congress, on the one hand, and nation-states, on the other, should they go beyond majority beliefs about what is legally permissible.

Thus, war-power and international rules are construed most often by political participants. A participant by word or deed asserts a legal position to which its fellows respond. For example, the President claims that it is his constitutional prerogative to control the commitment of American troops to combat so long as war is not declared; or Congress says that it may constitutionally pass legislation directing the President to end any use of force begun unilaterally by him within 60 days after its initiation unless he can obtain legislative approval of it. Similarly, a nation-state asserts the right to extend its territorial waters 200 miles out to sea. If these claims are explicitly accepted or acquiesced in by other participants, the law usually conforms accordingly, though some believe that constitutional law, as opposed to international law, may never be shaped in this fashion. If the claims are definitively rejected, the law remains as it was. During the interim between claim and concession or rejection, conflict between competing sets of legal requirements—or between beliefs about what the law requires, at one pole, and what is actually happening, at the other—can become so severe that realistically no law exists on the matter. The process is not surgically precise.

Moreover, any law, no matter how it is produced, risks disregard when it is vague and when it governs crisis situations. The more ambiguous a requirement, the more easily deviant conduct can be rationalized. And rationalization, even outright violation, becomes attractive when people believe that a requirement interferes with the emergency protection of their vital interests. Rules fixed by claim and concession tend to be vague and to govern vital interests. Resolution of legal issues by this process, accordingly, lacks not only surgical precision but also the stability possessed by law governing more humdrum matters.

Claim and concession can result in significant consensus nonetheless. The consensus is honored to achieve the common benefits of public order and predictable relationships, also to avoid retaliation from other participants should community beliefs about the rules be disregarded. The President or Congress is deterred from attempting to seize all war powers by the fear of severe retribution from other centers of influence in the country. More fundamentally, obedience springs from voluntary commitment to the rule of law: The President, Senators, and Representatives swear to uphold the Constitution when they take office, and most honor their oath for reasons in addition to fear that violation will lead to punishment.

19.   The most recent major flowering of this art came in mid-1975 when a 12-member Commission on the Organization of the Government for the Conduct of Foreign Policy issued its 278-page report, buttressed by seven volumes of appendixes. The Commission was established in 1972 as a joint congressional-executive body, by § 603(a) of the Foreign Relations Authorization Act of 1972. In full swing by April 1973, the group, its staff, and consultants worked long and expensively to produce the June 1975 recommendations. This effort was preceded by "more than 80 major studies of one aspect or another of foreign affairs organization in the three decades since World War II. Among the most prominent government studies have been the first Hoover Commission of 1949, the Wriston Committee of 1954, the Heineman Task Force of 1967, and the State Department's 'Diplomacy for the Seventies' program. Notable private studies include those contracted to the Brookings Institution in 1951 and 1959, the Herter Committee of 1962, and the American Foreign Service Association's 'Toward a Modern Diplomacy' of 1968." Spong, *Organizing the Government to Conduct Foreign Policy: The Constitutional Questions*, 61 Va. L. Rev. 747 n.2 (1975).

20.   Proposals of this sort have come in a variety of forms from a variety of people for a number of years. *See, e.g.,* the discussion in Henkin, "*A More Effective System" for Foreign Relations: The Constitutional Framework*, 61 Va. L. Rev. 751, 772-74 (1975); Spong, *The War Powers Resolution Revisited: Historic Accomplishment or Surrender?* 16 Wm. & Mary L. Rev. 823 & n.4 (1975); *cf.* American Soc'y of Int'l Law, The Constitution and the Conduct of Foreign Policy 2 (Wilcox & Frank eds. 1976). *See also* note 22 below and accompanying text.

21.   N.Y. Times, May 30, 1975, at 1, col. 1.

22.   In 1975 the Federation of American Scientists (FAS) began a campaign for "no first use" of nuclear weapons by this country without prior congressional approval. To this end, FAS urged passage of a joint resolution providing that

"[i]n any given conflict or crisis, whatsoever, and notwithstanding any other authority, so long as no nuclear weapons (or other weapons of mass destruction) have been used by others, the President shall not use nuclear weapons without consulting with, and securing the assent of a majority of, a committee composed of the:

> President Pro Tempore of the Senate and Speaker of the House of
>   Representatives
> Majority and Minority Leader of the House of Representatives
> Majority and Minority Leader of the Senate
> Chairman and Ranking Minority Member of:
>   Senate Committee on Armed Services
>   House Committee on Armed Services
>   Senate Committee on Foreign Relations
>   House Committee on International Relations
>   Joint Committee on Atomic Energy [now extinct]."

The constitutionality of any such resolution hinges on three issues: (1) whether the first use of nuclear weapons constitutes the *initiation* of a new military venture or whether it amounts simply to the *conduct* (strategy or tactics) of a larger undertaking; (2) even if the first use of nuclear weapons is termed "conduct," whether Congress nonetheless has authority to condition the use of nonconventional weapons by the President in waging any given conflict; and (3) *if* the President may constitutionally be denied the first use of nuclear weapons without prior congressional approval, whether Congress itself may delegate to a few of its members the authority to decide whether to give the Executive such approval when a need for speed or secrecy prevents his resort to Congress as a whole.

As noted below, a strong factual case can be made that nuclear first use is more akin to the initiation of a new armed action than to the conduct of a larger venture. The more this is the case, the more readily a constitutional basis can be found for requiring the President to have congressional approval before going nuclear. Even if such first use is deemed strategy and tactics, Congress has constitutional authority to impose certain constraints on the conduct of a military venture, *e.g.*, the geographical areas in which it may be waged, the length of time for American involvement, the maximum number of men and amount of money to be committed—and whether nonconventional weapons are to be used. How within these constraints the conflict is to be conducted, then, becomes a matter for executive discretion. Finally, it is probable that the legislators may constitutionally delegate crisis authority to a few of their number. Post-1789 practice provides firm indications that such would be acceptable—for instance, the frequent congressional delegations of crisis authority to another branch of government, the Executive. More fundamentally, practice since 1789 has read the Constitution to permit the realization of its enduring objectives through institutional arrangements responsive to the realities of the times. An enduring constitutional goal is congressional participation in decisions by this country to initiate the use of force. Given the realities of nuclear war, such involvement is not likely *unless* a congressional crisis committee exists to collaborate with the President quickly and/or quietly.

Proposals like the FAS joint resolution are attractive on five scores. (1) Passage of such a resolution (even if over executive veto) would explicitly affirm that nuclear weapons are not just another species of arms. Though in some cases their first use might limit conflict, the risks of first use remain staggering, whether viewed as the risk that tactical or selective strikes might evolve into general nuclear exchange or that limited strikes in one conflict might legitimize more deadly nuclear use in later conflicts. The seemingly unavoidable spread of nuclear technology and materials through the world heightens the need for affirmation that nuclear arms are different. (2) It is important that there be national consensus behind any first use of nuclear weapons by this country (whether the consensus develops before or after the fact). If a congressional crisis committee and the President both approved first use, that fact would assist consensus. (3) The workings of the committee would make more likely the forceful, independent criticism of any factual assumptions, technical opinions, and political judgments that may be leading an Executive to nuclear attack. (4) The committee could involve Congress in nuclear decisions while still safeguarding American capacity to move toward a first use rapidly or secretly if necessary. By dint of their small number, it is quite possible that these Congressmen could be quickly and secretly assembled, if such were required. Once at the White House they could easily be kept abreast of emerging developments—the basic facts of the situation at hand, realistic alternatives for dealing with it, as well as expert technical and political evaluations of the costs and benefits of each alternative. By dint of their own congressional responsibilities, these Senators and Representatives should already be aware of the country's overall foreign policy objectives and priorities. Such a group of Congressmen—more than the 535 Senators and Representatives en masse— should also prove willing to join with the President in risky action for war or peace, including the first use of nuclear weapons, should that seem essential to the long-term national good. (5) Use of a crisis committee should spread beyond the nuclear sphere. The notion of congressional delegation of emergency decision-making authority to a few of its ranking, internationally informed members has broad utility. Such a committee could provide a mechanism for significant legislative involvement in *all* decisions whether to initiate an American use of force when the President feels that these decisions must be made too quickly or quietly to involve Congress as a whole.

Chapter XI: The War Powers Resolution of 1973

1. Dep't of Defense Appropriations Act, Pub. L. No. 93-437, § 839 (1974). For other such limits *see* Glennon, *Strengthening the War Powers Resolution: The Case for Purse-Strings Restrictions*, 60 MINN. L. REV. 1, 13 n.30 (1975); Spong, *The War Powers Resolution Revisited: Historic Accomplishment or Surrender?* 16 WM. & MARY L. REV. 823, 851 n.164 (1975).

2. The necessary-and-proper clause received little attention at the Constitutional Convention. *See, e.g.*, 2 THE RECORDS OF THE FEDERAL CONVENTION 344-45 (M. Farrand ed. 1911). Recall, however, that a prime federalist objection to Confederation government was the dichotomy between its formal

powers, reasonably ample, and its impoverished authority over means necessary to implement them. Antifederalists during the ratification struggle strongly attacked the necessary-and-proper language. According to Hamilton, it and the supremacy clause were "held up to the people in all the exaggerated colours of misrepresentation as the pernicious engines by which their local governments were to be destroyed and their liberties exterminated." FEDERALIST PAPERS No. 33.

Madison in *Federalist No. 44* examined the problem in some detail. He argued that even without the necessary and proper language, Congress would control means: "Had the constitution been silent on this head, there can be no doubt that all the particular powers, requisite as means of executing the general powers, would have resulted to the government, by unavoidable implication. No axiom is more clearly established in law, or in reason, than that wherever the end is required, the means are authorized; wherever a general power to do a thing is given, every particular power necessary for doing it is included."

Madison argued, moreover, that it would have been impractical for the Constitution itself to attempt to deal more explicitly with means: "Had the convention attempted a positive enumeration of the powers necessary and proper for carrying their other powers into effect; the attempt would have involved a compleate digest of laws on every subject to which the constitution relates; accommodated too not only to the existing state of things, but to all the possible changes which futurity may produce: For in every new application of a general power: the *particular powers*, which are the means of attaining the *object* of the general power, must always necessarily vary with that object; and be often properly varied whilst the object remains the same."

Finally, Madison spoke to the possibility that Congress might attempt to usurp authority through necessary-and-proper legislation: "If it be asked, what is to be the consequence, in case the congress shall misconstrue this part of the constitution, and exercise powers not warranted by its true meaning? I answer the same as if they should misconstrue or enlarge any other power vested in them, as if the general power had been reduced to particulars, and any one of these were to be violated . . . . In the first instance, the success of the usurpation will depend on the executive and judiciary departments, which are to expound and give effect to the legislative acts; and in the last resort, a remedy must be obtained from the people, who can by the election of more faithful representatives, annul the acts of the usurpers."

Since 1789 congressional authority under the necessary-and-proper clause has been generously read in most instances. As Chief Justice Marshall said in McCulloch v. Maryland, 17 U.S. (4 Wheat.) 316, 421 (1819): "Let the end be legitimate, let it be within the scope of the constitution, and all means which are appropriate, which are plainly adapted to that end, which are not prohibited, but consist with the letter and spirit of the constitution, are constitutional." *See also, e.g.,* United States v. Oregon, 366 U.S. 643 (1961); Kennedy v. Mendoza-Martinez, 372 U.S. 144, 160 (1963). Note the suggestion that the necessary-and-proper clause is more sweeping in its grant of authority to Congress than are the enforcement provisions of the fourteenth and fifteenth amendments, in Cox, *Foreword: Constitutional Adjudication and the Promotion of Human Rights,* 80 HARV. L. REV. 91, 99-108 (1966). Congressional power to prescribe means has been judicially restrained, as a rule, only when it impaired civil liberties, *e.g.*, Kinsella v. United States *ex rel.* Singleton, 361 U.S. 234, 247 (1960). *See generally* L. Henkin, Foreign Affairs and the Constitution 78, 331-32 n.54 (1972).

Many have indicated that war-power legislation would be constitutional. *See, e.g., Hearings on War Powers Legislation Before the Senate Comm. on Foreign Relations*, 92d Cong., 1st Sess. (1971), at 7, 135 (Javits); 551, 554 (Bickel); 653-54 (William D. Rogers); 708 (Stennis); 774, 779 (Goldberg). *But cf.* William P. Rogers: "The question about whether a statute can change the President's constitutional powers or affect Congress['] constitutional powers is a very doubtful proposition." *Id.* 517. But, as will be noted in the text, there is a distinction between congressional authority to define the nature of constitutional powers, on the one hand, and the means for their realization, on the other. Rogers's comments seem to assume that war-power legislation does only the former.

3. 50 U.S.C. § 1541(b) (Supp. 1975). The Resolution as a whole covers §§ 1541-48 of the Code and is set out in Appendix C.

4. 119 Cong. Rec. 36,194 (1973).

5. 9 Weekly Compilation of Presidential Documents 1285-86 (1973). The text of the veto message appears in Appendix C.

6. Former Senator William B. Spong, Jr., of Virginia actively participated in these steps until January 1973. He has summarized them in two articles: *Can Balance Be Restored in the Constitutional War Powers of the President and Congress?* 6 U. Rich. L. Rev. 1 (1971); *The War Powers Resolution Revisited: Historic Accomplishment or Surrender? supra* note 1, at 824-37. Notable collections of divergent views on the wisdom of war-power legislation were compiled early in the process, during the 1971 Senate Foreign Relations Committee hearings cited in note 2 above and during earlier proceedings in the House. *See Hearings on Congress, the President, and the War Powers Before the Subcomm. on Nat'l Security Policy and Scientific Developments of the House Comm. on Foreign Affairs*, 91st Cong., 2d Sess. (1970).

7. S. Res. 85, 91st Cong., 1st Sess., 115 Cong. Rec. S7153 (daily ed. June 25, 1969). For further discussion of Congress and national commitments, *see* 48 Cong. Digest 193-224 (1969).

8. S.440, 93d Cong., 1st Sess. § 3 (1973). Jacob Javits was the guiding spirit behind the Senate approach. *See* note 33 below. *See generally* J. Javits, Who Makes War: The President versus Congress (1973).

9. The House of Representatives almost adopted a requirement designed to preclude congressional inaction. It would have provided that, within 120 days after the beginning of a military initiative by the Executive, Congress "shall either approve, ratify, confirm, and authorize the continuation of the action taken by the President . . . or . . . disapprove such action in which case the President shall terminate [it] . . . ." 119 Cong. Rec. 24,685 (1973) (Whalen amendment). But the most dyspeptic attack on the notion of ending an executive initiative by congressional *inaction* came in the Senate. Sam Ervin picked "invasion" to hammer home his point: "This measure is an absurdity. It says that when the United States is invaded, Armed Forces of the United States must get out of the fight against an invader at the end of 30 days if the Congress does not take affirmative action within that time to authorize the President to continue to employ the Armed Forces to resist the invasion. The bill is not only unconstitutional, but is also impractical of operation. In short,

it is an absurdity. Under it, the President must convert Old Glory into a white flag within 30 days if Congress does not expressly authorize him to perform the duty the Constitution imposes on him to protect the Nation against invasion." 119 CONG. REC. 25,093 (1973).

10. *See* Spong, *supra* note 1, at 828 n.41, 874.

11. 119 CONG. REC. 33,559 (1973).

12. 119 CONG. REC. 36,189 (1973); *see* Spong, *supra* note 1, at 823.

13. 119 CONG. REC. 33,557 (1973). Senator Eagleton has described his concerns at length in a book, *War and Presidential Power: A Chronicle of Congressional Surrender* (1974).

14. S. REP. No. 220, 93d Cong., 1st Sess. 34 (1973) (supplemental views of J. W. Fulbright). *See* Glennon, *supra* note 1, at 3-5 n.15.

15. *Hearings on War Powers: A Test of Compliance Before the Subcomm. on Int'l Security and Scientific Affairs of the House Comm. on Int'l Relations*, 94th Cong., 1st Sess. 93 (1975).

16. Section 8(c) further narrows the meager § 2(c) discretion given the President by its broad definition of "introduction of United States Armed Forces" to include "the assignment of members of such armed forces to command, coordinate, participate in the movement of, or accompany the regular or irregular military forces of any foreign country or government when such military forces are engaged, or there exists an imminent threat that such forces will become engaged, in hostilities."

17. *See* pages 197-98. Admittedly, there is controversy over whether Congress may "legislate" by concurrent resolution when the legislative process runs in reverse. The touchstone for those who think not is Ginnane, *The Control of Federal Administration by Congressional Resolutions and Committees*, 66 HARV. L. REV. 569 (1953). Executives especially have questioned legislation by concurrent resolution. It does deprive them of an opportunity to veto congressional limits on their initiatives. As a Congressman asked and the Legal Adviser to the State Department answered in 1975:

"MR. SOLARZ. . . . [I]s it your position that if the troops were sent in in the first place under the President's inherent constitutional authority that the concurrent resolution ordering them to be withdrawn would itself be unconstitutional or do you believe that the President would be constitutionally obligated to act in accordance with the provisions of the War Powers Resolution and withdraw the troops?

"MR. LEIGH. . . . I think it would be unconstitutional on the simple logic that if the President had the power to put the men there in the first place that power could not be taken away by concurrent resolution because the power is constitutional in nature. There might, however, be all sorts of reasons as to why the political process would force him to wish to comply with that concurrent resolution.

"There is a further question as to whether a concurrent resolution in this situation would have the dignity of law under the Constitution. I think a very strong argument can be made that a concurrent resolution in this situation would be insufficient and that the Congress must resort to the usual process for a statute and submit it to the President. If he disapproves it, it must then be pas[sed] over his veto by a two-thirds vote in each House." *War Powers Hearings*, *supra* note 15, at 91.

Precedent exists, however, for legislation by concurrent resolution. For instance, there was provision for ending presidential action by this means in two prominent war-power measures: the 1941 Lend Lease Act and the 1964 Gulf of Tonkin Resolution. It is also a fact of life that, if Presidents wish to have their constitutional cake by committing troops without prior congressional approval, it is not likely that they will be allowed to eat it too by denying simple majorities in both houses the right to call a halt.

It can be argued that precedents such as those just cited are not applicable because they "created a concurrent resolution procedure to control the exercise of authority delegated [by Congress] to the President," while the War Powers Resolution "does not delegate anything to the President. . . . It is . . . a procedural scheme for arranging an interchange in what is . . . a difficult area between the two branches . . . ." Accordingly, "to say that Congress would later by concurrent resolution take back what it had previously delegated overlooks the fact that nothing was delegated." *War Powers Hearings, supra* note 15, at 96-97 (remarks of Mr. Leigh); *cf.* Rostow, *Response,* 61 VA. L. REV. 797, 800-01 (1975): "There are some instances of true delegation between Congress and the Presidency in the field of foreign affairs. The President's discretion to change tariffs is a good example; only a statute could vest such authority in the President. However, in most cases a more accurate description is that a statute combines the overlapping powers of the Presidency and of Congress. In such instances, there is no delegation, but a pooling of the respective powers of the Presidency and of Congress. Thus in the Tonkin Gulf Resolution, the Formosa Resolution, and the Middle East Resolution, for example, language was carefully chosen to indicate that Congress and the President were making separate and also joint decisions, each exercising its own authority. No one attempted to draw a line marking the exact boundaries between the presidential zone and the congressional zone."

It is more likely than not, however, that Congress did delegate some authority to the President in the War Powers Resolution. To wholly disclaim that possibility, it is necessary to assume that the Executive has a constitutional prerogative to commit troops whenever and wherever he pleases, subject only to later restraint by a two-thirds vote of the Senate and House, overriding his veto. If, as is more probable, Congress has a constitutional right to vote on at least some troop commitments *before* they are made, then the Resolution does delegate to the President congressional approval to act in these cases if he thinks it necessary, subject to the deadline and concurrent resolution restraints in §§ 5(b) and (c).

18. *See* pages 198-99. Some assume that the President has a constitutional prerogative to defend American soil, perhaps no matter what Congress thinks. *Cf.* Senator Ervin's remarks in note 9 above and Legal Adviser Leigh's testimony to a House Subcommittee in 1975: "I [am] not sure that the Congress by imposing a condition subsequent on an appropriation which has not yet been fully expended could limit the President's power to carry out certain constitutional duties such as to defend the United States from hostile attack against its mainland territory. There is obviously no judicial decision on this but I would think that there would be a serious doubt as to the constitutionality of such a limitation if it were applied to prevent the President from defending the mainland territory of the United States from attack." *War Powers Hearings, supra* note 15, at 89.

19. *See also* Senator Javits: "If this is a statute, every part means something, whether it is written in subsection 2(c) or in section 3, as in the Senate bill." 119 Cong. Rec. 33,557-58 (1973).

20. 2 U.S. Code Cong. & Ad. News 2364 (1973).

21. 119 Cong. Rec. 33,555 (1973).

22. According to Representative Zablocki, the conference included § 2(c) "[i]n order to satisfy the Senate conferees"—"but it was intended as a statement of purpose and policy, a sort of sense of Congress." *War Powers Hearings, supra* note 15, at 32.

23. 119 Cong. Rec. 36,194 (1973). For further appraisal of § 2(c)'s mysteries, *see* Spong, *supra* note 1, at 837-41.

24. *See* pages 297-306 and note 25 below; *cf.* the Executive's rejection of the notion that the Resolution "delegates" any authority to him, note 17 above.

25. 119 Cong. Rec. 36,181 (1973); *accord*, the Legal Adviser to the State Department in 1975: "[W]e would not agree . . . that the specification of circumstances in which this power [the President's authority as commander in chief] might be used would be limited by section 2(c)." *War Powers Hearings, supra* note 15, at 11. *See also* note 26 below and accompanying text.

26. *War Powers Hearings, supra* note 15, at 90-91.

27. *Id.* 40.

28. Representative Zablocki's 1975 complaints are typical: "Clearly, it was not the intent of Congress to be merely informed of decisions already made. In the fullest meaning of partnership and shared responsibility in foreign affairs, it was the desire of Congress to have a participatory role in the process of decisionmaking.

"   . . . .

"Measured against that clear directive of intent, it is apparent . . . that the executive branch proclivity is toward evasive and selective interpretation of the War Powers Resolution." *War Powers Hearings, supra* note 15, at vi.

29. This distinction does make sense on one score under the Resolution as presently written. Reports by the President pursuant to § 4(a)(1) permit Congress to end his initiatives by inaction or concurrent resolution. That is not justifiable if the President is acting with explicit congressional authorization (whether by declaration of war or some other form of approval). Accordingly, if the Resolution were amended to require presidential reports at the outset of any hostilities, it ought also to be amended to prevent the termination under §§ 5(b) or (c) of ventures previously approved by Congress.

30. *War Powers Hearings, supra* note 15, at 2.

31. 2 U.S. Code Cong. & Ad. News 2351 (1973).

32. *War Powers Hearings, supra* note 15, at 38-39. It does appear that the Resolution was not directed at "hostilities" involving foreign mobs, international criminals, or the like. *See, e.g.*, the June 15, 1973, Committee on Foreign Affairs report on the House bill that underlay the ultimate Resolution: "The term 'war powers' may be taken to mean the authority inherent in *national sovereignties* to declare, conduct, and conclude armed hostilities with other states." 2 U.S. Code Cong. & Ad. News 2348 (1973) (emphasis added). But so long as another nation is the adversary, Congress defined "hostilities" broadly, as indicated in the text.

33. *War Powers Hearings, supra* note 15, at 69. The Senator had previously elaborated:

"Now it is perfectly true, that [the Senate] bill which contained an authority test as well as a performance test was not the bill adopted in the sense that the House approach was adopted without the authority test. We did adopt the House approach, the methodology being that it is a performance test, it is not an authority test. That is, did he or didn't he have constitutional authority?

"The minute he puts troops into hostilities or imminent danger of hostilities, the act begins to operate. And he does not have to tell us he is doing it, because the 60-day clock starts to tick if a report is required, and even if he fails to do a report, it still begins to operate and it is up to us to press the button so he loses all authority if we do not agree with his actions. Now this is the key to this whole legislation. If the President takes emergency action, his action is only good until Congress acts dispositively because we have the declaration of war authority." *Id*. 63.

34. *Id*. 87.

35. According to the Resolution's legislative history, "[A] *commitment* [or introduction] of armed forces commences when the President makes the final decision to act and issues orders putting that decision into effect." 2 U.S. CODE CONG. & AD. NEWS 2351 (1973).

36. *War Powers Hearings, supra* note 15, at 77.

37. See the terse accounts submitted by President Ford, Appendix C. "They are brief to the point of being in minimal compliance with the content requirements set forth in the law." *War Powers Hearings, supra* note 15, at 69 (remarks of Sen. Javits); *cf*. Thomas Ehrlich: "No one can expect preparation of a carefully reasoned, fully-developed brief within two days after a decision to use military force. But precisely for that reason, the requirement should have a useful impact. The need for justification to support a decision should be a strong incentive for a broader analysis of the impact of that decision than might otherwise be made. By requiring those in the Executive Branch to articulate the basis for an action, and to defend that basis, the Resolution will encourage them to think through their decisions more fully." *Response*, 61 VA. L. REV. 785, 788 (1975).

38. The legislators cannot expect much tactical and strategic information from the President unless he is confident that it will not leak; *e.g.*, Legal Adviser Leigh's remarks to a House subcommittee about the *Mayaguez* hostilities:

"Now let me say a word about this final assault action which involved movements of troops from various parts of the Far East into a position to be effective. The President was extremely apprehensive that there be no breach of security in advance of the time that they actually were landed, so there were strong arguments for not revealing that information—even to a select group of members—very much in advance of the time it was to occur.

"   . . . .

When I was speaking about the President's judgment of confidentiality, I was speaking in terms of an assumption on my part. I do not know what the President actually thought on this subject. I do know that he went to great pains to request the Members of Congress who came for the briefing in the Cabinet room that they maintain absolute security about this because breach of security might prejudice the carrying out of military operations.

"   . . . .

"Section 3 of the War Powers Resolution has, in my view, been drafted so as not to hamper the President's exercise of his constitutional authority. Thus, Section 3 leaves it to the President to determine precisely how consultation is to be carried out. In so doing the President may, I am sure, take into account the effect various possible modes of consultation may have upon the risk of a breach in security. Whether he could on security grounds alone dispense entirely with 'consultation' when exercising an independent constitutional power, presents a question of constitutional and legislative interpretation to which there is no easy answer. In my personal view, the resolution contemplates at least some consultation in every case irrespective of security considerations unless the President determines that such consultation is inconsistent with his constitutional obligation. In the latter event the President's decision could not as a practical matter be challenged but he would have to be prepared to accept the political consequences of such action, which might be heavy." *War Powers Hearings, supra* note 15, at 81, 100. *See also* Chapter VII, note 38 and accompanying text.

   39.   2 U.S. Code Cong. & Ad. News 2350-51 (1973).
   40.   *War Powers Hearings, supra* note 15, at 85. *But see id.* 3.
   41.   *E.g., id.* 64, 73 (remarks of Sen. Javits).
   42.   *Id.* 57 (remarks of Rep. Findley).
   43.   *Id.* 62 (remarks of Sen. Javits); *accord,* his views at 67-70, 73.
   44.   *Id.* 67.
   45.   *Id.* 63 (remarks of Sen. Javits).
   46.   Congressional umbrage at the missing references to § 4(a) (1) was met by Legal Adviser Leigh with various palliatives:
"There was nothing ulterior about this in any sense. We were not trying to mislead anyone. I think the factual situation was different as between the first case, the Danang sealift, and the other two. In the Danang sealift we were confident that we were not going to be involved in a section 4(a) (1) situation of hostilities, and in fact the President's orders required that the force avoid any kind of hostilities. We felt certain that that was going to fall under 4(a) (2) so we specified it in that case.
   "Now the other distinction is that we didn't know at the time we were required to make the report, which has to be within 48 hours, when we would complete the task of picking up refugees, and as it turned out it went on longer than either of the other two.
   "Now with respect to both the Cambodian and the Saigon evacuations, by the time the President made his report the last Americans and the last armed forces had already been taken out so that as lawyers we did not see that the specification of which of the three subsections of 4(a) was involved, was crucial to the operation of the mechanism which is established in section 5 of the War Powers Resolution because there would be no occasion for the 60-day period to even begin running.
   " . . . .
   "It seems that the real thrust of the question is why the President in his April 30, 1975 report referred to section 4 in general, and not to any particular subparagraphs in that section. We presume that the President did so because the events giving rise to that report did not seem to be limited to just one of the three subparagraphs in section 4(a).
   "Thus, although the events as known at that time indicated that hostilities may have existed between U.S. and communist forces, U.S. forces 'equipped

for combat' were also introduced in the 'territory, airspace or waters' of South Vietnam—the situation apparently provided for in section 4(a)(2).

"Furthermore, since the operation had terminated by the time the report was prepared, the question of possible congressional action under section 5 of the Resolution was moot; thus, a specific reference to 4(a) (1) was not needed to call attention to possible action under section 5.

". . . .

"[T]he first three war powers reports contain the phrase 'taking note of . . . .' You inquire whether this suggests anything other than a full binding legal responsibility upon the President. This phrase connotes an acknowledgement that the report is being filed in accordance with section 4 of the War Powers Resolution. No constitutional challenge to the appropriateness of the report called for by section 4 was intended." *War Powers Hearings, supra* note 15, at 9, 39, 40.

47. The evacuations sparked a brouhaha over what was statutorily permitted and over the broader question of the President's constitutional right to order armed rescues. *Compare, e.g.,* the views of Glennon, *supra* note 1, *with* those of Emerson, *The War Powers Resolution Tested: The President's Independent Defense Power,* 51 NOTRE DAME LAWYER 187 (1975). *See also, e.g., War Powers Hearings, supra* note 15, at 26-32.

48. 121 CONG. REC. 10,006 (1975). In making this request, the President did not concede any constitutional necessity to do so. The Legal Adviser to the State Department suggested that Mr. Ford "wanted the political support of the Congress in what he saw was going to be necessary, and the fact that he asked for it should not, in my view, be interpreted as an indication of his belief that in the absence of congressional action he could not have done the things that he did. On the other hand, he obviously wished to have congressional support and there remains the question of the financing of this evacuation." *War Powers Hearings, supra* note 15, at 18; *cf.* Woodrow Wilson's requests for prior congressional approval of his Vera Cruz and merchantmen ventures, pages 158-59 above.

49. The Executive disliked restrictions in the bill as it ultimately emerged, *e.g.,* its severe limits on rescuing non-Americans. *See* the description of the measure in Glennon, *supra* note 1, at 17-19, and Spong, *supra* note 1, at 852-53. *See also* Legal Adviser Leigh's objections, *e.g., War Powers Hearings, supra* note 15, at 19-20, 34-35.

50. Eagleton, *Congress's "Inaction" on War,* N.Y. Times, May 6, 1975, at 39, col. 2. *See also* Glennon, *supra* note 1, at 19-20 n.66.

51. *War Powers Hearings, supra* note 15, at 131.

52. *E.g., id.* 82 (remarks of Rep. Zablocki); Spong, *supra* note 1, at 855 n.180.

53. *See* Emerson, *supra* note 47, at 193.

54. On May 15, 1975, the legal adviser and legislative assistant to the Chairman of the Joint Chiefs of Staff explained the bombing to a House committee:
"In conducting an operation of this nature, there is only one mission involved . . .: To achieve the return of the crew, the vessel. Thereafter you must execute the safe extraction of the forces that were put in in order to accomplish the two primary missions.

"The potential enemy had the capability of reinforcing from the places on the mainland that were struck. To strike those places . . . in the judgment of almost every military man involved in the situation—and I say almost everyone because I have not talked to everybody, everybody I have talked to shares this view—was essential to save the marines on that island.

"Now, you are forced . . . to make a judgment between using adequate force and failing to use sufficient force to protect the men on the ground. That judgment is a very close one . . . in almost every instance, whether it is a platoon operation under a sergeant, a division operation under a general, or an operation of this nature under the direct command of the Commander in Chief. That is a tactical decision that is easy sometimes to Monday-morning quarterback. The question has to be what would you do if you were responsible for the men on the ground at the time the decision was made . . . .

"We recognized that of all the manifestations of power, restraint is one that is greatly recognized. That fact was constantly a consideration in the minds of the military planners involved in this operation. Restraint was a goal, but protecting American lives . . . was the first goal.
" . . . .

"Mr. WILSON. I would like to comment that as far as the air strikes on the mainland were concerned, the military judgment was made apparently that it was necessary, but I think that the strikes on the mainland, and I would like to hear the Colonel's response, probably in addition to their military significance served to let the Khmer Rouge know we were serious about this.

"MR. ZABLOCKI. It would serve as a deterrent to any further intentions of any country, including Cambodia.

"COLONEL FINKELSTEIN. We certainly hope it will have that effect." *Hearings on the Seizure of the Mayaguez Before the House Comm. on Int'l Relations*, 94th Cong., 1st Sess. 33-34, 34-35 (1975).

It seems likely that the bombing was meant both to protect American troops and demonstrate that America "cannot allow U.S. vessels to be seized with impunity" (remarks of Secretary of Defense Schlesinger in a May 21 interview). *Id.* 130. *See also id.* 42-43, 49.

55. According to May 14 testimony of the Deputy Assistant Secretary of State for East Asian and Pacific Affairs: "The Thai Prime Minister has called in our Chargé in Bangkok . . . and has in effect given us an aide memoire asking that our marines leave Thailand immediately." *Mayaguez Hearings, supra* note 54, at 16. The President had sent approximately 1,200 marines from Okinawa into Thailand when the crisis broke. Two hundred of them had then moved from there to the Cambodian theater. *Id.* 16, 43, 58.

56. *War Powers Hearings, supra* note 15, at 78. *But cf.* note 38 above, and Mr. Leigh's recognition that "the congressional leadership under the circumstances of the emergency action had been given an opportunity to express dissent or contrary views before the [President's] orders were *executed* [not before they were given]." *Id.* 81 (emphasis added).

57. *Id.* 61.

58. *Id.* 51; N.Y. Times, May 15, 1975, at 18, col. 7.

59. Address by Gerald R. Ford, Univ. of Kentucky, John Sherman Cooper Lecture, April 11, 1977, *reprinted in Hearings on a Review of the Operation and Effectiveness of the War Powers Resolution Before the Senate Comm. on Foreign Relations*, 95th Cong., 1st Sess. 327 (1977).

60. *Id.* 328.
61. *Id.* 328-30.
62. *See id.* 338-48. Perhaps most important among numerous proposed changes was the amendment that would have given operative effect to § 2(c)'s presently inoperative view that *prior* congressional approval is required for American use of force except in very limited circumstances. The impact of this amendment would have been softened only slightly by its expansion of the existing § 2(c) occasions in which the President may act alone to include (1) protecting Americans endangered abroad and (2) forestalling direct, imminent threats of attack on this country.
63. *See id.* 187, 322.
64. *Id.* 190. *See also* 126 CONG. REC. S4114 (daily ed. April 23, 1980).
65. *Hearings on Congressional Oversight of War Powers Compliance: Zaire Airlift Before the Subcomm. on Int'l Security and Scientific Affairs of the House Comm. on Int'l Relations,* 95th Cong., 2d Sess. 15 (1978). *See also* Editorial, *The War Powers Skirmish,* N.Y. Times, May 2, 1980, at A26, col. 1.
66. *See Zaire Hearings, supra* note 65, at 2-4, 16, 32.
67. The full text of the Church-Javits letter is in Appendix C. *See also, e.g.,* Gwertzman, *Senators Bid Carter Consult over Iran Under '73 War Curb,* N.Y. Times, April 25, 1980, at A1, col. 6; 126 Cong. Rec. S4109-16 (daily ed. April 23, 1980); *id.* S4192-93 (daily ed. April 24, 1980).
68. The State Department's Assistant Secretary for Congressional Relations, however, did write soothingly to the Chairman of the Senate Foreign Relations Committee. The Assistant Secretary said in part:
"As you know, your letter was received after the commencement of the rescue mission in Iran on which the President reported to the Congress on April 26. For that reason, the letter has in a sense already been overtaken by events.
"The President did not find it possible to consult with the Congress before commencing this rescue mission, in view of its extraordinary nature which depended upon absolute secrecy. Nevertheless, let me assure you that this Administration remains fully committed to the effective implementation of the consultation provisions of the War Powers Resolution to which you refer, and to the maximum possible cooperation between the Executive and Legislative branches in decisions which might involve the United States in hostilities." Letter from J. Brian Atwood to Frank Church, May 6, 1980.
69. *Cf.* Editorial, *The War Powers Skirmish,* N.Y. Times, May 2, 1980, at A26, col. 2:
"Congress adopted the War Powers Resolution to remind Presidents of their accountability for the use of troops. It created a formal procedure for consultation and an as yet untested requirement that Congress consent to hostilities lasting longer than 90 days.
"But for all its bark, Congress has always been reluctant to bite. Successive Presidents have committed forces to emergency operations on eight occasions without real consultation with key committee chairmen. President Ford reported after the fact on the military airlift of Americans out of Southeast Asia and on the rescue of the crew of the Mayaguez. But he did not report on the evacuation of civilians from Cyprus and Lebanon, nor did Mr. Carter report on airlifts into Zaire during an insurgency in 1977.

"The war powers debate actually flared up before the rescue mission, in response to Mr. Carter's threats of a blockade against Iran. That is scarcely a minor matter; it could involve a direct challenge to a warship, including a Soviet ship. As Senators Church and Javits of the Foreign Relations Committee asked even before the rescue raid, the military options the President keeps threatening clearly should be discussed with leading members of Congress. That view will have a sympathetic advocate in Senator Muskie, Mr. Carter's nominee for Secretary of State.

"The legal scholar Edward Corwin once observed that the Constitution is 'an invitation to struggle for the privilege of directing American foreign policy.' In that struggle, Congress too often confines itself to tactical details, ignoring strategic design. If the will is there, Congress can now insist on a larger role and give real meaning to its War Powers Resolution."

70.   Eugene V. Rostow has been among the most compelling critics of war-power legislation, the 1973 Resolution included. Such measures treat an "imaginary disease," in his view, one that resulted when congressional result-orientation was misdiagnosed as "presidential usurpation":

"That popular thesis [that the rules of constitutional balance were somehow violated in Indochina] is a myth. There was no presidential usurpation of Congress' war power in either Vietnam or Korea. . . .

"In the Korean War, and to a much greater extent during the war in Vietnam, we experienced naked political irresponsibility. First, the President and Congress, acting together in a constitutional mode that goes back to the time of Washington, made a series of decisions involving us in the wars. Later, when the wars became unpopular, many of the congressmen who had voted and voted and voted for them suddenly began to say that they were all the President's fault. They claimed that the President had involved the country in war through stealth and concealment. They argued that the difficulties were the result not of human mistakes in carrying out policies duly authorized and pursued, but rather of some structural imbalance in the Constitution. These representatives told their constituents, 'The President has stolen our clothes while we were swimming; we have never really authorized this Presidential war.' Then, having created the myth of presidential usurpation, Congress passed the War Powers Resolution to cure the imaginary disease.

"These events have had a significant effect on the spirit of cooperation between the Executive and Congress. When the Executive Branch deals with congressmen and senators who continue to vote for a war and then say, 'There's no one here but us chickens' after the war becomes unpopular, a mood of suspicion develops which is rather hard to allay. I personally have dealt with congressmen and senators about Vietnam, often reminding them that the Administration had long been trying to achieve goals which they had recommended in political speeches—reconvening the Geneva Conference, for example. Typically, their response was, 'I know that, but you must remember that I have to be elected in my district. The President has to do what must be done. I must take care of my reelection.' In short, a great many men slithered off the deck when the going got rough. This is simply a fact, not a reproach, something that happens in life.

"It is the ultimate reason why the War Powers Resolution and other structural remedies we have been considering are so unrealistic and unreal. President Johnson was very conscious of President Truman's experience in

Korea and of the political fact that Korea became 'Truman's War.' President Truman did not seek the support of a formal congressional resolution. President Johnson had the advantage of the SEATO Treaty, . . . the Tonkin Gulf Resolution, and a number of other congressional actions expressly designed to approve the decisions of four Presidents under the Treaty. This experience is what President Johnson had in mind when he observed, 'I knew that if I wanted Congress with me at the crash landing, they had to be with me at the take-off. But I forgot about the availability of parachutes.'" *Response*, 61 VA. L. REV. 797, 801-03 (1975).

71. *But cf.* the executive views in note 17 above. It is quite conceivable that the Supreme Court would agree to decide such a case if asked, and it is probable that the President would obey a decision against him. *See* pages 206-17 above.

Chapter XII: Why Not a More Direct Approach?

1. Q. WRIGHT, THE CONTROL OF AMERICAN FOREIGN RELATIONS 370 (1922).

2. Wright, *The Power of the Executive to Use Military Forces Abroad*, 10 VA. J. INT'L L. 43 (1969).

3. Falk, *International Law and the United States Role in Viet Nam: A Response to Professor Moore*, 76 YALE L. J. 1095, 1150-51 (1967); *cf.* Falk, *Response*, 61 VA. L. REV. 791-94 (1975). The language omitted from the quotation in the text stated: "No need is more paramount at the present time than to develop a Constitutional tradition of restraint upon the Executive's virtually discretionary power to commit the nation to war of any scope and duration." Quincy Wright, in the works cited in notes 1 and 2 above, also found the President's authority over war virtually unlimited by the Constitution. For example, he concluded in *The Power of the Executive to Use Military Forces Abroad, supra* note 2, at 54, that "the Constitution and practice under it have given the President, as Commander-in-Chief and conductor of foreign policy, legal authority to send the armed forces abroad; to recognize foreign states, governments, belligerency, and aggression against the United States or a foreign state; to conduct foreign policy in a way to invite foreign hostilities; and even to make commitments which may require the future use of force. By the exercise of these powers he may nullify the theoretically exclusive power of Congress to declare war."

Having taken so grim a view of existing constitutional restraints on executive authority, both Falk and Wright are unusually drawn to international limits. But while the President has exercised great control over the use of force during the last generation, it does not follow that (a) he wielded the same authority before the Cold War, (b) his practice during it was thought wholly constitutional, or (c) it will live on. For reasons already stated, the Constitution does not make the President sole arbiter of American war and peace—and there is a reasonable prospect that, even without resort to international restraints, executive dominance of the last generation can be lessened. Thus, while a direct constitutional ban on American aggression may well be desirable, it is not as crucial as Falk and Wright suggest.

4. Ware v. Hylton, 3 U.S. (3 Dall.) 199, 281 (1796); The Paquete Habana, 175 U.S. 677, 700 (1900). *See also* Moore, *The Justiciability of Challenges to the Use of Military Forces Abroad*, 10 VA. J. INT'L L. 85, 96 (1969).

5. *See generally* Q. WRIGHT, THE CONTROL OF AMERICAN FOREIGN RE-
LATIONS, *supra* note 1, at 3-9, 66-68, 161-75. *But see, e.g.*, the so-called Byrd
Amendment, in effect from 1971-77 to nullify the UN embargo on Rhodesian
chrome so far as United States purchases were concerned. It is currently constitutional for Congress to pass laws violating international obligations of
this country. *E.g.*, Whitney v. Robertson, 124 U.S. 190 (1888).

6. *See, e.g.*, Chinese Exclusion Case, 130 U.S. 581 (1889); Reid v. Covert,
354 U.S. 1 (1957); Moore, *The Justiciability of Challenges to the Use of
Military Forces Abroad, supra* note 4, at 96-100; Q. WRIGHT, THE CONTROL OF
AMERICAN FOREIGN RELATIONS, *supra* note 1, at 3-9, 66-68, 161-75.

7. Chief Justice Taney in Fleming v. Page, 50 U.S. (9 How.) 603, 614
(1850).

8. Clarence A. Berdahl in his WAR POWERS OF THE EXECUTIVE IN THE
UNITED STATES 223, 223-24 n.3 (1921). Berdahl's "doctrine," however, may
have been intended only for virulent aggression: the conquest and physical
absorption of the enemy. He cited *Fleming* in the context of "a complete
subjugation of one of the belligerents by the other, involving the conquest
and annexation of its territory and extermination of its government."

9. Chinese Exclusion Case, 130 U.S. 581, 603 (1889).

BIBLIOGRAPHY

(referenced to the text and notes)

Articles

Berger, *The Presidential Monopoly of Foreign Relations*, 71 MICH. L. REV. 1 (1972): 309-10 n.4, 313 n.6, 334 n.28, 336 n.50, 350 n.1, 352 n.9

Berger, *War-Making by the President*, 121 U. PA. L. REV. 29 (1972): 313 n.6, 314 n.19, 315 nn. 27 & 29, 328 n.77

Bestor, *Separation of Powers in the Domain of Foreign Affairs: The Intent of the Constitution Historically Examined*, 5 SETON HALL L. REV. 527 (1974): 312 n.1

Casper, *Response*, 61 VA. L. REV. 777 (1975): 348 n.66

Corwin, *Who Has the Power to Make War?* N.Y. TIMES MAGAZINE 14 (July 31, 1949): 140

Cox, *Foreword: Constitutional Adjudication and the Promotion of Human Rights*, 80 HARV. L. REV. 91 (1966): 358 n.2

Donahoe & Smelser, *The Congressional Power to Raise Armies: The Constitutional and Ratifying Conventions, 1787-1788*, 33 REV. OF POLITICS 202 (1971): 315 n.20, 317 n.43

Emerson, *The War Powers Resolution Tested: The President's Independent Defense Power*, 51 NOTRE DAME LAWYER 187 (1975): 365 nn.47 & 53

Ehrlich, *Response*, 61 VA. L. REV. 785 (1975): 363 n.37

Falk, *International Law and the United States Role in Viet Nam: A Response to Professor Moore*, 76 YALE L.J. 1095 (1967): 369 n.3

Falk, *Response*, 61 VA. L. REV. 791 (1975): 265-66, 369 n.3

Fulbright, *American Foreign Policy in the Twentieth Century Under an Eighteenth-Century Constitution*, 47 CORNELL L.Q. 1 (1961): 320 n.52

Ginnane, *The Control of Federal Administration by Congressional Resolutions and Committees*, 66 HARV. L. REV. 569 (1953): 360 n.17

Glennon, *Strengthening the War Powers Resolution: The Case for Purse-Strings Restrictions*, 60 MINN. L. REV. 1 (1975): 357 n.1, 360 n.14, 365 nn.47 & 49-50

Grosser, *The Evolution of European Parliaments*, 93 DAEDALUS 153 (Winter 1964): 349 n.70

Guggenheimer, *The Development of the Executive Departments, 1775-1789, in* ESSAYS IN THE CONSTITUTIONAL HISTORY OF THE UNITED STATES IN THE FORMATIVE PERIOD 1775-1789 (J. Jameson ed. 1889): 315 nn.21 & 23, 316 n.34

Henkin, *"A More Effective System" for Foreign Relations: The Constitutional Framework*, 61 VA. L. REV. 751 (1975): 355 n.20

Levi, *Unrest and the Universities*, U. CHI. MAGAZINE (Jan/Feb. 1969): 351 n.3

Levitan, *The Foreign Relations Power: An Analysis of Mr. Justice Sutherland's Theory*, 55 YALE L.J. 467 (1946): 310 n.4

Lofgren, *War-Making Under the Constitution: The Original Understanding*, 81 YALE L.J. 672 (1972): 70, 312 n.1, 313 n.6, 314 nn.13 & 15-16, 317 n.40, 319 n.48, 320 n.53, 331 n.6

Moore, *The Justiciability of Challenges to the Use of Military Forces Abroad*, 10 VA. J. INT'L L. 85 (1969): 353 n.2, 369 n.4, 370 n.6

Morgenthau, *The American Tradition in Foreign Policy, in* FOREIGN POLICY IN WORLD POLITICS (3d ed. Macridis 1967): 159, 178

Note, *The Supreme Court as Arbitrator in the Conflict Between Presidential and Congressional War-Making Powers*, 50 B.U.L. REV. 78 (1970): 353 n.2

Note, *The Supreme Court, 1968 Term*, 83 HARV. L. REV. 62 (1969): 353 n.2

Note, *The War-Making Powers: The Intentions of the Framers in the Light of Parliamentary History*, 50 B.U.L. REV. 5 (1970): 313 n.6

Putney, *Executive Assumption of the War Making Power*, 7 NAT'L UNIV. L. REV. 1 (1927): 343 n.29

Ratner, *The Coordinated Warmaking Power—Legislative, Executive, and Judicial Roles*, 44 S. CAL. L. REV. 461 (1971): 353 n.2

Reveley, *Constitutional Allocation of the War Powers Between the President and Congress: 1787-1788*, 15 VA. J. INT'L LAW 73 (1974): 312 n.1

Reveley, *Presidential War-Making: Constitutional Prerogative or Usurpation?* 55 VA. L. REV. 1243 (1969): 342 n.5, 348 n.67

Rostow, *Great Cases Make Bad Law: The War Powers Act*, 50 TEXAS L. REV. 833 (1972): 340 n.13, 353 n.2

Rostow, *Response*, 61 VA. L. REV. 797 (1975): 349 n.74, 361 n.17, 368-69 n.70

Schlesinger, *The Limits and Excesses of Presidential Power*, SATURDAY REVIEW (May 3, 1969): 348 n.65 (165), 349 n.69 (167)

Schwartz & McCormack, *The Justiciability of Legal Objections to the American Military Effort in Vietnam*, 46 TEXAS L. REV. 1033 (1968): 353 n.2

Spong, *Can Balance Be Restored in the Constitutional War Powers of the President and Congress?* 6 U. RICH. L. REV. 1 (1971): 359 n.6

Spong, *Organizing the Government to Conduct Foreign Policy: The Constitutional Questions*, 61 VA. L. REV. 747 (1975): 355 n.19

Spong, *The War Powers Resolution Revisited: Historic Accomplishment or Surrender?* 16 WM. & MARY L. REV. 823 (1975): 355 n.20, 357 n.1, 359 n.6, 360 nn.10 & 12, 362 n.23, 365 nn.49 & 52

Thayer, *Our New Possessions*, 12 HARV. L. REV. 464 (1899): 173

Wallace, *The War-Making Powers: A Constitutional Flaw?* 57 CORNELL L. REV. 719 (1972): 353 n.12

Wormuth, *The Nixon Theory of the War Power: A Critique*, 60 CALIF. L. REV. 623 (1972): 310 n.4, 315 n.22, 332 n.17, 341 n.22, 353 n.2

Wright, *The Power of the Executive to Use Military Forces Abroad*, 10 VA. J. INT'L L. 43 (1969): 265, 369 n.3

Books

D. ACHESON, PRESENT AT THE CREATION (1969): 135, 342 n.2

AMERICAN SOC'Y OF INT'L LAW, THE CONSTITUTION AND THE CONDUCT OF FOREIGN POLICY (Wilcox & Frank eds. 1976): 355 n.20

W. BAGEHOT, THE ENGLISH CONSTITUTION (1949 & 1964 eds.): 328 n.77, 348 n.68

B. BAILYN, THE IDEOLOGICAL ORIGINS OF THE AMERICAN REVOLUTION (1967): 313 n.10

C. BEARD, AMERICAN GOVERNMENT AND POLITICS (1920): 347-48 n.56

C. BERDAHL, WAR POWERS OF THE EXECUTIVE IN THE UNITED STATES (1921): 267, 315 n.33, 338 n.1, 343 n.26, 370 n.8

R. BERGER, CONGRESS V. THE SUPREME COURT (1969): 315 n.31

W. Binkley, The Man in the White House, His Powers & Duties (1959): 313 n.8, 315 n.30

B. Blechman & S. Kaplan, Force Without War (1978): 343-45 n.30

E. Borchard, The Diplomatic Protection of Citizens Abroad (1927 ed.): 144-45

E. Burnett, The Continental Congress (1941): 315 n.21

E. Corwin, The Doctrine of Judicial Review (1914): 331 n.4

E. Corwin, The President: Office and Powers 1787-1957 (4th rev. ed. 1957): 31, 55, 160, 164, 314 n.14, 328 n.79, 341 n.1

E. Corwin, The President's Control of Foreign Relations (1917): 309 n.2, 341 nn. 25-26 (130), 343 n.16 (143), 346 n.41

T. Eagleton, War and Presidential Power: A Chronicle of Congressional Surrender (1974): 360 n.13

A. Eden, The Memoirs of Anthony Eden: Full Circle (1960): 285

R. Fairfield, The Federalist Papers (1966): 312 nn.1 & 3, 313 n.9, 328 n.69, 331 n.4

M. Farrand, The Framing of the Constitution (1913): 316 n.36, 325 n.54

D. Fleming, The Treaty Veto of the American Senate (1930): 326 n.65

L. Fuller, The Morality of Law (1964): 351 n.5

W. Graves, America's Siberian Adventure (1931): 284

L. Henkin, Foreign Affairs and the Constitution (1972): 310 n.4, 314 n.14, 317 n.42, 319 n.47, 320 n.50, 338 n.2, 359 n.2

R. Hofstadter, The American Political Tradition and the Men Who Made It (1948): 321 n.66

R. Hull & J. Novogrod, Law and Vietnam (1968): 347 n.51

J. Javits, Who Makes War: The President Versus Congress (1973): 312 n.1, 359 n.8

A. Link, Wilson: Confusions and Crises, 1915-1916 (1964): 347 n.54

W. Lippmann, Essays in the Public Philosophy (1955): 163, 178, 348 n.62

K. Llewellyn, The Bramble Bush (1960): 1

M. McDougal & Associates, Studies in World Public Order (1960): 310 n.4, 314 n.16, 316 nn.36 & 38 (58-59), 317 n.42, 320 n.50, 326 n.65, 351 n.7, 352 n.9

A. McLaughlin, A Constitutional History of the United States (1935): 51-52

W. Malloy, Treaties (1910): 347 n.44

F. Marks III, Independence on Trial: Foreign Affairs and the Making of the Constitution (1973): 312 n.1

E. May, The Ultimate Decision: The President as Commander in Chief (1960): 313 n.6, 315 n.30

P. Mishkin & C. Morris, On Law in Courts (1965): 350 n.1

W. Munro, The Makers of the Unwritten Constitution (1930): 321 n.66

A. Nevins, The American States During and After the Revolution, 1775-1789 (1924): 315 n.26

J. Parton, Life of Andrew Jackson (1860): 341 n.24

J. Pomeroy, Introduction to the Constitutional Law of the United States (1888): 159

T. Roosevelt, An Autobiography (1922): 143, 161

E. Root, The Military and Colonial Policy of the United States (1916): 347 n.48

C. Rossiter, Seedtime of the Republic (1953): 315 n.20

C. Rossiter, 1787: The Grand Convention (1966): 328 n.79, 329 n.80

C. Rossiter, The American Presidency (2d ed. 1960): 168, 328 n.79

R. Russell, The United States Congress and the Power to Use Military Force Abroad (unpublished thesis, Fletcher School 1967): 315 nn.22 & 30

A. Schlesinger, Jr., The Imperial Presidency (1973): 312 n.1

A. Schlesinger, Jr. & A. DeGrazia, Congress and the Presidency: Their Role in Modern Times (1967): 133-34, 349 n.74

A. Sofaer, War, Foreign Affairs and Constitutional Power: The Origins (1976): 312 n.1

W. Taft, Our Chief Magistrate and His Powers (1916): 160

F. Thorpe, The Federal and State Constitutions (1909): 315 n.26

U.S. Dep't of State, The Right to Protect Citizens in Foreign Countries by Landing Forces (rev. ed. 1913): 147

L. Velvel, Undeclared War and Civil Disobedience: The American System in Crisis (1970): 351 n.3, 353 n.2

C. WARREN, THE MAKING OF THE CONSTITUTION (1937): 55, 317 nn.38 & 41 (60), 321 n.62, 330 nn.1-2 (100)

W. WILSON, CONGRESSIONAL GOVERNMENT (13th ed. 1901): 165-66

G. WOOD, THE CREATION OF THE AMERICAN REPUBLIC 1776-1787 (1969): 320 n.53

Q. WRIGHT, THE CONTROL OF AMERICAN FOREIGN RELATIONS (1922): 265, 313 n.6, 314 n.14, 320 n.50, 347 n.44, 370 nn.5-6

H. WRISTON, EXECUTIVE AGENTS IN AMERICAN FOREIGN RELATIONS (1929): 172, 313 n.7, 315 nn.21, 26 & 34, 319 n.47, 351 n.6

Cases

Baker v. Carr, 369 U.S. 186 (1962): 207-8, 217

Chinese Exclusion Case, 130 U.S. 581 (1889): 309 n.4, 370 nn.6 & 9

DeCosta v. Laird, 405 U.S. 979 (1972): 354 n.11

Durand v. Hollins, 8 Fed. Cas. 111 (No. 4186) (C.C.S.D.N.Y. 1860): 149, 345 n.33, 346-47 n.42

Fleming v. Page, 50 U.S. (9 How.) 603 (1850): 352 n.11 (177), 370 nn.7-8 (267)

Hart v. United States, 391 U.S. 956 (1968): 354 n.11

Holmes v. United States, 391 U.S. 936 (1968): 354 n.11

Holtzman v. Schlesinger, 484 F.2d 1307 (2d Cir. 1973), *cert. denied*, 416 U.S. 936 (1974): 353 nn.6-7 (212-14), 354 nn.8 & 10

Holtzman v. Schlesinger, 414 U.S. 1304 (Marshall, J.), 1316 (Douglas, J.), 1321 (Marshall, J.), 1322 (Douglas, J.) (Aug. 1-4, 1973) (opinions in chambers): 354 nn.9 & 16 (216)

Home Bldg. & Loan Ass'n v. Blaisdell, 290 U.S. 398 (1934): 349 n.1

Kennedy v. Mendoza-Martinez, 372 U.S. 144 (1963): 358 n.2

Kinsella v. United States *ex rel.* Singleton, 361 U.S. 234 (1960): 359 n.2

Martin v. Mott, 25 U.S. (12 Wheat.) 19 (1827): 148

Massachusetts v. Laird, 400 U.S. 886 (1970): 354 n.11

McArthur v. Clifford, 393 U.S. 1002 (1968): 354 n.11

McCulloch v. Maryland, 17 U.S. (4 Wheat.) 316 (1819): 358 n.2

Miller v. The Ship *Resolution*, 2 U.S. (2 Dall.) 1 (Ct. App. in Cases of Capture 1781): 314 n.15

Missouri v. Holland, 252 U.S. 416 (1920): 341 n.23

Mitchell v. Laird, 488 F.2d 611 (D.C. Cir. 1973): 353 n.6, 354 nn.13-15 (215-16)

Mitchell v. United States, 386 U.S. 972 (1967): 354 n.11

Mora v. McNamara, 389 U.S. 935 (1967): 354 nn.11-12 (214-15)

Nixon v. Administrator of Gen'l Serv., 433 U.S. 425 (1977): 354 n.17

Paquete *Habana*, The, 175 U.S. 677 (1900): 369 n.4 (266)

Powell v. McCormack, 395 U.S. 486 (1969): 350 n.1, 353 n.2

Prize Cases, The, 67 U.S. (2 Black) 635 (1863): 149, 342 n.8 (140), 345 n.34

Propeller *Genessee Chief*, The, v. Fitzhugh, 53 U.S. (12 How.) 443 (1851): 349 n.1

Reid v. Covert, 354 U.S. 1 (1957): 370 n.6

Sarnoff v. Shultz, 409 U.S. 929 (1972): 354 n.11

Scott v. Sanford, 60 U.S. (19 How.) 393 (1857): 171, 209-10

South Carolina v. United States, 199 U.S. 437 (1905): 349 n.1

Towne v. Eisner, 245 U.S. 418 (1918): 31

United States v. Butler, 297 U.S. 1 (1936): 349-50 n.1

United States v. Curtiss-Wright Export Corp., 299 U.S. 304 (1936): 346 n.42

United States v. Midwest Oil Co., 236 U.S. 459 (1915): 352 n.10

United States v. Nixon, 418 U.S. 683 (1974): 217, 346 n.38

United States v. Oregon, 366 U.S. 643 (1961): 358 n.2

Ware v. Hylton, 3 U.S. (3 Dall.) 199 (1796): 369 n.4 (266)

Whitney v. Robertson, 124 U.S. 190 (1888): 370 n.5

Youngstown Sheet & Tube Co. v. Sawyer, 343 U.S. 579 (1952): 70, 210-11, 342 n.5, 350 n.1

Congressional Hearings

Hearings on Assignment of Ground Forces of the U.S. to Duty in the European Area Before Senate Comms. on Foreign Relations and Armed Services, 82d Cong., 1st Sess. (1951): 342 n.11

Hearings on Congress, the President, and the War Powers Before the Subcomm. on Nat'l Security Policy and Scientific Developments of the House Comm. on Foreign Affairs, 91st Cong., 2d Sess. (1970): 313 n.6, 341 n.20, 346 n.39, 359 n.6

Hearings on Congressional Oversight of War Powers Compliance: Zaire Airlift Before the Subcomm. on Int'l Security and Scientific Affairs of the House Comm. on Int'l Relations, 95th Cong., 2d Sess. (1978): 257, 259, 367 nn.65-66

Hearings on Department of Defense Appropriations for 1974 Before a Subcomm. of the House Comm. on Appropriations, 93d Cong., 1st Sess. (1973): 342 n.14

Hearings on a Review of the Operation and Effectiveness of the War Powers Resolution Before the Senate Comm. on Foreign Relations, 95th Cong., 1st Sess. (1977): 256-57, 366 n.59, 367 nn.60-64

Hearings on Department of State Appropriations Authorization, Fiscal Year 1974 Before Senate Comm. on Foreign Relations, 93d Cong., 1st Sess. (1973): 342 n.13

Hearings on the Nomination of Alexander M. Haig, Jr., to be Secretary of State Before the Senate Comm. on Foreign Relations, 97th Cong., 1st Sess., Parts 1 & 2 (1981): 262

Hearings on the Seizure of the Mayaguez *Before the House Comm. on Int'l Relations,* 94th Cong., 1st Sess. (1975): 366 nn.54-55

Hearings on War Powers: A Test of Compliance Before the Subcomm. on Int'l Security and Scientific Affairs of the House Comm. on Int'l Relations, 94th Cong., 1st Sess. (1975): 360 nn.15 & 17, 361 nn.17-18, 362 nn.22, 25-28, 30 & 32-33, 363 nn.34 & 36-37, 364 nn. 38 & 40-45, 365 nn.46-49 & 51-52, 366 nn.56-58

Hearings on War Powers Legislation Before the Senate Comm. on Foreign Relations, 92d Cong., 1st Sess. (1971): 284, 315 n.22, 319 n.48, 346 nn.36-37, 350-51 n.3, 359 nn.2 & 6

Constitutions and Legislation

LIBRARY OF CONGRESS LEGISLATIVE REFERENCE SERVICE, THE CONSTITUTION OF THE UNITED STATES OF AMERICA (1964 ed.): 29-50, 273-76, & generally

B. POORE, THE FEDERAL AND STATE CONSTITUTIONS, COLONIAL CHARTERS, AND OTHER ORGANIC LAWS OF THE UNITED STATES (1878): 315 nn.27 & 29 (57)

Resolutions and statutes, 118, 122-30, 225-62, 287-93, & generally

Newspapers, Records, and Writings

AMERICAN STATE PAPERS, FOREIGN RELATIONS (W. Lowrie & M. Clarke eds. 1832): 278

ANNALS OF CONGRESS: 313 n.9, 321 n.63, 329 n.80, 335 n.41 (111-12), 346 n.42

BENTON'S ABRIDGEMENT: 312 n.4 (52)

COLLECTED PAPERS OF JOHN BASSETT MOORE, THE (1944): 147-48

COMPLETE WORKS OF ABRAHAM LINCOLN (J. Nicolay & J. Hay eds. 1907): 148

CONGRESSIONAL DIGEST: 359 n.7

CONGRESSIONAL GLOBE: 280-81, 340 n.15 (127), 343 n.24 (145)

CONGRESSIONAL RECORD: 297, 338 n.1 (118), 342 n.5 (136), 343 nn.18-21 & 27 (144 & 146), 346 n.35, 347 nn.47, 49, 51 & 53 (155-57 & 159), 350-51 n.3, Chapter XI generally

DEBATES IN THE SEVERAL STATE CONVENTIONS ON THE ADOPTION OF THE FEDERAL CONSTITUTION (J. Elliot ed. 1859 & 1861): Chapters III to V generally, 351-52 n.9

DEPARTMENT OF STATE BULLETIN: 342 nn.3-4 (135-36), 10 & 12 (140-42), 347 n.50 (157)

ESSAYS ON THE CONSTITUTION OF THE UNITED STATES (P. Ford ed. 1892): 331 n.12 (102-3), 338 n.56 (114)

FEDERALIST: A COLLECTION OF ESSAYS WRITTEN IN FAVOUR OF THE NEW CONSTITUTION, THE (J. & A. M'Lean 1788): 57-58, 96, 101-5, 109-13, 176, notes to Chapters III & V generally, 324-25 n.37, 326-27 n.67, 328 n.69, 352 n.9, 358 n.2

T. JEFFERSON, WRITINGS (Ford ed. 1895 & 1896): 152, 330 n.3

JOURNAL OF WILLIAM MACLAY, THE (1927): 347 n.46 (154)

JOURNALS OF THE CONTINENTAL CONGRESS (1905): 314 n.20, 315 n.32 (58)

MEMOIRS OF JOHN QUINCY ADAMS (C. F. Adams ed. 1875): 280, 342 n.7

MESSAGES AND PAPERS OF THE PRESIDENTS 1789-1897 (J. Richardson ed. 1897 & rev. ed. 1917): 278-80, 283-84, 340 nn.16-17 (127-28), Chapter VII generally

MILWAUKEE JOURNAL: 252

J. MOORE, A DIGEST OF INTERNATIONAL LAW (1906): 277, 281-82

NAVAL DOCUMENTS RELATED TO THE QUASI-WAR BETWEEN THE UNITED STATES AND FRANCE (1935): 278

NEW YORK TIMES: 307-8, 355 n.21 (224), 365 n.50 (252), 366 n.58, 367 nn.65, 67 & 69

PAPERS OF THOMAS JEFFERSON, THE (J. Boyd ed. 1958): 106

PUBLIC PAPERS OF THE PRESIDENTS: EISENHOWER, 1954: 285

RECORDS OF THE FEDERAL CONVENTION OF 1787, THE (M. Farrand ed. 1911): Chapters III to IV generally, 334 n.24, 336 nn.44 & 47, 337 n.53, 352 n.9, 357 n.2

UNITED STATES CODE CONGRESSIONAL AND ADMINISTRATIVE NEWS: 362 nn.20 & 31-32, 363 n.35, 364 n.39

WASHINGTON POST: 342 n.14 (143)

WEEKLY COMPILATION OF PRESIDENTIAL DOCUMENTS: 293, 359 n.5 (229)

WORKS OF ALEXANDER HAMILTON, THE (J. C. Hamilton ed. 1851): 140

WORKS OF JAMES WILSON, THE (R. McCloskey ed. 1967): 106, 314 n.19

WORKS OF JOHN ADAMS (C. F. Adams ed. 1853): 320 n.52 (61)

WRITINGS OF ABRAHAM LINCOLN, THE (A. Lapsley ed. 1905): 281

WRITINGS OF GEORGE WASHINGTON, THE (J. Sparks ed. 1836): 277

WRITINGS OF THOMAS JEFFERSON (Library ed. 1903): 71

INDEX

 VIRGINIA LEGAL STUDIES are sponsored by the School of Law of the University of Virginia for the publication of meritorious original works, symposia, and reprints in law and related fields. Titles previously published are listed below.

Studies Editors; Carl McFarland, 1967–73
Richard B. Lillich, 1973–

Central Power in the Australian Commonwealth, by the Rt. Hon. Sir Robert Menzies, former Prime Minister of Australia. 1967.

Administrative Procedure in Government Agencies—Report by Committee appointed by Attorney General at Request of President to Investigate Need for Procedural Reforms in Administrative Tribunals (1941), reprinted with preface and index 1968.

The Road from Runnymede: Magna Carta and Constitutionalism in America, by A. E. Dick Howard. 1968.

Non-Proliferation Treaty: Framework for Nuclear Arms Control, by Mason Willrich. 1969.

Mass Production Justice and the Constitutional Ideal—Papers and proceedings of a conference on problems associated with the misdemeanor, held in April 1969, under the sponsorship of the School of Law, edited by Charles H. Whitebread, II. 1970.

Education in the Professional Responsibilities of the Lawyer—Proceedings of the 1968 National Conference on Education in the Professional Responsibilities of the Lawyer, edited by Donald T. Weckstein. 1970.

The Valuation of Nationalized Property in International Law—Essays by experts on contemporary practice and suggested approaches, edited by Richard B. Lillich. v. I, 1972; v. II, 1973; v. III. 1975.

Legislative History: Research for the Interpretation of Laws, by Gwendolyn B. Folsom. 1972.

Criminal Appeals: English Practices and American Reforms, by Daniel J. Meador. 1973. Out of print.

Humanitarian Intervention and the United Nations—Proceedings of a conference held in March 1972, with appended papers, edited by Richard B. Lillich. 1973.

The United Nations, a Reassessment: Sanctions, Peacekeeping, and Humanitarian Assistance—Papers and proceedings of a symposium held in March 1972, edited by John M. Paxman and George T. Boggs. 1973.

Mr. Justice Black and His Books—Catalogue of the Justice's personal library, by Daniel J. Meador. 1974.

Legal Transplants, by Alan Watson. 1974.

Limits to National Jurisdiction over the Sea, edited by George T. Yates III and John Hardin Young. 1974.

Commentaries on the Constitution of Virginia (in two volumes), by A. E. Dick Howard. 1974.

The Future of the United States Multinational Corporation—Proceedings of a conference held in 1974, edited for the J. B. Moore Society of International Law by Lee D. Unterman and Christine W. Swent. 1975.

Dictionary of Sigla and Abbreviations to and in Law Books before 1607, edited by William Hamilton Bryson. 1975.

An International Rule of Law, by Eberhard Paul Deutsch. 1977. Out of print.

Mr. Justice Black: Absolutist on the Court, by James J. Magee. 1980.

International Regulation of Internal Resources: A Study of Law and Policy, by Mahnoush H. Arsanjani. 1981.